Accommodation Management: Perspectives for the International Hotel Industry

Edited by
Constantinos S. Verginis and Roy C. Wood

THOMSON

LEARNING

Australia • Canada • Mexico • Singapore • Spain • United Kingdom • United States

Accommodation Management: Perspectives for the International Hotel Industry

Copyright © 1999 International Thomson Business Press

The Thomson Learning logo is a registered
trademark used herein under licence

British Library Cataloguing-in-Publication Data
A catalogue record for this book is available from the British Library

First edition published 1999 by International Thomson Business Press
Reprinted 2002 by Thomson Learning
Typeset by Saxon Graphics Ltd, Derby
Printed in the UK by TJ International, Padstow, Cornwall

ISBN 1-86152-489-7

Thomson Learning
Berkshire House
168–173 High Holborn
London WC1V 7AA
UK

http://www.thomsonlearning.co.uk

Accommodation Management: Perspectives for the International Hotel Industry

Tourism and Hospitality Management Series

Series Editors:

Professor Roy C. Wood
The Scottish Hotel School, University of Strathclyde, UK

Dr Stephen J. Page
Massey University, New Zealand

Series Consultant:

Professor C. L. Jenkins
The Scottish Hotel School, University of Strathclyde, UK

Textbooks in this series:

Interpersonal Skills for Hospitality Management
M. A. Clark
ISBN 0 412 57330 X, 224 pages

Hospitality and Tourism Law
M. Poustie, N. Geddes, W. Stewart and J. Ross
ISBN 1 86152 181 2, 320 pages

Business Accounting for Hospitality and Tourism
H. Atkinson, A. Berry and R. Jarvis
ISBN 1 86152 470 6, 432 pages

Economics for Hospitality and Tourism
P. Cullen
ISBN 1 86152 179 0, 224 pages

Tourism in the Pacific
Stephen J. Page and C. Michael Hall
ISBN 0 415 12500 6, 352 pages

Managing Wine and Wine Sales
J. E. Fattorini
ISBN 0 412 72190 2, 184 pages

Researching and Writing Dissertations for Hospitality and Tourism
M. Clark, M. Riley, E. Wilkie and R. C. Wood
ISBN 1 86152 046 8, ca. 300 pages

The Business of Rural Tourism
S. Page and D. Getz
ISBN 0 415 13511 7, 240 pages

Human Resources for Hospitality Services
A. Goldsmith, D. Nickson, D. Sloan and R. C. Wood
ISBN 1 86152 095 6, ca. 240 pages

Hospitality Accounting, 5th edn
R. Kotas and M. Conlan
ISBN 1 86152 086 7, ca. 456 pages

Tourism in Developing Countries
M. Oppermann and Kye-Sung Chon
ISBN 0 415 13939 2, 192 pages

Corporate Strategies for Tourism
J. Tribe
ISBN 1 86152 752 7, 240 pages

Working in Hotels and Catering, 2nd edn
R. C. Wood
ISBN 1 86152 185 5, ca. 252 pages

Tourism Marketing
Les Lumsdon
ISBN 1 86152 045 X, 304 pages

Tourism in Scotland
R. MacLellan and R. Smith
ISBN 1 86152 089 1, 264 pages

Management Accounting for Hospitality and Tourism 3rd edn
R. Kotas
ISBN 1 86152 490 0, 352 pages

Books in this series are available on free inspection for lecturers considering the texts for course adoption. Details of these and any other titles are available by writing to the publishers Thomson Learning (Berkshire House, 168–173 High Holborn, London WC1V 7AA) or by telephoning on 020 7497 1422.

Contents

PART III: ISSUES IN HOTEL ACCOMMODATION

Series editors' foreword

The International Thomson Business Press Series in Tourism and Hospitality Management is dedicated to the publication of high quality textbooks and other volumes that will be of benefit to those engaged in tourism, hotel and hospitality education, especially at degree and postgraduate level. The Series is based on core textbooks in key areas of the curriculum. All the authors in the series are experts in their own fields, actively engaged in teaching, research and consultancy in tourism and hospitality. Each book comprises an authoritative blend of subject-relevant theoretical considerations and practical applications. Furthermore, a unique quality of the series is that it is student orientated, offering accessible texts that take account of the realities of administration, management and operations in tourism and hospitality contexts, being constructively critical without losing sight of the overall goal of providing clear accounts of essential concepts, issues and techniques.

The series is committed to quality, accessibility, relevance and originality in its approach. Quality is ensured as a result of a vigorous refereeing process, unusual in the publication of textbooks. Accessibility is achieved through the use of innovative textual design techniques, and the use of discussion points, case studies and exercises within books, all geared to encouraging a comprehensive understanding of the material contained therein. Relevance and originality together result from the experience of authors as key authorities in their fields.

The tourism and hospitality industries are diverse and dynamic industries and it is the intention of the editors to reflect this diversity and dynamism by publishing quality texts that enhance topical subjects without losing sight of enduring themes.

Series Editors
Dr Stephen J. Page
Massey University – Albany
Auckland
New Zealand

Professor Roy C. Wood
The Scottish Hotel School
University of Strathclyde
United Kingdom

Series Consultant
Professor C. L. Jenkins
The Scottish Hotel School
University of Strathclyde
United Kingdom

Notes on contributors

Antonio P. Adamo is Professor in Engineering at the École Hôteliere de Lausanne, Switzerland.

Tom G. Baum Ph.D. is Professor of International Hospitality Management and Head of Department, The Scottish Hotel School, University of Strathclyde, Glasgow, Scotland, UK.

Dr Roger J. Callan is Principal Lecturer in the Department of Hospitality and Tourism Management at The Manchester Metropolitan University, UK.

Kevin Donaghy is Senior Lecturer at Northern Ireland Catering College, Northern Ireland, UK.

Joseph E. Fattorini was, until recently, Sir Hugh Wontner Lecturer in Hotel Management, The Scottish Hotel School, University of Strathclyde, Glasgow, Scotland, UK. He is now an independent consultant and broadcaster.

Norman Geddes is a practising solicitor and Lecturer in Hospitality and Tourism Law, The Scottish Hotel School, University of Strathclyde, Glasgow, Scotland UK.

David A. C. Gee has recently retired as Lecturer in Hotel Management from The Scottish Hotel School, University of Strathclyde, Glasgow, Scotland, UK.

Cailein H. Gillespie is Lecturer in Hotel Management, The Scottish Hotel School, University of Strathclyde, Glasgow, Scotland, UK.

Professor Howard L. Hughes is at the Department of Hospitality and Tourism Management, The Manchester Metropolitan University, UK.

Colin Johnson is Director of Research and Development at the École Hôteliere de Lausanne, Switzerland.

Una McMahon-Beattie is Lecturer at the Department of Leisure and Tourism, University of Ulster, Northern Ireland, UK.

Dr Alison J. Morrison is Senior Lecturer in Hotel Management at The Scottish Hotel School, University of Strathclyde, Glasgow, Scotland, UK.

Dennis P. Nickson is Lecturer in Human Resource Management at The Scottish Hotel School, University of Strathclyde, Glasgow, Scotland, UK.

Christopher G. Rawstron is General Manager of the Hilton London Gatwick Airport Hotel and Honorary Lecturer at The Scottish Hotel School, University of Strathclyde, Glasgow, Scotland, UK.

Professor Udo A. Schlentrich is an independent consultant and Visiting Professor at The Scottish Hotel School, University of Strathclyde, Glasgow, Scotland, UK.

Constantinos S. Verginis is a Teaching Assistant in Accommodation and Financial Management at The Scottish Hotel School, University of Strathclyde, Glasgow, Scotland, UK.

Roy C. Wood is Professor of Hospitality Management at The Scottish Hotel School, University of Strathclyde, Glasgow, Scotland, UK.

Ian Yeoman is a Lecturer in the Department of Hospitality and Tourism Management at Napier University of Edinburgh, UK.

Introduction: managerial approaches to accommodation in hospitality organizations

1

Roy C. Wood

For students on courses in hospitality management, the terms 'accommodation studies' or 'accommodation management' usually circumscribe two principal subjects in the curriculum – front office/reception practice and housekeeping. Each of these areas embraces a number of activities relatively diverse in their consequences for the successful (or unsuccessful!) management of hotels. For example, housekeeping touches upon subjects now being increasingly refined into a new discipline, facilities design and management, subjects which include the study of areas as diverse as heating and ventilation engineering; kitchen planning; security systems installation; material selection and management; and environmental services such as lighting and plumbing. The traditional conception of accommodation studies within hospitality management courses is valid and important, but it is a comparatively narrow perspective on an area of activity critical to business success.

The strengths of the traditional approach are twofold. First, there is an emphasis on science, engineering and technology as a basis for accommodation management – for example, the physics of lighting; elementary mechanical engineering; and the deployment of information technology in the front office and elsewhere. Students even modestly successful in completing and understanding such a curriculum acquire a certain technical authority and this, indeed, gives rise to the second strength of the traditional approach – it allows prospective hospitality managers to understand specialists and increase their chances of avoiding being hoodwinked by over-enthusiastic and over-ambitious designers, engineers and computer hard- and software sales staff into purchasing systems and structures they do not really need, whilst at the same time furnishing knowledge which can be put to positive use in the design and redesign process.

The limitations to the traditional approach to accommodation studies teaching says much about the development of the sector in the last 30 years – especially in respect of hotels. First, the main strength of the traditional approach is also its principal weakness. It emphasizes technique and technical knowledge over managerial knowledge and imperatives, and in particular, the imperative to satisfy customer needs and wants. Ironically, this occurs because in seeking to make the manager a specialist (one might say multi-specialist if the range of subjects studied by hospitality management students is contemplated) there is a danger that discharge of the accommodation function becomes management-centred rather than customer-centred. At the level of reception and reservations systems this can be seen all too clearly in the many customized hotel information technology systems that slow check-in and check-out to a snail's pace even in the 'express' queue, and despite the dexterity of reception staff.

Second, over the last 20–30 years the hospitality industry and hotel sector have changed dramatically in terms of their operational philosophies and financial structures. As one instance, the concept of 'outsourcing' has become accepted as part of the fabric of hotel operations such that it is applied to a much greater variety of services than was historically the case. Whereas, for example, laundry was always a favourite candidate for external servicing, outsourcing has now been extended to most or all of some accommodation departments, in many cases by means of the tendered management contract or some other arrangement. Housekeeping services are a particular target in some large chain hotels for outsourcing. Indeed, across a hotel, the outsourcing of many functions can be more economic (because both the number and competitiveness of specialist companies servicing such needs have grown allowing purchasers to achieve cost savings); release management time for other customer-oriented activities; and displace risk.

Of course, it may be fairly objected that none of these things diminish the manager's need for specialist knowledge, because such knowledge is still required in order to ensure adequate stewardship of assets and inculcate the skills necessary to inspection and quality control. This is, indeed, a fair point. The extent of required specialist knowledge is more questionable. The traditional approach to accommodation management is heavy on technique and technicalities but achieves little in the integration of knowledge across (quite diverse) areas of expertise. Further, the highly technical basis that characterizes the traditional approach to conceptualization of accommodation management often ignores many relevant and important topics. There is thus not only a lack of integration between the traditional components of the curriculum, but between these and other germane topics.

One of the most important influences on the changing nature of accommodation management at the operational level has been the standardization of hotel operating procedures. This standardization, notably in chain hotels, has led to a certain 'deskilling' of hotel managers in some areas, with specialist knowledge being reserved to strategic managers and enshrined and communicated to others via operations manuals. Similarly, the planning of major hotel refurbishments or even hotel new-builds may involve operational managers but specialist skills are 'bought-in' and mediated through experienced senior personnel at head-office level. The changing nature of corporate hotel management has meant that materials selection and management, together with provisions for wear and tear, depreciation and even planned obsolescence, are a joint responsibility of the company centre and the unit management team together with specialists, such that control, treatment and monitoring procedures are 'built-in' from the start. Thus, for example, the selection of new carpets for a hotel refurbishment will incorporate *de facto* the specification for appropriate cleaning methods and techniques, and since standardized operating procedures are synonymous with some degree of standardization of products (in the broadest sense), inclusive specifications reduce the need for localized specialist knowledge in key areas of managerial activity, including accommodation management. At the same time, it is important to note that in developing standardized operating procedures, many hospitality organizations have facilitated the *enskilling* of unit management teams in other functions, for example in training, quality control, unit monitoring and direct customer service.

The interplay between markets, technology and the corporate philosophy of hotel companies had led to many subtle changes in the hotel manager's role in the last two decades. To some extent, it is possible to see a diminution over time in the requirement for certain kinds of *detailed* specialist knowledge and skills that were once regarded as a *de rigueur* aspect of hotel managers' training. Building on the traditional 'mein host' or 'being there' style of management traditionally associated with the hotel sector (Guerrier, 1987), managers are more than ever required to have heightened faculties of alertness and awareness in respect of customers' reactions to the products and services on offer. It is not so much that the need for specialists and specialist knowledge has been consciously diminished, but rather that the need for those with a holistic aware-ness of the hotel business has increased in parallel with a more discerning and more demanding clientele, and the need to more effectively centralize certain specialist func-tions in order to ensure organizational effectiveness, economies of scale and, ulti-mately of course, the profitability and wider success of the business in a highly competitive environment. Changes within hotel businesses in response to the latter imperative have also encouraged the rise of the 'holistic' manager in that through the 'delayering' of management at unit level, the reduction in size of unit management teams, and the 'empowerment' of supervisory staff with responsibilities that were once the province of management, managerial roles and responsibilities are much wider, arguably requiring that what are regarded as 'desirable' skills be distributed amongst more and different levels of personnel.

At this point, it is appropriate to look outside of hotel corporations for a moment and consider the kind of skills necessary for the very large number of small and medium-sized hotel enterprises (SMEs) in respect of accommodation management. Given that the majority of these businesses are owner-managed or part of small chain holdings, they represent diversity in every sense. Surely, then, it is here that a genuine need might be located for traditional accommodation management skills? At one level, the answer is undoubtedly 'yes'. Anyone who has stayed in a British boarding house, or a small hotel, will be aware of the variability of standards and the tendency, evident especially in smaller units, for the 'public' aspects of the premises to be managed as if it were an extension of the proprietor's home. Often, these establishments appear to be crying out for someone who has skills in basic design, colour and materials coordination, and maintenance strategies. There are a number of problems with such a view, however. First the variability of accommodation standards is part of the appeal of the small firms sector in so far as the broad clientele who utilize the services of such establishments tailor their expectations of the quality of facilities (see Wood, 1994). Second, a very large number of units operating in this sector do not have the resources to implement changes in facilities in line with the dictates of higher level aesthetic and design con-siderations. Finally, of course, the fact that many such units *are* extensions of propri-etors' homes means that they are furnished accordingly and in respect of materials management at least, require a different treatment to that which would be required in a highly standardized and capitalized hotel chain.

The foregoing depiction of the small firms section of the British hotel industry is necessarily a caricature. There are many small and medium-sized hotels which are highly capitalized, well-designed and constitute a recognizably 'advanced' product (and this applies not only to the recent fashion for small 'designer' hotels). In the SME sector within the hotel industry they remain a minority, but a significant minority. Equally evident in Great Britain are the vast number of 'faded' hotel properties that benefited from the improvement grants paid out in the wake of the 1969 Development of Tourism Act and where little else has been changed (save for routine decoration) since. Travel in continental Europe and you will encounter variations on the same themes (Seymour, 1985). It is usually recognized that the SME sector has a generalized need for more and better management skills and much has been done in the UK to supply training for 'small business' managers and proprietors. Whilst, as far as the hotel sector is concerned, it is possible to construct an argument in favour of training in specialist skills relating to accommodation management (as traditionally construed), these have to be located within a framework or hierarchy of desired and desirable skills and techniques, especially given the high level of business mortality in the hotel SME sector.

THE DIMENSIONS OF ACCOMMODATION MANAGEMENT

Thus far in this chapter, 'accommodation management' has been loosely defined in terms of the traditional conceptions of housekeeping and front-office management. As the earlier discussion indicated, however, accommodation management is much more than this. Indeed, in a very literal sense, hotel management *is* accommodation management, or at least the largest part of it is. The traditional emphasis in hospitality education placed on food and beverage management and the fact that food and beverage management responsibility is one of the key career routes to a hotel general managership obscures, first, the fact that the overall financial contribution of accommodation to hotel revenues normally exceeds that of food and beverage; and second, that food and beverage revenue generation is, for many hotels, a highly problematic area (Riley and Davis, 1992). One might speculate that the privileged status accorded to food and beverage in the hospitality industry derives from the fact that a core element is the manufacture or production of a tangible good or goods – and despite the fact that we now live in an economic culture dominated by services, there is still a tendency to regard the manufacture of goods as in some way 'superior' to the provision of services.

Whatever the case, it is of course true that some hotels are 'food and beverage led' even if the majority are 'accommodation led' (i.e. derive the bulk of their revenue from the sale of accommodation). These terms, though enjoying reasonable currency in the hospitality industry, are in a sense highly misleading. For example, the growth of conference and banqueting trade for those hotels able to take advantage of such business may mean that a unit is food and beverage led, and that the greatest managerial efforts are directed towards marketing such services. It does not *necessarily* mean, however, that the revenue generated by such activities is greater in significance in terms of contribution to profitability than accommodation lets, i.e. sale of bedrooms. Of course, this is a crude example but one which emphasizes that, if talking about hotels being food and beverage led, it is necessary to clarify whether this means that net profit contribution is higher than for other services.

Leaving food and beverage for the time being, it is useful to discuss the core elements of what constitutes 'accommodation management' in the context of hotels (and, indeed, accommodation provision more generally). As indicated earlier, the term 'facilities management' is becoming more fashionable as a portmanteau label for describing the management of buildings and their wider environment. The generic concept of facilities management is explored later in the book but in the broadest sense, the term draws attention to both the totality of external and internal systems and processes of management pertaining to a property, examining how these interact. Such a view of accommodation management is useful in directing attention towards the interplay of factors that affect or influence users' experiences of buildings. 'Facilities' do not, however, operate in an economic and social vacuum, for each building has a purpose – in our case the care of travellers and others staying away from home.

The hotel thus exists in an environment or market that both influences, and is influenced by, the activity of individual hotels and the hotel industry more generally. Any market consists of two primary elements – demand and supply – and hotels have varying powers, depending on whether they are individually owned, members of consortia or of chains, to influence demand and supply. To understand how the hotel industry operates therefore, some knowledge of the supply of accommodation, its nature, extent and interaction within the market, is both useful and necessary, as is some comprehension of how hotels market *themselves*, i.e. how they seek to influence consumer choices and with what wider effect. An understanding of the context of provision, of markets for hotel accommodation services, also requires some understanding of the extent to which other organizations seek to regulate these markets – for example, government through the legislative framework; tourism organizations through their collective promotion of an area or region or through hotel grading schemes; and other organizations involved in the latter process such as automobile associations, or private enterprises solely dedicated to hotel inspection and grading.

Emphasis has thus far been given to the supply-side aspects of markets, and this indeed is a major impetus to the study of the context of provision in this book. There are at least three reasons for this. First, factors bearing on the supply (and its effect on management) of accommodation have, comparatively speaking, been either ignored or only implicitly treated in many of the surveys of hotel accommodation management previously undertaken. Market supply is thus an area long overdue for some detailed attention. Second, thus far analyses of the demand for hotel accommodation have proved at best descriptive or confined to the technical assumptions of disciplines such as economics (see, for example, Cullen, 1997 who does, however, show how economic analysis might be beneficial beyond mere description in analysing demand for accommodation). Descriptive analyses of demand for accommodation, whilst always useful, are usually either theoretically or market research derived, meaning that they are frequently, though not invariably, static in nature. Finally, and perhaps most important, is the observation that studies of the demand for particular products and services, not just hotel accommodation, tend, at their least sophisticated, to marginalize the influence that the market for supply has on the overall market state. As a generic, disciplinary level, economics and marketing texts will at least implicitly show how the behaviour of 'suppliers' in an industry can influence demand for the industry's products and services, for example through advertising, pricing and so on. Behavioural economics has not, however, had a great deal to say on hotel accommodation specifically, on hotel organizations' attempts, through their managements, to influence markets. To a small extent, therefore, the 'supply-side' dimension of accommodation management is given greater weight here, although more through the examination of specific topics than from the point of view of encompassing economic analysis.

If the context of accommodation management in hotels is important then so is departmental management of accommodation. The operational management of accommodation functions is both an essential aspect of organizational maintenance (the execution of practices and procedures convenient and necessary to a hotel) and the satisfaction of customer needs and wants (ensuring, crudely, that organizational maintenance is turned to good use, i.e. satisfied customers and acceptable financial performance of the hotel). The departmentalization of hotel functions is as old as hotels themselves, though in the contemporary hotel industry, departmentalization is not necessarily always an accurate guide to the execution of specific functions. Problems of functional departmental separation and of integration of all of a hotel's activities have been the subject of several analyses (e.g. Shamir, 1978) all now somewhat dated. Nevertheless, even in the smallest hotels, some basic functional separation is normally effected between different aspects of accommodation management. As indicated earlier, the two most distinctive features of departmentalization are front office and housekeeping to which can be usefully added areas such as hotel engineering and maintenance and conference and convention management (often overlapping with food and beverage functions to create a 'conference and banqueting' department). The various labels employed in this context are somewhat less important than the complexity of missions and tasks that fall under the respective umbrella titles.

The hotel building exists in a local 'space'. The immediate management of the facility extends to the boundaries of that space which are often outside the main, physical, building, including grounds, access roads/drives, car parks and so on. The hotelier has some responsibility, often legal, more frequently moral, for the maintenance and security of these external areas as well as of internal spaces. This may involve much interaction with other local businesses, local government and other organizations who have a stake in the immediate environment. Disclaimers about the hotelier's legal liability for x, y and z though sometimes enjoying the force of statute, are meaningless to the hotel guest who cannot park, or feels the grounds or access to the hotel are unsafe because poorly lit, or has to walk 40 yards from a taxi to the hotel entrance in pouring rain because of parking congestion in the hotel forecourt. Local residents may raise environmental objections to the activities of the hotel: these may relate to traffic congestion, noise from a popular public bar within the hotel, the behaviour of guests leaving the hotel and a myriad other things. In short, to speak of the departmental management of hotel accommodation often ignores these 'immediate external' factors that matter to guests and the local population alike, problems which are often directed to front-line staff in one of the accommodation departments who may have limited powers or ability to effect action satisfactory to the guest. Departmental management in hotel accommodation is thus about both external and internal aspects of the management of space. Conventionally, the front office and reception department is the interface between these two dimensions. Clearly, however, most of a hotel's accommodation 'departments' are focused inwards, on the satisfaction of guest demands *within* the hotel. These dimensions are explored within this book from a perspective that seeks to give a flavour of both the functional tasks that fall within the ambit of the various departments as well as emphasizing the contribution of each department, in performing (or underperforming on) these tasks, to the satisfaction of customer needs and wants. In this respect, accommodation management in hotels is concerned principally with shelter, comfort and security, in creating an environment that is distinctive of the hotel, but reminiscent of guests' homes; that facilitates freedom but also offers control (see Wood 1994).

THE SCOPE OF THIS BOOK

This text is intended as an introduction for those approaching accommodation management for the first time, as students or as practitioners. It is not intended to be an extensive or comprehensive 'manual' of how to 'run' accommodation in the hotel industry. Rather, its purpose is to highlight key areas of activity and performance and to locate these in a wider context, to show, as it were, how accommodation might at the unit level fit into the bigger picture or framework of provision for the tourist and traveller. To this end, the book is divided into three sections.

The first section is 'The context of provision' and as the title implies, examines the framework alluded to above. Thus, Colin Johnson examines the broad state of supply of accommodation in the hospitality industry, focusing principally on hotels. Following this, Roger Callan writes on an ever-controversial issue in the UK and elsewhere, namely the construction and reliability of hotel grading schemes. At the time of writing, the UK's new Labour Government is committed to a universal grading and classification scheme which it hopes to achieve by voluntary means. More generally, for the practising hotel manager, grading schemes can be the stuff of nightmares or of dreams. Many hoteliers perceive such schemes as, variously, unfair, poorly constructed and unreliable. Callan's pioneering work on this topic is well known to academic colleagues and offers a rare combination of theoretical and practical interest and insight of value to industry managers.

In the next paper, Alison Morrison addresses the important issue of marketing hotel accommodation. The hospitality industry has one of the highest, if not the highest, rate of business failure of all industrial sectors. Barriers to entry to the industry are low, meaning that anyone with reasonable capital can set up as a hotelier. Indeed, many so called hotels and guest houses are converted domestic residences. Often, the very smallest businesses are run by those with no prior experience of the hotel industry, nor any formal qualifications in hotel management. Business failure can occur for many reasons, but a lack of marketing awareness and skills is an especially important source of inadequacy in the hotel sector. Morrison's paper thus also contributes to both a theoretical and practical understanding of the nature and benefits of marketing in the hotel business.

Following this, Joseph Fattorini returns to the question of hotel stock from the perspective of the physical, financial, investment that hotel buildings represent, reminding us that a knowledge of real estate principles is just as important to the hotel manager as marketing, personal selling or any of the other myriad skills necessary to effective functioning. As Fattorini reminds us, outside of the US both operators and academics have tended to marginalize the importance of real estate considerations, somewhat puzzling given the amount of investment hotel premises usually represent.

In his paper, Tom Baum reminds us of the relationships that exist between the accommodation sector and the local and national state, giving important context to the nature of relationships between the industry and government policy. Such relationships are widely ignored in the current literature on the hotel industry. Their importance lies in the mutual influence that exists at national, local and area tourist board level; the exploitation (or lack of it) by hotels of the services of independent or government-related organizations in marketing their properties and training their staff; and the extent to which, at the structural level, future policy can be developed by hotel and tourist organizations to the benefit of each.

The final paper in this first section strikes a different if no less important note. Norman Geddes explores the legal framework for the operation of hotel services with a particular slant on United Kingdom aspects of accommodation law. This article is not intended as a substitute either for more detailed study of the law as it applies to hoteliers, or for employing a good lawyer! Rather, the intention is to give a basic outline of the kinds of responsibilities hoteliers have in the UK and to consider these in a European Union context.

Section two of this book focuses on the internal aspects of accommodation management by which is meant those key performance areas that bear directly on the management of the accommodation unit. Constantinos Verginis offers a statement of the principles of front office management and considers enduring issues relating to the front office as custodian and guardian of the first impressions conveyed to customers. Christopher Rawstron writes on the critical issues facing modern hoteliers in housekeeping services from the perspective of a hotel general manager. In both cases, again, the objective is not to offer some detailed 'manual' of practice but to identify general trends, principle task elements and key aspects of customer orientation. This is followed by Antonio Adamo's paper on hotel engineering and maintenance, an area of management often played down in the UK but where managerial knowledge can be helpful in informing important capital expenditure decisions as well as planning for short-term operational variations in service engendered by maintenance needs. Udo Schlentrich focuses on a phenomenon that is in a sense both an essential aspect of the context of provision and, increasingly, an important element of a departmental function in hotels in the form of conferences and banqueting. Schlentrich concentrates on conferences and conventions, now a major source of business for many hotels, ranging from small half-day seminars to full-scale conventions that take over whole cities. Finally in the second section, David Gee concentrates on the emerging 'umbrella' subject of facilities management and design. Increasingly, this label (or at least the 'facilities management' part of it) is coming to represent a generic approach to the management of accommodation, not only in hotels, but in all kinds of buildings. Gee focuses on facilities management applications to hotels which includes such areas as security.

In the book's final section, 'Issues in hotel accommodation' a number of topics are examined which bear on the wider concerns of hotel accommodation management. In an era of renaissance in hotel design, Cailein Gillespie examines some of the recent trends in this area and their relevance for the marketing of the hotel product. Dennis Nickson outlines the importance of human resource management to hotel accommodation services in the context of increasing emphasis on total quality management and empowerment. Una McMahon-Beattie, Kevin Donaghy and Ian Yeoman, in contrast, focus in detail on one of the currently 'sexy' areas of hotel management – yield management, particularly in respect of the sale of hotel bedrooms. In an age when hotel organizations are increasingly sensitive and open to the applications of yield management techniques to accommodation, this useful summary of key features of policy and procedure is timely. Joseph Fattorini returns us to consideration of the 'real estate' aspects of accommodation management by examining current practices, procedures and debates attendant on hotel valuations. The last paper in the section, by Howard Hughes, focuses on the role of hotels in entertainment. In the 'golden age' of British hotels, few larger establishments were without their regular string quartet or pianist. This tradition has somewhat died out but hotels still play a critical role in the field of entertainment, and not simply in the large pleasure palaces of Las Vegas. The staging of entertainment is used as a device for filling hotels in periods of low occupancy, but the industry also employs entertainers to deliver diverse products as part of the hotel experience. Hughes' paper re-establishes the importance of this area and considers some of the managerial implications for running entertainments of varying kinds.

All of the topics covered in this book should be of interest to students of hospitality management but it should be emphasized once again that in matters of detail and specialization, other relevant texts should be consulted. The particular emphasis taken here is a managerial one. The book's main objective is to give a sound introductory sense of the breadth and scope of accommodation management in hotels beyond the narrower confines of 'traditional' approaches. Given the existence and availability of certain physical, economic and human resources, the management in respect of hotel accommodation requires effective skills to coordinate and control such resources in a manner that does not compromise unduly that manager's time, ability and resources to fulfil other aspects of their responsibilities. At the same time, it is essential that the appropriate weight be given to the importance of accommodation in the hotel product. Accommodation is *not* simply about meeting and greeting people, checking them in, cleaning their rooms, and repairing the plumbing. It is the managing of what hotels 'do', and in this context, it is hoped that this book makes some small contribution to restoring accommodation management to its central role in hotel management.

REFERENCES AND FURTHER READING

Cullen, P. (1997) *Economics for Hospitality Management*, London: International Thomson Business Press.

Guerrier, Y. (1987) 'Hotel managers' careers and their impact on hotels in Britain', *International Journal of Hospitality Management*, **6**(3), 121–30.

Riley, M. and Davis, E. (1992) 'Development and innovation: the case of food and beverage management in hotels', in Cooper, C. (ed.) *Progress in Tourism, Recreation and Hospitality Management*, Vol. 4, London: Belhaven Press.

Seymour, D. (1985) 'An occupational profile of hoteliers in France', *International Journal of Hospitality Management*, **4**(1), 3–8.

Shamir, B. (1978) 'Between bureaucracy and hospitality – some organizational characteristics of hotels', *Journal of Management Studies*, **15**, 285–307.

Wood, R.C. (1994) 'Hotels and Social Control', *Annals of Tourism Research*, **21**(1), 65–80.

Part I
The context of provision

The supply of accommodation | 2

Colin Johnson

INTRODUCTION

This chapter presents key issues in relation to supply and demand in the international hotel industry. The structure and size of the industry is outlined, together with an analysis of the relationship between tourism and the hotel business. Major themes of importance in the short and medium term are identified and assessed. Key international players are identified, and growth strategies practised by international hospitality corporations are examined and discussed.

DEFINING A HOTEL AND HOTEL CORPORATION

We begin by reviewing several definitions of hotels and similar establishments in order to provide a clear basis for discussion. Although there is an increasing amount of research being conducted in the field of hospitality management, problems occur at a very basic level in defining what the hotel industry is, and specifically in deciding what constitutes a hotel, and therefore a hotel corporation. If one cannot even agree on the basic definition of a hotel, then it becomes extremely difficult to treat data and quantify the industry.

General definition

The World Tourism Organization (WTO) regularly provides data on hotel capacity around the world, and remains a valuable source of information. Their definition is a worthwhile starting point (Todd and Mather, 1995: 7):

> Hotels and similar establishments … are typified as being arranged in rooms, in number exceeding a specified minimum; as coming under a common management; as providing certain services, including room service, daily bed-making and cleaning of sanitary facilities; as grouped in classes and categories according to the facilities and services provided.

Problems often exist at the country level, however, where translation of these terms varies considerably. For example, interpretations may include: hotels, private hotels, residential hotels, guest houses, boarding houses, lodging houses, bed and breakfasts, inns, pensions, motels, auberges, posuadas, and so on, which in different countries may or may not fall within the remit of a hotel *per se*.

Often in the US, hotels are referred to as lodging properties, and Go and Pine (1995: 25) use a general definition of 'lodging firms including motels, in competition, and producing goods and services of a like function and nature'. In Europe, according to industry analysts Dresdner Kleinwort Benson, the problem is compounded, owing to the peculiarly diverse range of provision (Slattery *et al.*, 1996). Standard industrial classification (SIC) schemes have been developed in both the UK and the USA, with hotels and other residential establishments appearing as section 884 in the UK and under SUC 70 (with sub branch 701) in the United States.

Definitions by relationship

Slattery *et al.* (1996) categorize a hotel through one of the following five relationships:

- owned;
- leased which includes properties which are rented as well as sale and leaseback hotels;
- management contracts with equity – which may be seen to be a growing trend in face of increasing competition;
- management contracts (equity free) the most common form of contracts particularly amongst major hotel brands (although variable, the time-scale has often historically been 20 years or more with 3 per cent of turnover and 10 per cent of gross operating profit (GOP), though the time span is diminishing and according to Kleinwort Benson Securities terms of 2 per cent of turnover and 8 per cent of GOP are being negotiated, again due to increased competition); and
- franchised hotels owned and operated by independent hoteliers and chains who pay a franchise fee to operate their hotel under a major brand, thereby giving access to reservation systems, corporate marketing, training and purchasing: not all major brands franchise due to difficulties of maintaining quality standards with franchisees; major brands that are franchised are Hospitality Franchise Systems, (Cendant), Holiday Inn Worldwide, (Bass) and Choice Hotels (Accor, Marriott International, Hilton Hotels Corporation and ITT Corporation also franchise to a lesser degree).

Within some European countries, franchising of hotels is still relatively new, but with recent agreements (such as with Friendly Hotels in 1997 as the master franchiser of Choice Hotels in the UK), this form of expansion is likely to be a major form of development (Slattery *et al.,* 1996).

Turning to hotel corporations (that is, companies that have management over one or more hotels) definitions become convoluted as hotel companies may be involved in at least three separate 'industries'. These include:

- companies involved in constructing, developing and owning hotel buildings, e.g. Marriott;
- companies involved in managing hotels (with or without equity in the hotels under management, e.g. Hilton International); and
- franchising companies that develop hotel chains without being involved in either owning hotel buildings or managing hotels, e.g. Choice Hotels, Cendant (Lewis, Chambers and Chako, 1995).

An additional element of confusion also appears through 'invisible' hotel companies operating with little outward presence to the public. These may be of significant size, but manage hotels under different brand names. Another factor that is not generally realized by the public is that they may stay in a brand A hotel that is owned by company X, marketed by company Y and managed by company Z. Olsen *et al.* (1998), propose as a definition for a multinational hospitality corporation 'a company that sets up its headquarters in one country and has business operations and affiliations in more than two countries'. It is clear, however, after all of the discussions and definitions attempting to circumscribe the sector that the hotel business may be regarded as a major industry that is truly international in scope. It is not uncommon for major hotel corporations to operate in more than 60 countries. The industry itself encompasses thousands of hotels, with millions of rooms owned, managed or leased by government agencies, pension funds, giant chains, independent operators, real estate investment trusts (REITs) (in the USA) and other investors.

RELATIONSHIPS BETWEEN THE INTERNATIONAL HOTEL BUSINESS AND THE TOURISM INDUSTRY

The hotel industry is an important subset of the international travel and tourism industry, with major tourist destinations usually determining where key hotel developments will occur. Figure 2.1 shows details of regional growth in tourism over the period 1990–96. As may be seen, East Asia/Pacific show by far the strongest growth, with an average annual growth of 8.6 per cent. Second in order of magnitude is the Middle East, (admittedly starting from a very low base), which recorded 7.9 per cent growth. Recent developments in both regions, however, underline how volatile tourism may be, with the uncertainties over economic, political and social developments in many Asian nations affected by currency fluctuations and the fall in intra-Asian tourism, and stability in the Middle East far from certain at this stage.

According to the World Travel and Tourism Council (WTTC, 1995) travel and tourism is the world's largest industry generating 11 per cent of the global gross national product. Whilst experts may differ over whether tourism is really 'an industry' (Davidson, 1994), the immensity of revenues generated under the tourism banner is undeniable. By 1994 the average increase in international tourism receipts had surpassed world exports in commercial services. Tourism receipts accounted for just over 8 per cent of total world exports by 1996, and over 35 per cent of the total world exports of services (WTO, 1997). The details may be found in Table 2.1.

There have been vigorous attempts in recent years by the WTTC to lobby governments and official agencies about the importance of travel and tourism to national

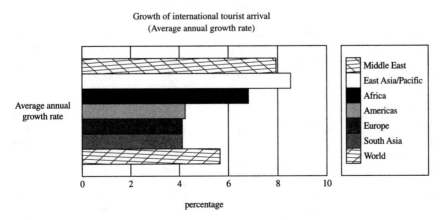

Figure 2.1 Growth of international tourist arrivals by region, 1990–96
Source: World Tourism Organization, *Tourism Market Trends*, 1997: 8

Table 2.1 Tourism receipts compared to world exports of merchandise and commercial services, 1994–96 (thousands of millions of dollars and percentage).

	Value			Yearly change (%)		
	1994	1995	1996	1994	1995	1996
Merchandise	4,215	4,920	5,100	16.2	19.5	3.5
Commercial services	1,037	1,170	1,200	1.7	12.6	2.6
International tourism receipts	352	399	425	9.5	13.6	6.5

Source: World Tourism Organization (1997: 3)

economies, with the contention that the industry now produces $3.4 trillion annually (International Hotel Association, 1996), and is set to double in output in the next decade (WTTC, 1995).

The international hotel industry

Table 2.2 provides a useful overview of the scope and magnitude of the industry throughout the world.

The World Tourism Organization drawing upon additional statistics from the International Hotel Association (now the International Hotel and Restaurant Association), illustrate that, in terms of revenues, Europe accounted for the largest share with 39.5 per cent or US$ 100 billion, followed by the Americas with US$ 81 billion (32 per cent). Europe and the Americas again hold first and second place of total hotel establishments (with 55 and 28 per cent respectively); in terms of hotel rooms the two areas

Table 2.2 The size and scale of the hotel industry worldwide, 1995

Region	Revenue (US$ m)	Hotels[1] (no)	Rooms (000)	Tourism receipts (US$ m)	Employees (000)
Africa	**6,300**	**10,769**	**384**	**7,165**	**1,259**
Caribbean	7,917	5,290	165	12,484	278
Central America	1,200	1,160	48	1,530	232
North America	62,133	66,943	3,754	75,310	2,268
South America	9,845	14,576	527	10,814	1,284
Americas	**81,095**	**87,969**	**4,494**	**100,138**	**4,062**
Northeast Asia	23,733	10,192	759	33,594	1,120
Southeast Asia	12,841	13,211	565	27,908	731
South Asia	3,083	3,663	143	3,647	472
Australasia & Pacific	6,602	10,082	234	12,099	539
Asia-Pacific	**46,259**	**37,148**	**1,701**	**77,248**	**2,862**
Middle East	**9,238**	**4,735**	**179**	**7,244**	**455**
European Economic Area	87,491	151,945	42,365	174,714	1,874
Other Europe	22,521	19,178	1,127	32,939	805
Europe	**100,012**	**171,123**	**5,492**	**207,653**	**2,679**
Totals	**252,904**	**311,744**	**12,249**	**399,448**	**11,317**

[1] Registered hotels
Source: World Tourism Organization, 1997: 36.

hold 45 per cent and 37 per cent respectively, and 44 per cent and 37 per cent of bed capacity. Although Asia-Pacific only commands 11.9 per cent of total hotels, due to the higher average size of property, their share of room and bed capacity is higher at 14 per cent. Staff to room ratios demonstrate interesting intra-regional variances, with the highest in Africa at 3.5 employees per room, the Middle East (2.5:1) and then Asia-Pacific (1.7:1), and Europe (0.5:1) (WTO, 1997). It should also be noted that, in terms of revenues, when the multiplier effect is taken into consideration, (which, for example in the US has been calculated at approximately 2), then the true worth of the industry in relation to profits, tax revenues for governments and employment may be more appreciated.

INDUSTRY DEVELOPMENT

The historical development of the international hotel industry has been well documented (see Litteljohn, 1985; Litteljohn and Roper, 1991; Jones *et al.*, 1994; Go and Pine, 1995), with the nascent international industry developing symbiotically with US airlines. The year 1946 saw the birth of the first international hotel chain with the founding of Inter-Continental by Pan American Airways. Thereafter followed Hilton and Sheraton, whose strategy was to create small pieces of American *terra firma* in distant lands for the US businessman. According to the seminal study of Dunning and McQueen (1982), eight of the top ten international hotel companies were American owned. Of their total population of 81 companies operating 1025 hotels with 270,646 rooms, 22 or 27 per cent were US owned companies operating 508 hotels with 56 per cent of internationally operated rooms.

It is interesting to note that there were already signs of some significant European presence, with six companies being domiciled in the UK and five in France. There was at that time only one transnational corporation from a developing country (India). These key industry names are still familiar today and have achieved increased recognition as brands which have been stretched into different market segments (e.g. Marriott Courtyard, Holiday Inn Express). This does, however, mask significant changes in company ownership.

Forces for change on the industry

Although the hotel industry often appears to be conservative and somewhat slow to embrace change, major transformations have taken place as a result of several irrevocable external factors. Many writers have identified key trends in business on the demand side at the macro-level, including Porter (1990), Go and Pine (1995), Lovelock (1991,1992), and Kostecki (1995). The International Hotel Association, in applying these trends specifically to the hotel industry, distinguished the major factors that have affected the industry in the last decade (see Table 2.3).

Supply-side developments 1970–97

In response to these changes on one side of the economic equation, there have been irreversible structural changes in supply. In just two decades, the industry has careered in a 'white-knuckle ride' from unprecedented expansion and development, through the resulting depression and over-supply, and then back to new 'lean and mean' franchise and management contract companies that are aggressively facing the 1990s and the

Table 2.3 Major events driving change, 1985–97

Ideological shift to free market economies	Fall of the US dollar from unprecedented heights (which later was to come back up)
Global recession and recovery	The Gulf War
Corporate downsizing and cost containment	Increase in buying power by consumer and corporate groups
Lower valuation of hotel assets	Increased interest by the capital market community in hotels
Life style changes, two income households increasingly demanding short break vacations	Growing disposable income in parts of the developed world
Tax reform in the United States	Crash in the real estate market
The inception and advancement of the information age and technology advancement	

Source: Modified from IHA, 1996: 30.

new millennium with anticipation and confidence. The major supply-side events of the past two decades are summarized in Table 2.4.

Some of the major issues which arise from the developments summarized in the above table and which will be discussed below are: a) ownership changes; b) mergers and acquisitions; c) diversification; and d) branding.

Ownership changes

For many decades the international hotel industry was the domain of 'USA Hospitality Inc.', large US lodging chains that had expanded throughout the world following a set pre-scription to cater for the wishes of the US business executive travelling abroad. However, a marked change during the past 15 years has been the emergence of first, European, and then Asiatic and other internationally owned chains. Asian influence was initially led by the Japanese, but was later picked up by Hong Kong and Thai hotel owners.

More recently Asian markets have been affected by turbulence resulting from distur-bances in their financial markets, with Inter-Continental being sold by Saison, and Dusit Thani selling off Kempinski. Kundu (1994) believes that a key difference between estab-

Table 2.4 Supply-side developments 1970–97

Increase in international competition	Development of multiple brands
Overcapacity	Escalation of mergers and acquisitions
Increasing number of consortia	Importance of franchising as a form of international involvement
Emergence of new markets in eastern Europe, Asia, South America	Divestment of acquisitions by airlines
Rise in importance of sustainable development and responsible environmental hotel-keeping	Related diversification into cruise-liners, health care, gambling and timeshare
Growing importance of gaining competitive advantage through technology and marketing methods	Recognition of importance of 'human factor' in service quality provision
Emergence of Real Estate Investment Trusts (REITs) as major shareholders of hotel properties	Proliferation of strategic business alliances
Rise in importance of secondary locations	

Source: Adapted from Kundu (1994) and IHA (1996).

lished multinational enterprises (MNEs) from developed economies and newly established MNEs emanating from developing nations is that the latter are pursuing niche strategies, in contrast to the expansionist strategies of the former, who have a preference for developing competitive advantage through the use of cheap financing while relying on international experience coupled with advanced management and marketing skills.

It is of interest that, in the Asia-Pacific region, the hotel sector is dominated by the major internationals, but there is also a strong group of regional chains which exert a significant presence in the area. As markets for four and five star hotels are approaching saturation levels, it is likely that chains will seek to develop their presence in the mid-price sector either through franchising or by acquiring chains in those categories. It is notable that franchising has not, to date, proved popular in certain countries such as Australia, and that multinational groups are focusing upon a certain range of countries, with no apparent pattern behind their choice of location (Wise, 1993). As income levels continue to rise, there will also be increased outbound travel from these nations, and the challenge will be, therefore, to select the correct market niches in order to sustain the properties in the region during volatile times.

Latin America and the Caribbean are other areas marked for international expansion, but again there are regional major participants, such as Grupo Posados based in Mexico City, Allegro Resorts based in the Dominican Republic, and Sol Melia from Spain.

Mergers and acquisitions

As may be seen from Table 2.5, the pace and scale of mergers and acquisitions have increased at an unprecedented rate throughout the last decade.

Table 2.5 A sample of mergers and acquisitions in the international hotel industry 1987–98

Year	Company Acquiring	Company Acquired	Value
1987	Ladbroke PLC	Hilton International	$1.07 billion
1987	Aoki Corp.	Westin	$540 million
1988	Seibu/Saison	Inter-Continental	$2.2 billion
1988	Wharf International Holding	Omni	$135 million
1989	New World Development	Ramada	$540 million
1989	Bass PLC	Holiday Inn	£125 million
1990	Accor SA	Motel 6	$1.3 billion
1991	HFS	Days Inn	$250 million
1992	Four seasons	Regent (25% stake)	$122 million
1993	HFS	Super 8	$125 million
1994	ITT Sheraton	Ciga	$530 million
1994	Forte	Meridian	$445.9 million
1994	Starwood	Westin	$1.58 billion
1995	HFS	Travelodge & Knights Inn	$185 million
1995	Marriott	Ritz Carlton (49% stake)	$200 million
1996	Hilton	Bally Entertainment	$3 billion
1996	Granada	Forte	$5.9 billion
1996	Doubletree	Red Lion	$1 billion
1997	Starwood	ITT Sheraton	$8.23 billion
1997	Marriott	Renaissance	$1.6 billion
1997	Promus	Doubletree	$4.64 billion
1997	Patriot	Carnival Hotels	$1.024 billion
1998	Bass	Inter-Continental	$2.9 billion

Source: The Economist (10 January 1998) and Olsen *et al.* (1998).

Deals worth $4.5 billion were completed in the first nine months of 1997, with a further $20 billion under negotiation (*The Economist*, 1998). This may be attributed in a large part to the over-building in the industry after the 1980s boom followed by the cyclical slump of the early 1990s. Size continues to remain a major source of competitive advantage, due to economics, technology and logistics affording economies of scale, especially through the use of computer reservation systems, purchasing and marketing.

Another major factor for change in recent years is the emergence of the Real Estate Investment Trust (REITs) from the US, which has accelerated the pace of concentration in the industry. REITs are corporate structures similar in nature to property trusts; they have exemption from US corporate taxation provided that they meet certain criteria concerning their composition and method of generating and disposing of income (for example, 75 per cent of income must come from rents and other income directly related to real estate, 95 per cent of taxable income must be distributed to shareholders) (DeRoos, 1998). Initially REITs were interested in the US domestic scene, but have lately played a more international role (see Chapter 5).

International investors are targeting Europe in particular at the end of the 1990s because the price of hotel assets has been bid up in the US. As a result, a greater standardization of European hotel stock is anticipated, with increasing emphasis on investment analysis, a more important role played by asset managers, and the increasing divorce of ownership and management. Due to several convergent factors the outlook for increases in hotel profits and property values in continental Europe is very positive. Major contributing factors include:

- cyclical recovery of European economies;
- demographic trends with ageing populations, resulting in a wealthier and more numerous middle-aged and retiree population;
- accelerating development of the service sector, which increases demand for hotel services;
- potential for lowered costs, through restructuring and consolidation;
- increased leisure demand, especially for short-break holidays; and
- lack of new building in recent years (Nilsson, 1998).

Many investors see the European hotel business as ready for consolidation, with only 20–25 per cent of the hotel stock in some form of chain ownership, management or other affiliation. It has been regularly forecast that national brands will disappear as the industry becomes pan-European (*Hotels*, May 1998: 6). This view, however, is not accepted by all industry professionals, with the Chief Executive Officer of Scandic Hotels, a substantial Scandinavian regional chain, presenting a strong argument for essential differences between European cultures, tax structures and consumers that militates against global brands in the hospitality industry (Nilsson, 1998).

Diversification

Hotel corporations are increasingly diversifying into related service industries, including health care, cruise liners, gaming and time-share. Marriott, Accor, Hyatt Hotels Corporation and Holiday Inns have all expressed interest in different health-related projects. Marriott has built certain life-care retirement communities, Accor has created a subsidiary 'Hotelia' and Hyatt has two 'Classic Residence' projects, which are assisted-living retirement communities, giving residents access to nursing and other support services as they grow older. Many major hotel corporations (including Hilton, Promus, and Club Méditeranée), are also investing heavily in gambling facilities and casinos, with traditional locations such as Las Vegas being developed, along with 'newer' sources such as riverboats and Native American reservations.

Timeshares have enjoyed something of a shaky reputation in many countries, largely because of dubious marketing practices. Major players in the industry are now anxious to stress that due to stricter regulations, and with reputable companies (such as Marriott) joining the field, the business is now more respectable. Leading holiday exchange companies such as RCI and Interval International quote strong growth in recent years, and estimate that the business in the US alone is worth something like US$ 6 billion. There are three basic types of timeshare – fixed week, floating week within season, or points, which can be used anywhere at any time subject to restriction. There are 4500 timeshare resorts worldwide in 81 different countries. Less than 1.7 per cent of the potential market has been penetrated in the US, only 1 per cent in the UK and a lesser percentage elsewhere in the world. The UK has the majority of European timeshare owners (some 700,000). Most of these consist of beach properties in Spain or Portugal. Sales and marketing typically cost 40–60 per cent of sales, against a cost of property acquisition of 20–40 per cent.

Branding

Although service companies have traditionally been slower to adopt marketing initiatives than fast-moving consumer good (FMCG) products (Lovelock, 1991), throughout the past decade more sophisticated marketing techniques have increasingly been used by hotel corporations, including brand segmentation. Now commonplace in the industry, Choice Hotels was one of the first companies to develop a multi-branding approach, with a range of different offerings to appeal to each price segment. Three-quarters of business travellers and two-thirds of leisure travellers are brand-conscious when choosing their hotel (*The Economist*, 1998). Three-quarters of all hotels in the US are part of a chain, but in the rest of the world, the percentage is less than 25 per cent. Renaghan (1998) draws attention to the problems inherent in branding in the international hotel business. On the one hand there is a need for standardization that is the essence of branding, bringing identity and comfort to the guest. On the other, there is the need to satisfy increasingly multinational customers while respecting constraints imposed by local conditions. There may well be opportunities for regional chains or independent hotels with chain affiliations to practise the 'think global, act local' mantra advocated by global strategists.

Key considerations in branding

As with many other elements of hotel development, location is important, in gateway cities, business centres, or leisure/resorts. Advances in information technology have facilitated mass customization, enabling the tabulation and recall of customers' individual needs and tastes, which can result in a personalized service on a worldwide basis. Relationship marketing is seen to be a major marketing initiative in recent years that will increase in importance as the lifetime value of the client is evaluated and exploited. Clear brand identity and positioning is essential, as is communication to the marketplace that the company is competing either on quality or price (and not getting stuck in the middle).

KEY INTERNATIONAL PLAYERS

Throughout the past 25 years the names of the top 20 companies have remained fairly consistent. Belying the names, however, are ownership changes with, for example, Hilton Hotel Corporation selling off its international operations to Ladbroke, the UK gaming corporation, which then managed the properties as Hilton International. Inter-Continental was in May 1998 acquired by Bass, who already own the Holiday Inn brand worldwide. Smaller chains such as the up-market Kempinski group have in the past decade been bought and sold by the Thai hotel corporation Dusit Thani. In terms of the international hotel industry, there are evident differences if one compares solely in terms of hotel and rooms, or in terms of international spread. The principal companies are as follows:

- **US Ownership**
Starwood Lodging Trust (owns ITT Sheraton and Westin brands)
Cendant (owns Hospitality Franchise Systems)
Patriot American
Choice Hotels International
Marriott International (owns Ritz Carlton)
Hyatt International and Hyatt Hotels Corporation
Radisson Hotels International
Promus Corporation (owns Doubletree brand)
Hilton Hotel Corporation
Delta Hotels
- **UK Ownership**
Holiday Inn Worldwide (Owned by Bass)
Inter-Continental (owned by Bass)
Forte (owned by Granada Group)
Hilton International (owned by Ladbroke)
- **French Ownership**
Accor
Club Méditerranée
Société du Louvre
- **Thai Ownership**
Dusit Thani
- **Japanese Ownership**
Nikko Hotels
Tokyu/Pan Hotels
- **Chinese Ownership**
Shangri-La
- **Spanish Ownership**
Grupo Sol Melia
NH Hotels
- **Scandinavian Ownership**
Scandic Hotels

• **German ownership**
Dorint Hotels
Kempinski Hotels
Steigenberger Hotels
• **Indian Ownership**
Omni Hotel
The Taj group
• **Miscellaneous**
Southern Pacific (Australasia)
Four Seasons/Regent (Canadian)

Table 2.6 compares the changes in brand names and growth in hotels and rooms that have occurred over the past quarter of a century.

The enormous growth in the industry is clear, recording an increase of close to 300 per cent in rooms, from approximately 500,000 to nearly 2 million. Multiple brands are also in evidence, with seven out of the top ten chains comprising multiple brands (Mosser, 1995). As previously mentioned, foreign involvement by hotel corporations dates back to the 1960s, and has been seen to be a major developmental strategy by companies faced by saturation in the domestic market and the prospects of higher returns in developing regions. Figure 2.2 shows the coverage of major chains internationally. Olsen *et al.* (1998) also highlight that in 1995, among the top 25 hotel corporations, 15 companies were operating in 18 to 68 countries, and that 54 of the world's top 100 hotel chains had operations in three or more countries.

Table 2.6 The international hotel industry 1970–96
Top ten hotel chains

1995 *1970*	Rooms	Hotels
1. Hospitality Franchise Systems	**490,000**	**5,300**
1. Holiday Inns Inc.	*182,513*	*1,293*
2. Holiday Inn Worldwide	**386,323**	**2,260**
2. ITT Sheraton Corp.	*59,600*	*225*
3. Best Western International	**295,305**	**3,654**
3. Howard Johnson Corp.	*39,500*	*425*
4. Accor	**279,145**	**2,465**
4. Best Western Motels	*37,500*	*1,300*
5. Choice Hotels International	**271,812**	**3,197**
5. Hilton Hotels Corp.	*46,500*	*88*
6. Marriott International	**251,425**	**1,268**
6. Ramada Inns Inc.	*35,625*	*352*
7. ITT Sheraton Corp.	**130,528**	**413**
7. Quality Courts Motels	*30,670*	*397*
8. Promus Corp.	**105,930**	**809**
8. TraveLodge International	*26,000*	*452*
9. Hilton Hotel Corp	**101,000**	**245**
9. Master Hosts International	*25,000*	*888*
10. Carlson Hospitality Worldwide	**91,177**	**437**
10. Trust House Forte Ltd.	*20,000*	*225*

Source: Hotels, July 1997: 48; July 1995.

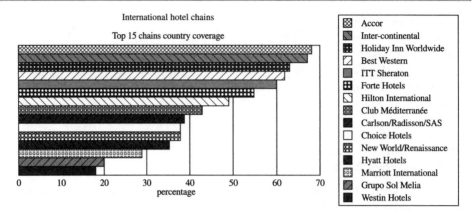

Figure 2.2 International representation
Source: Hotels, July 1996.

Although it may be seen that there are over one dozen truly international hotel corporations, there are also two other types of large hotel corporation – national corporations (e.g. Red Roof Inns, domestic to the United States), and regional corporations (i.e. those hotel corporations that have many hotels in their own country, and in the near vicinity, for example Scandic with representation in the Scandinavian countries; Southern Pacific in Asia-Pacific; and Protea in Africa).

Table 2.7 provides an interesting insight into the coverage of corporate hotels. As may be seen, there are more than three times the number of corporate hotels owned by hotel chains in the Americas than in Europe, whilst in other regions of the world ownership by hotel chains is negligible.

GROWTH STRATEGIES ADOPTED

Todd and Mather (1995: 107) argue that 'there are still no truly global players in the sense that no company has representation, in depth, in all countries of the world in which there is a hotel market'. This view has been reinforced by Andries de Vaal from Deloitte & Touche Consulting, who believes that although corporate clients increasingly want a global service which offers a discount for using a single chain worldwide, only a small number of hotel chains have properties in more than 60 countries, and even chains with wide networks operate in less than a third of the world's total nations

Table 2.7 Corporate hotels by region (no. of hotels)

	Total	**% of total**
Americas, of which:	15,570	71.3
USA	14,396	65.9
Europe	4,512	20.7
Asia-Pacific	1,309	6.0
Africa	273	1.2
Middle East	177	0.8
Total	**21,841**	**100.0**

Source: Todd and Mather (1995: 77).

(*Financial Times*, 31 January 1997: 19). Olsen *et al.* (1998) take an opposite view, arguing that globalization has emerged as an important trend in the hospitality and tourism industries since the last decade.

For the hotel sector of any country to expand and receive investment there are two clear prerequisites: an expanding economy which stimulates domestic demand and international business travel, and a growing tourism industry that is attractive to international leisure visitors (Todd and Mather, 1995). Although providing a broad picture, this does, however, hide disparities between regions, with, for example 82 per cent of business being accounted for by domestic demand in North America, whilst in Africa and the Middle East foreign demand accounts for 76.1 per cent of business.

According to Dunning (1993:11) a global corporation is one that practises an integrated strategy towards value-added activities in each of the major regions of the world. Clearly, therefore, with representation in Africa, Asia, Europe and the Americas, there are at least several hotel corporations that merit the term 'global'. As well as size (with the number of properties being cited as the key target), there are also a number of other criteria used by hotel corporations to assess their success. These include (Todd and Mather, 1995: 107):

- depth in specific markets;
- structural changes – enabling a higher return on investment;
- product improvement;
- extension or refocusing of branding;
- increased investment in marketing and distribution;
- diversification into related areas; and
- a combination of the above and other options.

Certain companies have, however, stressed numerical targets, including Holiday Inn, Choice, Accor and Marriott.

Growth through non-equity involvement

It has been noted by several sources, notably Dunning and McQueen, (1982), Olsen *et al.* (1992), Kundu (1994), Lewis *et al.* (1995) and Slattery *et al.* (1996), that non-equity forms of expansion, and especially franchising have increased in importance in recent years. Indeed it has been suggested that 'franchising will be the primary engine driving growth' (Olsen, 1993: 63). The power of a franchise brand is a function of its size and the ability of the franchiser to drive demand into the hotels. It follows that the rate of expansion is a critical element in determining the success of a franchise operation. From the point of view of the international operator, there are two crucial factors to be considered when expanding internationally: first the franchiser's willingness and ability to supply the financial and human resources to the international franchisees, and second the availability and quality of suitable licensees, franchisees, or partners in the target countries.

Franchising has been the 'major success in the development of corporate hotel keeping in the US over the past forty years' (Slattery *et al.*, 1996: 86), with franchised properties in the US outnumbering company-owned units by more than six to one (Kundu, 1994). Consequently it is now being viewed as a major vehicle by chains both within and outside the US. Despite this expansion in the US, at this stage really only Holiday Inn and Choice Hotels International may be regarded as attaining any measure of success internationally. One of the largest franchisers, Hospitality Franchise Systems,

(HFS), has been pursuing an aggressive worldwide expansion programme throughout the 1990s, and created a new division (HFS Global Services) to accelerate international growth and development. Fairly recently Regent International entered the franchise market – the first luxury hotel group to offer their services as an alternative to the marketing consortia route that luxury hotels often follow. There is an inherent problem in the expansion of franchising in the UK and mainland Europe due primarily to the age of the hotel stock (which was developed before the era of standardization and brand specification). Most hotels do not conform to the basic requirements behind major franchise brand demands (Slattery *et al.*, 1996). To date, only two hotel companies (Choice and Accor) have developed specifications that are flexible enough to accept the older European mid-range hotel stock.

Olsen (1993) identifies several generic strategies that have been employed by multinational hospitality firms as follows.

- Exporting core technology that has been developed in the home country. There are numerous examples which include Accor, Forte, Choice, Oberoi and Club Méditteranée.
- Broad-based competitive positioning developed through the belief that the international customer has homogeneous needs and reasons for travel.
- Exporting of management expertise.
- Development of strategic alliances characterized by joint ventures, management contracts and master franchise agreements.
- Destination/location advantage. This approach is designed to maximize the firm's presence in as many key international areas as possible. This has been a definite, if at times not particularly successful, policy for hotels which have been aligned strategically with airline companies including PanAm, Swissair, Air France and Scandinavian Airline Systems. In addition to this strategic linkage, there has also been an attempt by firms to locate in as many market areas as possible (sometimes regardless of the competition).
- The drive for technological advantage. As firms attempt to compete in an increasingly competitive and combative environment, attempts have been made to differentiate through their strategic use of information technology. As long ago as 1982 Dunning made the point about advanced technology and easier technology, believing that more powerful companies would possess a clear advantage over smaller players. This viewpoint may now be doubted. Although it came as something of a surprise to Dunning and Kundu (1995) in their research, Go and Pine (1995) reported upon an industry trend whereby economies of scope have been *reduced* through technology, with virtually all private, small-roomed properties having access to global distribution systems through reservation companies acting as intermediaries.

Market entry and international expansion

Olsen *et al.* (1998) warn of the complexities involved in international expansion, and the need to appreciate different cultural norms and business dealings. A useful matrix (Figure 2.3) is proposed that represents four dimensions of risk: political, legal/economic, demand generator (which comprises the mix of attractions destinations possess so as to produce the level of business required by investors), and investment. Each cell of the matrix demonstrates the method that may be adopted by hospitality firms

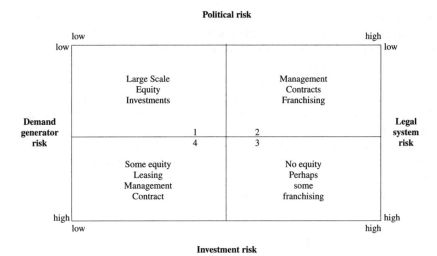

Figure 2.3 Risks and market entry relationships for hospitality businesses
Source: Olsen *et al.* (1998).

moving into new markets. The mode of market entry may range from Foreign Direct Investment (FDI), as used by Forte Hotels with the Hotel Bristol project in Warsaw, Poland, to no equity (franchising, as used by Choice International and other predominantly franchising corporations). There are also many other forms that may be used such as management contracts, leasing, joint ventures, and strategic alliances.

As may be seen from cell one, where there is relatively little risk politically, legally or on the demand side, investors are naturally more keen to invest larger shares of capital. Moving to cell three, where there are both higher legal and political risks coupled with lower potential demand, investors are unwilling to give large shares of equity, and look for other expansion methods such as franchising. This was the situation in the mid-1990s in eastern central Europe, as the former eastern bloc nations were seen by hospitality corporations as still highly volatile, politically, socially and economically, with unclear property rights and low domestic demand. Happily for the peoples of these nations (especially Poland, the Czech Republic and Hungary), the situation is now significantly more stable, and many international hotel corporations are unveiling expansion plans for the region.

CONCLUDING REMARKS

The international hotel industry has undergone irrevocable changes in the last two decades. Key structural changes have often occurred due to spectacular growth in the tourism industry notably in the emerging markets of south-east Asia The situation towards the end of the 1990s, however, has changed dramatically for the worse, with many financial analysts predicting that the Asian economic crisis will continue to have serious consequences in the medium to long term. There have also been fundamental changes in distribution methods by hotel corporations (especially through non-equity forms), that has resulted in significant increases in the size of hotel corporations.

Many hotel operators have attempted to create sustainable advantage through technology, either to improve operations, or to augment guest services. Especially important are advances in internet systems and the development of loyalty-based programmes focusing upon the lifetime value of the client, rather than the value of the property. Operating internationally has become increasingly competitive, complex and frenetic. Concentration and consolidation in the industry has continued through major merger and acquisition activity. Many corporate developers and investors still believe, however, that there are exceptional opportunities for investing in European hotel stock. Olsen *et al.* (1998) make the point that with current environmental challenges, success in the international marketplace is dependent upon commitment to appropriate value-added competitive methods. Increasingly, international hospitality firms are being governed by 'information managers' with the financial expertise, acumen, strategic vision and intent, striving to keep their corporation ahead of the pack as the industry develops in an increasingly multifarious and sophisticated form towards the close of the century.

REFERENCES AND FURTHER READING

Davidson, T.L. (1994) 'What are travel and tourism: are they really an industry?' in Theobold, W. (ed.) *Global Tourism*, Oxford: Butterworth-Heinemann Ltd, 20–6.

DeRoos, J. (1998) 'Exploring the U.S. REIT phenomenon and its impact on the European hotel industry', presented at the Cornell University European Hotel Industry Strategy Conference, London, 5–7 May 1998.

Dunning, J.H. (1993) *Multinational Enterprises and the Global Economy*, Wokingham: Addision-Wesley.

Dunning, J.H. and Kundu, S.K. (1995) 'The Internationalisation of the Hotel Industry – Some New Findings from a Field Study', *Management International Review*, **35**(2): 101–33.

Dunning, J.H. and McQueen, M. (1982) 'Multinational Corporations in the International Hotel Industry', *Annals of Tourism Research*, **9**, 69–90.

The Economist (1998) *Travel and tourism: special report*, 10 January.

Go, F. and Pine, R. (1995) *Globalisation Strategy in the Hotel Industry*, London: Routledge.

International Hotel Association (1996) *Into the New Millennium*, Paris: The International Hotel Association.

Jones, C., Nickson, D. and Taylor, G. (1994) 'Ways of the world: managing culture in international hotel chains', in Seaton, T. (ed.), *Tourism: The state of the art*, Chichester: John Wiley and Sons, 626–34.

Kostecki, M.M. (1995) *Marketing Strategies for Services*, Oxford: Pergamon Press.

Kundu, S.K. (1994) 'Explaining the globalisation of service industries: the case of multinational hotels', unpublished Ph.D. thesis, Rutgers University, New Jersey, UMI, Ann Arbor.

Lewis, R.C., Chambers R.E. and Chacko, H.E. (1995) *Marketing Leadership in Hospitality*, New York: Van Nostrand Reinhold, 2nd edn.

Litteljohn, D. (1985) 'Towards an economic analysis of trans-/multinational hotel companies', *International Journal of Hospitality Management*, **4**(4): 157–65.

Litteljohn, D. and Roper, A. (1991) 'Changes in international hotel companies' strategies', in Teare, R. and Boer, A. (eds.), *Strategic Hospitality Management*, London: Cassell, 194–212.

Lovelock, C.H. (ed.) (1991) *Services Marketing*, Englewood Cliffs, NJ: Prentice Hall.

Lovelock, C.H. (ed.) (1992) *Managing Services,* Englewood Cliffs, NJ: Prentice Hall.

Mosser, F.W. (1995) 'What a difference a generation makes', *Cornell HRA Quarterly*, **31**(2): 1.

Nilsson, R. (1998) 'The branding challenge: will national identities remain the dominating factor or will international brands succeed?', address by R. Nilsson, President and CEO Accor, The Inaugural Cornell University European Hotel Industry Conference, London, 5–7 May.

Olsen, M.D. (1993) 'International Growth Strategies of Major US Hotel Companies', *Travel and Tourism Analyst*, 3, London: Economist Intelligence Unit.

Olsen, M.D., Tse, E.C.Y. and West, J. (1992) *Strategic Management in the Hospitality Industry*, New York: Van Nostrand Reinhold.

Olsen, M.D., Tse, E.C.Y. and West, J. (1998) *Strategic Management in the Hospitality Industry*, New York: Van Nostrand Reinhold, 2nd edn.

Porter, M.E. (1985) *Competitive Advantage*, New York: The Free Press.

Porter, M.E. (1990) *The Competitive Advantage of Nations*, London: Macmillan.

Renaghan, L. (1998) 'The branding challenge: will national identities remain the dominating factor or will international brands succeed?' paper presented at the Cornell University European Hotel Industry Strategy Conference, London, 5–7 May 1998.

Slattery, P., Fechley, G. and Savage, M. (1996) *Quoted Hotel Companies: the world markets 1995*, London: Kleinwort Benson Research.

Todd, G. and Mather, S. (1995) *The International Hotel Industry*, London: The Economist Intelligence Unit.

Wise, B. (1993) 'Hotel Chains in the Asia Pacific Region', *Travel and Tourism Analyst*, 4, London: The Economist Intelligence Unit.

World Tourism Organization (1997) *Tourism Market Trends, The World 1997*, Madrid: World Tourism Organization.

World Travel and Tourism Council (1995) *Travel and Tourism's Economic Perspective*, Brussels: World Travel and Tourism Council.

3 Hotel grading schemes

Roger J. Callan

This chapter will examine a range of hotel grading schemes employed in the UK. The discussion will be limited to UK schemes in order to provide relative depth to the explanation and development. The UK hotel industry is probably graded more than any other hotel industry and the schemes discussed will cover a range of approaches, which will serve to illustrate the different types of hotel grading systems which are operated elsewhere in the world. To undertake this task in detail would produce a book in itself (see Callan, 1992; 1993; 1994a; 1994b; 1995; 1998). The explanation, therefore, has been limited to exploring the major developmental stages and operating characteristics of a number of schemes, together with a cursory reference to other schemes.

During the early part of the century, only the motoring organizations and Michelin classified hotels for travellers. The rapid growth of tourism after the Second World War brought with it the need for some form of hotel registration or classification to ensure the monitoring of standards in a burgeoning number of hotels. By 1970 only five European countries had national classification schemes: Belgium, France, Greece, Norway and Spain. By 1980 this number had risen to 22.

Early research for the English Tourist Board into the choice criteria for serviced accommodation indicated that only 10 per cent of consumers used national guides to assist with their hotel selection. Since that time there has been a progressive development of national and commercial schemes. The major hotel classification and grading schemes consist of those run by the National Tourist Boards (England, Scotland, Wales, Northern Ireland, Isle of Man, Guernsey, Jersey), the motoring organizations (Automobile Association [AA] and Royal Automobile Club [RAC]) together with a number of commercial guides: Egon Ronay, Good Hotel Guide, Michelin, and Which? Hotel Guide published by the Consumers' Association.

REGISTRATION, CLASSIFICATION AND GRADING OF HOTEL ACCOMMODATION

In order to understand the discussion which follows, it is necessary firstly to define the terms: registration, classification, and grading.

Registration

Registration is simply a recording of establishments on a register which may or may not require inspection. The establishment would not normally need to comply with particular specifications other than legislation pertaining to fire precautions, hygiene and so on, which *can* be viewed as a form of *minimum* standards.

Classification

Classification is where the stock of accommodation is sub-divided into categories. Each category consists of specified facilities, such as the proportion of private bathrooms, minimum size of rooms, full-length mirrors and so on. Each country may classify differently, having a number of categories covering self-catering accommodation, guest-houses, hotels and motels, or *different* classifications for different *types* of accommodation. The number of levels within each classification will signify the range of facilities that it is possible to measure. For example, there may be up to six classes for hotels, but rarely more than three for guest houses. Classification does not imply a *qualitative* element, only that specified facilities and services are provided, with the overall understanding that the establishment is clean and well maintained.

Grading

Grading is often confused with classification, but it implies entirely different criteria. Grading is a qualitative assessment of the facilities described under classification. Grading will assess how *good* or *bad* are the facilities or services offered.

The purpose of registration

Registration is a procedure which applies when a hotel meets specified minimum criteria. It will then be entered on to the register of the national tourist board. Three major reasons are suggested for the introduction of hotel registration: consumer protection, tourism planning and marketing.

Hotel registration in the UK is not a new concept. It has been in existence in the Channel Islands since the end of the Second World War and exists in a compulsory form, not only there but in Northern Ireland and the Isle of Man. In the UK mainland, the Development of Tourism Act (1969) provided for compulsory registration, classification and grading, but this provision has never been implemented. Voluntary registration was introduced by the English, Scottish and Wales Tourist Boards in 1974. Opposition to compulsory registration has, in the main, centred around the cost of operating such a scheme.

Statutory registration

As the years have passed, is there any evidence to support accommodation registration, compulsory or otherwise? The Consumers' Association has supported compulsory registration and quality grading for some time and called for its implementation. The view has been expressed that a major weakness of the national Crown classification (see below, pp. 34–36) is that, as there is no compulsion, many of Britain's finest hotels have not joined the scheme, which therefore misrepresents the range of hotels which are available.

The strongest call for a statutory scheme came (in 1992) from the National Economic Development Council's Working Party on Competitiveness in Tourism and Leisure. They believed that considerable progress had been made by the hotel sector and the Tourist Boards to get a credible official scheme in place:

> It might be thought that the hotel industry would regard a mandatory scheme to be to its own advantage, since it would enforce minimum quality levels and reduce the incidence of unacceptable quality in that part of the industry which tends to

damage the latter's image as a whole. (National Economic Development Council, 1992: 32).

The Working Party went a step further and recommended that a mandatory scheme should be reconsidered:

> Once the industry has a comprehensive scheme, the industry's trade associations and the Tourist Boards should consider afresh whether a grading and classification scheme would be more beneficial if it were mandatory. The new Department of National Heritage should keep this under close review. (National Economic Development Council, 1992: 33).

The Government may be unconvinced of the need for statutory registration, classification or grading, as they appear to favour deregulation. A possible solution may be that a national registration and grading scheme should follow the example of the Wales Tourist Board and be operated by a private sector company, supported by the national tourist boards and the motoring organizations.

The benefits of classification

The classification of service accommodation into categories and the assessment of the presence of a range of facilities and services can assist both governments and consumers in a number of ways. The analysis of such categories of accommodation can provide government with a more detailed source of data. At the same time it is possible to identify those types of accommodation which require development and possible financial support. Further, consumers and the travel trade are able to identify more accurately the accommodation which they require. However, it is debatable whether classification, even if statutory, would actually eliminate substandard hotels. It could eliminate those which fall below a particular level of provision of tangible facilities, but would probably do little to change the *quality* of these facilities, or affect the performance of service providers.

A classification system will include certain facilities and services incrementally in each classification. Provision will be made for particular types of accommodation such as farm-houses, lodges and guest-houses. An inspection process is required to monitor the criteria, with non-compliance resulting in some form of penalty. Such penalties should be subject to an appeals procedure. In a fast developing hospitality industry, regular reviews of criteria are essential to ensure that the classifications match the needs of the customers. The arguments for compulsion presented under registration apply equally to classification. A voluntary scheme makes if difficult or impossible to realize the benefits of classification detailed above. Voluntary classification is often associated with sales promotion, in that to gain an entry into Tourist Board publications, the Board must first inspect and classify the property.

The concept of quality grading

It was stated earlier that there is a confused use of the terms 'classification' and 'grading'. The *provision* of facilities should be seen as classification. Grading as a term is appropriate when assessment moves beyond the provision and availability by attempting to assess the quality or degree of service provided.

The confusion about the term 'quality grading' is also apparent amongst hotel operators. Many hoteliers have provided additional equipment and facilities in their rooms which tended to increase their classification level, rather than attempting to improve the *quality* of their existing services. Such moves could take them into new market segments, by holding say four crowns rather than three, in which they are unable to satisfy the additional needs of the customer. These are real dangers as hotel classification and grading are, particularly for the independent operator, a valuable and cost effective promotional tool. Thus, grading schemes can be viewed, in essence, as a proxy for quality as they aim to represent the quality of a hotel for a guest who has no previous experience of that hotel. Such grades give rise to customer expectations; when managers and staff meet or exceed these expectations they can be seen to have provided quality service.

Some elements of the guest experience cannot be assessed by a grading scheme. Incidents which are identified as 'non-routine' (namely those services which the guest does not expect the hotel to provide in the normal course of events) are often in the forefront of the customer's mind when evaluating the quality of the return hotel stay. These types of non-routine incidents are often the most memorable when making a judgement of service quality. Such incidents cannot be included in either a quality assurance programme, or quality grading. Although these specific non-routine experiences cannot be assessed, some provision can be made within the grading criteria to assess the flexibility of the service providers, or their willingness to respond to requests for assistance.

ENGLISH TOURIST BOARD (ETB)

Historical background

In the mid 1960s, due to the increase in the scale and rate of growth of UK tourism, it became clear to the Government that it could no longer stand aside from the industry. In 1968 the Government announced its intention to introduce three measures:

- a hotel development incentive scheme;
- powers to register and classify tourist accommodation; and
- introduction of powers to give selective financial aid for particular tourist projects.

The Development of Tourism Act (1969) was passed on 25 July 1969, confirming these powers and establishing the Tourist Boards for England, Scotland and Wales. In 1971 the ETB commissioned consultants to examine and report on the operation of existing registration and classification schemes and to devise and cost a system of hotel registration. The principle recommendations were to introduce statutory registration and classification on the basis of self-classification.

The proposals were submitted to the Government in April 1972 but they suggested that the Tourist Boards introduce a voluntary scheme to be reviewed after a number of years. The voluntary classification system was introduced by the English Tourist Board in 1974; it allocated numbers from one to six for each of three categories: bedrooms, services and meals, the higher the number in each category, the wider the range of facilities. The system provided 216 possible classifications from 1.1.1 to 6.6.6. The system was not readily understood and did not lend itself to display signs for use on premises, perhaps the most important means of making the public familiar with a classification system. The scheme did not contain a qualitative element. As the scheme did not allow for routine inspection, hotels could submit enhanced information to the Board in order to gain higher points than they were rightfully allowed.

After four years of operation of the scheme, the Tourist Boards were uncertain as to whether their original objectives could be achieved through a voluntary system. The question was reviewed by a committee chaired by Professor J. Beavis. The subsequent report was known as the 'Beavis Report' (Beavis, 1979). Following the deliberations of the committee, which are too detailed to discuss here, the ETB in 1981 rationalized the three-way system and represented the bedroom category only with roses, which were displayed on signs outside each listed property. The classification was based on information supplied by the hotelier, although the ETB claimed that it was increasingly involved in verification.

The introduction of the Crown scheme

Following extensive consultation with the hotel industry and other relevant parties, the three national Tourist Boards devised and introduced the Crown classification inspection-based scheme in 1985, to replace the 'Roses scheme'. The Crown scheme would operate throughout England, Scotland and Wales, using the same crown symbol, the same classification criteria and the same 'code of conduct'. Each classified establishment would be inspected annually to ensure that national standards would be maintained. It was reported that by August 1987 the total of establishments who had applied to join the scheme was 10,000 and many of the major hotel groups and consortia were participating. Stirrings of dissent from operators and customers about the rigidity of the scheme were already being voiced.

The ETB commissioned research to measure consumers' awareness of the scheme and their recognition of the crown symbols. Approximately 2500 consumers were targeted. Only 4 per cent of adults in Great Britain were spontaneously aware that the ETB had a rating system for hotels and other accommodation, and 11 per cent of those knew that the symbol used by the ETB was a crown.

The English Tourist Board received much criticism for its awarding of five crown classifications. Some 200 properties were awarded five crowns compared with 22 AA five-star properties. In order to combat the criticism, the ETB announced a new five gold crown category. The maximum number of five gold crown establishments was to be 30. The announcement went some way to mollify the opposition of the major hotel groups to the scheme, whose major criticism was the lack of qualitative assessment. The gold crowns have never been officially withdrawn, although they were superseded by the introduction of quality grades.

ETB quality grading

A significant proportion of the hotel industry as represented by the BHRCA (British Hoteliers, Restaurateurs and Caterers' Association) had, for some time, opposed the introduction of any form of grading. Quality grading had been introduced by the Scottish Tourist Board in the summer of 1985, but the debate in England was to continue for some time.

In January 1988 a consultation document was issued entitled 'Crown classification scheme – taking account of relative quality'. The document included a questionnaire which was distributed to all registered members of the Crown scheme and other interested parties by the Regional Tourist Boards of England and Wales. In the questionnaire, hoteliers were asked whether the Crown classification should be only for hotels or cover the spectrum of serviced accommodation. The documents issued by the England and Wales Tourist Boards proposed two ways of assessing an establishment's quality, rather than just classifying its facilities.

- Option A   Quality grading should be an integral part of the classification, unifying subjective and objective elements.
- Option B   Quality grading should be assessed separately from facilities and present them as an *addition* to the Crown classification (known as the 'Scottish Option').

The 'Scottish option' was supported by the Regional Tourist Boards but the BHRCA were opposed. Each side undertook research and presented evidence to support its case without a final agreement. The ETB decided to proceed with quality grading expressed as a separate epithet as operated by the STB.

In February 1992 the ETB announced the introduction of the additional quality grade of 'De Luxe'; this followed a similar decision by the Scottish Tourist Board in January. The grade was to apply to all types of establishments from top hotels, guest-houses and inns to bed and breakfast and self-catering. A listed or one crown bed and breakfast or guest-house could still achieve a de luxe grade if what it provided (although limited in range) was to an exceptionally high quality standard.

The lodge category

With the development of the budget hotel sector, it became clear that budget hotels did not fit easily into existing classification systems. In November 1992 the ETB announced the launch of a new lodge category for the national classification and grading scheme. The scheme had moons as its symbol, placing lodges in three bands by awarding one, two or three moons. Quality grading used the same terms as the Crown scheme (approved, commended, highly commended and de luxe). Unlike the Crown scheme, grading was compulsory for all establishments seeking classification; all lodges were to be inspected for both facilities and quality, and must show both assessments.

In the Spring of 1994 the then Tourism Minister, Iain Sproat, announced a review of the Crown classification system. He strongly opposed the scheme, believing that it confused the consumer. He asked the ETB to look at more effective alternative systems such as those of the AA and RAC. Subsequent developments of combined co-operation of scheme operators will be addressed later in the chapter.

SCOTTISH TOURIST BOARD

Historical background

Scotland made its own unique contribution to the establishment of a national classification and grading system through the establishment of 'A Working Group on Registration and Classification of Tourist Accommodation' which produced the 'Sneddon Report' in 1980. The Sneddon Committee established a sub-committee that considered in detail the various options for a classification scheme. It proposed that the existing ETB three-category scheme of bedrooms/services/meals was confusing to the customer, and that this should be replaced by a single category system. A three-way voluntary self-classification scheme allowing establishments to evaluate facilities under three categories (bedrooms, services and meals) was introduced for the accommodation guides in 1982. As with the ETB scheme, there was a maximum of six points in each category.

A Highlands and Islands Development Board working party's activities subsequently resulted in an investigation of hotel grading which was undertaken and reported in the Inverness, Loch Ness and Nairn Research Project, in June/July 1984. The investigation not only formulated a pilot grading scheme, but tested it with inspectors in the field. Amongst several recommendations, two are selected as particularly significant, as they led to the establishment of the current grading system. These were that there was both a need and demand for a new national accommodation classification and grading scheme, ideally for all accommodation types, but in the first instance confined to hotels, guest-houses and self-catering properties; and second that the Scottish Tourist Board should itself set up and administer this new scheme (Inverness, Loch Ness and Nairn Area Tourist Board, 1984: 23). The results of the report led to the establishment of the STB grading scheme which was the forerunner of the schemes adopted by the ETB and WTB.

Quality grading

The first criteria for classification and quality grading were issued in 1986. One noticeable omission from the quality criteria was a reference to food. Dining-room criteria referred only to the physical surroundings and equipment. The grading officers worked from a 24-point assessment form, covering the six broad areas: exterior; bedrooms; bathrooms, washbasins and toilets; public rooms including bars; dining room and/or restaurants; and hospitality and service. Of those establishments inspected by the Autumn of 1986, 80 per cent had opted for classification and grading. The grading of food and beverages were included in the scheme in 1988. The growing acceptance of the grading scheme was indicated by marketing consortium, Inter-Hotels, who made the scheme a provision of membership. Hotels must be four crown 'commended'.

Overnight stays by the inspectors were to be once every three years; in the intervening two years the Board would conduct a day-time inspection. There were exceptions to this rule, for example a highly commended establishment would be visited each year, as well as any establishment with more than 50 rooms, or any bed and breakfast which was 'commended'. An establishment could appeal against a grading. There would be a second visit from a different inspector. If the establishment was still unhappy with the result they could appeal to the Overseeing Committee. There were approximately 12–15 appeals each year, about 50 per cent of which were upheld.

The scheme was generally well received and was seen as a role model for the ETB and WTB. The Scotland *Where To Stay* guide 1990 listed 2407 establishments, 53.6 per cent (1291) of which displayed an award or award-pending (STB Quality, 1989a). Because of quality grading, the scheme attracted more backing from corporate hotel groups than did the ETB scheme. Mount Charlotte Group were strongly supportive of the scheme, claiming that: 'We will be marketing strongly on the strength of the scheme, particularly in the United States and Europe. The most important aspect of the scheme is that people now have a definition of a quality hotel and they can buy accordingly' (STB Quality, 1989b: 4).

A study commissioned by the STB in 1992 indicated better levels of performance by classified and graded hotels: bed occupancy in 1991 showed an increase of 9 percentage points between classified and non-classified hotels, which rose to 10 in 1992. Graded hotels were 9 percentage points ahead of ungraded in 1991, rising to 11 in 1992. Room occupancy showed consistent margins of 8 percentage points between classified and unclassified in 1991 and 1992, and graded and ungraded in both 1991 and 1992 (Centre for Leisure Research, 1993: 20). The contentious issue of allowing establishments to be classified without grading was resolved when the STB announced its intention to make the grading mandatory for all serviced accommodation seeking its endorsement.

WALES TOURIST BOARD

Historical background

In 1981 the Wales Tourist Board (WTB) became the first mainland tourist board to inspect all establishments featured in its brochures. In the 1970s there was a system of self-classification operated by the Board. When verification was introduced in 1981, 65 per cent of establishments inspected did not have the facilities and services which they claimed to have.

Crown classification scheme

The development of the Crown scheme followed the same or similar patterns to that of the ETB. Identical classification criteria to those of the ETB were issued in March 1987. In 1989 the WTB attempted to respond to the BHRCA suggestion of separate registers for different accommodation, by differentiating sectors such as hotels, guest-houses, farmhouses within different sections of their guidebooks.

Quality grading

By March 1988 the WTB announced its plans to introduce the Scottish system of grading to its Crown classification scheme. Hoteliers accused the WTB of precipitative action by failing to wait for the ETB decision to accept the Scottish model, or make quality an integral part of the crowns. The WTB based its decision on its own consultations, being the views of 770 establishments, 73 per cent of which were in favour of the Scottish system, while only 26 per cent favoured an integral scheme, combining classification and quality grading in one category.

Other developments 1990–94

The WTB made clear its intention to press ahead with the privatization of its services. It was proposed that accommodation grading would be the first service to be privatized, with the WTB Head of Trade and Consumer Affairs as director. By March 1990 the first stage of privatization was completed with the formation of the grading company, Tourism Quality Services. The company was to be subsidized by the WTB in the first three years of operation.

AUTOMOBILE ASSOCIATION

Historical background

The AA first began hotel inspection in 1908 and appointing hotels in 1910 when it was difficult for their motoring members to find hotels which offered acceptable meals and accommodation. The stars were the inspiration of the AA Secretary of 1911, Stenson Cooke, who decided to use them as a designation in a similar fashion to the brandy trade. The award of the black stars was also made by the Royal Automobile Association (RAC) and the Royal Scottish Automobile Association (RSAC). A joint scheme for the three organizations was established in 1950 which operated until it was terminated in 1973.

The black, red and white stars

In 1974 a new appointment scheme using black, white and red stars was introduced. Black stars were retained for service hotels, white stars to denote motor hotels, motels and similar establishments. Red stars indicated that AA inspectors considered the establishment to be of outstanding merit within its classification. The 1984 review of hotel classification led to the removal of the white star classification from the 1986 guide.

Quality grading

The AA introduced its first quality awards in 1981, the 'H, B and L' awards. These symbols were to indicate to the customer that a higher standard existed in each area (hospitality, bedroom, public areas) than would normally be found in the star classification. These subjective awards were viewed as a success by highlighting individual areas of excellence. Red star hotels were those which were considered to be ahead of all the three subjective awards and thus reflected an overall level of excellence.

In 1988 the AA published the results of a major research exercise which involved a strategic review of the relevance of the AA hotel classification system to consumer requirements. This was achieved by a detailed evaluation of the existing requirements for each star level. The results of the research brought the announcement late in 1989 that a subjective percentage quality rating would be shown alongside three to five star hotels in the 1990 AA guide, the remaining classifications to be quality graded in 1991. The AA had followed the lead of the National Tourist Boards and shown their quality assessment as an additional grade to the classification band. The next stage in the quality improvement process was a move to make accolades for good food less élitist and to broaden the spectrum of establishments which could be recognized. The AA/BHRCA liaison committee developed and proposed the new five rosette scheme. This wider range was not intended to devalue the rosette awards, but to identify more establishments offering enjoyable food that was particularly worthy of note.

Other developments

Branded hotels

In October 1993 the AA introduced a new hotel classification category-branded hotels. These were to be listed after the star category entries under each town or city, and be identified with the brand logo. To be eligible the hotel groups had to have a national profile with at least ten establishments consistently providing uniform standards of accommodation and catering. The 1994 AA guide to Hotels in Britain and Ireland featured 328 branded hotels. In addition to the criteria for entry given above, hotel groups who had an international presence of at least four hotels in the UK would also be eligible. Hotels would be subject to inspection in the usual way. Branded hotels had to make a choice; they could be shown with brand logo or a star classification, but not both.

Town house hotels

The AA introduced the new Town House Hotel classification in 1993. These were to be character properties offering accommodation in city centres, each with its own individual style, although guests could expect a minimum number of qualities common to all: bedrooms of AA four-star standard; reception service available day and night; room service meals; a selection of snacks or light refreshments; and English or high-quality continental breakfast, served in bedrooms or in a restaurant. Any public rooms were to be of similar quality to the rest of the establishment. It was confirmed that ten establishments (seven in London) met these criteria and were entered in the 1995 guide. The Town House Hotels were to be identified by a symbol in the guide, and be listed under a town or city after stars but before branded hotels.

ROYAL AUTOMOBILE CLUB

Star classification

To map the development of the black star classification would parallel the AA explanation already provided. As the organizations followed similar developments only major differences will be highlighted. The revised classification specifications in 1987 were almost identical to those of the AA. Changes in 1989 were, in the main, in line with those announced by the AA with a few additions.

Quality grading

Blue letter merit awards

In the Autumn of 1987 new quality awards were announced which were applicable to one to four star hotels; five star hotels, however, were excluded from the scheme, as they were already expected to provide the highest standard. The merit awards were granted for one year only and would be reviewed at the end of that year. An award was made in three areas and a hotel could obtain one, two or three awards:

H – hospitality and service granted to those hotels when the quality of hospitality and service is superior to that expected in its classification;

C – comfort granted to those hotels where the overall comfort of the bedrooms and public rooms is superior to the general run of hotels within its classification; and

R – restaurant granted when the cuisine at a hotel is of higher standard than is normally expected within its classification.

Blue ribbon award

This award was introduced at the same time as the blue letters and is the premier award of the RAC, one to four star hotels being eligible for the award. To be considered for a blue ribbon, a hotel must first receive the three merit awards. In addition, the hotel must have the almost indefinable quality of 'guest awareness' amongst management and staff.

EGON RONAY

Historical development

Egon Ronay came from a family of Hungarian restaurateurs. He wrote columns for the *Daily* and *Sunday Telegraph* newspapers and published his first guide in 1957. The development and growth of influence of his guides was considerable, selling 90,000 copies in 1982 and 100,000 copies in 1987.

Quality grading

The hotels for entry in the ERG (*Egon Ronay Guide*) are not classified and then quality graded, but are awarded a score which takes account of the 'overall experience' whilst at the hotel. The score is expressed as a percentage and then divided into grades:

De Luxe   80–100 per cent
Grade 1   70–79 per cent
Grade 2   50–69 per cent

Restaurants are assessed separately from a hotel. Stars reflect 'excellence' in the cooking, and crowns the degree of 'luxury' in the restaurant. The hotels are assessed on the basis of 21 factors with different weightings which are then added to a final percentage score. Bonus or penalty points can be added by the inspector based on outstanding impressions, be they positive or negative. A clear distinction between ERG and the National Tourist Boards and Motoring Organizations is that ERG are not interested in the detailed specification of facilities. They would not measure rooms or itemize the contents. The percentage score, it is believed, is simple for the consumer to understand, namely if it is 90 per cent it is perceived as excellent, if 50 per cent it is a pass. Fifty per cent is the minimum grade. A hotel which scored below this, but was accepted for entry, would be identified with an 'H' only. Another unique feature which Ronay brought to his hotels and restaurants guide was a series of quick reference lists so that the consumer could refer to hotels with particular characteristics. In the Autumn of 1997 the guide, no longer operated by Egon Ronay, failed to pay fees to some of its reviewers. The organization went into liquidation. The guide was re-acquired by Egon Ronay who planned to re-launch it during 1998.

GOOD HOTEL GUIDE

Historical development

Hilary Rubinstein, a journalist, launched the *Good Hotel Guide* (GHG) in 1978. Rubinstein claimed that until he started the GHG the public could discover little about the character of a hotel from printed sources. He indicated that the hieroglyphic guides of the AA and Michelin, valuable though they were, were no substitute for critical appraisal where the readers can be given the feel of an establishment and be alerted to its weaknesses as well as its strengths.

Quality assessment

The assessment scheme for GHG differs from those examined so far. Until 1981 the guide relied entirely on readers 'recommendations', but at that time part-time inspectors were introduced to monitor differences in readers' opinions. The GHG does not classify or grade the hotels in the guide. A hotel would not be rejected because it lacked some tangible provision, although comment about its absence might be made in the write-up. The guide has no pretensions to comprehensiveness either by hotel type or geographical coverage; the entries in the main are generated by the consumer and tend to be smaller privately owned hotels rather than corporate chain operations. Value for money is, however, a key criterion for selection. Inspectors are now used to resolve three situations: first when the GHG is worried about the absence of feedback from consumers about a hotel; second, when they receive ambivalent reports; and finally, when there is concern about the veracity of the opinion expressed, or when entries are noticed in guides such as the *Good Food Guide* and seem worthy of investigation.

MICHELIN GUIDE

The *Michelin Guide* (MG) for the UK was first published in 1911; it was withdrawn in the early 1930s, and re-introduced again in 1974.

Quality assessment

In many respects the *Michelin Guide* is a publication surrounded by mystery. It is impossible to determine the criteria which are used for classification and grading, and the inspectorate employed by the company prefer to remain incognito. The *Michelin Guide* does not publish accommodation standards; they look for standards of cleanliness, upkeep and comfort that their readers tell them they require. Like the Egon Ronay and *Good Hotel Guide*, the *Michelin Guide* does not charge for an entry and does not accept advertising.

The hotels are 'graded' by numbers of black pavilions represented by a 'house' symbol: **5** – luxury in the traditional style; **4** – top class comfort; **3** – very comfortable; **2** – comfortable; **1**- quite comfortable; also symbols for 'simple comfort' and 'other recommended accommodation at moderate prices'. All symbols are also shown in red when the establishment has 'a peaceful atmosphere and setting'. The non-availability of any criteria prevents the hotelier from deliberately seeking a higher Michelin grade, as additional requirements cannot be determined. The impression presented by Michelin is that much of the inspection is of a subjective nature.

WHICH? HOTEL GUIDE

The Consumers Association (CA) had published Hilary Rubenstein's *Good Hotel Guide* for 11 years up to 1990. The CA announced the publication of a new guide, the *Which? Hotel Guide*, in September 1990.

The criteria for inclusion in the guide were 'it should be a good place to stay' and 'it should have that extra something setting it apart from others of its kind'. This applied as much to the luxury hotel as to the three-room bed and breakfast. The main concern of the guide was to identify: friendliness that makes every guest feel like someone special; freshness of approach – the sign that hoteliers enjoy their work; freedom for the guest, to be themselves, rather than feel that they have to conform to the 'house style'; and value for money, namely that the customer feels that the stay was worth every penny.

An entry in the guide is a descriptive passage, one to two pages in length. There is no 'classification' or 'quality grading' but entries are distinguished with three special award symbols. A casserole denotes that customers can rely upon a *good meal*. A £ denotes that the hotel offers especially *good value* at whatever price level. A leaf denotes that the hotel is in an exceptionally peaceful situation.

OTHER SCHEMES

Limitations of space prevent a detailed explanation of the development and operation of a number of the UK schemes, however a very brief description is provided.

Northern Ireland Tourist Board

A compulsory grading scheme was developed in the 1970s. The complexity of its operation led to the development of a classification scheme in 1992, which is almost identical to that operated by the Irish Tourist Board. Although a 'classification' scheme, there are a number of 'quality criteria' which, if not met could lead to failure to achieve a particular classification. Thus the terminology is a source of confusion.

Isle of Man Tourist Board

The Isle of Man operated a compulsory registration scheme under 11 separate accommodation registers. In 1985, compulsory grading was introduced, the grades being represented by 'keys'. In 1992 the ETB crown classification and quality grading scheme was adopted for the island. It is currently the only part of the UK which operates the Crown scheme on a *statutory* basis.

States of Jersey

The first part of the UK to introduce a non-commercial hotel classification scheme (1932). The scheme was re-designed in 1948 and again in 1990. There are currently two statutory registers: hotels with grades of 1–5 suns; and guest-houses with 1–3 diamonds. The statutory scheme is in two parts – a basic registration standard, which every establishment must achieve, and a grading standard which reflects by comparability the standard of hotels one to another.

States of Guernsey

A statutory accommodation and grading regime was established in 1948. The scheme has undergone a number of changes but currently has two registers for hotels and guest-houses. The hotels are graded with 1–5 crowns and the guest-houses graded A–D. Hotels are graded under four sections with a maximum of 1000 points being awarded; an arithmetical score places the hotel in the appropriate grade. Similarly, guest-houses have nine sections with a maximum score of 250. The current scheme is under review.

Other commercial hotel guides

Ashley Courtenay

First published in 1934. Hotels are inspected by anonymous husband and wife or partner teams who report as typical consumers and are unpaid except for the reimbursement of expenses. Hotels are not graded but assessed under general headings such as 'comfort' and 'value for money'. Hotels are charged a fee for entry, graduated according to the number of rooms.

Johansens

The guide does not contain chain hotel entries and hotels are not graded, being either recommended or excluded. Assessment comes from three sources: freelance inspectors; guest's report cards and spontaneous letters written by Johansen's customers. The guide is a high quality colour publication with strong photographic content for which the hotelier pays a fee.

Grading and classification by tour operators

Some tour operators offer their own hotel classifications or grades rather than explain the national schemes to their clients. This can present a confusing picture for the customer, particularly if the operator's grade is higher than that awarded by a national scheme. New regulations came into force on 1 January 1993 which require all operators to list official 'star' ratings alongside their own classification for EU hotels.

IMPACT OF PRODUCT BRANDING

National and international companies are increasingly engaging in defining a particular product; giving it a brand name and then promoting into specific segmented markets. Many chain operators do not regard hotel grading systems as appropriate to their products and would prefer the customer to judge 'value for money' implied by the brand.

The demand for clear comparable international standards will grow with the increasing use of global distribution systems to link airlines, hotels, agents, car hire, road and ferries, and which will deliver reservations internationally within seconds. It is claimed by some that a comparison of hotels by a travel agent is easier to understand when using brand names than a disparate set of classification and grading criteria. The recognition of brands as an important influence in the field of hotel classification and grading has been identified by the Automobile Association, as previously discussed.

RECENT DEVELOPMENTS

The Crown scheme operated by the mainland National Tourist Boards has been dogged by disagreements over its effectiveness since its inception in 1987. The Department of National Heritage called for a review of the Crown scheme in 1995 but little initial progress was made due to the conflicting interests of the tourist boards and the motoring organizations. In 1996 the Tourism Society (Tourism Society, 1996) produced a consultative document which had widespread industry support and this provided a spur to bring the discussions to a conclusion. In February 1997 the STB announced a breakaway from the discussions to develop its own scheme based on quality criteria. The ETB, AA and RAC continued to develop a scheme which was primarily classification. The WTB withheld its decision but later opted for the STB approach.

The essential difference in views is that the ETB/AA/RAC schemes assess the facilities of an establishment (taking into account some quality measures), whilst the STB/WTB scheme is based on quality assessment, with some account being taken of facilities at the four and five star level. Stars will be awarded by the former schemes for hotels and, at the time of going to press, another symbol (yet to be decided) for guesthouses, bed and breakfasts and farmhouses. The STB/WTB scheme will award stars for all establishments. To add even more confusion to the situation, if a Scottish or Welsh hotel also wishes to attract customers through the AA guide, it will be independently assessed and awarded different stars, based on different criteria to their national schemes. Far from meeting the government's desire to see a national harmonized scheme, the current position presents a more confusing picture than ever for the customer.

CONCLUSION

The development of the hotel product in the UK has resulted in increasing diversity with individual types of properties satisfying the needs of particular market segments. Brands specifically identify some of these products, but classification schemes attempt to reduce diversification by funnelling all hotels into a range of inflexible criteria. This lack of flexibility linked with some operators' wishes to obtain higher classifications, whether they are appropriate for their market segments or not, produces confusion and criticism from both operators and customers.

It can be suggested that a grade expressed simply in a non-contentious way is what the customer requires. Hoteliers may have many different views but many independent operators see the grades as important marketing tools which they would not be without. Similarly, consumers have differing expectations from a scheme; some see international uniformity and simplicity as the key; another, flexibility that recognizes customer expectations that vary by location, type of property and purpose of stay.

The re-organization of the mainland tourist board schemes has taken place. It has presented the customer with a very confusing picture, this is in contrast to the purpose of the review. While the ETB and the motoring organizations base their schemes primarily on classification and Scotland and Wales major on quality, the process of change has not produced 'harmonization'. Failure to produce a voluntary national scheme acceptable to the customer may well encourage government intervention along the lines of their manifesto to establish a statutory basis for registration, and possibly classification and grading. It seems certain, however, that the development of, and debate about, hotel grading will continue for some time.

REFERENCES AND FURTHER READING

Beavis, J. (1979) 'Consultative committee on registration of tourist accommodation', report to the National Tourist Boards, London, August.

Callan, R.J. (1992) 'Jersey's hotel grading scheme: an idiosyncratic approach', *International Journal of Contemporary Hospitality Management*, **4**(3), 30–36.

Callan, R.J. (1993) 'An appraisal of UK hotel quality grading schemes', *International Journal of Contemporary Hospitality Management*, **5**(5), 10–18.

Callan, R.J. (1994a) 'Statutory hotel registration and grading: a review', *International Journal of Contemporary Hospitality Management*, **6**(3), 11–17.

Callan, R.J. (1994b) 'European hotel classification – boon or burden?', *Hospitality*, October, 14–17.

Callan, R.J. (1995) 'Hotel classification and grading schemes, a paradigm of utilisation and user characteristics', *International Journal of Hospitality Management*, **4**(3), 271–83.

Callan, R.J. (1998) 'Attributional analysis of customers' hotel selection criteria by UK grading scheme categories', *Journal of Travel Research*, **36**(3), 17–31.

Centre for Leisure Research (1993) *Scottish occupancy survey 1992: a report to the Scottish Tourist Board*, Edinburgh: Centre for Leisure Research, Heriot-Watt University, March.

Development of Tourism Act (1969), London: HMSO.

Inverness, Loch Ness and Nairn Area Tourist Board (1984) 'Classification and grading of tourist accommodation, summary report and recommendations', study sponsored by Scottish Tourist Board working with the Highlands and Islands Development Board and the Inverness, Loch Ness and Nairn Area Tourist Board, June/July Vol.1.

National Economic Development Council (1992) *Tourism competing for growth*, Working Party on competitiveness in tourism and leisure, London: National Economic Development Council, July.

STB Quality (1989a) 'Scheme is a winner, says the trade', *STB Quality*, December, 1.

STB Quality (1989b) 'Marketing is crowned with success', *STB Quality*, December, 4.

Tourism Society (1996) *Tourist accommodation classification and grading schemes*, London: Tourism Society, January.

4 Marketing hotel accommodation

Alison J. Morrison

INTRODUCTION

Over the last 30 years marketing has become established as a recognized academic discipline. The likes of Kotler (1988), Porter (1980) and Levitt (1988) have produced respected literature, models and theories of a generic nature. Buttle (1996) and Middleton (1994) have dominated hospitality and tourism marketing. However, amid such commendable scholarship it is perhaps easy to lose sight of the simplicity of the marketing process. So let us begin this chapter by putting marketing into perspective. Marketing is as old as civilization. It is the origin of business, starting with simple bartering and then evolving into the centralized exchange process of a town market (Wearne and Morrison, 1996). If we think of a market trader, literally taking a product to the marketplace, then the following simple approach applies. Generally, the market trader will:

- seek to secure a prime, prominent position, or attractive site, for their stall which will draw the attention of potential customers;
- ensure their product displays obvious attractive features and/or the trader can persuade and illustrate the less explicit features;
- be sensitive to consumer spending power, flexible and open to negotiation within certain profit-making parameters;
- be in tune with consumer behaviour, buying patterns and the value of building a rapport/relationship in order to develop repeat business and word-of-mouth advertising;
- shout out loud into the marketplace about the existence and benefits of their product, have an eye-catching stall, and use aggressive sales techniques; and
- adopt strategies of co-operation and networking amongst fellow traders, suppliers, officials and loyal customers to position their product in a wider marketplace.

So we can see that marketing is fundamentally about trading in a marketplace, applying a customer orientation which is designed to achieve a sustainable competitive advantage. Fletcher (1990: 2) believes that marketing is 'applied common sense, an attitude of mind and its maxims so obvious once stated that it is hard to believe firms do not naturally follow them'. Where complexity of the process arises is in endeavouring to build or expand a market, and from the necessity in an open market to compete against other businesses for the available market share. Wearne and Morrison (1996: 2) define marketing as:

> the process of creating, or making available, products and services which satisfy market needs and wants. The marketing process involves careful planning by management to allow for a large number of market variables. All these market variables

are caused by the separate requirements and preferences of people who, when grouped together, comprise the market.

Planning of the marketing process takes into account the main inter-related components which are generally accepted as people, product, place, price, promotion and positioning. So how does the marketing process interact with hotel accommodation? Currently, primary hotel accommodation places are termed hotels, budget lodges, and resorts. Each term is meant to describe a type of place where one can expect a certain style of service and product mix. The amount of total revenue a hotel receives from the sale of its main product – accommodation – will vary according to the style of operation. For example, in traditional full-service hotels it may amount to c.60 per cent, in budget lodges c.95 per cent, and in hotel resort properties c.50 per cent. According to the Hotel, Catering, International Management Association (HCIMA, 1998) the UK hotel industry average is 49.7 per cent of revenue. Furthermore, capital investment in hotels is substantial, and has a strong correlation with the state of underlying operating conditions in a particular market. Both these factors are clearly illustrated in Table 4.1 relative to the level of hotel investment in 1997. In the cities of London and Edinburgh a combination of market level and location combine to have a significantly higher level of investment per room when compared to a hotel of a similar market level outside of a large city (Croydon).

Whatever the style and level of capital investment, revenue from accommodation is clearly highly significant to the overall profitability of the hotel business. As such, the maximization of occupancy and room rates represent a primary, continuous concern for hotel management. Currently, this is taking place within an increasingly aggressive competitive environment. Consequently, the objective of the hotel accommodation marketing process is to influence consumer behaviour in a positive manner in order to maximize the economic yield from hotel accommodation and to achieve a sustainable competitive advantage. This can be achieved through the marketing process, expenditure on which averaged 2.6 per cent of expenses within the UK hotel industry in 1997 (HCIMA, 1998). Thus, this chapter focuses on the key current marketing processes, issues and challenges facing suppliers of hotel accommodation. This is presented within the framework of the six Ps: people, product, place, price, promotion and positioning.

PEOPLE

In line with a philosophy of consumer orientation, the starting point in hotel accommodation marketing planning must always be people and their characteristics, needs and

Table 4.1 Level of hotel investment 1997

Hotel	No. rooms	Approx. price (£m)	Price per room (£)	Vendor	Purchaser
Sheraton Belgravia, London	89	27	303,370	ITT Sheraton	Harilela Hotels
Selsdon Park, Croydon	170	17	100,000	Private	Principal Hotels
Balmoral, Edinburgh	145	35	241,379	Bank of Scotland	RF Hotels

Source: HCIMA (1998: 23).

wants. They represent the life-blood of every hotel enterprise – without them it would literally die from lack of business. According to the Henley Centre (1996), the profile of hospitality consumption is changing, reflecting what is termed 'postmodernism', where symbols have been elevated over substance. The Centre suggests that the hotel consumer of the 21st century will exhibit the following range of characteristics:

- be volatile, older and discerning;
- desire a spectrum of convenient and entertaining services almost any time and any place;
- be confident in purchasing;
- expect a wide choice in all markets; and
- demand value for time as well as value for money.

Mere consistency, reliability and efficiency is no longer considered sufficient to maintain a competitive advantage. Furthermore, it is important to recognize that 'people' may take on various forms, such as, families, females, business persons, private and public sector organizations, societies and associations, none of which are mutually exclusive categories. For example, hotel companies, especially in the economy and mid-priced segments, are marketing to capture the third-age, or 'grey pound', 50 to 75 year-old market segment.

Generally, this segment has been identified as having a high disposable income with demands of its own. They have above average literacy, loyalty and credit worthiness, and are experienced consumers with a considerable degree of sophistication. This, then, suggests to us the benefit of dividing up the marketplace into groupings of 'people' who share common characteristics, needs and wants. Such groupings are called market segments, and each has its own set of expectations and benefits which they seek to have satisfied. The range of the computerized property management systems (PMS) which are used in many hotels today can facilitate this process by providing vital sales and marketing information which can be 'mined' in order to identify the profile of various people who are currently using the hotel, and as a source for 'prospecting' for future business. With this knowledge or 'market intelligence' the components of the marketing process can be more accurately directed. Variables which can be generally used to categorize this information into identifiable market segments are:

- purpose of stay away from home e.g. leisure, business, visiting friends and relatives;
- socio-demographic people type e.g. family, empty-nesters (people whose children have left home), 'greys';
- geographic origins of consumer e.g. domestic, overseas;
- psychographics and life-style variables e.g. gourmet, romance, golfing;
- benefits sought and product usage behavioural segmentation e.g. relaxation, cultural enrichment, fitness, parent respite;
- purchase cycle and price e.g. weekly, annual, corporate rate, short-break package;
- hotel products or strategic segments which compete within the same market place e.g. Sheraton, Hilton, Inter-Continental; and
- multiple segmental measures to identify niche in apparently homogeneous mass markets e.g. leisure/empty-nester/gourmet/short-break package.

Clearly, a hotel will rarely be able to orientate itself to all 'people' nor would this be realistic in terms of its physical and operational capabilities. Therefore, management must decide which segment(s) of the market they intend to try and capture; which requirements of that segment of the market they intend to satisfy; and whether the business has the physical, financial and human resources to do it. For example, the segments and their characteristics presented in Table 4.2 have been matched to different types of hotel which they would potentially find appealing. In the contemporary marketplace it would be overly simplistic to believe that market segmentation was a clear-cut, simple to apply process which seldom fails. Never before has hotel accommodation management been faced with such an array of volatile consumer behaviour and patterns. It is really rather irritating. Once you have taken the trouble to group a person in one market segment they really should stay there! This is not the case – the lines between segments are increasingly becoming blurred.

The reality is that people are moving in and out of segments, reacting to their different business and life-style circumstances. What we are now seeing can be termed 'people occasions' (Henley Centre, 1996). For example, the person who buys the hotel product for a business occasion one week, may the next week be looking to purchase for a leisure, family, romantic, or sporting occasion. This suggests that one person may be represented in multiple market segments as the occasion dictates, and at different stages dependent upon their life-cycle position. This indicates the importance of building up a strong relationship with, and sensitivity to, people in the marketplace, identifying their characteristics, needs and wants. This enables effective management of demand, married to appropriate hotel product development, in a way that develops loyalty and retention across the range of hotel occasions people may wish to experience. Buttle (1997) refers to this as 'owning the customer' for life – not just one occasional visit. This approach is evident in the policy of Radisson Hotels World-wide which has developed products to attract the teenager, travelling with parents, market. If captured, these brand conscious young persons could be won over to being a 'Radisson guest' for life – as they move through their teenage years into careers, marriage, and old age. This corresponds to the teenager being able to differentiate Radisson, as a strategic segment, from the range of competitor hotel groups such as Marriott, Hilton, or Sheraton.

PRODUCT

Within each hotel product type are a number of core hotel accommodation product lines, such as self-contained, fully serviced apartments/suites, separate timeshare or

Table 4.2 Relationship of market segment and characteristics to hotel type

Market segment	Characteristics	Hotel type
Nature lover	Landscape and scenery, passive experience	Traditional, full-service country house hotel
Rest seeker	Tranquillity, pampering, comfort	Health spa
Discoverer	Cultural enrichment, access to heritage, natural environment, active experience	Castle hotel with wide range of sporting activities available in the local environment
Traditionalist	Safety, no surprises, familiar surroundings	Long established town house hotel with a 'club' atmosphere
Contact oriented	Social interaction, personalized/customized service	Independently owned, personally managed small hotel
Family oriented	Multi-age activities, amusements, entertainment, safety, parent respite	Resort hotel with leisure centre, supervised crèche/children's club

self-catering lodges, family rooms, twin/double/single/honeymoon and so on. Auxiliary product lines can include catering, beverage and bar, entertainment, business services, shops, personal services, leisure and sports facilities, and merchandise. There is limited potential for differentiating the core hotel accommodation product lines through architectural and interior design, although of course there are unique hotel products (see Box 4.1 and Chapter 13).

Box 4.1:   The Ice Hotel

The Ice Hotel in Jukkasjarvi, Swedish Lapland, is a vast igloo that accommodates up to sixty people. Guests can stay from December until May, when melt-down happens. Construction starts in October, when 3,500 tonnes of snow are combined with 1,000 tonnes of ice hewn from the Tornealve River. Out of this material a thirteen bedroom hotel is designed, complete with check-in desk, vodka bar and furniture, including ice tables and chairs, a sparkling chandelier, a fireplace and even ice glasses. White weddings take on a new dimension in the ice chapel where, in 1997, 60 couples 'tied the knot' in front of an ice cross, with the congregation seated on ice pews covered in reindeer skins. Less appealing may be the first night in sub-zero temperatures in the honeymoon suite! (*Britannia 360 Skyscene,* Winter 1997/98).

The basis of any hotel is to provide a mixture of physical products and services to enable people to sleep, eat and meet in a safe place to the satisfaction of the whole gamut of human experiences. However, rarely does someone want to experience everything on the one occasion. Thus, hotel operators are required to make decisions as to what products and services to offer, and in what combination (see, for example, Box 4.2). This results in the setting of a portfolio of a hotel's core and auxiliary products – its product mix – which is targeted at defined market segments and adapted to the environment in which it operates. Even the large, international, corporate group hotels, such as Hilton, do not operate a universal, inflexible product mix formula. It recognizes the importance of taking into account cultural considerations. People's views of the world and the society in which they find themselves are conditioned by the country of their origin and the society which shaped their beliefs and values. Knowing this, many of the large successful Asian hotels have developed their facilities to meet the demands of Western cultures, while still retaining some of the charm and mystery of their own environments.

Box 4.2:   Holiday Inn Kidsuites

Holiday Inn have developed a product concept called 'Kidsuites' in jungle, circus and pirate themes. These are children's rooms within rooms for adults. For a small premium, families with children between the ages of 4 and 12 can enjoy board games, electronic games, confectionery, puzzles and videos.

It can be observed that for the operator of a hotel, marketing is the means by which they can turn the core accommodation into a desirable product by adding value through service and design, combining physical form and attributes, and symbolism such as status and life-style statements. The key to success is to appeal to a specific group of customers, with a strong concept which provides a valid sustainable competitive advantage for customers to consider. In this way hotels, through customization, can clearly differentiate themselves within identified fertile, market segments. It has been identified that hotel accommodation consumers do not merely buy tangible products, they buy the expectation that they will receive a range of less tangible benefits. In this respect, product branding is used to provide a unique identity, reassuring potential customers that they will receive the range of benefits they seek. It helps to produce a consistent, differentiated, image in consumers' minds that facilitates recognition and quality assurance. In this way, branding bestows added value upon a product that can transcend the basic physical attributes. It is created by:

- advertising;
- people's experience of the brand;
- the sorts of people who use or are associated with the brand;
- belief that the brand is effective; and
- appearance of the brand (see Boxes 4.3 and 4.4).

Box 4.3:   Cliveden Hotel Company

The Cliveden hotel company has its eyes on expansion, but don't expect its name to start appearing over the doors of historic buildings around Europe. The Managing Director believes that the company is too small to attempt to create a brand out of the Cliveden name. To date, the portfolio consists of Cliveden itself, the famous stately home on the banks of the River Thames, the Town House, near London's Sloane Square, and the Royal Crescent in Bath. More hotel projects in the UK and Europe are in the pipeline as the company seeks to build a group of 'distinctive' hotels. Rather than use the Cliveden name directly, the group will aim to trade off the hotel's reputation for high-quality service. They are more concerned with branding the quality and standards so guests who go there will say 'This is what we recognise and it is exactly what we expected'. This policy is already working to the advantage of the Town House (*Caterer and Hotelkeeper*, 30 October 1997: 68).

Box 4.4:   Greenalls Hotel and Leisure

Greenalls hotel interest is represented by the following brands. De Vere Hotels are four and five star hotels which have unique character, including The Grand Brighton, The Belfry golf resort and Cameron House overlooking Loch Lomond. Village Leisure hotels combine an informal blend of hotel leisure club, pub and restaurant under one roof at ten locations. Premier Lodges are conveniently, comfortable and suitable for all the family, and there are over 45 accessible locations across the UK. Each is complemented by a friendly local pub or restaurant. Finally, there is Premier Inns which is a small select group of traditional country inns.

Different hotel companies approach brand building in a variety of ways. For some, it is implicit in the strength of a group's reputation for distinctiveness and high quality service. For others, it is a means of explaining the nature of the product and service and explicitly categorizing a portfolio of diverse products into standardized 'brand bundles' designed to appeal to specific markets segments.

PLACE

When used relative to the marketing of hotel accommodation, it is generally accepted that 'place' has two meanings. The first refers to the physical location of a hotel, and the second refers to the distribution systems used to make the product accessible to intermediary organizations who are involved in the 'selling' process, and prospective consumers. Traditionally, location and distance to travel to a hotel have been primary determinants of a hotel's success, and to a large extent this continues to hold true. Certainly, proximity to places where people want to engage in other activities is considered to be advantageous. This may be associated with:

- transportation types (airports, motorways, railways, ferry ports);
- leisure activities (shopping, sports, sight-seeing, theatres); and
- business (conferences, training, exhibitions).

Conversely, more peripherally positioned hotels in rural and coastal locations hold their own attraction. This is often based on their remote location, natural environment and distinctive local culture. People's perceptions of a place are generally dictated by its geographic location. Whichever market segment the hotel targets, the location requires to match expectations. For example, for whom does the 'place' hold the greatest appeal – business persons, tourists, domestic/overseas visitors, sports enthusiasts, and/or families? The answer to this question will influence markets of operation and geographic reach. Generally, people buy the hotel product on the basis of the information which they have available and not on product inspection. This information requires to attempt to make a largely 'intangible' product become more 'tangible' and persuasive. Consequently, in terms of the marketing process, there requires to be a strong emphasis on the quality of information produced and its effective dissemination, processing and transmission to the target market through carefully selected distribution channels.

Still significant and powerful tools in this process are hotel directories widely referred to by the travel trade and individual consumers. In addition, large hotel groups benefit from the ability to cross-sell their properties internationally (see Boxes 4.5 and 4.6). However, management of this function is becoming more complex as technologically driven innovations to the distribution system and its configuration continuously alter business practices. Table 4.3 summarizes the key electronic distribution alternatives and describes each of the components. These provide an indication of the different type of organizations, media types, financial benefits and costs involved in distributing hotel accommodation. Each hotel requires to design the most effective system relative to their markets operation, which delivers a surplus of financial benefits over associated costs.

Box 4.5: British Travel Agents' Accommodation Register

The Atlantic Hotel on the Isles of Scilly scarcely needs an extra push to its marketing efforts. Its average occupancy in 1996 was 98.6 per cent. But hotel owner George Teideman is not complacent. He believes that high-street travel agents can provide useful top-up bookings for his property, hence his support for a new register aimed at encouraging the travel trade to sell UK hotels. When the British Travel Agents' Accommodation Register was officially launched in March 1997, 850 properties in the UK had signed up at a cost of £175 per year, including every hotel in the Forte network. Commission rates for accommodation reservations quoted in the Register range from 8 per cent to 12 per cent. Since its launch, a further 400 hotels have signed to the Register. In the first year, ABTA has covered the £10,000 of distributing the publication to all its members. A CD-ROM version was distributed to agents in November 1997, making it easier for them to search for a property (Conway, 1997: 60).

Box 4.6: Best Western Hotels cross property selling

Best Western Hotels is a marketing consortia which was first established in 1946 to promote independently owned hotels and currently has a membership of 3700 properties. It produces an atlas and hotel guide which lists all Best Western Hotels by country and town in alphabetical order. Reservations can be made through travel agents or directly with Best Western using its computerized reservations system. This international network of hotel properties and reservation systems facilitates cross-selling and referral amongst the membership.

Table 4.3 Components of the electronic distribution system: a descriptive

Centralized reservation systems (CRS)	All information needed to make a reservation e.g. product specification, price, quality, availability, etc. is consolidated within a computerized centralized reservation system. The large hotel groups, consortia, and specialist reservation companies, have their CRSs permanently linked to the GDSs.
Global distribution systems (GDSs)	Four dominate travel bookings worldwide: **Amadeus/System One** (Lufthansa, Air France, Iberia); **SABRE** (American Airlines); **Galileo** (United Airlines, BA, KLM, US Air, Swissair); and **WORLDSPAN** (TWA, North West, Delta). Through these systems travel agents have accurate, real-time information on a hotel's rates and availability.
Hard storage devices	Devices such as CD-ROM are strictly information retrieval sources, with no interaction between end-supplier and end-user. The producers of such media include GDSs, travel organizations such as the AA, and NTOs.
Internet	It is predicted that consumers will commence to make their own reservations as hotel room databases become available on the Internet, thus replacing traditional methods. All hotel intermediaries have a Web site. Travel Web has grown to become the leading electronic hotel catalogue with brochures for over 8000 properties, representing 26 chains and many independent properties. In 1997, the on-line travel market was worth $1 billion.
Marketing consortia	Can be described as a grouping of hotels, most of which are single, independently owned hotels. They share corporate costs, such as marketing, while retaining independence of ownership and operation. These organizations can be either location or market specific. Within a hotel consortia a hotel is less tied than in other types of affiliation.

continued overleaf

Table 4.3 *continued*

National tourism organizations (NTOs)	Increasingly moving towards a leadership role in the coordination of tourism marketing activities. Specifically, in the form of integrated destination management systems, developed through collaboration with software houses and government agencies e.g. Integra and the Scottish Tourist Board.
Reservation companies	A specialist retail outlet for the hotel product offering. They are CRS driven and have access to GDS. In effect these organizations act as brokers, holding stock of available rooms for sale to all interested parties.
Switch companies	Evolved to act as an intermediary between the CRSs and GDSs. Such companies include **THISCO**, **Ultraswitch** and **Wizcom**, which enables smaller groups to connect via them. Switch companies are unwilling to offer this service to small firms, who are not able to offer sufficient reservations income to cover permanent linkage costs.
Travel agents	Retailers of the composite tourism product of which hotel accommodation is part. Acting as an agent for participating hotels they distribute their products, which entitles the agent to a commission of 10–12 per cent on the sale.
Web/interactive TV	Enables the customer to interact digitally with the Internet through their own television, PC and some purchased hardware and software, using the likes of Cable connections. This is known as WebTV. It is already used in the US, and collaboration between British Telecom and BSkyB has resulted in the launch of British Interactive Broadcasting. This illustrates the opportunity to reach the customer almost directly, and in real-time.
Wholesalers/ tour operators	Consolidate the component of the tourism product into a package which can be sold through distribution systems to the public. They do not sell direct to the public but through outlets such as travel agents or airline sales offices.

Sources: Buhalis and Main (1997); Emmer *et al.* (1993); Welch (1996)

PRICE

Price represents a significant strategic decision for all hotel accommodation operators, and is an important device for 'creating' consumers. It acts as a product cue, making a statement to consumer groups about the nature, accessibility, status association, perceived risk, quality and competitive differentiating features of the product they are purchasing. As such, it helps to determine the consumer mix and conversely, whatever consumers mix is targeted by a hotel will determine the price. For example, luxury products positioned in affluent markets at a premium price may be an essential requirement to maintain an image of exclusivity (see Box 4.7).

Box 4.7: The Royal Crescent Hotel, Bath

The Royal Crescent Hotel was acquired by Cliveden plc in 1997 which committed a £2.5m investment. The desire is to offer something unique. This prompted the decision to build a health spa within the hotel, reflecting Bath's origins, rather than a traditional health centre. Guests are also offered the chance to fly in the Royal Crescent's own hot-air balloon, or journey along the canals in the hotel's own 1920s river launch. Management believe that such extras are important to attract an affluent market segment. The target achieved room rate is £200, and the aim is for occupancy levels of 75 per cent (Anon, 1997: 68).

Price can be used to perform a variety of different functions which include:

- maximizing access and providing a broad market appeal;
- restricting access and limiting product offers to target markets;
- controlling demand in times of seasonality; and
- controlling demand in location relative to prime location versus 'off-the-beaten-track'.

Hotel grading and classification schemes, such as those administered by the Automobile Association, Royal Automobile Club, and the regional tourist boards, determine broad parameters of accommodation price (see Chapter 3). In addition, price is generally based on:

- perceived value to guests provided by the hotel product and services;
- spending power of target market segments;
- market demand for hotel facilities and services prevailing at the time;
- intensity of competition offered by other hotel operators;
- capital investment, fixed and variable cost recovery; and
- the level of commission paid to intermediary organizations in the distribution system.

The 'rack rate' is the term given to the regular published room rate. In a perfect market it is set as a result of cost-plus pricing which is based on a simple formula:

(operating costs + capital recovery + profit)/forecasted number of guests = price

Unfortunately, rarely is there such a thing as a perfect market. Therefore, rack rate in many instances has become a sort of starting price for parties to enter into negotiation downwards. The volatile nature of the hotel accommodation market causes fluctuations in demand. This dictates that short-term tactical pricing be used frequently, and that different rates may apply at different times of the year, week or even day. This is due to the need to generate rapid demand shifts in order to overcome unused accommodation capacity. An unoccupied, unsold, hotel bedroom is revenue lost forever. Key causes of unused hotel room capacity arises from:

- seasonality (vacation-taking patterns, weather);
- sudden, unexpected market fluctuations (terrorism, political unrest, air strikes, changes in foreign exchange rates, economic recession); and
- competitive activity 'spoiling' or 'matching' market activity.

Regularly, special offers are publicized in the media designed to attract guests on price, to fill rooms at a time when it has been identified that demand will be low, or even non-existent (see Box 4.8).

Thus, tactical pricing has become a recognized feature of hotel accommodation marketing, as a means of effectively managing the overall financial 'yield' from the stock of hotel accommodation. Yield management is the term used to describe the process of managing revenue against demand in hotel accommodation operations. Yield represents the actual revenue achieved, compared with the potential revenue if all the capacity is optimally used at the rack rate. Hotel accommodation managers require to balance the market segments they deal with in ways best calculated to improve yield (see Chapter 15).

> **Box 4.8:   Travelodge January price sale**
>
> At over 120 locations nation wide, a 2-night stay in a comfortable, spacious Travelodge room now costs just £19.95 per room, per night. Rooms are available at this specially reduced rate from January 6th to February 15th, 1998, but to qualify you must make your reservation for 2 consecutive nights before January 21st.

PROMOTION

Promotion is all about stage-managing an illusion using the base physical attributes of the hotel accommodation product, in a way designed to satisfy psychological and life-style needs and aspirations of the targeted market segments. As such, the objectives of promotion can be divided into three main types:

● reinforcement and market retention of existing clientele;
● creation of new ideas and attitudes to attract new consumers/markets; and
● effecting a change, converting negative to positive attitudes of disenchanted people.

Thus, promotion is concerned with image and relationship building over time and at different stages in the consumption process such as:

● decision choice stage;
● after-decision confirmation/reassurance;
● during experience/consumption; and
● post-experience to encourage loyalty/retention.

The promotional mix is designed to communicate the existence of a hotel and its products through a variety of information feeds, the main forms of which are:

● physical presence of the place – external and locational;
● interior design and layout;
● recommendations from frequent consumers (word-of-mouth);
● publicity and public opinions;
● advertising activities;
● brochures and other promotional materials;
● attitudes and appearance of staff;
● prices, value and special offers;
● ambience;
● people who patronise/are associated with the hotel; and
● name/brand/symbol/logo.

In fact, the methods of promoting hotel accommodation are diverse as is evidenced through the following selection of approaches and illustrations.

1. Repeat custom can be achieved by adding value through guest services designed to capture particular market segments (see Box 4.9).

Box 4.9:   Corporate executive guest services

Corporate executives on the road who clock up hundreds of bed nights in the line of duty provide the bread-and-butter business for most hotels, but the competition for their custom is fierce. In October 1997, Holiday Hospitality finished trials of a new Business Complete package specifically targeted at business travellers. For a supplement of £39.50 on top of the rack rate or the corporate rate negotiated by the client's company, the guest received an upgrade to executive room, car parking, full English breakfast, £30-worth of telephone calls, £20-worth of fax calls, postage and photocopying, and a consumer designed 'instant office' kit. It also included an in-room film, newspaper and magazines, premium brand toiletries, laundry for one shirt or blouse, a goodie box of sweets and games, and as much beer, wine and soft drinks as they could drink from the minibar. Similar packages, tailored to the appropriate market level, are being developed by Forte, Radisson Edwardian Hotels, Inter-Continental, and Sheraton (Conway, 1998: 70).

---

2. The hotel accommodation product can be customized by providing a value monopoly through personalizing communication (see Box 4.10).

Box 4.10:   Hatton Headlines

To our friends:
We hope you all had a very enjoyable Christmas and are rested and relaxed ready to enjoy the excitement that the New Year always brings.

The frantic, but thoroughly enjoyable activity of Christmas has rounded off a hugely successful year for us all and we too are enjoying a few days calm before our own New Year Celebrations.

During the Autumn months, four more of the manor house bedrooms at Hatton Court were completely refurbished, including the four poster bedroom, which has benefited from the installation of a 'twin tub' whirlpool bath. The launch of the new audio-visual facilities in the Severn Room has attracted great interest from local business media, more than fulfilling our expectations. More importantly, it provided a superb venue from which to enjoy England's football success in Rome!

On the downside, no further confirmed reports have been received as to the whereabouts of Freddie the Fox, but rumour has it he is about to launch a career in the media with his own cartoon strip. The new dining style at The Snooty has been well received by the hotel guests and locals, with the new evening menu being offered in all areas of the hotel. Following suggestions from the staff we have also repainted the hotel exterior and changed the outside lighting, signage and uniforms. We hope you like their ideas as much as we do. Across the county line in Castle Combe, fears for the health of Dolittle the pet cockatiel have been laid to rest. We have been assured that his insistence on pulling out his plumage is an indication of his desire to find a mate. The two hotels can't agree on which is the biggest handicap, a fox that has gone AWOL or a 'sexually frustrated parrot'. There's a bottle of champagne for the wittiest rhyming solution! Studley Priory, our sister hotel near Oxford, has come to the end of a two year extensive refurbishment programme,

creating some of the most impressive bedrooms and bathrooms in the group. This has been our most challenging adventure to date due to the age and fragility of the building, but we are extremely pleased with the end result. We hope you will be able to visit us soon, details of our January blues offer are on the reverse of this letter. In the meantime the search is on to find Freddie, and a single female cockatiel with a morally casual attitude.
We look forward to seeing you soon.

Yours,
Russell Pendregaust MHCIMA
Groups Operations Manager

PS: Details of our Valentines Weekend and Easter Break Holidays are now available should you require them. For further details contact the hotel of your choice.
Source: The Hatton Hotel Group (Hatton Court Hotel, Upton St Leonards, Snooty Fox Hotel, Tetbury, The Castle Inn, Castle Combe, and the Studley Priory, Oxford)

3. It is possible to formulate co-operation and cross-promotional activities, which are mutually beneficial for consumers and companies (see Box 4.11).

Box 4.11:   Greenalls, Radisson Edwardian and Hastings Hotels

To ensure coverage in London and Northern Ireland, Greenalls Hotels and Leisure have special arrangements with Radisson Edwardian and Hastings Hotels. They are all marketed within one Leisure Break brochure. This provides prospective consumers with a wide range of product types, locations and pricing levels.

---

4. Operators can link into consumer life-styles through reader offers in newspapers, journals and magazines associated with the target market segments (see Box 4.12).

Box 4.12:   Readers' Offer – Spring Destinations

The Glasgow Herald newspaper, in association with Hotel Connections, is pleased to offer readers the Spring Destinations Hotel Offer, valid from February 7 to May 3 1998. You and your family could enjoy two nights' dinner, bed and breakfast from as little as £60 per person. We are pleased to offer 10 hotels that would make the ideal location for a relaxing Family Break this Spring. Every hotel has a wide choice of leisure facilities and things to keep you busy. The hotels also provide special services for young children such as baby listening and crèche services, as well as early dining for younger people (*Herald*, 21 January 1998: 21).

---

5. Operators can solicit the endorsement of the hotel accommodation product through reputable editorial which has significance to members of the target market segment (see Box 4.13).

Box 4.13:   HOTEL SPOT CHECK 'Hotel du Vin & Bistro, Tunbridge Wells – the perfect mid-range hotel'

By the time we checked out, I was still praising the efficiency and friendliness of the young staff. The Hotel du Vin is the very best sort of mid-range hotel and back in the car my only complaint was that we had stayed for just one night. Service: good, Location: good, Food & Wine: excellent (*The Sunday Times*, 4 January 1998: 12).

---

6. It is possible to devise sales promotions which facilitate giving and reward of a personal or corporate nature (see Box 4.14).

Box 4.14:   Whitbread Leisure Vouchers

By giving Whitbread Leisure Vouchers to your family and friends you give them more fun and more choice, at 3000 outlets throughout the UK. As well as being the perfect gift, Whitbread Leisure Vouchers are bought by many companies for use in staff reward schemes and sales promotions, and for consumer gifts. Can be used in Travel Inn and Marriott hotel brands.

---

7. Companies can develop loyalty schemes, whereby guests are rewarded in the form of gaining benefits from frequent use of a specific hotel group (see Box 4.15).

Box 4.15:   Holiday Inn Priority Club World-wide

Each time you stay at a Weekender Plus rate or any other qualifying rate you can collect points with our Priority Club programme which recognizes the loyalty of frequent travellers by providing exclusive hotel benefits, special Hertz car rental tariffs and exciting award options, such as a free weekend and special activity awards. Membership normally costs US$ 10, however, if you join before 30 September 1998 the membership will be waived. You can also earn Priority Club points for Hertz car rentals.

---

8. Organizations can forge alliances with high profile chefs or restaurant brands to raise the market profile of the hotel through its food and beverage outlets (see Box 4.16).

Box 4.16:   Hotel restaurant alliances

Long regarded as an unwelcome and unnecessarily costly facility, the hotel restaurant is now becoming a revenue-generator in its own right, as well as a means of raising a hotel's profile. Granada is engaging Marco Pierre White to take over such places as the Oak Room in Le Meridien, London and the restaurants in the

Randolph, Oxford and the Queens Hotel, Leeds. The company's Posthouse division is looking to even more exotic themes to boost business. A pilot Mongolian Barbecue franchise restaurant is being introduced in two Posthouses, while Regal Hotels is planning to introduce ten themed bars to its hotels in the next year. Raymond Blanc has opened a *Petit Blanc* in Forte's Queen's Hotel, Cheltenham (Sangster, 1998: 53).

POSITIONING

Positioning is what happens when all the marketing components of people, product, place, price and promotion come together. It is not about the hotel accommodation core product, it is what is created in the minds of the target consumers as a result of the combined effect of the marketing process. As a consequence, a hotel has become 'positioned' in the minds of consumers and is given an image. According to Ries and Trout (1981) this can be described as a battle for the consumer's mind. When a significant number of people hold similar perceptions about a hotel, it has what is called market position. Over the life-cycle of a hotel business it may become necessary to reposition. If the marketer has done their job well, the hotel accommodation will have captured the consumer's mind, with positive reputation (market opinion), image (pictorial perception) and associations (descriptive terms which have emotive connotations) (see Box 4.17).

Box 4.17: Small, exclusive hotel positioning

In 1997, the Cliveden plc resigned from the marketing consortium Leading Hotels of the World. The organization, whose membership is by invitation only, prides itself on having within its ranks the cream of the hotel industry. However, the hotel felt that it was not well served by Leading, as it does not represent small exclusive hotels like Cliveden. It gives a confused message to its clients to be represented beside 500-room hotels in Manila which look like office blocks. Management believe that Clivenden will get more value out of working closely with API, a US-based consortium of travel agents which focuses on small exclusive hotels at the top end of the market (Anon, 1997: 68).

Essentially, a good positioning strategy is to achieve awareness through marketing, which is capable of fulfilment. Without credibility and a sustainable competitive advantage it is unlikely that a satisfactory position can be achieved for a hotel. This emphasizes the integral nature of marketing, which is concerned with more than activities external to the physical hotel. The positioning messages have to be followed through effectively within the internal environment as depicted in Figure 4.1.

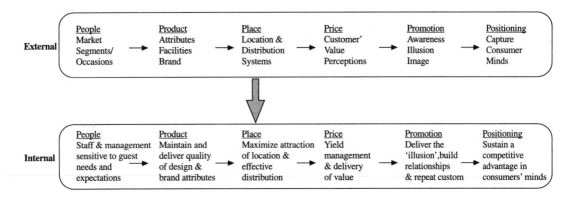

Figure 4.1 6 Ps of marketing: external and internal environments

CHAPTER SUMMARY

For each independently owned, and corporate hotel organization, the marketing process will have its unique set of factors, components and functions. Relative to the tourism industry in general, this is recognized by Seaton (1996: 4) who asserts that: 'Marketing principles can be applied to any hotel enterprise but there are differences between organizations in operational scope and impact arising from differences in financial resources, control of the market, degree of integration with other tourism enterprises and consumer volumes'. Thus, it is difficult, if not unwise, to prescribe a universal approach to marketing planning and strategy. What has been presented in this chapter is an insight into the marketing of hotel accommodation and current trends at one point in time. The reality is that the dynamism of markets and, indeed, the hotel industry itself, dictates that the marketing process is like a kaleidoscope – the picture changes with each revolution. Therein lies the excitement and challenge for marketers of hotel accommodation, as we seek to capture the minds and hearts of guests, in providing them with a unique experience on one occasion, which will live in their memories for many more visits to come.

REFERENCES AND FURTHER READING

Anon. (1997) 'Flying a High Standard', *Caterer and Hotelkeeper*, 30 October: 68–9.

Britannia Airline (1997) In-flight magazine, Winter 1997/98.

Buhalis, D. and Main, H. (1997) 'Catalysts in Introducing Information Technology in Small and Medium Sized Hospitality Organizations', *HITA 97*, Edinburgh: HITA.

Buttle, F. (1996) *Hotel and Food Service Marketing*, London: Cassell.

Buttle, F. (1997) 'Owning the Customer', paper presented at the HCIMA Annual Conference, Stratford-upon-Avon, October.

Conway, H. (1997) 'The Agents' Secrets', *Caterer and Hotelkeeper*, 13 November: 60–1.

Conway, H. (1998) 'Rewards of Loyalty', *Caterer and Hotelkeeper*, 15 January: 70–1.

Emmer, R., Tauck, C., Wilkinson, S. and Moor, R. (1993) 'Marketing Hotels Using Global Distribution Systems', *Cornell HRA Quarterly*, **34**(6), 80–9.

Fletcher, K. (1990) *Marketing Management and Information Technology*, London: Prentice-Hall.

HCIMA (1998) *The Hospitality Yearbook*, London: HCIMA.

Henley Centre (1996) *Hospitality into the 21st century: a vision for the future*, London: Henley Centre.

Herald (1998) 'Readers' Offer – Spring Destinations', Glasgow, 21 January: 21.

Kotler, P. (1988) *Marketing Management: Analysis, Planning, Implementation and Control*, Englewood Cliffs, NJ: Prentice-Hall, 6th edn.

Levitt, T. (1988) *The Marketing Imagination*, New York: Free Press.

Middleton, V. (1994) *Marketing in Travel and Tourism*, Oxford: Butterworth-Heinemann.

Porter, M. (1980) *Competitive Strategy: Techniques for Analysing Industries and Competitors*, New York: Free Press.

Ries, A. and Trout, J. (1981) *Positioning: The Battle for Your Mind*, New York: McGraw-Hill.

Sangster, A. (1998) 'Whatever Next', *Caterer and Hotelkeeper*, 1 January: 53–5.

Seaton, A. (1996) 'The Marketing Concept in Tourism', in Seaton, A. and Bennett, M. (eds.), *Marketing Tourism Products*, London: International Thomson Business Press, 399–420.

The Sunday Times (1998) 'Hotel Spot Check', 4 January: 12.

Wearne, N. and Morrison, A. (1996) *Hospitality Marketing*, Oxford: Butterworth-Heinemann.

Welch, S. (1996) 'Can Independents Ride on the Superhighway for World-wide Marketing?', paper presented at the IAHMS Symposium, Harrogate.

Accommodation strategy and accommodation stock in the hotel industry

5

Joseph E. Fattorini

In this chapter we examine the dynamics of accommodation strategy and how they effect the level of accommodation stock. Traditionally the focus of accommodation and hotel management courses has been what might be termed the 'retailing' of hotel services to customers. By 'retailing' we mean selling hotel rooms, meals, conferences, leisure facilities and the variety of other services that are offered in hotels. This focus is not surprising as most hotel managers spend most, if not all of their time, concerned with these activities. However, it has long been understood that it takes more than successfully retailing these various services to customers to run a profitable hotel. Hotels are complex and very expensive capital assets. Successful hotels must be both well managed *and* return a sufficient level of profit relative to the price paid for them. This chapter is concerned with the second of these features.

Before becoming immersed in the subject, it has already been noted that most hotel managers spend little or no time concerned with strategic questions of hotel acquisition or disposal. It is therefore pertinent to ask why should they need an understanding of the issues involved. One reason is, as we see below, that there is a trend towards the separation of ownership and operation in hotels. Yet owning a hotel is not necessarily the same as owning other forms of property. The success or failure of the investment is often dependent on the competence of the operator. Thus the relationship between owner and operator can be crucial and, not surprisingly, mutual understanding of each other's objectives is a prerequisite. This chapter will hopefully help managers understand what owners' objectives and strategies are and consequently help managers assist the owners in achieving them.

A second reason for studying this area is that the managers today may well wish to become the owners of tomorrow. A number of commentators have suggested that hospitality management education is failing fully to prepare students for eventual promotion to senior management positions by concentrating on operational issues rather than the broader skills they will require (Lewis, 1993; Slattery, 1997). Furthermore, a number have specifically suggested that hotel real estate education is one area of specialized, if advanced, knowledge that might be usefully studied in order that students have the capability to move into senior roles as they progress through their careers. Indeed it is interesting to note that in the US, where the division between ownership and operation is more advanced than in the UK and continental Europe, hotel real estate classes often appear in the curriculum of hospitality management degree programmes and on occasions provide an area of specialism for more advanced students. For those seeking a more detailed discussion of this topic see Wilson (1995) and Mayer (1998).

STRATEGIC FOCUS AND 'DUALITY' IN HOTELS

At the heart of modern strategic management thinking is the concept that successful companies match internal corporate resources to opportunities in the marketplace. In other words you find out what you are good at, find customers who are prepared to pay for this skill and then concentrate on that activity. Implicit in this concept is the understanding that this area of expertise will be necessarily limited. This has been a driving force behind the break-up of many industrial conglomerates, with managers and investors having greater faith in focused companies that operate in one industry area than in a large sprawling collection of companies with no real connection between them. In the hotel sector we have seen this with the demerging of Lonrho, a conglomerate which felt it could provide more value for its shareholders by selling its hotel groups, Metropole and Princess. Indeed, in this case it was hard to see the connection between these two hotel groups (one largely concentrated on the UK conference market and the other on Caribbean resorts) let alone the connection between hotels and Lonrho's African trading and mining interests.

In hotels there is a further dimension to this question of strategic focus. In any hotel business there are two quite different business activities. One is the retailing of rooms and other services to guests. The other is investment in property. The strategies involved in these two business activities are quite different. The retailing of hotel services involves issues of branding, customer service, marketing and distribution. It involves satisfying very large numbers of customers, each one making a relatively small purchase. Conversely, owning property, particularly hotels, involves making long-term, large scale investments. The issues here are the enhancing of asset value through 'project feasibility, project financing, and financial control in cooperation with a management contract company' (Go and Pine, 1995: 37). Put another way, operating hotels is about making a very large number of quite small decisions, owning hotels is about a much smaller number of very big decisions.

It is important to note that an understanding of this 'duality' in the industry is important for a hotel company's success. In an analysis of twelve UK hotel company case studies Stewart (1996: 191) noted that the 'ability of the hotel operator to recognize, adopt and exploit a dual perception of the business' was 'an important contributory factor to the success of any [hotel] company'. He goes on to note 'It is via the expert matching of the inherent and potential value of the property in terms of environment, location and size to the retailing of accommodation, food, liquor and leisure that the potential capital gain attributable to the property may be realised'.

This evidence from Stewart's study is important for two reasons. It shows that hotels need to be thought of as investments and treated as such if they are to be successful in the long term. It is to this quality of hotels that the chapter turns next. However, Stewart's study also notes that the 'environment, location and size' of the hotel must be matched to the appropriate accommodation, food, liquor and leisure retailing skills. Thus where ownership and operation are divorced, both owner and operator must have a clear idea what the other has to offer and seeks to gain from their relationship. Where ownership and operation are by the same person or company they must be competent in, and able to, combine the skills of both.

HOTELS AS INVESTMENTS

Hotels differ from other forms of property investment in a number of ways. This feature has been noted by several writers, although they have often tended to emphasize different aspects of the character of hotel property. Hattersley (1990) notes how hotels tend to be single-use buildings with facilities such as bedrooms and bathrooms that cannot easily be converted to other uses. Furthermore he points out that hotels usually carry out all of their business in one building to the exclusion of other tenants, and that they carry out the whole of their business in the same building. Similarly, Leonard (1992: 35) emphasizes the differences between hotels and other forms of commercial property, suggesting three basic differentiating factors:

- hotels are labour intensive businesses;
- hotels must resell the 'leases' on their space (bedrooms) each day; and
- hotels must care for customers 24 hours a day, unlike offices and retailers which are usually empty at night.

Alternatively an analysis of hotels and motels as investments in the US by Rushmore (1992: 239), lists a quite specific selection of 'unique investment elements' although this list is oriented to those who would wish to buy a hotel:

- as much as 25 per cent of the total property value may be accounted for in furniture, fixtures and equipment;
- as retailers hotels and motels require well trained, specialist managers; and
- hotels and motels may come with large inventories of expendable items such as food and beverage and linen.

Whilst each of these writers has suggested a variety of ways in which hotels are different from other forms of property, the overall message is quite clear. They all stress the limited use to which the properties can be profitably put. Butler *et al.* (1994) also emphasize the 'single-use' nature of hotel property, but go further by pointing out that this feature tends to be exacerbated as hotels have cycles of supply and demand that do not always affect other types of property. It is to the external environment of hotels and fluctuations in demand and supply that we now turn.

The cyclical nature of hotel demand

In discussing the cyclical nature of hotel demand we must add two other features of hotels to that of their limited use. The first feature is that hotels, particularly in terms of accommodation, have a fixed supply and have no substitute. The second feature to add is that hotels take a long time to build and open. The first feature, fixed supply, is important because the demand for hotel facilities is rarely fixed or even stable. Over a weekly cycle we see demand fluctuate between weekdays and weekends. This is particularly noticeable in city centre hotels focused on business travellers who will tend not to travel at weekends. These hotels try to increase demand at weekends with discounted city breaks and other packages aimed at leisure travellers. We also see demand fluctuate over an annual cycle with high and low seasons for leisure travel. Hotels in highly seasonal resorts may offer discounted packages in the off-season or in some cases even close when demand slackens.

Nevertheless, perhaps the most important cycle, particularly in developed economies like those of the UK, US, and continental Europe, is the cycle of the economy. Demand for hotel rooms is particularly sensitive to the state of the economy. In economic upturns, demand tends to be particularly strong especially from business travellers. This is because companies are expanding, new opportunities are opening up and existing units need visiting, all of which require businesses to set employees, managers and others to travel where they will often require to stay overnight. Conversely, in downturns and recessions, business travel is often one of the first areas of the corporate budget to be trimmed. As companies retrench and delay investment in new opportunities they can considerably reduce their need for business travel.

This means that over the course of an economic cycle hotels are faced with both an opportunity and a threat. In the upturns, a fixed supply of rooms and rising demand from customers allows hotels to charge higher prices. In a downturn, the opposite is true with declining numbers of customers and the same number of rooms leading to reduced prices and more aggressive discounting. Evidence for this is more than simply anecdotal. In an analysis of hotel room rates in the US (the hotel market most similar to that in the UK) Rushmore (1994) demonstrates that room rates increase faster than other prices (using the Consumer Price Index or CPI) in periods of strong occupancy and lag behind the CPI in periods of weak occupancy. As he points out, 'using sophisticated yield management programmes, modern lodging facilities can ride the demand curve and maximize the room rates charged as the market permits. As a result hotels generally offer significant upside potential during economic recoveries' (Rushmore, 1994: 139).

This quality or ability of hotels to 'ride the demand curve' and outpace prices elsewhere in the economy makes hotels a very attractive investment in buoyant economies. Evidence for this is widespread, but perhaps the most significant example in recent years in the UK was the spate of hotel company flotations and other activity on the stock market in 1996. Beginning with Granada's purchase of Forte, the market saw the flotation of Millennium and Copthorne, Scottish Highland Hotels, Macdonald Hotels, Jarvis Hotels, Thistle Hotels and Cliveden. The impact of these flotations is clear when we consider that whilst 1994 saw UK hotel flotations worth US$ 36 million, and in 1995 the figure was US$ 2 million, 1996 was an extraordinary year with flotations totalling US$ 2,905 million (Allison, 1997).

A stock market flotation is only part of the story though. The money raised from this and other sources of finance can be used to invest in existing properties, and perhaps more importantly, to finance new developments. Existing and prospective hoteliers see the fixed capacity, rising occupancies and rising room rates of existing hotels during economic upturns and decide that the best way to exploit this prosperity is to develop new hotels. Unfortunately, given that new hotels change an otherwise fixed supply of rooms, they inevitably have a diluting effect on levels of occupancy and room rates. This is particularly true in small markets where the addition of new hotel supply can have a devastating impact on the market levels of occupancy. Indeed, research shows a generally negative correlation between hotel room sales and new hotel construction (Rushmore, 1994).

This negative correlation tends to be exacerbated by the second feature of cyclical demand changes in hotels attended to earlier: hotels take a long time to build. Before building a hotel, a developer must first find, evaluate and purchase a suitable site. This is followed by planning, finance raising, and eventually building the hotel. Therefore from inception to the first paying customers can be a period of several years. This is quite long enough for growth in the wider economy to have slowed, reducing overall demand for hotel accommodation with the added dilution effect of the new hotel property compounding the effect of already reducing occupancy and room rates.

In the UK and US this dilution has been made even worse by the provision of incentives to build hotels that frequently led to the development of marginal properties. In the UK the Development of Tourism Act 1969 gave rise to the Hotel Development Incentive Scheme. This scheme provided grants and loans for buildings and fixed equipment for work begun before April 1971 and completed by April 1973. The maximum grant available was £1000 per bedroom, which at that time was approximately one-quarter the capital cost. Estimates over this period suggest that around 2000 bedrooms per year were added to the total room stock and investment in hotels increased sixfold (Medlik and Airey, 1978). In the recession that followed initiated by the 1973 oil crisis and lasting until 1975, properties built and managed by inexperienced developers and managers suffered, particularly in London (Stewart, 1996). Similar supply gluts appeared in the US, first with the popularity of real estate investment trusts (REITs) at the beginning of 1970 which, like the UK, was followed by the oil crisis in 1973. A second example of this type of incentive to development was found in the US after the deregulation of the savings and loan industry and changes to tax laws that made hotel development particularly attractive to US investors. Much of the blame for the problems suffered by the US hotel industry in the 1990 recession has been attributed to this period of overbuilding (Rushmore, 1994).

Structural change and hotel demand

As well as changes in demand for hotels emanating from the cycle of the economy, some commentators have suggested that we see fundamental changes in demand for accommodation from a changing economic structure. The structural theory of business travel was developed by Paul Slattery of Kleinwort Benson Securities (1990) and is further described in (amongst others) Litteljohn and Slattery (1991), Slattery and Litteljohn (1991) and Slattery and Boer (1991) and describes one type of change in the demand for accommodation, i.e. business travel. The structural theory deals only with business travel and as Slattery and his team at Kleinwort Benson have themselves suggested, changes to the structure of the non-business traveller market are likely to become increasingly important in the demand for hotel facilities (Slattery *et al.*, 1996).

The essence of the structural theory is as follows. Slattery suggests that demand for business travel is determined by the structure of an economy rather than simply by growth or absolute levels of GDP. He identifies three distinct phases of growth and development in national economies which in turn influences business travel demand. Those nations in phase one have economies dependent on extractive industries or manufacturing. Economies in this phase have very few hotels, usually centred in large commercial centres. These serve incoming business people and are frequently foreign owned brands. Regions in this phase include Africa, Latin America and Eastern Europe. Phase two is a period of rapid growth, characterized by the UK in the 1980s, where the economy moves from a manufacturing base towards an economy dominated by services. This shift towards a service industry dominated economy leads to an increase in business travel as more people need to travel to sell, manage and administer in service businesses. Much of continental Europe is currently experiencing a rapid growth in its service sector and is thus in phase two. Finally, phase three is the position currently occupied solely by the UK and US. Here the rapid growth of hotels has ceased and the industry matures. This is often characterized by industry consolidation. This has been particularly true in the UK in the late 1990s where short to medium-term concerns are pointing to an extended period of consolidation as investors seek to maximize cost savings and generate growth. Langston (1998: 38) notes,

> because of the fragmented nature of the industry, most commentators are agreed that consolidation will be a feature for some time. With well over 60 public and private companies of varying size operating in the sector, there is much potential for rationalisation.

Similar sentiments were expressed in a *Financial Times* report on a major hotel industry conference with the headline 'Hotel Sector Faces Period of Consolidation' (Daneshkhu, 1998).

Thus the level of business demand for hotels is felt to be related to the structure of the underlying economy. However it is important to note that many commentators have not accepted this concept of the structural theory for business demand (for criticisms of the theory see in particular Hughes, 1993 and 1995). Although Hughes (1993: 309) concedes that the theory is 'intuitively plausible', he suggests that it is overly simplistic, and based on 'invalid comparisons over time and between countries'. He notes that there is no evidence that growth in service businesses leads to a concurrent growth in business travel and furthermore, that to suggest that the proportion of the economy occupied by services will dictate the level of hotel growth, is not borne out by the evidence. In particular he is critical of the way Slattery suggests that an economy enters phase three, and is supposedly dominated by its service sector when the service sector exceeds 50 per cent of GDP. Hughes notes that Sri Lanka, Panama, Zambia and Malaysia all had service sectors that accounted for over 55 per cent of GDP even in 1981 and Belgium, the Netherlands, Denmark and Sweden had service sectors more dominant than that found in the UK in 1981 yet they are all phase one economies within the theory. Yet Hughes asks 'Have they experienced substantial hotel growth? A straightforward relationship of hotel demand with service importance seems too simplistic' (1993: 310). Notwithstanding this criticism, the structural theory of business demand has gained wide currency in the industry and amongst some academics. Undoubtedly this is due in no small part to the fact that it is 'intuitively plausible' and that its suggestion of a paradigm shift in the demand for hotel accommodation seems to provide evidence for bullish or optimistic predictions about hotel growth outside the UK and US.

A second aspect of structural change has also been emphasized by Slattery (Slattery *et al.*, 1996: 5) and appears to be rather less contentious. In their June 1996 share valuation overview, *A Golden Age for Hospitality,* Slattery, Feehely and Savage suggest that 'the main source of demand growth is the 40–64 year age group which will account for circa 30 per cent of the UK population by the turn of the century'. They point out that this group of 'babyboomers' have had families who have now left home, have paid off their mortgages, already own most white and brown goods they need (dishwashers, televisions and so on) and may well have two incomes. This provides them with very high levels of disposable income which they appear increasingly happy to spend on leisure activities outside the home, like leisure breaks in hotels. Furthermore, repurchase is the only way to enjoy these activities again, the enjoyment of hedonistic activities is itself a spur to repurchase and such activities are viewed culturally as enhancing customers' standards of living. Slattery *et al.* point out that growth in leisure oriented demand is not restricted to the UK either, noting the World Travel and Tourism Council projections that between 1995 and 2005 travel and tourism is expected to double in size in nominal terms and increase spending in real terms by 54.6 per cent (clearly, these figures will need to be revised in light of the 1997/8 crisis in many Asian economies).

Drawing these structural and cyclical influences together, it is clear that demand for accommodation is very heavily influenced by the external environment. What complicates the picture is that the supply of accommodation is relatively fixed, leaving prices fluctuating as demand rises and falls. Additions to the accommodation stock may well appear very attractive in times of strong demand, but their addition can dilute occupancy, room rates and profitability across the market, and given the time taken to build hotels, might very well be too late to take advantage of the demand that stimulated construction in the first instance. Underlying all this, there appears to be large shifts in the structure of the economy and market which can fundamentally change demand for hotel accommodation. All these features must be considered by owners of hotel property and evaluated when buying or selling accommodation stock. Beyond these macro factors a wide range of micro, short-term and opportunistic factors influence buyers and sellers which are largely dependent on the circumstances of the day. Some of these have already been outlined above, for example in the UK, the Hotel Development Incentive Scheme; and in the US, cheap financing from REITs and the deregulated savings and loans industry. This discussion now turns to examine some of the current motivations, macro, micro and opportunistic, of hotel buyers and sellers, particularly in the UK market.

THE BUYER'S PERSPECTIVE

As we have already noted, the UK hotel industry remains heterogeneous with well over 60 public and private companies of varying size operating in the sector in addition to the many small single owner-managed enterprises. This is not new, and as Stewart (1996) has pointed out, there has been a gradual consolidation of the industry in the period since 1945. During the modern period of consolidation there are several key themes.

First a number of companies are keen to create a critical mass. Small groups like Regal Hotels recognize that they can no longer compete whilst they remain restricted to small markets and unable to market themselves further afield. Allied to this, these groups recognize the advantages that can be found in economies of scale. Alongside the reduction of non-revenue generating facilities in hotels, hotel companies are keen to reduce costs incurred by head offices and other administrative functions. By buying groups of hotels, profitability across the newly expanded group can be much greater. For publicly quoted and traded companies, these acquisitions are particularly important where they enhance earnings.

Second, a feature of many recent hotel acquisitions has been that they have come from overseas. This feature was particularly noticeable from south-east Asian investors. A similar interest from Asia was evident in the late 1980s in the US, a phenomenon termed 'asset evolution' by Olsen et al. (1991: 216–14). During this period, US hotel companies sold a large proportion of their assets to become an industry based largely on management contracts and franchises. This was done in order to lighten their balance sheets and create more impressive returns on assets. A particularly powerful group of buyers of hotel assets during this period were the Japanese. Initially they bought 'quietly and moderately', only later paying high or even above market prices that bought these sales of hotel property to wider attention. The strategy behind these acquisitions was, Olsen et al. (1991) suggest, that paying higher prices for later acquisitions would raise the total portfolio value of properties bought 'quietly and moderately' before. By raising the value of the portfolio the Japanese buyers gained greater leverage and could acquire yet more property. Despite being described by Olsen et al. as a strategy of 'sound logic', this now has the appearance of a classic investment bubble, and Saison's sale of Intercontinental to Bass may well be the first of a number of Japanese hotel sales. In the UK, recent interest in hotel property has tended to come from Malaysia and Singapore and has been largely centred on London hotel property. The impact of currency fluctuations and these countries' need to service foreign currency debt is not yet clear, however many feel that it could impact on London hotel prices (Day, 1998).

Other significant overseas buyers of hotel property in the UK have been US Real Estate Investment Trusts (REITs). As described above, their influence on the US hotel property market has not always been entirely benign. Even so, as they find domestic acquisitions harder to come by they are increasingly looking overseas for suitable property. A full description of the structure of REITs is beyond the scope of this chapter, but it is worth outlining their main features. Initially set up to provide an incentive to invest in property development, REITs enjoy tax advantages including freedom from corporate tax. In return for this tax break they must distribute 95 per cent or more of their taxable earnings to shareholders in dividends, and in most cases, they may not operate the properties they own, in other words they act simply as landlords. However a small number of REITs enjoy a tax loophole that gives them so called 'paired share' status, allowing them to act as landlord and operator yet still holding on to their tax advantages. Three of these 'paired share' REITs, Starwood Lodging, Patriot American Hospitality and more recently, healthcare REIT Meditrust, have shown an interest in or have actively bought UK hotel property. The most important deal so far has been Patriot's purchase of Arcadian, which was also part owner in the rapidly expanding Malmaison chain. Many in the industry as well as politicians, commentators and academics have raised concerns about the power of 'paired share' REITs to outbid others in purchasing hotel companies and property (for example see Walsh, 1998) and the signs are that their power is likely to be curbed. Nevertheless REITs provide an interesting example of how distortions in the market can occur when incentives are introduced by legislators.

THE SELLER'S PERPSECTIVE

Alongside the buyer's desire to consolidate their position in hotel markets, there must be a corresponding number of willing sellers. Yet, like buying, selling is increasingly seen as a strategic business decision. Kay Dymock of JLW Hotels suggests 'owners/investors should look at optimising sale price by selecting the timing of marketing the property relative to the trading performance of the hotel. It may take two to three years to reposition or effectively asset manage the hotel prior to sale' (cited in *Hotels: Investment Outlook*, 1998: 5–10). For many owners the willingness to sell is driven less by necessity than by a desire for strategic focus in the remaining group. The most obvious targets for this type of sale are difficult, marginally profitable or even loss-making properties/sites. Sometimes, other operating companies feel that they can turn these difficult properties around or that they can be converted to a different use. Other properties may be disposed of because they fall outside the company's core area of operations or they target non-core business.

In some cases, the move into a limited number of brands of hotels can lead to disposals of either individual properties or whole collections of hotels. For example, Swallow Hotels disposed of hotels without swimming pools. Swallow had made swimming pools and leisure facilities a key part of its brand package in targeting the business market, a package which was compromised by a limited number of sites that did not live up to full brand expectations. Whitbread decided to concentrate on two brands/markets, Marriot and Travel Inn. Those non-core hotels from the Lansbury brand that failed to fit into either portfolio were sold to Regal Hotels (where they did fit into the Regal brand) in early 1997 for £64.5 million (Day, 1998). Similarly, Stakis have put a number of properties up for sale. However, in their case, the motivation is less that the properties do not fulfil brand promises than that Stakis are seeking capital to finance a vigorous programme of internal refurbishment and expansion.

Finally two other groups of recent sellers in the UK are worth mentioning. During the recession of the early 1990s a number of banks and other institutions became unwilling owners of hotels after companies defaulted on loans. They see the current high values being placed on hotel property as making it an ideal time to sell their hotels. Many have been able to sell at prices above those they had provided for and clear their books. Similarly, they have used current high prices to put pressure on their 'bad book' of hotels (those with high levels of debt) to sell property and clear debts. The second group of sellers worth noting are those wealthy individuals who have also been tempted by the high prices being paid for hotel property to sell what they feel is at, or near the top, of the market (Day, 1998).

DIVORCING OWNERSHIP FROM OPERATION

A recurring theme throughout this chapter, mentioned in various contexts, has been the separation of ownership and operation. This process is much more advanced in the US than in the UK. However, as it becomes increasingly popular in markets outside the US it is worth discussing how the relationship between owner and operator has evolved. Go and Pine (1995) note that a critical issue in the owner's selection of a management contracting operator is human resources. As service businesses are highly dependent on their staff, poor quality personnel will almost inevitably lead to poor business performance. With wage levels in many countries varying little across the industry, effective recruitment, training and retention policies are the key features owners look for in any prospective operator.

Beyond human resources policies, Go and Pine (1995) refer to two International Hotel Association (IHA) reports which are useful in charting the main trends in the evolution of management contracts (IHA, 1988, 1993). Owners are seeking more flexible terms which allow them to end the contract if the operator fails to live up to expectations or if they decide to sell the hotel. Owners are also seeking contracts that last for shorter periods of time. They may well seek minimum performance levels too. Operators for their part are becoming more involved in putting equity into projects, or alternatively being asked to forego their part of the fees until the hotel is maintaining a level of cashflow sufficient to pay off its debt. The IHA noted, however, that finding satisfactory ways of implementing many of those features that both parties were happy with was proving difficult. Even so, the established position of management contracts within the industry was underlined by the 1993 report. It noted that during the recent (1991) recession, large international brands like Hilton, Intercontinental, Ramada, Meridien and Holiday Inn maintained far higher levels of profitability than their smaller rivals. As owners have become more focused on profitability and maintaining a strong return on their properties and whilst they have the opportunity to run their hotels under these brands by management contract, consolidation in this way seems set to continue.

SUMMARY

This chapter has outlined some of the ways that accommodation stock is influenced by factors within the wider economy. It has also shown how hotel owners devise strategies to deal with these environmental influences. As the hotel industry, particularly in the UK, consolidates over the next few years, managers, whether as retailers of hotel services or as managers of hotel assets must become more aware of the value of their properties. Although there appears to be a shift towards the management contract based industry of the US, the UK and Europe may chart its own course, leaving hotel ownership in the stewardship of operators. Either way, managers and companies will find success through a knowledge of, and ability to combine, the skills of owner and operator.

REFERENCES AND FURTHER READING

Allison, S. (1997) 'The Equity Market in European Hotel Stock', paper presented at the 'What are Hotels In and Throughout Europe Worth?' Conference, London, 29 September.

Butler, J.R., Benudiz, P.P. and Rushmore, S. (1994) 'Hotel Lending in the 1990's: Amateurs Beware', *Cornell HRA Quarterly*, **35**(6), 39–46.

Daneshkhu, S. (1998) 'Hotel Sector Faces Period of Consolidation', *Financial Times*, 25 March, 38.

Day, C. (1998) 'Deals Deconstructed: Lessons for Interpreting the Current Market and Discerning Trends – The UK Market', paper presented at the 'What are Hotels In and Throughout Europe Worth?' Conference, London, 29 September 1997.

Go, F. and Pine, R. (1995) *Globalisation Strategy in the Hotel Industry*, London: Routledge.

Hattersley, M. (1990) 'Valuation of Hotels', *Journal of Valuation*, **8**(2), 143–65.

Hotels: Investment Outlook (1998) 'Maximising Real Estate Opportunities', *Hotels*, January, 5–10.

Hughes, H. (1993) 'The Structural Theory of Business Demand: A Comment', *International Journal of Hospitality Management*, **12**(4), 309–11.

Hughes, H. (1995) 'The Structural Theory of Business Demand: A Rejoinder to Slattery', *International Journal of Hospitality Management*, **14**(2), 117–18.

IHA (1988) *Hotels of the Future: Strategies and Action Plan*, Paris: International Hotel Association.

IHA (1993) *The Case for Hotel Management Contracts*, Paris: International Hotel Association.

Kleinwort Benson Securities (1990) *UK Hotels PLC: The Decade Review*, London: KBS.

Langston, J. (1998) 'The Ghost of Fawlty Towers', *Investors Chronicle*, 9 January, 35–8.

Leonard, S. (1992) 'A Hotel is More Than Real Estate', *Hotels*, **26**(7), 35.

Lewis, R.C. (1993) 'Hospitality Management Education: Here Today, Gone Tomorrow', *Hospitality Research Journal*, **17**(1), 273–83.

Litteljohn, D. and Slattery, P. (1991) 'Macro Analysis Techniques: An Appraisal of Europe's Main Hotel Markets', *International Journal of Contemporary Hospitality Management*, **3**(4), 6–13.

Mayer, K.J. (1998) 'Hospitality Real Estate Education – A Review and Proposed Research Agenda', paper presented at the Third Annual Graduate Education and Graduate Students Research Conference in Hospitality and Tourism, Houston, USA, 8–10 January.

Medlik, S. and Airey, D.W. (1978) *Profile of the Hotel and Catering Industry*, London: Heinemann, 2nd edn.

Olsen, M., Crawford-Welch, S. and Tse, E. (1991) 'The Global Hospitality Industry of the 1990s', in Teare, R. and Boer, A. (eds.) *Strategic Hospitality Management*, London: Cassell, 213–25.

Rushmore, S. (1992) *Hotels and Motels: A Guide to Market Analysis, Investment Analysis, and Valuations*, Chicago, Ill: Appraisal Institute.

Rushmore, S. (1994) 'An Overview of the Hotel Industry: Past Present and Future', *The Real Estate Finance Journal*, Spring, http: //www.hvs-int.com/frcareer.htm.

Slattery, P. (1997) 'Are we heading for mediocrity', *Hospitality*, July/August 1997, 24–5.

Slattery, P. and Boer, A. (1991) 'Strategic Developments for the 1990s: Implications for Hotel Companies', in Teare, R and Boer, A (eds.) *Strategic Hospitality Management*, London: Cassell, 161–5.

Slattery, P., Feehely, G. and Savage, M. (1996) *A Golden Age for Hospitality*, London: Kleinwort Benson Securities.

Slattery, P. and Litteljohn, D. (1991) 'The Structure of Europe's Economies and Demand for Hotel Accommodation', *Travel and Tourism Analyst*, **4**, 20–37.

Stewart, D. (1996) *Hoteliers and Hotels: Case Studies in the Growth and Development of UK Hotel Companies 1945–1989*, Glasgow: Search Publications and Consultancy Services.

Walsh, D. (1998) 'Over-rich and Over Here', *Caterer and Hotelkeeper*, 12 February, 62–4.

Wilson, R.C. (1995) 'Hospitality Real Estate: A Relevant Hospitality Course', *Hospitality and Tourism Educator*, **7**(2), 31–5.

Accommodation development: a public sector perspective

6

Tom G. Baum

INTRODUCTION

The contemporary accommodation sector is one that is characterized by diversity in terms of the age, history and size of its units of operation; ownership structure; and geographical dispersal. It is a sector which confounds generalization in that seeking a framework for the meaningful comparison of the accommodation stock of, for example, Hong Kong with rural Ireland is elusive if not pointless. In most countries, the accommodation sector that we see today is a response, over an extended period of time and varying from location to location, to evolving market demand in the destination's key segments, whether leisure travellers; business visitors; conference and convention delegates; pilgrims visiting a holy shrine; or a combination of some or all of these. In this process of development, whether 200 years as in the case of many European countries or 30 years in, for example, Singapore, there has been an important interplay between the roles of the private and public sectors, roles which have changed over time according to economic and political considerations but both of which have been important in shaping the accommodation sector as we find it today. At the heart of the debate over public versus private responsibilities in the accommodation sector is consideration of whether the sector is an economic area in its own right (which then merits treatment on purely commercial and competitive terms alongside any other sector of the economy) or whether it is an essential ingredient in the wider business and leisure tourism infrastructure, without which other areas of the economy cannot operate (in which case the argument for a greater level of state involvement is strengthened).

In this chapter, discussion will focus on the varying roles which public sector agencies, especially tourist boards play in the development and regulation of the accommodation sector. Chapter 3 addressed the specific issue of accommodation grading. This has, traditionally, been one responsibility in which the public sector, generally tourist boards, have played an important part. This chapter will only consider grading in the wider context of the regulatory role which the public sector has in accommodation development.

The public sector and its various agencies influence the extent, location and character of accommodation development in a number of ways and consideration of these varying influences is at the core of this chapter. At one level, the relationship between accommodation development and the role of public sector agencies can be located within the framework of tourism and wider economic policy in the sense that public intervention in the area has clear policy development objectives, whether these relate to expanding the tourism industry or creating employment for construction or hotel workers. In this sense, government and its agencies seek to implement specific policies and consequent measures which will have a direct and causal effect on their main concerns, which are facilitating more tourists or reducing the numbers in receipt of unemployment benefit. This model of policy development and implementation is articulated at a conceptual level by Pressman and Wildavsky (1973: xv, in Hall and Jenkins, 1995):

> Whether stated explicitly or not, policies point to a chain of causation between initial conditions and future consequences. If X, then Y. Policies become programs when, by authoritative action, the initial conditions are created. X now exists. Programs make the theories operational by forging the first link in the causal chain connecting actions, giving them stability and internal coherence.

This model assumes that the actions of public intervention will make a direct contribution to meeting overall policy objectives, whether in tourism or in a wider economic context. In other words, facilitating or financing the building of additional hotel stock, or refurbishment of existing properties, or supporting the marketing of them, will directly contribute to an increase in the number or quality of visitors to that location whilst at the same time providing local employment during the building or up-grading phase – in both cases, tangible economic benefits will be seen and there will be an expansion of the local economy in this application of Keynsian economic thinking. The thinking behind the UK's Development of Tourism Act (1969) and measures such as the Hotel Development Incentive Scheme, similar legislation in the Irish Republic (the Grant Scheme for Hotels and Guesthouses, 1978, and the Hotel and Guesthouse Reconstruction and Development Scheme, 1985) (Deegan and Dineen, 1997) as well as measures to boost hotel supply in Turkey during the late 1980s are examples of initiatives of this kind. In both the UK and Irish examples, the administering agents on behalf of government were the respective tourist boards but the investment was publicly justified in terms of its support for national tourism objectives.

Public intervention in accommodation development may also be rather more *ad hoc* and have little direct relationship to tourism policy objectives. Funding for accommodation build and refurbishment in Northern Ireland has been made available through European Union sources (for example, the first Operational Programme for Tourism and the INTEREGG (Inter-regional Development Programme) for border areas) from the late 1980s but such initiatives had few direct links to tourism policy except as an expression of vague optimism in the aftermath of the 1985 Anglo-Irish agreement. Similarly, the quasi-independent (but government controlled) International Fund for Ireland (IFI), established in 1986, expended some 20 per cent of its monies (in excess of £55 million) on tourism infrastructure projects on both sides of the border. The focus in the accommodation sector was on private sector amenities through the addition of conference and leisure facilities to existing establishments with the objective of extending the season and making the border regions more competitive. At that time, this objective was laudable but delivered little in increased tourism activity because of the prevailing political situation. The long-term benefits may only be realized in the context of a more stable political environment in Ireland since 1994. Scepticism about this model of intervention is well expressed by Deegan and Dineen (1997: 206) when they state:

> Evaluating the IFI expenditures is difficult because no formal studies have been undertaken … . The funds did represent an important additional injection to the sector. The extent to which these may have led to windfall gains for the operators involved or displacement of business from non-assisted operators is conjectural though a definite possibility since the 'reconciliation' more than the 'economic' motive for support may have been paramount.

It would be a mistake to think of the role of the state in the development of accommodation solely in terms of financial incentives and support although this is clearly the most 'visible' and direct role. Probably the most visible role is that of marketing and promotion. For many small accommodation units, placement in the appropriate tourist board accommodation guide is their only annual promotional activity. As Chapter 3 has shown, the role of public agencies is also strongly (but not exclusively) associated with quality enhancement through accommodation grading schemes. Planning regulations (a public concern) can also have an important impact on the character of accommodation stock through the preservation of existing buildings, land zoning controls and restrictions on the type and height of buildings permitted. Fire and other health and safety measures can also impact on the design and refurbishment of accommodation facilities. In many countries, the public sector also plays an important part in the initial training and subsequent further training of accommodation sector employees, thus providing significant public subsidy to operations both large and small. This contribution, in turn, can make a significant difference to operational standards and business profitability.

INCENTIVIZING ACCOMMODATION INVESTMENT

The role of the public sector in the financing of hotel development takes two forms. The simplest and one that is of decreasing significance in most developed countries, involves the state or its agencies acquiring or building accommodation units which they then operate or lease to public or private companies. This form of state involvement was the standard approach within the planned economies of Eastern Europe until the early 1990s but was also to be found in the UK through British Transport Hotels (BTH) and British Airport Authority (BAA) hotels at Gatwick, Heathrow and Stansted airports. In Ireland, the successful and expanding Great Southern Hotels Group (GSH) remains in public ownership and other examples of state accommodation investment are Irish Country Cottages, developed by Shannon Development as a new accommodation product concept and subsequently privatized. To some extent, BTH and GSH came into the public domain by default with the privatization and re-structuring of the railways. In Newfoundland, the provincial government built four key hotels in the 1970s as a specific instrument designed to encourage the growth and development of tourism to the island. Originally operated in the public sector, they were subsequently operated by Holiday Inn and were privatized in the late 1990s. At a local level, the municipal governments of a number of towns in Iceland have built and operate hotels as a public amenity necessary to support the development of other sectors in the local economy, generally the fishery. Moves to increased private sector ownership of the economy in many countries has led to a decline in this form of public involvement in the accommodation sector.

A rather more common model and one which is designed to stimulate the private sector rather than retain control in the public domain, is represented by the range of investment incentives which governments operate in order to encourage the private sector to invest in accommodation facilities and refurbishment. In this, the principles are common with incentives available to companies across the economy and widely used to attract major multinational investment in the manufacturing area (Rolfe *et al.*, 1993). As we have seen, incentives may be offered at a transnational level within the European Union (Wanhill, 1993) but in the accommodation sector the most common model is at the level of national or regional government. Here, a number of different approaches to incentivization can be identified (Baum and Mudambi, 1996). These include the following.

Grants

These involve the transfer of financial or in-kind resources from the taxpayer to the accommodation facilities developer, who then has no obligation of repayment. This form of support may be given by granting publicly-owned land to the developer. This approach entails a number of risks and problems from the point of view of the grant agency, particularly the possibility that the recipient will liquidate the project without repayment being required. Grants to cover part of the project remain an important strategy for economic development agencies – the Hilton project in Belfast is in receipt of about 40 per cent of total costs from public funds while the RF Hotels development in Cardiff Bay has benefited to a similar level. Grants may be offered with the attachment of certain strings. For example, schemes operational in Ireland in the 1980s to encourage the provision of bed and breakfast facilities in farms and private homes of the west and south-west, required letting for a period of five years after which operators could choose to withdraw from the accommodation sector.

Infrastructure development

Upgrading of airports and recreational facilities, subsidies for employee training and the provision of services all come under this heading. As with grants, the development authority does not benefit directly from the success of a project but there are important differences in that the accommodation developer does not retain ownership of the resource and there is little incentive to liquidate the investment. Furthermore, this form of support cannot be finely targeted and the benefits frequently extend beyond any one specific developer.

Tax Concessions

Typically, these involve favourable changes to the developer's property and/or profit tax liability. Tax concessions provide positive incentives to the developer because the benefits only accrue if the project is successful. Concessions may be offered over an extended period of time as with the creation of tax-free zones or, more commonly, developers and operators can be offered a 'tax holiday' for the start-up period of the project. Some tax benefits against operational liabilities such as those relating to training may also be offered.

Loans and loan guarantees

Loans and loan guarantees permit accommodation developers to access development funding at, frequently, favourable rates because of government intervention. Loans make direct use of public funds and, therefore, their availability will be limited. The incentive to succeed is greater than is the case with grants as any residue after business failure goes to the lender not the developer. Loan guarantees support private bank loans but do not involve the direct outlay of public funds unless businesses fail, so this method is rather more efficient.

Interest subsidies

This method uses public funds to reduce the cost of borrowing to developers, usually from private banks. It does not influence the level of commitment which developers make to the long-term of the project.

The above measures are frequently administered by tourist boards or similar agencies. With this range of financial support mechanisms available to public sector agencies, their potential influence on the location, structure and character of accommodation is considerable. This influence can be used to alter the supply structure at a national level as happened in Turkey in the 1980s with incentives to invest in hotel stock on the Mediterranean and Aegean coasts and is part of a strategy to develop Egypt's Sinai and Red Sea resorts over the coming decade. However, the negative impact of financial incentives can be seen in the number of newly built bed and breakfast properties in the west of Ireland, subsequently taken out of the tourist accommodation stock and contributing to 'bungalow blight' in the area.

MARKETING ACCOMMODATION

The marketing and promotion of accommodation (considered in more detail in Chapter 4) is probably the most visible aspect of the public sector's role in relation to the industry. Most tourist boards publish an accommodation guide or a series of guides to reflect location or type of accommodation (hotels, self-catering, guest-houses and so on). This role has, in the past, been offered as a complementary service to establishments which meet specified facilities and quality criteria. While charging for inclusion in the guide is now normal practice, it is generally offered to businesses at a highly subsidized rate. Promoting the operation was, and in most situations remains, an important 'carrot' in the attempts by tourist boards and similar agencies to raise the overall standards of accommodation stock.

Over the past 20 years, the general trend has been towards marketing partnerships, designed to ensure that those businesses which benefit from promotional efforts on their behalf contribute to the costs of such promotion. Large accommodation operators and those which are part of major groups invest significantly in free-standing marketing and this, generally, does not attract public subsidy. However, the micro- to medium-sized businesses which, numerically, dominate the accommodation sector of most countries, do not have a tradition of significant investment in marketing and, alone, cannot make a significant impact in key market segments. Tourist board promotion through guide books, representation at travel fairs and similar initiatives represents their main market access route. The possible downside of the tourist board guide is that it has created a level of complacency about marketing amongst small accommodation businesses. An insert in 'the guide' can be seen as a marketing panacea when, in reality, analysis of buying behaviour suggests that only a minority of potential guests actually use this source for information.

Recent years have seen the growth of electronic marketing, particularly via the internet. This has given small accommodation businesses a low cost, potentially high impact promotional route which bypasses normal distribution channels managed by tourist boards. There are an increasing number of small accommodation businesses which have their own web site and accept bookings over the internet. However, there has been relatively little research on the costs and benefits of such systems for small businesses and the overall impact of internet marketing for small accommodation businesses will not be seen for some years.

As a general assessment of marketing accommodation and the role of public agencies, it is fair to say that the more mature the destination, the role of tourists boards in the marketing of individual properties declines so that in the US, for example, federal involvement is not an option and at a state or local level the focus is on the destination, not the specific product.

REGULATING AND RAISING THE STANDARDS OF ACCOMMODATION

One of the key objectives of public sector, generally tourist board, involvement with the accommodation sector is to support the raising of operational and service standards within all businesses in a destination or country. The reduction or elimination of 'rogue operators' is an important step in enhancing overall destination image and, with it, strengthening the appeal of the location from a marketing perspective.

Two approaches, 'carrot' and 'stick' can be used to encourage improvements in the quality of accommodation on offer and these frequently go hand in hand. Positive inducements may be through the accommodation grading scheme which can be used to recognize both quality and improvement (see Chapter 3). In addition, tourist boards frequently sponsor national or regional tourism awards which include accommodation categories aimed at the establishment and key personnel working in it. In Singapore, for example, the prestigious Tourism Awards recognize the best performing hotels, the hotel with the best service, the best marketing campaigns by hotels and awards for key posts in hotels – 'Receptionist of the Year' and so forth.

The 'stick' approach is to require specified minimum standards before accommodation units are recognized by the tourist board, included in marketing campaigns, able to participate at trade fairs and permitted to use the public insignia of approval and recognition; in Ireland this is represented by the green shamrock. Sanctions may also be applied through the grading scheme with the possibility of a reduced level within either the facilities or service categories or both. As a final sanction where grant, loan or other financial incentives to upgrade or refurbish exist tourist boards as common administrators of such schemes can influence their allocation to businesses other than those which meet various operational, safety and training criteria.

SUPPORTING HUMAN RESOURCE DEVELOPMENT AND TRAINING

The accommodation sector, especially in its more traditional forms (hotels, guesthouses) is labour intensive and assessments of its quality are closely allied to the quality of service which is delivered. This is particularly true of the micro- and small- to medium-sized enterprises which, numerically, dominate the sector. While labour intensity is not such an important component in self-catering complexes or in the growing budget hotel sector. quality of personal service can still be an important dimension in achieving business competitiveness. Increasingly, the overall quality of service which is delivered within the accommodation sector is accepted as a key component of a destination's competitiveness and the institutional arrangements which have to be put in place in a country such as Singapore in support of this service quality culture are critical to the international reputation which that destination has achieved (Council for Hospitality Management Education [CHME], 1998).

The rationale for state involvement in education and training for accommodation stems from the wider justification which is expressed for the expenditure of public monies in support of the development and marketing of the sector in general. This is based on the structure of the industry, primarily its small and medium-sized enterprise (SME) focus which makes marketing, in particular, difficult at a destination level; its geographical dispersion and the contribution which tourism makes to regional and local development in areas where few economic alternatives exist; and the relationship which exists between accommodation and its wider natural and cultural environment – it is both consumptive and supportive of local resources which generally fall under public ownership or management.

Education and training for the sector is accepted, in part, as a public sector responsibility within the context of general state investment in the development of its skills base in key areas of the economy. The extent to which the state invests in education and training is a good indicator of the importance which is attached to the accommodation sector within overall economic planning. This reasoning is reinforced by the widely held belief that a sector dominated by SMEs and which has a strong presence in remote and peripheral locations has a limited capacity to meet its own skills requirements and, in order to develop towards international competitiveness, requires public investment in both its entry-level skills base and in the further development of the workforce. In some contexts, notably in the developing world, international tourism also demands skills which are not necessarily readily available within the local economy, reflecting the cultural and language demands which international tourists place upon a local workforce. This argument, for example, justifies the level of joint investment which the public and private sector in Australia have made in the development of Japanese language skills and cultural familiarization to support accommodation marketing investment in that segment.

Finally, the accommodation sector has the capacity and offers a variety of employment opportunities to support the entry or re-entry to the workforce of those who might otherwise remain marginalized and there is a widely held perception that it is in the public good to support this form of labour market participation through technical and social skills training. This argument applies to groups such as the disabled as well as to recent immigrants and other members of minority communities as well as those seeking skills updating prior to re-entry to the workforce.

In recognition of the role which skilled personnel play in the delivery of accommodation services, it has long been accepted that there is a level of public responsibility for the provision of a skilled workforce for the industry. This responsibility is most evident through public funding of the initial education and training which those at school, college and university receive in preparation for their entry to the industry's skilled workforce on graduation. Hotel craft and management education, in the public sector, has a history of close to 100 years, mainly in the food and beverage area but the growth of 'rooms division' education in reception and housekeeping, while slower, has taken place over a similar timeframe. Most programmes of study combine college learning with industry placement and training, through a form of apprenticeship or internship and, therefore, public sector investment is complemented by an input from the private sector. The nature of this partnership varies. In the UK and a number of other countries, the relationship between public and private sector is relatively loose but the German 'dual system' ensures strong partnership commitment from employers, the local administration through the chambers of commerce and the public college system (Rutter, 1992).

In most countries, public investment in and commitment to this area of vocational education has provided a major if unheralded subsidy for the sector and one which has not been subject to significant critical assessment and evaluation as to its impact and benefits. The relatively small proportion of employees in the accommodation sector with formal pre-entry training in the UK raises important questions about cost and benefit which remain largely unaddressed. There are a wide variety of publicly funded or subsidized courses (full and part time) from initial skills training to postgraduate university study and these are offered throughout the country. Similar patterns of provision can be found in other countries.

In addition to public support for training within the college and university system, there has also been a long-standing commitment in many countries to supporting the upgrading of human resources amongst those already in employment in the accommodation sector. In the UK until the mid-1980s, this support took the form of a dedicated Industrial Training Board for the hotel and catering sector, the Hotel and Catering Industry Training Board (HCITB) (subsequently, the HCTB and, after privatization, the Hotel and Catering Training Company and the Hospitality Training Foundation – HtF). In its original form, the training activities of this statutory agency were funded through a training levy based on a percentage of payroll which was imposed on all employers in the sector and which could be 'clawed back' through the up-take of approved training programmes. With the ending of the levy scheme, public funding was and still is channelled through the agency from a variety of different sources and special initiatives, the New Deal and NVQ assessment structures to name but two. Whilst the levy scheme no longer operates in the UK, it has been introduced in the sector in both Malaysia and Singapore within the last five years as one formal mechanism of ensuring private sector commitment to training. With the ending of the statutory base for HCITB and its Northern Ireland counterpart, part of the role in this respect has been adopted by economic development agencies in various parts of the UK. In Scotland, Tourism Training Scotland (TTS) is a body established by Scottish Enterprise and Highlands and Islands Enterprise (TTS, 1996: 4): 'to transform Scotland's competitive position in tourism, through promoting quality training and career development for all who work in the industry, to ensure that a world-class quality of service is enjoyed by all visitors to Scotland'.

This mission translates into three inter-linked objectives:

- to generate an industry wide commitment to training and staff development;
- to attract and develop high calibre staff through relevant initiatives and professional qualifications; and
- to provide easy access to quality training and advice which meets the needs of the industry.

TTS supports training at all levels within the industry and, through its parent agencies as well as Local Enterprise Companies (LECs), ensures that training is accessible to all businesses in the sector and this includes accommodation operators of all sizes. The prime objective of the sponsoring agencies sees training as an arm of economic development whereby enhanced skills and quality of service contributes directly to the overall economic prosperity of a destination and this, in turn, allows the sector to grow and increase the level of local employment.

Pre-dating the HCITB by a number of years is CERT (the Council for Education, Recruitment and Training for the Tourism Industry) in Ireland which, as an agency focusing on hotel and catering alone, was established in 1963 and maintains a strong and influential role in the education and training of hospitality employees. CERT is responsible to the Minister of Tourism (although originally established as a Labour Ministry agency) and receives its funding from both the exchequer and the European Union. The Irish situation provides an integrated approach to all levels of education and training for accommodation, both within the college system and in industry. CERT coordinates the implementation of all aspects of government policy in the area of education and training for hospitality – researching industry's education and training needs; recruitment of craft trainees; design of the training programmes; funding of training in schools and colleges through EU and state subvention; and the provision of in-company training. CERT's role is both comprehensive and cohesive and, thus ensures close affinity between the development of national tourism policy and the strategies which meet its human resource objectives. The target-driven approach to tourism development which has dominated Irish tourism policy since 1987, has also translated into education and training targets which were modified through regular review so as to ensure that skills match the product and service focus of market development. Flexibility and responsiveness allow CERT to put in place initiatives which cater for the specific needs of selected sectors – subsidy for training executives within small accommodation businesses is one example while the formalization of a tradition of in-company training for entry level managers into a certified programme is another. The contribution of European and national funding is critical to existing CERT provision and this will be subject to considerable change in 1999.

ACCOMMODATION AND THE ROLE OF ECONOMIC DEVELOPMENT AGENCIES

We have already noted the training initiatives which economic development agencies such as Scottish Enterprise or their local partners (Local Enterprise Companies (LECs) in Scotland and Training and Enterprise Companies elsewhere in the UK (TECs)) undertake in the accommodation sector. In addition, these agencies have the power and remit to support the development of the sector with a particular emphasis on up-grading facilities and improving business performance. The agencies also have the ability to manage the size of the accommodation stock – in a mature destination such as the Highlands and Islands of Scotland for example, the issue is not one of increasing the stock but of upgrading the quality of what is there so the efforts of the development agencies have been directed at this in terms of both physical and human capital.

Central government economic initiatives also can impact on the accommodation sector and its development. One of the key labour market challenges which the sector faces is that of skills shortages. The issue of sector image is, probably, at the heart of this problem (Wood, 1997). Springboard UK is a joint public and private sector partnership which has the objective of raising the profile of careers in the accommodation (and wider tourism) sector so that it becomes the career of first choice amongst school leavers and mature entrants. Public commitment and funding to this project is influenced by the clear economic development purpose of making the sector more competitive and, as a result, its contribution to national wealth greater.

CONCLUSION

With the increasing focus of tourist boards on, primarily, marketing functions, other roles are being either discontinued or allocated to other agencies in the public or private sector. The wide-ranging development and training activities which are sponsored by economic development agencies provide good examples of this. The administration of accommodation grading schemes, for example, has been contracted out by Bord Failte Eireann (the Irish Tourist Board) to a private company. In a mature, efficient and competitive accommodation market, it may well be that a 'withering away' of state involvement is appropriate. The lack of public regulation and an emphasis on self and market regulation in the US, beyond health and safety, points to how this can be achieved. In countries where there remains a preponderance of independent micro and small enterprises in accommodation, it is unlikely that the state role will disappear entirely in the foreseeable future.

REFERENCES AND FURTHER READING

Baum, T. and Mudambi, R. (1996) 'Attracting Hotel Investment: Insights from Principal-Agent Theory', *Hospitality Research Journal*, **20**(2), 15–30.

Council for Hospitality Management Education (CHME) (1998) *In the world of hospitality ... anything they can do, we can do better*, a study commissioned by the Joint Hospitality Industry Congress, London: CHME.

Deegan, J. and Dineen, D.A. (1997) *Tourism Policy and Performance: The Irish Experience*, London: International Thomson Business Press.

Hall, C.M. and Jenkins, J.M. (1995) *Tourism and Public Policy*, London: Routledge.

Rolfe, R.J., Ricks, D.A., Pointer, M.M. and McCarthy, M. (1993) 'Determinants of FDI Incentive Preferences of MNEs', *Journal of International Business Studies*, **24**(2), 335–55.

Rutter, D. (1992) *Catering Education and Training in Germany*, London: Hotel and Catering Training Company.

Tourism Training Scotland (1996) *Improving Standards ... Increasing Profits*, 1996 Annual Report, Glasgow: Scottish Enterprise, Inverness: Highlands and Islands Enterprise.

Wanhill, S.R.C. (1993) 'European Regional Development Funds for the Hospitality and Tourism Industries', *International Journal of Hospitality Management*, **12**(1), 67–76.

Wood, R.C. (1997) *Working in Hotels and Catering*, London: International Thomson Business Press, 2nd edn.

Accommodation, hotels and the legal framework

7

Norman Geddes

INTRODUCTION

The operation of all businesses requires some knowledge of the law. This is of particular importance where the business involves regular contact with the general public. The hospitality industry clearly falls into this category and it is vital that the management of a successful hotel be aware of the legal framework within which they must operate. There are many fields of law which will have influence on the conduct of the business. The ones on which we wish to focus are those which affect the management of the unit and its relationship with customers.

Fundamental to this will be the law of contract. This regulates the rights and obligations of the parties who are dealing with each other and a knowledge of the principles of contract law is important. Regardless of whether or not a contract exists the law places upon all of us an obligation to conduct ourselves in a manner which should not cause harm to others. For the protection of the public, the law of tort (delict in Scotland) places an obligation on us all to conduct ourselves in a manner which should not cause harm to others. This will of course impact upon the manner in which any business should be run. It is not only deliberate actions which can lead to such harm, but also negligent actions. This idea of protection of the public has been extended within modern times by creating many specific areas of protection for the public, generally referred to as consumer protection. Thus, specific obligations are placed upon all businesses not to mislead the public or cause them harm.

The issues of contract and tort law form part of the civil law thus regulating the relationship between the individual parties. In consumer protection law the obligations are extended and criminal penalties introduced. A breach of the consumer protection provisions is regarded as an offence against society with the result that the party breaching the provisions is guilty of a criminal offence and may be punished by the courts. In order to emphasize the requirement for protection of the public by the law these duties have been extended to envisage general criminal responsibility of the obligants. The officers and management of a company or business are criminally responsible for their actions in the conduct of the business and its effect on others.

All of these issues are regarded as provisions of national law and each nation makes its own provisions. However, within the European Union, each member state has agreed to accept laws made by the Union and they impinge on the national laws. There is now a massive body of law from the European Union and it does in fact have supremacy over national laws. If the terms of a national law conflict with the terms of any European Union law, the European Union law will prevail and the courts are obliged to confirm this. There are very many examples of European Union law which could affect the hotelier but one of major importance which we shall consider is the Directive on Package Travel, Package Holidays and Package Tours.

Let us therefore consider those branches of the law which are important to the management of a hospitality business.

THE LAW OF CONTRACT

A basic knowledge of the law of contract is vital to the successful operation of any business. All goods and services sold and provided involve a contract with the customer and all supplies and services received involve contracts with suppliers. Contracts are made between a hotel and a customer when, for example, an individual books a room in a hotel or a company books a conference. Such contracts are usually set out in writing so that each party is aware of the terms and conditions to which they are agreeing. It is not necessary, however, for all contracts to be expressed in writing. Many contracts can be made orally or even based solely on the actions of the parties involved. It is harder to prove the existence of such contracts in the absence of any written evidence. Thus, a customer ordering a meal or a drink is completing a contract with the hotel. The menu will provide terms for the contract and other terms will be implied e.g. service, quantity and quality.

Requirements of a contract

Although it is not always necessary for a contract to be made in writing, there are certain requirements which must be met for a valid contract to be constituted. The parties entering into the contract must have legal capacity to enter such relations. There must also be agreement between the parties and an intention to be legally bound. In addition, contracts must not be for an illegal purpose. In England, though not in Scotland, there must be consideration. Each of these requirements shall now be examined in more detail.

Legal capacity

In England and Wales, anyone over 18 years of age may enter into a contract, provided that they are not insane or intoxicated. Persons aged under 18, minors, may only enter into contracts for necessaries. Necessaries are 'goods suitable to the condition in life of the minor to his requirements at the time of the sale and delivery' (Sale of Goods Act 1979, Section 3 (3)). Booking a hotel is unlikely to be considered a necessary, while purchasing a meal may be necessary. The minor's circumstances, the facts, and the cost of the accommodation or meal would all be relevant.

In Scotland, the position is regulated by the Age of Capacity (Scotland) Act 1991. In Scotland, people of 16 years of age or over have full legal capacity. Contracts entered into by 16 or 17 year olds may however be set aside if the contract is to their serious detriment. People under 16 may contract for items normally contracted for by people of their age and circumstances, provided that the contract is reasonable. This is again unlikely to include hotel bookings.

Agreement

A valid contract will not be constituted unless the parties to the contract are in agreement over its terms. Contracts require an offer by one party which is accepted by the other. In our example of a company booking a conference to be held at a hotel, the parties must agree on all elements of the contract, for example price, before the contract exists. Where the hotel offers to provide the conference service for £2,000, but the company responds by saying it is only willing to pay £1,000 there is no agreement and so no contract. The company's response is called a 'counter offer' and is treated as a new offer. The contract will be concluded only if and when the parties finally agree on the contractual terms, including the price.

Offers may be communicated by letter, fax, email or, as discussed earlier, orally in person or by telephone. The method of acceptance is usually determined by the terms of the offer. Where an acceptance is posted, it is valid from the moment it is posted and not just when it is received by the offeror.

A hotel may have a standard form of contract which it uses to contract with other parties. Difficulties may arise when the hotel contracts with another business which also has a standard form of contract. A 'battle of the forms' then takes place. It is not possible to accept one standard form contract with another. The party which sends the last standard form which is accepted by the other party to the contract will have their terms to be held as prevailing.

Intention to be legally bound

A contract will only be entered into if both parties intend to enter legal relations. Consent must be given freely by both parties to the contract.

Consideration

In England and Wales, though not in Scotland, it is a requirement of a contract that there be a consideration. Thus only in Scotland will a promise be enforceable. In England, each party must either give the other something of value or provide them with a service. The consideration does not, however, require to be adequate.

Illegality

Contracts which are illegal or contrary to public policy cannot be enforced. The case of *Hamilton v Main* (1823) involved a contract which promoted sexual immorality. A customer gave the landlord of a Public House a promissory note for £60 for staying in the Public House with a prostitute. The landlord was not allowed by the courts to enforce the promissory note for payment.

Express and implied terms

Express terms

In England and Wales, express terms are divided into conditions and warranties. Breach of a condition of a contract will allow the contract to be cancelled by the injured party who can then claim damages. When a warranty is breached, the contract may not be cancelled, but damages can be claimed. In Scotland, there is no such distinction between conditions and warranties. A material breach of contract will allow the contractual party to cancel a contract.

Implied terms

Some terms are incorporated into a contract even though they are not expressed in the contract. The terms must be so obvious that the parties believed that there was no need to express them in the contract for them to be implied.

Exclusion clauses and the Unfair Contract Terms Act 1977

It is possible to attempt to exclude certain items from an agreement by way of a clause in the contract. Exclusion clauses which are incorporated into a contract may be upheld at common law. They may however be ineffective under the terms of the Unfair Contract Terms Act 1977 (UCTA). UCTA applies where one party, a business, seeks to exclude their liability through a contractual term or notice. A hotel may, for example, seek to exclude its liability for death or personal injury to its guests. Under the Act, such a term in a contract or notice is void. Clauses which seek to exclude other types of liability such as damage to property will only be included if it is fair and reasonable to do so.

Invalid contracts

It is possible to challenge a contract which has been entered into on several grounds. Where one party to the contract is persuaded to contract by a false statement, the contract may be challenged on the grounds of misrepresentation. A contract can also be challenged if there has been a mistake, or in Scotland, an error. A unilateral mistake is one in which a party to the contract is mistaken as to one element of the contract. This may arise where a hotel offers a customer a room at a certain price per night, but this customer thinks the price is per week. Such a contract would be void. Where both parties make the same mistake, the contract will be void on the grounds of common error. Similarly where parties must understand each other's intentions, a mutual mistake will arise and the contract will be void.

Termination of contract

Contracts come to an end on the passing of certain events. The contract will terminate when it is performed in accordance with its terms and conditions. Where a company has a contract with a hotel for a function, the contract will terminate once the function has taken place and the contract terms have been satisfied. The contract will also terminate in England and Wales when a condition is breached and in Scotland when a material breach occurs. When it is no longer possible to perform a contract through no fault of either party, frustration will arise and the contract will again terminate.

As nearly all hotel and restaurant managers are aware, many customers seek to cancel a booking at the last minute or simply fail to turn up after a booking has been made. A booking which has been accepted is a legally binding contract and may be enforced against the customer. Traditionally, hoteliers and restaurateurs did not usually seek to enforce the contract but due to the increasing prevalence of this problem many do now seek to enforce their legal rights against the customer. There have been several successful court cases recently where the hotelier/restaurateur has succeeded in obtaining damages from the customer for breach of contract in these circumstances. The hotelier/restaurateur is obliged by law to mitigate their loss by attempting to re-let the room or table. If this is unsuccessful then the loss will be the anticipated income from the booking less the cost of serving it, e.g., the cost of food, and operators will be entitled to damages for this loss.

Privity of contract

The concept of privity of contract dictates that only those who are parties to a contract may seek to enforce its terms.

TORT/DELICT

At common law

The law of tort, or delict in Scotland, regulates our conduct in relation to others. Whereas the criminal law imposes penalties for breaches of the rules and norms of society in general, tort law finds us liable to make reparation civilly for harm done to others. Reparation generally means paying compensation for injury or harm caused to someone else or their belongings. The Scots law of delict has developed in a quite different manner to the English law of tort, but in the most important aspect, negligence, the law is now quite similar and the same principles may be applied.

Donoghue v *Stevenson*

The modern law of negligence is based upon the judgement in the famous 'Snail in the Bottle' case – *Donoghue* v *Stevenson,* 1932 AC562. It was alleged that Mrs Donoghue had called at a cafe with a friend who had purchased a bottle of ginger beer for her. The drink was supplied in an opaque bottle and when Mrs Donoghue poured out the last of the drink a decomposed snail emerged from the bottle. Mrs Donoghue complained that she had suffered shock and gastro-enteritis and had to be off work for some time. She sought compensation for her injury. The principle of privity of contract meant that she had no claim against the owner of the cafe as she herself had not purchased the drink. She therefore sought to claim in delict against the manufacturer of the drink and the House of Lords awarded compensation against the manufacturer. In the judgement it was stated that we all owe a duty of care not to harm each other. We must conduct ourselves in such a way that others will not be harmed by our acts or omissions and we owe this duty to all parties whom we might reasonably consider could be harmed by our action or failure to act.

Although *Donoghue* v *Stevenson* was a Scottish case the judgement in the House of Lords is authoritative in English law also and the principle has thus been followed in many other legal jurisdictions.

Thus, tort must be kept in mind by the management of a hospitality business. They must exercise care in the operation of all aspects of the business, otherwise they may face financial claims from parties who suffer loss as a result of their actions or negligence. The condition of the premises or fittings within it; the quality and condition of food and drink; the efficiency of the staff; the accuracy of the advertisements and documentation – all must be considered carefully and kept under review.

The requirements

In order to succeed in a claim the injured party must establish that:

- he/she was owed a duty of care;
- the duty of care was breached by an act or omission;
- he/she has suffered injury or loss; and
- the injury or loss was as a result of the breach of duty – 'causation'.

If they can establish all of these points then they will be entitled to reparation to restore them to the same position as they were in before the incident. They will be entitled to recompense for all losses which followed naturally from the incident and which might reasonably have been expected to follow from the negligent act or omission. Of course, when someone has suffered physical injury it is often not possible to reinstate their health as before. They are entitled to financial compensation for their injury and the court will award an amount which it believes compensates for the injury sustained plus an amount for any actual loss incurred, e.g. loss of wages.

Vicarious liability

It is important for business operators to bear in mind that the employer will generally be held responsible for any loss occasioned by the actions of an employee. This principle of vicarious liability applies where the employee was at the time of the incident acting in the course of his employment. The courts have construed in very wide terms what may be regarded as in the course of employment and in practice, the employer usually will be held liable.

Contributory negligence

Where the injured party has in some way contributed to the incident or the extent of his injury any award of compensation may be reduced by the percentage which the court considers relates to the extent of their own contribution.

Statutory liability

The laws of tort and delict are largely based on the common law recognition of the duties which we owe to others. We have indicated the chain of causation which the claimant must prove in order to obtain reparation and in some instances it may be difficult to prove this. In certain circumstances, the law places a direct duty of care on certain people. This will commonly be where an obvious requirement for care can be seen to exist and parliament has passed legislation to regulate matters. Examples which are of particular interest to the hospitality industry are: occupiers' liability; innkeepers' liability; licensing legislation; and certain aspects of the food safety and food hygiene laws.

Occupiers' liability

Under the Occupiers Liability Acts 1957 and 1984 (in Scotland the Occupiers Liability (Scotland) Act 1960) the occupier of a building or land is given particular duties in relation to members of the public entering the premises. In simple terms, the occupier must take reasonable care to ensure that anyone entering the premises will not suffer injury. This envisages a duty to ensure that the premises in their entirety are in a safe condition and that nothing is done or omitted to be done which could lead to injury. The obligation is to take reasonable care.

Innkeepers' rights and obligations

At common law and under statute the Hotel Proprietors Act 1956 (HPA), an innkeeper has certain rights and obligations. An 'innkeeper' is not just a hotelier. The Act defines an innkeeper as one who holds his establishment out as offering sleeping accommodation to any traveller who presents himself without having to book in advance. At common law, an innkeeper is bound to receive all travellers who call at his premises requiring food and/or accommodation. This obligation applies provided the travellers are willing to pay a reasonable sum, are in a fit state to be received, the innkeeper has vacant accommodation and, if required, adequate provision of food.

An innkeeper who does not meet these obligations may be charged with a criminal offence (see section on criminal responsibility hereafter) and may also be liable in civil damages to the offended traveller. Innkeepers may not therefore choose their clientele. They must also provide food and drink to travellers at all times and may not use late arrival as an excuse for not serving a traveller (*R* v *Ivens,* 1835). The food to be provided, however, may be limited by the provisions available and the hour of day. There is no requirement to provide a four course meal to someone arriving at midnight and an offer of sandwiches, for example, would be reasonable.

The traveller must be fit to be received and willing to pay a reasonable sum. The innkeeper may therefore request payment in advance in order to establish this first, but the charge must be reasonable. 'Fit to be received' does permit innkeepers some discretion in receiving guests in that they may decline them on the basis of standard of dress or their behaviour (*Rothfield* v *North British Railway Company*, 1920). The law accepts that there are hotels of different standards and that innkeepers may require a particular standard of dress or behaviour in keeping with the standard of the hotel. If all bedrooms are occupied they need not provide accommodation (*Browne* v *Brandt*, 1902).

The innkeeper is also deemed to be an insurer of all luggage and goods which a traveller brings to his premises. There is no requirement to show negligence on the part of the innkeeper in order to claim compensation for property which has been lost. The innkeeper is therefore said to have strict liability for the guest's belongings (HPA S.I.) (*Carpenter* v *Haymarket Hotel,* 1931 and *Shacklock* v *Ethorpe Ltd,* 1939). However, innkeepers may restrict their liability if they display a Schedule Notice in terms detailed in the Schedule to the HPA. The appropriate notice must be displayed in a prominent place visible to the guest completing registration. The restriction on liability will not however apply where the loss occurred as a result of the default, neglect or wilful act of the innkeeper or their employee or where the goods were accepted specifically for safe-keeping. The innkeeper is entitled to exercise a lien upon a resident's belongings to cover payment of his bill for accommodation. This means that if an innkeeper's bill is unpaid, goods may be retained pending payment and if payment is not made, the innkeeper may proceed to sell the goods and apply the sale proceeds to the bill in question.

CRIMINAL RESPONSIBILITY

The background

As mentioned earlier, management and employees of a company or business should be aware that they may be held to be criminally responsible, not only for their own actions or negligence but also for the actions or negligence of other employees. It is therefore advisable to ensure that suitably trained staff are employed with adequate and serviceable equipment provided and a suitable system of management supervision in operation.

Many people may consider crime to be represented by the traditional 'intentional' crimes, e.g., theft, assault, murder, and so on, but there are now many forms of statutory crimes, often enacted by parliament with a view to public safety or consumer protection. We have already indicated above the criminal responsibility of innkeepers for their actions at common law and in terms of the HPA. Many other statutes which can give rise to criminal liability will be encountered in the hospitality industry and these include the Food Safety Act 1990, the Licensing Acts, the Health and Safety at Work legislation, the Trade Descriptions Act 1968, as well as regulations such as the Package Tours Regulations.

The recent movement towards strict liability in many aspects of the law means that there need not be intention to commit a crime. Many of these recent statutory provisions do not require any intention and the crime is committed simply when the incident occurs. No proof of criminal fault is required. Thus, false or misleading advertising; unsafe food; dangerous work places; failure to deal with waste products; serving alcohol outside licensing hours; and many other situations can give rise to criminal charges.

In many cases the company itself will be prosecuted and will be responsible for any penalty, as in *Sunair Holidays* v *Dodd* (1970) and *Wings Ltd* v *Ellis* (1984), both of which related to incorrect information in brochures, and were charged under the Trade Descriptions Act 1968. However there have been instances of officers and employees of a company being held responsible, as illustrated in *R* v *OLL Ltd & Kite* (1994). The company operated a leisure activity centre. Four young people died on a canoe trip in Lyme Bay which had been organized by the company. Both the company and its managing director where convicted of manslaughter in relation to their involvement in the incident which led to the deaths. The managing director was sentenced to three years imprisonment and the company was fined £60,000.

The due diligence defence

In relation to some statutory criminal offences, the 'due diligence' defence to a charge is made available. To successfully plead this defence the company or employee must prove that they had taken all steps which could reasonably be taken to avoid the offence being committed. This defence will not be accepted lightly by the courts but has been successfully pleaded in relation to some statutory offences, e.g., *Byrne* v *Tudhope* (1983) in regard to licensing law, specifically selling liquor outside licensing hours and *Tesco Supermarkets Ltd* v *Nattrass* (1972) in regard to the Trade Descriptions Act, specifically misleading advertising. In order to succeed in the defence the company will require to prove that they had taken all steps reasonably possible, for example by training staff and establishing appropriate systems to endeavour to ensure that an offence may not be committed. This defence will not be available unless the statute in question specifically makes provision for its availability.

The Food Safety Act, 1990 (the FSA)

There are various offences stated in this Act for which a company and its officers may be held responsible. The principal ones are:

S.7   Rendering food injurious to health.
S.8   Selling food and complying with food safety requirements.
S.14   Selling food not of the nature, substance or quality demanded.
S.15   False advertising, describing or presentation of food.

The principal aim of the Act is consumer protection and the construction of these four main offences is designed to catch any situation which may mislead or cause injury to the public. Food safety is at the moment an area of particular public concern as a result of several recent high profile food scares. Management personnel should therefore be vigilant in complying with food safety regulations and recommendations. For a serious offence the maximum penalty would be imprisonment for up to two years and/or an unlimited fine. For less serious offences the maximum penalty would be a fine of up to £20,000.

Offences under licensing legislation

The principal statutes are presently the Licensing Act 1964 for England and Wales and the Licensing (Scotland) Act 1976 for Scotland. These contain very detailed provisions on liquor licensing the terms of which are beyond the remit of this chapter. It should however be noted that there are many provisions for criminal offences contained in the Acts and they are fertile ground for the conviction in the courts of companies and their employees.

The main offences which commonly arise involve the sale of alcohol:

- outwith licensing laws;
- below the permitted age;
- in a volume below the specified measure; and
- which is not of the specified quality or strength.

Offences under the Acts will generally lead to a fine but perhaps the greatest penalty is that they can lead to loss of the liquor licence with massive financial repercussions.

Licensees should also be aware of The Weights and Measures Acts, 1963–1985 and The Weights and Measures (Sale of Wine) Order, 1976, all of which deal with measures in relation to the sale of alcohol while The Price Marking (Food and Drink on Premises) Order, 1979, requires the display of a list of prices for all items. All of these make provision for criminal penalties if their terms are breached.

Health and safety at work legislation

There is a substantial and rapidly expanding body of legislation dealing with the protection of employees in the workplace. The principal statute is the Health and Safety at Work Act, 1974, but much of the law is passed as regulations often implementing European Union initiatives. The volume of legislation is too great to detail here but the general principle is that the employer is responsible for the safety of the workplace and the employees within it and must ensure that there are in use safe working practices utilizing safe equipment. There are many provisions for criminal penalties on employers where employees are injured as a result of breach of the regulations and penalties can be severe.

The Trade Descriptions Act, 1968

This is an early example of consumer protection legislation designed to protect the consumer from false and misleading descriptions on goods. It contains provisions for the prosecution of businesses who breach its terms.

Regulation of package holidays

It is essential for the management of a hotel to have knowledge of their obligations to customers who book accommodation. The rights of customers have recently been greatly increased with particular reference to package holiday bookings, by regulations passed under the European Union's consumer protection programme. Having recognized the importance of the tourism industry to member states and seeking to increase consumer protection as well as promoting competition, the European Union (EU) passed the Directive on Package Travel, Package Holidays and Package Tours (Directive 90/314/EEC) ('the Package Travel Directive'). By harmonizing laws of the member states, the Directive gives the same protection to consumers throughout the Union regardless of the different legal systems, which operate in each country. The Directive had to be implemented by each member state and in the UK this was done in the Package Travel, Package Holidays and Package Tours Regulations 1992 ('the Regulations'). The effect of the Regulations is to give consumers additional protection to that which they formerly enjoyed under common law.

The package

In general terms, the Regulations describe a 'package' as being the pre-arranged combinations of at least two of:

 (i) transport;
 (ii) accommodation; and
 (iii) other tourist services.

In practice, the package will usually involve the combination of transport and accommodation.

The regulation extends the rights of consumers in several ways. Recognizing that most package holidays are booked through travel agents ('the retailer'), the Regulations make the retailer responsible as well as the holiday company ('the organizer'). They are made responsible for the accuracy of all information given to the consumer including in particular, the brochure. Important provisions of the package may not be altered without the agreement of the consumer and there are restrictions on any variations to the price. In the event of the elements not being of the standard promised then the organizer and the retailer may require to compensate the consumer.

Other regulations

Other regulations of which a hotelier should be aware include the Immigration (Hotel Records) Order, 1972, which make it an offence not to keep a register of all residents and the Tourism (Sleeping Accommodation Price Display) Order, 1977, which require all hotels and guest-houses comprising four or more letting bedrooms to display prominently at the entrance the price list of accommodation. Failure to do so is punishable by a fine.

CONCLUSION

In this age of onerous regulation and consumer protection, businesses of all types require some knowledge of the laws affecting them. Where the business is devoted to the service of the public, as in the hospitality industry, this knowledge becomes vital to the success of the business. It can be seen from the terms of this chapter that in many instances specialist legal advice will be required in connection with a particular circumstance. However, some general knowledge of the main areas of law having influence on the operation of the business is likely to enhance its success and assist in avoiding unwanted problems.

REFERENCES AND FURTHER READING

Cork, J. (1988) *Tourism Law*, London: Elm Publications.
Davidson, J. and Miller, K. (1991) *Employment Law in Scotland*, Edinburgh: T and T Clark.
Field, D. (1988) *Hotel and Catering Law in Britain*. London: Sweet and Maxwell, 5th edn.
MacCormack, M. (1984) *What they don't teach you at the Yale Law School*, London: Fontana.
Pannett, A. (1992) *Principles of Hotel and Catering Law*, London: Cassell, 3rd edn.
Poustie, M. (ed.) (1999) *Hospitality and Tourism Law*, London: International Thompson Business Press.

Part II
Key performance areas

Front office management

Constantinos S. Verginis

THE IMPORTANCE OF FRONT OFFICE

The term 'front office' was originally introduced in the US, but is now used internationally. It is a term used to cover the following sub-units of the hotel: reception, concierge, switchboard, reservations and guest relations. However, as hotels vary in size and type these sub-units may not always be present as distinct entities, and the front office department will thus vary in nature, size and definition from hotel to hotel. Despite the size or the type of the hotel, however, the front office department is in many ways the 'heart' of the hotel. One reason for this is that the sale of rooms generates over 50 per cent of a hotel's revenue and profit; it is imperative, therefore, that the front office department is organized to maximize sales. However, revenue and sales generation is not the only reason that the front office is the 'heart' of the hotel. Just as important is the fact that it is the first contact that a guest or a potential guest has with the hotel. This might be through the switchboard, in the process of making a reservation over the telephone, or by entering the hotel to check-in or to make an inquiry. Furthermore, in city centre business hotels in particular, where guests are often on short business trips, arriving late one night, checking-in, and departing early the next morning, it is often the case that the front office might be the only department with which they interact during their entire stay. In these cases, the guest's perception of the level of service provided by the hotel will be based entirely on the level of service provided by the front office.

This stresses the importance of the front office for repeat business. Even if the hotel's rooms meet guests' expectations, but the service provided by the hotel personnel is not as good as the guest anticipates, then they might not return and, furthermore, may even communicate negative publicity about the hotel to others. It is very important, therefore, to ensure that the guest's contact with the front office will be a positive one. In addition, the information obtained about guests during the reservation and registration process, such as address and telephone number, can be used in order to advertise hotel promotions, functions or other activities. It is clear therefore that the front office is a strong marketing tool that generates business for a hotel. It is the centre for guest activity. It is the hotel department where guests check-in, request information about the services that the hotel provides, and at the end of their stay where they settle their bill and check-out.

Beyond that, the front office department is the communication centre of the hotel, providing information to the other hotel departments, such as guests' requirements, or arrival times, and through the switchboard dealing with incoming calls. The front office also generates profit, indirectly, for other departments of a hotel, such as restaurant bookings handled by the concierge, and the up-selling of the hotel in general. Up-selling of the hotel means that whilst a guest is staying at the hotel, already using some of the hotel services, the hotel personnel are promoting other services that the hotel is offering. For example, guests often inquire at the concierge about dining possibilities. The concierge then suggests and perhaps persuades the guest of the virtues of the hotel's restaurant.

Although the front office, in terms of size, is not usually the largest hotel department, it is essential to organize it with great care in order to maximize sales revenue. Front office management, like any other form of management is about organizing and controlling people and other resources in order to achieve specific objectives. These objectives derive from the company's mission statement. The mission statement defines the organization's business, states its vision and goals, and articulates its main philosophical values (Pearce, 1982). The front office department, however, should have its own mission statement, in addition to the company's. In this way, the department's goals and objectives are clear for all front office personnel, and they can relate all their decisions to it. Box 8.1 is an example of a front office mission statement from the Heathrow Marriott Hotel.

Box 8.1:   Example of a front office mission statement

It is our mission to give fellow associates, guests and others with whom we come into contact, a constant variety of pleasant experiences that are personally satisfying and that make us all happy and prosperous. Your mission is to sharpen your social skills and provide yourself with pleasant experiences that make you a happy person.

The blend of personalities you bring to the team creates a unique image and set of attributes which differentiate us from other hotels in the area. If we continue to improve our skills, we will fulfil the needs and wants of those who have the choice. Our guests have that choice as well as our associates.

We can only influence this choice by satisfying expectations through providing the benefits, services and the delivery thereof in a fashion that is appealing, credible, logical, and fair.

The individual role each of you plays has a vital effect on the team as a whole and its efficiency.

You as Shift leader, by your leadership skills and motivation are the one to guide and help those junior associates under your control. You are the one they will copy in dress and appearance. By your attitude and efficient but friendly manner geared to guest service and satisfaction at all times we can be assured of motivated personnel and satisfied guests. Leadership by example is the key word.

You as a Receptionist/Cashier/Switchboard operator when the hotel is at its busiest, it will be your calm efficient and friendly guest approach that will ensure that all guests queries are kept to a minimum. Your smart appearance, efficient yet well-informed and friendly caring manner will set the standard for the guest's stay with us. Because lobby and telephone contact is the first and the last impression the guest will have with the hotel, it is your role to act as our ambassador, and to ensure the guest returns time and time again. We rely on you to maintain the consistency of service our guests have come to expect.

Reprinted with kind permission of the author, Adam Salt.

FRONT OFFICE STRUCTURE

A hotel's size and objectives determine the organizational structure of the front office. It is usual for different hotels of the same hotel chain to have different front office organizational structures. There are, nevertheless, certain common features to all aspects of front office organization because, necessarily, there are certain functions that every front office must carry out, whether the hotel is large or small, resort or business, five star or bed and breakfast. In larger hotels, though, it is easier to separate some of the jobs performed by front office personnel and thus create some specialization. Table 8.1 shows the typical organizational structure of a large five star hotel's front office.

The Front Office Manager is responsible for the front office department. In the US, however, the term Rooms Division Manager (RDM) is in common use and often preferred. However, the position of RDM also has additional requirements for housekeeping services. The position of Front Office Assistant Manager is often found in large properties. In contrast, smaller properties do without any separate management position and assign managerial duties to a senior shift leader or a reception manager. As previously mentioned, different hotels often have different front office organizational structures. The one characteristic, however, that commonly shapes successful front office departments is the presence of a culture in which teamwork thrives. It is only through teamwork that a front office will achieve the goals set by its mission statement. Furthermore, it is only by working together, as a team, that the department members will both start and continue to work successfully through busy times, very busy times and not so busy times. It is also very important that all front office personnel maintain a positive working relationship with all other hotel departments. A hotel functions through a team effort, not through independently acting departments.

Table 8.1 Front office structure

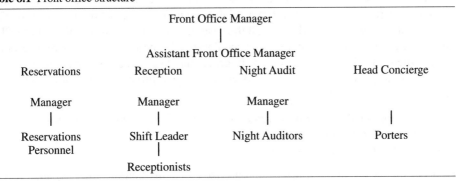

OPERATIONAL ASPECTS OF FRONT OFFICE

This section will cover the main actions involving front office that a hotel guest will have to go through when staying at a hotel, namely reservation, checking-in and checking-out. The process is summarized in Table 8.2.

Reservations

The reservations department is often part of the front office. In many hotels, however it is regarded as, or actually is, an independent department. In both cases, it affects

Table 8.2 The front office process

Guest Action	Front Office Task
Reservation	Check room availability on the required date and for the required duration. Record the booking. Retrieve the booking information before arrival.
Arrival and Registration	Check booking details and registration. Allocate room(s) and issue key(s).
Check-out	Check and present bill. Receive payment.

greatly the smooth running of the front office and the hotel in general. It is usually the second contact, after the switchboard, a potential guest has with the hotel. It is, therefore, to a certain extent, up to the reservations personnel to convince the guest to make the reservation. In other words, the reservations section is the sales department of the front office, and thus a profit centre for the department and the whole hotel. Furthermore, it affects the whole department in the sense that reservations determine occupancy levels, which then determine personnel levels and the rostering patterns of the front office and other hotel departments.

The reservation procedure usually begins with an inquiry by a potential guest about room availability on a specific day and for a specific period. The inquiry, by the guest, can be communicated to the hotel in a variety of ways. The most common method is, of course, the telephone. Such inquiry may, however, be made by facsimile, or in person, and increasingly, in the case of many international hotel chains, over the internet. Furthermore, international hotel companies have central reservations offices and systems (CROs or CRSs) that have on-line computer access to every hotel in the chain, and can thus rapidly check for room availability and make the actual reservation. This means that a person in the UK can call the (usually free) telephone number of the CRO and make an inquiry about hotel room availability in the US, or anywhere else in the world where the chain is represented. In order that a reservations agent can process a reservation inquiry effectively, any system must have three core functions that allow them to:

1 check room availability on the required date and for the required duration;
2 record the reservation; and
3 retrieve the booking at any time.

None of this is problematic with computerized systems that are fully integrated with every aspect of the hotel function. Modern software packages allow the reservations agent to perform all three of the above functions. However, small hotels and bed and breakfast establishments may not be able to afford computerized systems. More importantly, both large and small operations that do run such systems must always have a manual backup procedure. Unfortunately, system crashes and power failures do happen and therefore a manual backup procedure is necessary to ensure the continuation of the smooth running of the hotel. Such manual systems can include the following.

● The bedroom book, a book that has a list of the hotel's room types and numbers down the side of each page, and next to them space for the guest's name and other information. Each day is a different page of the book. This is suitable only for very small hotels because entering the guest's name on every night of his stay increases the amount of writing to be done. An example of a bedroom book page is shown in Table 8.3.

- The conventional chart, a development of the bedroom book. A conventional chart lists the hotel's room types and numbers down the side of each page, and the dates of the month across the top of the page. An extract from the conventional chart may look like the example in Table 8.4. The conventional chart is simple to operate, and is more efficient than the bedroom book.

Table 8.3 Bedroom book (extract)

Date: 3 February 1998

Room	Name	Particulars
101 (S)		
201 (D)	Smith	Vegetarian
301 (T)		
401 (S)	Jones	Early check-out
501 (D)	King	

Table 8.4 Conventional chart (extract)

Month: February 1998

Room	1st	2nd	3rd	4th	5th	6th	7th
101 (S)			←	Smith	→		
201 (D)							
301 (T)							
401 (S)			←	Jones	—	→	
501 (D)			←	King →			

- The density chart is a development of the conventional chart. It is mainly used in large hotels with standardized rooms. The receptionist, or the reservationist, does not reserve a specific room, rather they book one room of the particular type requested (e.g. single). The actual room allocation is done on the arrival date, or even just upon arrival. Table 8.5 shows a typical density chart page. The major advantage that the density chart offers is its greater flexibility than the two previous systems.

Table 8.5 Density chart (extract)

Density chart for 1st February 1998						Density chart for 2nd February 1998					
Singles						**Singles**					
32	31	30	29	28	27	32	31	30	29	28	27
26	25	24	23	22	21	26	25	24	23	22	21
20	19	18	17	16	15	20	19	18	17	16	15
14	13	12	11	10	9	14	13	12	11	10	9
8	7	6	5	4	3	8	7	6	5	4	3
2	1	-1	-2	-3	-4	2	1	-1	-2	-3	-4
Doubles						**Doubles**					
32	31	30	29	28	27	32	31	30	29	28	27
26	25	24	23	22	21	26	25	24	23	22	21
20	19	18	17	16	15	20	19	18	17	16	15
14	13	12	11	10	9	14	13	12	11	10	9
8	7	6	5	4	3	8	7	6	5	4	3
2	1	-1	-2	-3	-4	2	1	-1	-2	-3	-4

The specific requirements and the size of the property determine the choice between these three types of backup system. Both manual as well as computerized systems require similar, if not the same, information. Typically this information includes:

- date of the booking;
- length of stay (in number of nights), or departure day;
- estimated arrival time;
- room type (single, double, suite) and number of rooms;
- number of persons per room and room rate;
- name of the guest;
- contact telephone number;
- address;
- name and telephone number of the person that made the reservation if different;
- company name;
- accounting instructions (e.g. prepaid, payment on departure, bill to company);
- special requests (e.g. room on a high floor);
- if the reservation is guaranteed or not (not guaranteed reservations may be released after 6pm on arrival date);
- if the reservation is guaranteed by credit card the credit card number, name on the credit card and expiry date;

- the name of the person that took the reservation;
- the date that the reservation was made;
- status of reservation (e.g. confirmed, to be confirmed, or waiting list);
- the way the reservation was made; and
- if confirmation was sent.

Computerized systems usually offer greater accessibility than manual ones. They can also be configured to produce a number of reports necessary for the smooth running of the front office operation. At a later stage of this chapter, reports will be dealt with in detail.

Confirmation of reservations is very important for both the hotel and the guest. It shows professionalism, and especially in cases where the reservation is made over the telephone or the internet, provides the guest with some assurance that they are indeed expected to stay at the hotel at the chosen time. Confirmation is also useful for the hotel because it is a way of double checking each reservation. If there is a misunderstanding (especially over the telephone), or an error it is likely that the guest will detect it and will contact the hotel about it. It is always best to detect mistakes earlier rather than later because this might save the hotel or the guest embarrassment or discomfort.

Overbooking is another important issue for reservations. Overbooking means deliberately accepting more bookings than the hotel has capacity for. Some companies do apply an overbooking policy in order to achieve occupancy and profit maximization. Overbooking is a controversial issue in many countries, with a leading case in the UK being *British Airways Board* v *Taylor* (1975). In this instance, the airline could not accommodate a passenger because it had overbooked the flight. The court case, questioning if this was a criminal offence or not, was taken to the House of Lords, but it had to be dismissed on technical grounds unconnected with the central issue. Until the status of overbookings is clarified, hotels are likely to continue to engage in the practice. Hotels overbook for two main reasons. First, because there is often a number of guests that do not have guaranteed reservations. A guaranteed reservation means that the guests guarantee that they will show up. Guaranteeing a reservation is a method that many hotels use in order to protect their revenue from guests that fail to show up. The most common method of guaranteeing a hotel reservation is by credit card. In the case of a guaranteed reservation, if the guests fail to show up, the hotel will charge them the room rate. The second reason is that often a number of guests with guaranteed reservations fail to show up. It is not unusual for a city centre hotel to have a 10 per cent no show rate every weekday. In such cases many Front Office Managers overbook the hotel by that, or slightly smaller, percentage, trying to maximize the hotel's revenue.

Overbooking, however, might prove to have a boomerang effect for the hotel. The purpose of overbooking is profit maximization. If the hotel finds itself in the unfortunate situation that it is overbooked and every guest shows up, both the short-term and long-term occupancy and profit benefits vanish for the following reasons. In this situation, the hotel will have to find rooms for the guests that cannot be accommodated. This is called 'booking out' or 'walking' the guests. This raises the issue of what the hotel is liable for. Since in such circumstances the hotel effectively breaches its contract with the guest, it is liable for compensating the guest by providing alternative accommodation and bearing the costs of additional travel (e.g. taxis). So, in this case there is no short-term profit for the hotel. Furthermore, it might represent a long-term loss for the hotel as well. The 'walked' guest understandably will not usually be pleased with the hotel's conduct (unless 'walked' to a hotel far superior to the one originally booked) and this might deter the guest from returning. Furthermore, such conduct may encourage the guest to share their bad experience with friends and colleagues, which might lead to long-term loss for the hotel. Overbooking is, however, not always deliberate. Hotel guests that stay in the hotel and decide to extend their stay may cause the hotel to overbook. In such cases, the hotel has the option of refusing the existing guests' requests to extend their stay, or risk an overbooking situation.

Check-in

Checking-in a guest is a further important task that front desk personnel have to undertake. Receptionists have to perform a multiple task, they must be polite, put guests at ease and make them feel welcome, at the same time efficiently performing the following duties:

- checking that the registration details on the registration card are correct and legible;
- checking with the guest that the details of the booking are correct;
- verifying that the guest knows the room rate and what it includes;
- checking that the room is allocated and ready;
- checking for messages for the guest or any other special requests; and
- issuing the room key.

Registration

The most common method for checking-in guests is the registration card. The registration card contains information required of the guest. The registration details required of the guest can be classified into two distinct categories. First is information necessary for the hotel to operate that the hotel is legally obliged to obtain, and keep for a certain period. These usually include the guest's:

- name;
- address;
- nationality;
- passport number; and
- signature.

Other information usually required by the hotel includes:

- date of arrival and departure;
- time of arrival;
- number of guests per room(s);
- payment method and deposit information;
- room number;
- rate and what it includes; and
- who handled the guest's registration.

Room status must be checked before the room allocation and more importantly before the guest registration. That is done to avoid sending a guest to an unserviced or even occupied room. There are many ways to keep track of a room's status. This is most commonly done with computerized systems. Using these systems, as soon as they service a room the hotel cleaners call the housekeeping office to report that the room has been serviced. The housekeeper then changes the room's status on the computer.

Check-out

Check-out is usually the last contact with the hotel that a guest has on any particular stay. If the guest has this far had a positive experience it is very important that this remains the case at check-out. If the guest did not have such an experience whilst staying at the hotel, it is even more vital to get everything right at the check-out so that the last experience, often the most memorable, is a good one. The principal functions of the check-out are therefore to settle the guest's bill or accounts, whilst rendering their last experience of the hotel's administration a positive one.

This account was opened at the check-in stage and there are certain principles that have to be followed regarding guest's accounts. These are:

- they must be always up to date and accurate;
- the postings from different hotel departments must be easily identifiable, and accompanied with a description on what was consumed. This helps guests to identify exactly what the transaction is for, and therefore avoids unnecessary inquiries;
- cash sales must be separately posted, because through sales transactions the hotels accountant prepares the cash flow statement for the hotel; and
- the system of records must be easy to operate and economic in terms of time and maintenance costs.

Many computerized accounting systems perform these functions. Originally, hotels used a book called a ledger. This is a manual system that is time consuming and therefore very few hotels still use it. Most hotels today use computerized systems. With a computerized system most functions are automated, resulting in both rapid and accurate results. Furthermore, control procedures are integrated in these computer packages. These control procedures include:

- goods in the form of cost control;
- accommodation, ensuring that all rooms are charged at the correct daily rate;
- telephones, guaranteeing that all telephone calls made are allocated so that the hotel does not lose any revenue;
- separately recorded cash transactions in order to avoid cash discrepancies; and
- bad debts by alerting the front office personnel when guests exceed their credit limit.

Methods of payment are another consideration during the check-out. The most common methods of payment are:

- cash;
- credit and debit cards;
- bank transfers;
- cheques;
- vouchers; and
- bills sent to the company that made the reservation, provided that there is prior credit agreement between the hotel and the company.

Express check-out is an option that has been developed because of the widespread use of credit cards for payment. At the check-in stage, or at any other time during the stay, the guest indicates that they will be settling the bill with a credit card and gives their credit card imprint to the reception. On departure the guest does not pass by the front office at all (in some hotels they must pass by the front office to sign the bill), the cashier charges the bill on the guest's credit card and mails the guest a copy of the final bill together with the credit card slip. Express check-out is a very good way to reduce the pressure on the front office during busy periods. It is however, very important that the guest's bill is accurate and that they are not overcharged.

Another consideration regarding the check-out is personnel levels at the front office. In a city centre hotel, mainly occupied by people on business, the busiest hours are early in the morning. In a resort hotel on the other hand the busy check-out times are affected by a group's departures and are usually later on in the day. Finally, front office personnel should take the check-out as an opportunity to offer the guest additional services, such as to book a room in the hotel for the future, and also to gather feedback on the guest's stay. Feedback is gathered by either direct inquiry by the front office personnel or by encouraging the guest to complete a guest satisfaction questionnaire. The purpose of gathering feedback is to see if the guest's experience of the hotel was pleasant and if not, to identify areas where the service quality does not meet standards.

Night audit

Night audit is another essential element of the front office department. A typical night audit shift would be between 11pm and 7am (or as called in the industry, the 'graveyard shift'). The function that night audit performs is one of auditing the front office department, and in many cases other revenue generating departments within the hotel as well. Furthermore, night audit is the main link between the front office and the accounts department of the hotel. Despite this, night audit personnel require no special knowledge of accounting although clearly such knowledge can be helpful.

Each shift, morning, afternoon and night, must balance up all payments received before going off duty. Night audit check that all postings and balances are correct, check all guests' accounts before next day's departure, and, finally, close the overall balance. It is quite usual that during the night, night auditors will also deal with some check-ins and post some transactions. This has to be done before the final balance is totalled. Furthermore, there may be transactions from other departments to be posted, such as restaurant, bar and room service, and they have to be posted before the final balance. Finally when the day's overall balance is closed the night auditors will have to print the management reports which summarize the day's trading activities, and next day's reports for all the hotel's departments, such as the departure and arrival lists for the front office.

Night audit through the above mentioned responsibilities also functions as an internal auditor. By identifying mistakes, they can point out to the relevant manager the areas in which their employees require more training and development. This can result in the provision of better service to the hotel's guests. In many hotels, the senior night auditor is also the night manager, responsible for the overall smooth running of the hotel during that shift.

SOCIAL AND PSYCHOLOGICAL ASPECTS OF FRONT OFFICE MANAGEMENT

Hospitality and Social skills

We all come across terms such as 'hospitality', 'providing a service', and 'accommodating the guest's needs'. It is therefore necessary to try to define these terms in order to avoid misunderstanding. Hospitality is the concept of anticipating and satisfying all guests' (reasonable) wants and needs. The terms 'wants' and 'needs' cover both material requirements (a good bed, a pleasant meal), as well as psychological benefits, such as making a guest feel welcome. Providing a service, on the other hand, is the process of satisfying guests' needs and therefore it combines what is done with how it is done. The quality of the service provided, though, is not measurable by any 'hard' criteria. It is a matter of perception, and accordingly varies from guest to guest, deriving from guests' prior expectations and current state of mind. It is apparent that the provision of service involves guest/hotel personnel interaction.

It was mentioned at an earlier stage of this chapter that the front office department is the most visible department of the hotel. Typically, guests look to front office personnel to answer questions, provide directions, suggest restaurants, accommodate their future reservations, whilst at the same time attending to the department's operational duties. It is, therefore, apparent that the hotel relies heavily on front office personnel to convince their guests about the quality of service that the hotel is providing. This is not an easy task but it involves the following key areas of activity.

- Good personal and uniform appearance is the key to a positive first impression, and therefore needs to be constantly monitored. Good personal appearance covers areas such as grooming, hairstyle, fingernails, and jewellery. Good uniform appearance means that each day the uniform must be clean and properly pressed, and shoes must be coordinated with the uniform.
- Facial expression must communicate willingness to offer assistance, emphasized by direct eye contact and a warm smile.
- Proper posture and body language are important means of visual communication at all times and particularly during the first encounter, and must convey alertness, enthusiasm and the willingness of personnel to attend to guests' needs.
- Every guest must be addressed with a welcome salutation, and most importantly, a positive attitude must be projected at all times, and the guest's name must be used as often as possible (when known).
- If the front office personnel are unable to help with guests' problems, despite making every effort to do so, they should volunteer to offer other alternatives before the guest asks for it. Box 8.2 gives examples of how to deal with difficult guest relation situations.

Box 8.2:   Examples on how to deal with difficult guest relation situations

Difficult guest relations situations are situations that most front office personnel have experienced or will experience at some point of their career. For these situations, it is very important to listen carefully to the guest's problem and try to resolve the problem as efficiently as possible. The following eight steps can be used when confronted with such a situation.

1. Listen carefully to what the guest is saying without interrupting. By doing that you can identify their feeling, an important first step to gain their trust that you will try to resolve the problem. Look for something in the guest's remarks that you can agree with. By using this approach, you can often avoid an emotional argument.

2. Filter through to the real problem by asking questions regarding the problem. It is important to realize at this stage that dealing with the problem itself is more important than dealing with the feelings, the guest's or yours, associated with it.

3. Develop alternative solutions. In many instances when the guest is very angry and highly emotional, their feelings interfere with their logic. In some cases, the guest might not accept the first solution that you suggest. By offering other possible solutions to the problem, the guest will realize that you are trying to solve the problem and furthermore will have to stop and reason in order to make a choice. In order to make that decision the guest must put their emotions aside. Tell the guest what you can and what you cannot do, and never blame a colleague or any other person.

4. Act immediately. Nothing reassures/calms an angry guest better than an immediate response to the problem. It is important that the guest actually sees you try to solve their problem, and always follow up with the guest when you have dealt with the problem.

5. Never make a promise that you cannot keep.

6. Refer problems that are beyond your authority or control.

7. Give the guest your undivided attention. Look directly at the guest at all times and keep your cool.

8. Finally, always be pleasant, use the guest's name as often as possible and thank the guest for bringing the matter to your attention.

MANAGEMENT ASPECTS

Pricing and yield management

One of the most important managerial aspects of the front office department is pricing. Pricing is an extremely important function because it affects the volume of sales and profit maximization for the hotel. Pricing in the hotel industry, like any other industry, nominally follows the rules of supply and demand. The target of the hotel's pricing policy is to strike the optimum balance between supply and demand in order to maximize the hotel's profits. There are two main approaches to pricing. One approach is cost based, such as the Hubbart formula or cost plus pricing. Cost based methods are based on the following general approach. The costs related to one room rental are identified and then a fixed rate of return (this rate is determined by the hotel operator) is added to calculate the selling price. The second method is market based, such as price followship and prestige product pricing. Hotels that use this method identify what the consumer is prepared to pay for a specific service and then they manage their cost structure accordingly, trying to achieve the desired rate of return. In reality, only big international companies can afford to do detailed market and demographic analysis in order to determine this. Even these companies, however, use a combination of cost based and market based pricing techniques in order to determine their selling price. Despite the pricing policy that a hotel decides to adopt, the fact remains that a hotel room is a perishable good/service (if a hotel room is not sold for a night it is lost revenue, since it cannot be stored and sold the next day) and this must always guide pricing decisions.

Smaller companies and independent operators, realizing that larger companies conduct detailed market research for pricing purposes, often follow the pricing trends set by these bigger companies. The advantage of this strategy is that they remain competitive. The problem however is that chains can use this behaviour to their advantage. By reducing their room price, hotel chain operators can 'force' independent operators out of business. This is because if a hotel is part of a chain and follows this strategy the chain's profits will support the loss making hotel (at least for a short period of time). On the other hand, an independent hotel that does not make any profits will go bankrupt, leaving a greater market share for the chain operated hotel. When the larger market share has been secured and competition reduced, the chain operated hotel can then increase room rates and become profitable again. This is a strategy that is usually employed by new entrants to a market, and is called market penetration strategy.

The pricing policy to follow is determined by the characteristics of the hotel(s) and hotel's guests. The guest's characteristics that influence the hotel's pricing policy are length of stay and meal requirements; alternative eating facilities in the hotel's locale; guests' spending power and price sensitivity; and homogeneity. A typical city centre hotel in a major European city, for example, tends to attract business people during the week and leisure weekend break guests during the weekend. The first segment is characterized by usually short stays; most people on business only travel between Monday to Friday. Their meal requirements vary from just breakfast (if they have prior lunch arrangements) to breakfast, business lunch and maybe room service dinner. Their spending power again is usually higher than the typical leisure guest because their company will normally be paying. This results in smaller price sensitivity and greater spending power. Corporate or business rates, therefore, are typically higher than weekend rates.

The hotel's characteristics relate to its grade, size, and market position and marketing strategy. A five star hotel will follow a different pricing policy to a bed and breakfast establishment, because of all the additional services that are expected from a five star hotel. Again, a small hotel will not be as capable as attracting large groups and conventions as a larger hotel. Finally, marketing issues such as competition have serious implications for the pricing policy of the hotel. A city centre hotel in Hong Kong, for example, with average yearly occupancy rates above 98 per cent will have a different pricing policy than a hotel in London, where the average occupancy rates are closer to 78 per cent.

There are a number of other issues that both independent as well as chain operated hotels must consider in relation to their pricing policy. These are price variations due to different room types (single, double, suite, view from the room), number of occupants per room, and market segments or types of guest. A typical hotel will have a room rack rate and a variety of other room rates available for different market segments. These could be a corporate rate, weekend rate, group rate, and conference rate to name just a few. Furthermore, apart from the set rates, hotels usually have contracts with tour operators, travel agencies and other companies that generate a lot of travel, such as banks. It is not unusual for a hotel, therefore, to have many other rates apart from the rack rate. Another pricing consideration is what should be included as part of any rate. The simplest term is the room only rate. Other rates could include breakfast, or lunch, or dinner, or all of these, what is usually called a full board rate. Finally, despite the adopted pricing policy, it is worthwhile pointing out that after a specific number of rooms are sold (this number is the break-even point of a hotel for that day) every other room sale contributes directly to the hotel's profits.

Hotel companies have started using yield management to try to maximize their profits (see Chapter 15). Yield management, originally used by airline companies, is based on the principle of supply and demand, but it concentrates on specific market segments and time periods. It is concerned with what sales mix to accept for a specific period (day, week, month, or even year) and what percentage of the total hotel's capacity is allocated for each specific market segment in order to maximize revenue, and therefore profits. Based on future bookings and booking forecasts, using yield management the hotel operator adjusts the hotel room price to achieve the optimum balance between supply and demand for the specific period.

Control

Control in a hotel's front office is very important, as indeed it is in every department as well as in every type of business. The objectives of every control system are to establish specific targets, monitor the performance to see if these targets have been met, and finally if necessary take corrective action to meet these targets. A number of areas can and must be controlled. The most common for the front office, however, are cash/revenue sales, guest satisfaction and night audit, the last dealt with earlier in the chapter.

Management observation is always a good way of controlling the smooth running of any department. Management, however, is not there 24 hours per day, 365 days per year. Reports, therefore, are necessary for every manager to control the department's function and performance, reports that must be accurate as well as adapted to the needs of the specific property, and, furthermore, to those of the specific manager. This is because apart from the reports that are produced for the senior managers and head office, every departmental manager, and in this case the front office manager, must be able to choose what information and reports are necessary. This avoids the problem of information overload.

A typical set of reports that are widely used by many front office managers include the occupancy report, which summarizes the previous day's occupancy rate and average room rate. It can be broken down by room type, so that the manager can see which room types and rates were popular during a day/period and which were not. The revenue report, apart from giving the total room revenue for the day, also gives the manager the average room rate for the day (total room revenue divided by the total number of rooms sold). Every front office manager has a target budget for both occupancy as well as average room rate. These two reports can help the manager to see if the department is meeting the set budget or if corrective action is needed. Revenue can also be broken down by rate, so a manager can identify which are the most popular rates and plan accordingly. The revenue report also breaks down the total revenue figure by method of payment (cash, credit card and vouchers). Cash and other receipts can then be checked against these reports. The arrival list is, as the name suggests, a detailed list of the day's arrivals. The departmental manager bases the department's rostering on the arrival list as well as the departure list. Usually arrival lists include special requests as well as information necessary for a correct room allocation, such as requests for non-smoking rooms. A departure list is a list with all the departures that are expected for the day.

The front office department generates most of these lists; most are generated, by the night shift, including the night auditing team. Some of them, however, are useful to other departments as well. A good example is the departure list that the housekeeping department can use to organize personnel levels. All of these lists also serve the purpose of manual back up in the unfortunate case of a computer breakdown. There are many more reports that can be generated in addition to the above. Some of these are:

- VIP guest report, includes arrival and departure information of VIP guests that arrive that day, as well as their room rate, special requests, and why they are on the VIP list;
- special requests report, for all arriving guests (such as non-smoking room or vegetarian meals required);
- no shows report, guests with reservations (guaranteed or not) that failed to show up the previous night;
- rooms out of order report, listing all the hotel rooms that are out of order: the purpose of this report is to avoid the allocation of these rooms to arriving guests, as well as to inform maintenance which rooms are out of order and why;
- messages report, a report that lists all the guests arriving that day and who have messages or parcels waiting for them so that the receptionists can arrange these messages to be in the guest's room prior to the arrival;
- maintenance report, lists all maintenance work to be carried out during the day;
- credit limit report, lists the credit limits that the hotel's credit controller has allocated to each guest: if guests exceed their credit limit the hotel can either request payment or increase their limit;
- in-house guests report, lists all the guests that are staying in the hotel; and
- vacant rooms report, lists all rooms that are vacant.

Most information supplied by these reports is already in the hotel's computer. These reports serve two main purposes. First, they act as backup in the case of a computer failure. The second use of these reports is by hotel employees who do not work in an office, such as maintenance personnel, and therefore do not have constant access to this information.

Another aspect that the management might want to control, apart from cash and revenue in general, is guest satisfaction. This is very important because a satisfied guest will come back and will communicate the positive experience to others. A dissatisfied guest on the other hand not only will not come back, but may deter others from using the hotel by communicating the negative experience they had whilst staying there. In small establishments this tends to be done, mainly, by direct personal contact. A member of the management team, such as the front office manager, will inquire about a guest's stay either during the stay itself or at the check-out point. In larger properties and chains, the procedure is less personal. Guest satisfaction questionnaires are widely used by many companies for the purpose of getting feedback on customer satisfaction. Usually these questionnaires are left in the guest's room and ask the guest to grade, on a specified scale, the various experiences that they have had in the hotel. These could include check-in, breakfast, a meal, and the room's décor, size and cleanliness. They also ask for comments about members of the hotel's personnel in terms of whether they were either exceptionally good or bad at their job. Many hotel operators take guest satisfaction questionnaires very seriously, and many heads of department's bonuses are directly related to their results.

PERSONNEL

Providing a good quality and effective service in front office is directly related to personnel. The right personnel can make a significant difference to the quality of the service offered. Furthermore, proper and continuous training in collaboration with the previously mentioned control procedures is essential to the success of the front office department. This, however, involves finding as well as keeping the right personnel. High personnel turnover always has negative results. The way to avoid this is by providing appropriate personnel levels, keeping the personnel motivated, having welfare and appraisal systems in place and ensuring career development possibilities for all personnel. Personnel issues are discussed further in Chapter 14.

IT AND EQUIPMENT

Technological advances have changed the ways hotels operate, and emerging technologies will continue that trend, including sales force automation, seamless reservation systems, paperless management and interactive services. The international hotel industry spends more than £1 billion on technology every year. There are many fully integrated computer systems readily available nowadays. These systems integrate front office with all food and beverage outlets; reservations; central reservations (if the hotel is part of a chain); the accounts department; conference and banqueting; sales and marketing; and more. Apart from in-house computerized systems, it is also common to find in a front office online credit card charging equipment and computerized guestroom key machines.

All this equipment can contribute greatly to providing a better service. Technology is a tool that is adopted in order to make all front office personnel more efficient and enable them to provide a better service to hotel guests, and not a replacement of traditional hospitality and personal contact. Technological equipment and computers cannot make a guest feel welcome. Moreover, although equipment is there to help the front office personnel provide a better service such personnel must be very careful not to ignore the guests. For checking a guest in, the use of a computer is necessary in most hotels these days, all personnel however, must make a conscious effort not to pay more attention to the computer screen than to the guest.

CONCLUDING REMARKS

This chapter has briefly discussed the functions of a hotel's front office department. The functions were grouped into three main categories, namely operational aspects of front office; social and psychological aspects of front office management; and management aspects. Many authors and practitioners would argue that the front office department is the most important in the hotel, because, more than any other, it generates more revenue for the hotel not simply through the sale of bedrooms but via the promotion of other hotel outlets such as restaurants. However, the importance of the front office department stretches beyond revenue generation, it being also the communication centre of the hotel, coordinating all the other departments aiming to provide the hotel guests with a level of service that will meet, or even exceed, their expectations.

REFERENCES AND FURTHER READING

Abbott, P. and Lewry, S. (1993) *Front Office: Procedures, Social Skills and Management*, London: Butterworth Heinemann.

Dix, C. (1979) *Accommodation Operations*, Plymouth: Macdonald and Evans Ltd.

Jones, C. and Paul, V. (1993) *Accommodation Management*, London: BT Batsford Ltd.

Pearce, J.A. (1982) 'The company mission as a strategic tool', *Sloan Management Review*, Spring, 15–24.

Vallen, J.J. (1985) *Check-In – Check-Out: Principles of Effective Front Office Management*, Iowa: Wm. C. Brown Publishers.

9 Housekeeping management in the contemporary hotel industry

Christopher G. Rawstron

This chapter focuses on modern methods of managing the housekeeping department within hotels where the overall aim of hotels is running an enterprise achieving an agreed level of profit and therefore a targeted return on the capital employed within the business. Over the last 20 years there have been many significant changes in the ways that hotels are managed and the housekeeping department has been no exception. These have been accelerated due to the economic circumstances of the 1980s and 1990s: in order to ensure survival, the strategic focus of the hotel industry has changed radically in terms of both its expectations of profit generation, and in modernizing aspects of hotel management processes.

Nowhere is this more evident than in the housekeeping department. Many of the practices and procedures in the housekeeping department have changed and new focuses and activities have been introduced to meet customer and business needs. This chapter will explore these new approaches to housekeeping management and give an overview of the systems and procedures increasingly evident in many businesses as means of ensuring that the aims of the hotel business as a whole are achieved. The housekeeping model being discussed may be transported to any hotel whether large or small, the only adjustment required being one of scaling up or down.

ROLE OF HOUSEKEEPING DEPARTMENT

First, it is essential that the actual role and purpose of the housekeeping department within the hotel is clearly defined. The housekeeping department's main role and purpose is of course to provide clean and serviced bedrooms on a daily basis to the agreed standards. In addition, all corridors and public areas, like the hotel lobby, should be neat, clean and tidy, again to the agreed standards. In some hotels the role may be extended to guest services like valet, laundry and dry cleaning and turndown, all of which the customer may pay for separately or as a premium on the standard room tariff.

However, the role of the housekeeping department also has additional aspects that are not always immediately evident. These include recruitment, training and development of people; strict control of costs like toiletries and linen; managing suppliers to ensure product specification and delivery schedules are adhered to; and maintaining the bedroom product to the standards set and agreed within the hotel whilst adhering to statutory law and health and safety standards. Most importantly of all, the housekeeping department supports the hotel's business as a whole. Since running hotels is about selling bedrooms, the housekeeping department is challenged with providing let-able rooms, day in and day out, and they can never have a day off. In some hotels this is more challenging than others, for example in airport hotels which both attract transient passengers and sell bedrooms 24 hours a day, with customers arriving and departing at all hours. The added caveat of delayed flights where a large number of bedrooms are required at very short notice all adds to the pressures that the housekeeping department has to deal with and overcome. Within any hotel, the housekeeping department is normally the biggest department and employer, where its staff work largely unsupervised and are substantially empowered in their daily tasks and routines. The majority of this work and effort occur out of sight and mind of the customer, and for this reason the housekeeping department is often the unsung hero within the hotel.

ROLE OF THE KEY PLAYERS

Within the housekeeping department there are four key roles that people will be employed to undertake, i.e. Housekeeping Assistant, Floor Housekeeper, House Porter and Housekeeping Manager. Whilst this is not an exhaustive list, i.e. additional roles like valet and seamstress occur but are rare and job titles vary, they need to be clarified so that performance may be measured and accountability delegated relative to the overall aims of the housekeeping department.

Role of the Housekeeping Assistant

This role was described as the Chambermaid in the past, but has been renamed to increase flexibility and to recognize that it is a job now popular with men as well as women. Servicing bedrooms is clearly the key role of the Housekeeping Assistant, and this must be achieved within agreed guidelines. Each bedroom, once serviced, should be to the same high standards of cleanliness, and the set-up of the room should be to the hotel's specification, i.e. in terms of location and presentation of toiletries, or the way that the bed is made (for example in respect of the latter, the use of 'hospital corners' which sets a particular standard relating to the way that the sheets are folded under the mattress). The Housekeeping Assistant has a certain responsibility for customer liaison and is often questioned by customers as to the hotel's facilities or local amenities. The reporting of maintenance duties is a key factor in ensuring that the customer's experience meets with expectations and the Housekeeping Assistant would be responsible for reporting any defects. Vacuuming corridors, stocking trolleys and disposing of refuse and linen are other duties to be undertaken. All of these tasks will need to be completed to agreed productivity targets set within the hotel. These may be measured in minutes, or by the volume of rooms serviced in a shift. This will be explored and elaborated upon in greater depth later in the chapter.

Role of Floor Housekeeper

The Floor Housekeeper is, as the name suggests, a supervisor in charge of a floor or a number of floors within the hotel. The Floor Housekeeper's primary responsibility is managing the Housekeeping Assistants working within this agreed area and supervising the quality and efficiency of their work. Once a room is serviced by the Housekeeping Assistant the room is not passed to reception as let-able until the Floor

Housekeeper has firstly checked that all relevant standards are in place and the room is ready for the customer. The Floor Housekeeper is then accountable for 'handing back' rooms to the front office to let.

A key focus on training and development of the Housekeeping Assistant forms a large part of the Floor Housekeeper's responsibility whether it be training and inducting new starters or re-training and corrective training of existing staff. It is vitally important that all training is recorded, however quick a session may be, for continued measurement of employee performance. The Floor Housekeeper will also assume responsibility for equipment and cost control within their area and for liaison with other departments in the hotel like maintenance and concierge. Guest liaison forms part of their role, as with Housekeeping Assistants. However, the Floor Housekeeper should adopt a proactive role and challenge customers on their perceived level of satisfaction, offering further assistance as appropriate. Other duties include management of linen, refuse, cleaning chemicals and computer input into the hotel's property management system (PMS) (e.g. in terms of rooms that are ready to be let to guests, or reporting maintenance requirements). In some hotels where multi-skilling is a key focus, in order to reduce the number of Floor Housekeepers some Housekeeping Assistants may be developed and classified as 'self-checking', where their work is only checked on an *ad hoc* or random basis. This can benefit the employee by an enhancement to their basic wage plus a cost saving to the hotel in a reduction in the number of Floor Housekeepers.

Role of the House Porter

The House Porter could be described as the jack (or jill!) of all trades and has a number of varied duties like sweeping fire exit corridors, back of house areas, lifts, bins, the delivery of guest laundry and stocking of Housekeeping Assistants' cupboards. It may also include conducting minor maintenance, e.g. changing light bulbs. Generally reporting to the Floor Housekeeper, the House Porter is the key trouble-shooter to undertake whatever tasks, within reason, to ready the housekeeping department for daily guest arrivals.

Role of the Housekeeping Manager

Formally (and still sometimes) known as the Head or Executive Housekeeper, the Housekeeping Manager is the person with the ultimate accountability for the department in terms of staff deployment and development, operational standards and profitability. They have a controlling and directing role of staff within the department, liaising with customers to ensure complete satisfaction whilst managing costs, achieving targets and observing relevant regulations like COSHH (Care of Substances Hazardous to Health).

Delegation, communication, guidance and direction are key skills required in a successful Housekeeping Manager. Human resource planning activities including recruitment, induction, training and the creation of flexibility within the workforce are key priorities to ensure that each and every day the hotel's bedrooms are properly serviced and prepared for arriving guests. Overall, the Housekeeping Manager accepts accountability for standards of cleanliness, maintenance and financial performance within the housekeeping department. In the contemporary hotel business it is this role that has seen the most significant change in recent years where the image of 'lady of the house' has vanished and been replaced by systems and controls to encourage effectiveness and flexibility. The following sections of this chapter will examine in more detail the human resource management aspects, and management systems and control within the housekeeping department as they prevail in many of today's hotels.

HUMAN RESOURCE MANAGEMENT

As previously stated, the housekeeping department is normally the largest employer within any hotel. It is therefore important that there are efficient human resource management practices in place (see also Chapter 14).

The largest proportion of the housekeeping labour force will work as Housekeeping Assistants who can be full-time, part-time, casual, short-term contracted, evening only shifts, week-end only shifts, students and agency workers. In very large hotels the number of Housekeeping Assistants may be in excess of 100 employees. The role of the Housekeeping Assistant, whilst relatively low-skilled in practice, is physically demanding and as a result there is a high turnover of staff. The complexities of managing such a range of staff with different contracts, as well as ensuring that there are always enough staff to service the business, reinforces the need for a truly effective human resource plan. In many locations within the UK and particularly in London, where hotels generally are larger than in the provinces, there is a continual shortage of Housekeeping Assistants. For this reason agency workers are utilized to fill gaps. Whilst employment of agency staff allows the Housekeeping Manager flexibility to service all of the bedrooms there are drawbacks to using agencies, such as additional costs; low levels of training; low levels of motivation; lack of loyalty to the hotel; and loss of productivity.

Any human resource plan for the housekeeping department should focus on the following areas:

- recruitment;
- induction and training;
- feedback – job chats and appraisals; and
- development and succession planning.

Recruitment

Recruitment should be an ongoing process where the various methods of recruitment are constantly refocused. Job specifications and job descriptions need to be clearly defined to ensure that, along with an effective interviewing process, the most suitable candidates are employed. The cost of recruitment is considerable. In addition to advertising and management time, there is the training cost when a new employee starts, and an associated loss in productivity until they are fully trained.

Induction and training

There is a higher drop out in the first four weeks of employment than at any other time. Therefore the hotel and departmental induction processes are vital to ensure that a new employee is properly welcomed to the unit; provided with all job relevant information; trained as appropriate; and then eased into the job, perhaps working alongside a colleague for the first two weeks. It is important that new employees are not 'dropped in at the deep end', e.g. not asked to service a full complement of rooms on their third day, since this is likely to increase staff turnover. The training must be comprehensive and might make use of visual aids, like photographs, to show how a bedroom should be prepared, and checklists to act as a reminder. Training is ongoing and must be recorded in an effective manner. Where budgeted expenditure allows, a dedicated Housekeeping Trainer can be very effective in assisting with induction and training, as well as managing future training requirements.

Feedback

Time needs to be allocated to conduct job chats and appraisals with all employees. Job chats are more informal and should occur every three months, lasting no more than 30 minutes, allowing quality exchanges about the job between the Housekeeping Assistant and their immediate boss. Appraisals, held approximately every six months in most large hotels, are more in-depth, taking longer and requiring thought in advance of the meeting. The appraisal is more structured and, to be effective, all comments are usually recorded on appropriate special forms. Following an appraisal meeting there will be action for both parties. It provides a focus for critical feedback and praise to be facilitated in a two way discussion that is controlled and effective.

Feedback from the employees of the department provides useful information in terms of morale and motivation of the team. In addition, new ideas may be generated for improvements to policies or procedures and standards, or just better ways of making more profit. Feedback given to the employees of the department can identify areas of success and areas that require further improvement within the department as a whole.

Development and succession planning

Following employee appraisals, personal development plans can be established to identify employees who are seeking more responsibility and therefore it becomes possible to channel and focus certain training to provide a successful succession planning process within the department, for example a Housekeeping Assistant can be developed to self-checking status, and then developed to a Floor Housekeeper and so on. The benefits of this process are numerous, and include cost savings on recruitment, better employee retention and a more highly motivated workforce. Hotels that have achieved the Investor in People (IiP) award will already be practising these procedures and approaches to human resource planning and consequently IiP is an award that every hotel should consider endeavouring to achieve (see Chapter 14).

Ultimately having an effective human resource plan will benefit the housekeeping department in a number of ways, most usually in addressing:

1 a high degree of motivation and morale within the team;
2 reduced labour turnover and hence savings on the cost of recruitment;
3 reduction on the reliance of employment agencies;
4 maintenance of the high level of standards in the department;
5 a 'can do' and flexible approach; and
6 effective rostering and ability to drive and maximize productivity levels within the department.

PRODUCTIVITY

Due to the ever increasing focus on profit generation within hotel management, productivity is a key influence on the level of profit generated by any department. In the housekeeping department, productivity relates primarily to the number of rooms a Housekeeping Assistant is able to service in a shift to the agreed standards. Finding the optimum balance of rooms serviced to standards achieved will vary from hotel to hotel. However, typical targets are three rooms per hour in budget standard accommodation to 15 rooms serviced in an eight hour shift in four star standard accommodation. Clearly as the number of rooms to be serviced increases, the standard of the end result will diminish and will impact on morale, motivation and employee turnover. Therefore the expectations of the customer and the standard of the hotel are key influences in the productivity levels to be set by a Housekeeping Manager. The size of the room is also important when comparing rooms across a range of hotels, e.g. suites normally count as two standard rooms in terms of cleaning time.

Incentivization can be an effective management tool to improve productivity and hence the profitability of the department whilst giving something back to the employee in return. Typical examples of this are additional wages for cleaning rooms to a consistently high standard that do not require checking by a Floor Housekeeper (i.e. the aforementioned 'self-checking' Assistants). Another example may be as simple as additional wages for servicing rooms in a shift over and above the normal target. All incentives should be governed by the following three criteria:

1 they should be easy to implement;
2 they should be easy to measure and control; and
3 they should be self-financing.

Incentivization is also an effective tool in managing other costs within the housekeeping department and this will be elaborated upon in the next section.

To ensure that productivity targets, once set, are consistently achieved effective rostering techniques are required. There is a fine art in ensuring that there are always enough Housekeeping Assistants on duty to cope with demand whilst at the same time avoiding over-staffing. Key features of efficient rostering are:

1 evaluating start times of staff in relation to departure times of guests;
2 analysis of arrival and departure numbers compared to stay-overs;
3 approximation of the number of late departures, e.g. aircrews;
4 awareness of day let volumes;
5 awareness of peaks and troughs in occupancy;
6 optimizing levels of supervision, i.e. Floor Housekeepers and levels of support, i.e. House Porters to the Housekeeping Assistants;
7 managing holiday entitlement and sickness; and
8 employing a range of people who can work at all times the business demands, e.g. in some hotels rooms are serviced throughout the night.

All in all the strength and success of human resource management within the housekeeping department will play a critical role in the overall success and profitability of the department and the hotel as a whole.

MANAGEMENT CONTROL SYSTEMS

There needs to be a number of management control systems in place that are able to supervise and measure the housekeeping department at every level. This is for two specific reasons:

1 to evaluate the success or otherwise of the housekeeping department in terms of standards and profit; and

2 to ensure that the goals and objectives set are achieved harmoniously alongside those of the hotel as a whole.

The following discussion covers the areas in housekeeping where management control systems are of particular and contemporary relevance.

Standards achievement

Clearly, despite all the pressures and focus in modern hotels on productivity and profit generation, this can and should not be at the expense of standards within the housekeeping department. The word standard needs some clearer definition. In each area of activity and performance in the housekeeping department there should be an agreed target of achievement. The most important of these would be bedroom cleanliness, which circumscribes areas such as tops of pictures; under the bed; and behind the credenza unit; in addition to the usual areas like vacuuming of carpets; clean and dusted work tops; and smear free polished mirrors. These standards are also transported to back of house areas like fire exit stairwells and goods lifts. The public areas and toilets are an important area of any hotel and normally the responsibility of the Housekeeping Manager, again all require agreed standards of cleanliness. There may be surfaces like marble, granite or terracotta tiling present which require special attention, and normally necessitate a separate contract with a specialist cleaning company. Standards of cleanliness must therefore be set taking into account the style and resources of the hotel. Once standards are agreed, the target is obviously to achieve and adhere to them, day in and day out. When standards are not being achieved is when the department will begin to lose sight of its objectives and not deliver its targets as laid down in the overall plan within the hotel. It has previously been stated that the role of the 'Lady of the House' is no longer evident and neither are the 'White Glove' checks of the past. Today there is a more systematic approach to standard delivery and some examples are as follows.

The checklist

The person responsible for monitoring a given task may have a checklist to be completed once the task is completed, e.g. the Floor Housekeeper on checking the standard of a Housekeeping Assistant's work. The example checklist in Table 9.1 shows the detail required to carry out a competent check of a bedroom. These are time consuming, as one would envisage. However, there should only be an agreed number completed each day, on a rotation basis, in order to cover every bedroom and every Housekeeping Assistant within a given time period.

Checklists may also be utilized for public area cleaning or for tasks that have many individual points, all of which are critical to overall success. An example of this would be the House Porter having a checklist for their shift, showing the numerous duties to be undertaken in that shift and perhaps the sequence in which such duties are to be executed. This also acts as an effective tool to ensure that some unmeasurable tasks are also completed. Overall, checklists are very effective in controlling and measuring standards, informing the employee as to what will be checked, serving as a memory jogger, and as a hard copy record of performance that can be measured and maintained over time and across the department.

Table 9.1 Housekeeping checklist

Date:	Room No:		
BEDROOM	**TICK**	**BEDROOM**	**TICK**
Lights off when finished		Top of headboard	
Lights all work		Bedspread, DND, breakfast card	
Wardrobe: 8 hangers & straight		Under bed	
Spare pillow in bag		Tops of pictures	
Trouser press works & dust free		Room dusted	
TV works & dust free		Room hoovered	
Remote control works		**BATHROOM**	
Clean room service menu		Bath grouting	
Guest directory: Three paper		Bath tiles	
Three envelopes		Chromework	
Two fax sheets		Towels – on sink 2 hand	
Merchandiser – leisure break		Above bath 2 bath sheets	
Mirrors clean & smear free		Over bath 1 bath mat	
Drawers: hairdryer		Shower curtain clean & folded	
1 laundry bag		Toilet	
1 shoe shine		Toilet rolls x 2	
1 laundry list		Toiletries on tray: 2 gel	
1 Bible		2 shampoo	
Cupboard: 1 empty kettle		1 shower cap	
2 glasses & coasters		2 soap	
Tea tray		2 glasses	
2 cups & spoons		Ice cup behind tray	
Tea, coffee, sugar, milk		Hygiene bags	
Bin – empty		Bin – empty	
Tops of lamps		Sink	
Windowsill		Mirror	
Curtains & nets		Tissue x 1 box	
Chairs		Floor	
Telephone-notepads & pencil		Back of door	
Yellow Pages & Phone Book			

Self-checking maids

Despite extensive revision in industry job titles the term 'self-checking maid' still remains to describe Senior Housekeeping Assistants who are paid more or incentivized to deliver the agreed standard in everything they do. Therefore, to become a self-checking maid an employee must first demonstrate an ability and commitment to delivering the agreed standards. Once in place their work will be checked on an *ad hoc* basis and if it is not to the required standard, they may be penalized or lose their self-checking status. This philosophy may be transported to other parts in the housekeeping department like public area cleaners, House Porters and linen staff. Naturally it has the benefit of reducing the level of supervision required within the department and therefore enhancing profits, without affecting or reducing standards.

MANAGEMENT BY WALKING ABOUT (MBWA)

Management By Walking About (MBWA) whilst more *ad hoc* is an effective way of measuring standards within the housekeeping department. This includes not only walking the floors or back of house areas but by sometimes being resident overnight in the hotel and sampling the product. This should be encouraged at all levels within the hotel from the General Manager down to the front line staff. Naturally it needs to be controlled and available only during the trough periods of business. Following the bedroom experience or by walking around the department, positive comments or troubleshooting ideas should be fed back to the Housekeeping Manager for action, and there needs to be a control system in place recording feedback and measuring corrective action as appropriate. In discussing standards it should *always* be remembered that standards should be set in line with customer expectations and the profit needs of the business.

PURCHASING

Purchasing forms a large part of the Housekeeping Manager's role who, in larger hotels is often accountable for expenditure of many hundreds of thousands of pounds. This is clearly one area where the profitability of the department can be affected if the purchasing and consumption of the various products and supplies are not effectively managed. The primary areas of purchasing that fall under the control of the Housekeeping Manager are:

1 bedroom supplies – e.g. toiletries, laundry bags, breakfast cards;
2 cleaning supplies – e.g. air freshener, bleach, cleaning products;
3 TCMF (tea and coffee making facilities) – e.g. tea/coffee sachets, sugar, milk and biscuits;
4 uniforms – e.g. for Housekeeping Assistants/Porters;
5 working replacements – e.g. shower curtains, crockery, glassware, vacuum cleaners, trolleys; and
6 linen – bed sheets and towelling.

In large organizations there would normally be a procurement department who will agree, on a company-wide basis, the relevant costs and specifications of the vast majority of the aforementioned items. In this case there will be a nominated supplier that the Housekeeping Manager must use to purchase the goods. In addition there will be levels of quality and agreed delivery times which the supplier needs to adhere to at all times.

In smaller hotel companies or in stand alone hotels, their will be a greater freedom with regard to purchasing. However, in both cases the Housekeeping Manager will need to be focused on both the purchase of supplies and their consumption once received in the hotel. At any one time large amounts of the hotel's money will be tied up in the purchasing of these products, therefore stockholdings have to be managed accordingly whilst ensuring that supplies do not run out. The list of the items shown above can be further classified into:

(a) consumable – bedroom supplies, cleaning supplies and TCMF; and
(b) assets – uniforms, working replacements and linen.

The Housekeeping Manager will adopt a different philosophy for purchasing and control of these two groups as follows. For consumables (so called because they are bought in to be consumed and then discarded) there will be a standard set-up for each room indicating the number of soaps, shampoos, tissues or coffee sachets that should be displayed. Actual consumption of these items can be forecast with reasonable accuracy in line with anticipated hotel occupancy. It is vitally important that the hotel does not run out of consumables at any time, therefore a stockholding would normally be in place where staff can requisition their needs on a daily or weekly basis. Additional caveats relating to pilferage and wastage need to be factored into the forecast for consumption and the causes of these phenomena addressed separately, as part of the control process. The Housekeeping Manager will therefore be targeted to spend within agreed limits on consumables and this would be recorded on the hotel's profit and loss account accompanied by detailed consumption reports in each area. The Housekeeping Manager will also be responsible for reconciling delivery notes and invoices and authorizing payment of these invoices once agreed.

In respect of assets (not assets in the true sense of the term relating to the hotel's balance sheet) uniforms, working replacements and linen need to be managed differently to consumables in terms of their purchase and control. In respect of uniforms, once the specification is agreed the required number of uniforms will be purchased for employees. They in turn sign for their uniform and have a responsibility to maintain it to the agreed standard in line with the hotel's image policy. Uniforms will be bought at irregular intervals in the main, and therefore purchased in larger quantities which will result in the phasing of the expenditure in the profit and loss account over a period of time.

The term 'working replacements' covers a multitude of items like vacuum cleaners, trolleys, skips, cutlery, crockery, glassware, shower curtains, blankets, curtains, bedspreads, bathrobes and so on. Due to the fact that these are normally all in use within the department, inventories need to be kept to manage their use and replacement requirements. Clearly these items will possibly break or wear out, therefore a phased purchase programme will be needed to ensure that there are funds available to purchase a small amount each month on an ongoing basis. Larger costs like vacuum cleaners (a 600 bedroomed hotel may require up to 50 in place) may be capitalized which means it will not be charged to the housekeeping account or phased over time, but registered as depreciation.

Finally here, linen (bed-linen and towelling) are traditionally seen as problematic in terms of control within the housekeeping department. The contemporary hotel has moved away from running laundries in-house, with all the problems associated with human resource and plant, to contracting the service out to professional laundry companies. Such deals are normally structured around a lease rental where there will be a wash cost per item plus a stock-loss charge made on a monthly or quarterly basis. Control of linen is problematic due to the possible scale of the operation (e.g. a typically busy 600 bedroom hotel would have over 5000 items of soiled linen per day all of which need to be classified and counted prior to leaving the hotel bound for the laundry). This makes consumption difficult to manage. In some locations, particularly airports, the guests may pilfer the linen (e.g. as an extra towel for the beach). Guests on occasion feel that this is their right given the room rate they are paying. Clearly this is not the case and stock-loss of linen needs to be tightly managed, although it is difficult or even impossible to manage the customer pilferage aspect.

The other major area of control in linen is a measure of the quality of the linen. Suppliers will normally be contracted to supply linen to an agreed standard (e.g. size of sheets or weight of towelling). However due to the complexities of their business, suppliers can, on occasion, deviate from these standards or supply reject articles like sheets with holes or torn towelling. It is important that the hotel identifies these and 'rejects' them, therefore requiring a replacement and negating the charge. The ever increasing need to improve control of linen and to work closely with suppliers has seen the evolution of the 'bonded linen room'. A bonded linen room is where the laundry supplier operates the hotel's linen room and manages the linen on behalf of the hotel. This would cover receiving of deliveries, stocking housekeeping cupboards on the bedroom floors, counting and classifying soiled linen, and dispatching back to the laundry. There is a charge for this service. However the Housekeeping Manager has less to worry about in respect of the linen and can therefore focus more time and energy in other areas.

Deep cleaning schedules

In addition to the daily servicing and cleaning of the bedrooms there is a need for schedules to accommodate the cleaning of items such as curtains, nets, bedspreads, shower curtains and carpets (shampooing). Clearly these cleaning tasks do not require to be undertaken daily, therefore an agreed cleaning programme will need to be in place. The standard should be set taking into account hotel occupancy. Following this, a rolling programme needs to be in place to undertake the required cleaning on a rota basis to ensure that the entire hotel is covered within a given period of time. Normally deep cleaning of this type is contracted out to a specialist cleaning company, where the rolling schedule is controlled by the Housekeeping Manager and expenditure is phased accordingly in the hotel's profit and loss account.

BUDGETS AND KEY PERFORMANCE INDICATORS

Prior to each financial year the budget will be set for the hotel. Overall this relates to the sales and profits to be achieved for the coming year. Included within this are the departmental accounts where the housekeeping department will be allocated expenditure targets on payroll and direct expenses. These targets are subdivided into monthly expenditure and further broken down as follows:

- payroll – Housekeeping Assistants (productive) and House Porters, Floor Housekeepers and Housekeeping Managers (non productive); and
- direct expenses – bedroom supplies, TCMF, working replacements, cleaning supplies and laundry and dry cleaning.

The actual expenditure targets are set in consideration of current performance and results for last year. In addition productivity norms that have been agreed will drive their own payroll targets. Larger hotel organizations are able to ascertain this information across all of their properties and benchmark the targets to standardize across the organization as a whole. The budget figure will be the actual cash expenditure allowed and the key performance indicator is the measuring of the effectiveness of the department in achieving the budget expenditure. This can be further explained by examining the specific areas of payroll and direct expenses.

Payroll

The housekeeping department will be allocated an annual budget expenditure for wages. This will be based on the forecast hotel occupancy or rooms let and is made up of the various elements within the housekeeping payroll (i.e. Housekeeping Assistant's pay, House Porter's pay, Floor Housekeeper's pay and so on, including all employees within the housekeeping department). The budget will include all employer National Insurance contributions and in some cases a contribution to the holiday pay reserve. The following example best illustrates this. Assume a 150 bedroom hotel with forecast annual occupancy of 82 per cent for the coming financial year. The housekeeping payroll budget for the year is £186,300. This can be expressed as a payroll per room let, i.e. the total rooms let for the year divided into the budget expenditure which equals £4.15 for the total department. This can be further broken down as follows:

	£ per room let
Housekeeping Assistants	2.70
House Porters	0.40
Floor Housekeepers	0.70
Housekeeping Manager & general	0.35
TOTAL	**£4.15**

This information will prove useful to the Housekeeping Manager, and measuring the payroll per room let allows management the opportunities to examine all areas within the housekeeping department in terms of how effectively the payroll is being managed in line with the budget target. However, in reality, the forecast occupancy will change overall and fluctuate throughout the year (i.e. there will be peaks and troughs) therefore the Housekeeping Manager must manage these variations in the business whilst always achieving the target.

The fixed cost or non-productive cost (i.e. all payroll costs other than Housekeeping Assistants) will become a larger proportion of the overall target when occupancy is low and hence make it more problematic for the Manager. However when occupancy is high the only additional requirements are Housekeeping Assistants at £2.70 per room let and the target is thus easier to achieve, with the fixed payroll cost being smaller pro rata. As a result the Housekeeping Manager has to phase expenditure with the target being overspent with low occupancy but underspent with high occupancy resulting in the overall expenditure balancing back to the original target of £4.15 for the year.

Direct expenses

These are costs directly associated with the housekeeping department other than the payroll. These are dealt with in a similar way to the payroll, where the annual budget is set and this is measured per room let. Continuing with the same example the hotel would have expenditure targets as follows:

	Annual Budget (£)
Bedroom Supplies	20,202
TCMF	15,700
Working replacements	22,450
Cleaning supplies	6,730
Laundry and dry cleaning	74,075

On the basis of the annual occupancy being 82 per cent the expenditure per room let is indicated below:

	£ per room let
Bedroom supplies	0.45
TCMF	0.35
Working replacements	0.50
Cleaning supplies	0.15
Laundry and dry cleaning	1.65

With this information the Housekeeping Manager can measure consumption and wastage therefore managing effectively the expenditure within the department. Since direct expenses are only incurred when a bedroom is let, any fluctuations in occupancy will not require as in-depth management as the housekeeping payroll in terms of phasing costs, and consequently the expenditure of direct expenses is measured either monthly or per financial period within the hotel. The Housekeeping Manager must ensure that they do not lose sight of the need to achieve and exceed financial targets that are set in the overall business plan of the hotel whilst at the same time balancing this between delivery of agreed standards and employee welfare.

Centre of Excellence

In order to pull all the various activities and foci within the housekeeping department together, Table 9.2 shows the criteria necessary to achieve a 'Centre of Excellence' in housekeeping in the contemporary hotel industry. The twenty points listed cover all areas and activities within the housekeeping department, setting the standard to be achieved on a consistent basis. All points are important and all play an integral part in the overall success of the department. The entire housekeeping team should be aware of the importance of their role and duty to participate in delivery of the criteria to achieve the Centre of Excellence.

Table 9.2 Housekeeping Centre of Excellence in the contemporary hotel industry

1. Impeccably cleaned bedrooms
2. Enough equipment and all in working order
3. Consistent delivery of agreed standards
4. Effective team work at all times
5. Good communication with each other and other departments
6. High standard of uniforms and immaculate personal presentation
7. Fully staffed at all times
8. Impeccably cleaned public areas of the hotel
9. Ongoing training programme with regular reviews
10. All suppliers deliver products to agreed specification
11. High degrees of staff morale
12. Planned maintenance programmes and effective systems of reporting
13. Impeccable back of house standards
14. Effective cleaning schedules
15. Defect reporting procedure

16 Agreed job description in place
17 Regular job chats and appraisals
18 Working to agreed productivity levels
19 Incentivization in place at all levels
20 Profit targets are consistently achieved

**Anything and everything undertaken in housekeeping must fit into the
'Centre of Excellence' criteria**

The contemporary hotel industry will continue to view hotels as a business where each department within the hotel is a sub-business contributing their own achievements and profits to the overall organization. Therefore, the housekeeping department being the 'engine room' of the hotel needs to be well positioned to deliver its goals and objectives in order to ensure the ongoing and future prosperity of the whole business.

REFERENCES AND FURTHER READING

Jones, U. (1986) *Catering: Housekeeping and Front Office*, London: Edward Arnold.
Jones, C. and Paul, V. (1993) *Accommodation Management: a Systems Approach*, London: BT Batsford Ltd, 2nd edn.

10 Hotel engineering and maintenance

Antonio P. Adamo

In this chapter we consider the engineering aspects of hotel construction and management. From actual construction to renovations; from installations to decoration; from operations to maintenance; from heat and refrigeration to computers and telecommunications; from energy management to waste disposal; modern hotel managers are faced daily with hundreds of decisions concerning the technical functioning of their hotels and hence, engineering. We will start from general technical notions and then proceed to more complex questions such as: technical installations in hotels; hotel construction; hotel planning and design; hotel safety and security; physical plant maintenance; and concepts of applied hotel ecology.

PRELIMINARY REMARKS

The notion of engineering comes from the Latin root 'genius'. In the 17th century the French Marshal Sebastien Le Prestre de Vauban (1633–1707) coined the expression 'military genius' to indicate specifically 'the construction and maintenance of military buildings, fortifications and highways'. The corresponding scientific discipline was named 'ingénierie', whence the English term 'engineering'. With the further development of science and technology this original definition came to include all kinds of applied technical disciplines, such as mechanical engineering, civil engineering, chemical engineering, genetic engineering and so on. Today the term engineering indicates the study and execution of an industrial project, including its technical, economic, ecological and social aspects and involving the coordinated efforts of a multitude of specialists. The major objective of engineering is the optimization of the means necessary to solve a given technical problem.

For the modern hotel manager a basic knowledge of engineering is needed because the hospitality industry has gone from its modest, domestic beginnings to a truly industrial activity. To be successful in this field the hotel manager has to be familiar not only with service techniques, financial management, gastronomy, oenology and the like, but also with construction techniques; technical installations; and sanitary, electrical, electronic, refrigeration, heating, ventilating and air conditioning equipment. Whether dealing with new construction or renovation, remodelling or modernization, preventive or corrective maintenance, the hotel manager is constantly confronted with engineering problems. In addition, the efficient functioning of technology ensures the comfort and safety of hotel guests. It is therefore important that the hotel manager is able to understand these issues and, above all, be capable of informed discussion with the diverse consultants and specialists involved in various forms of engineering projects. Self-confidence comes from knowledge. However, the purpose of this chapter is not to seek to make proficient plumbers, electricians, fully-fledged engineers or architects of its readers. Rather, the aim is to give exposure to engineering as applied to the hospitality industry, to give a taste for technical problems and their possible solutions and to mention some typical engineering situations and references that may stimulate further study.

GENERAL NOTIONS

Hotels are basically buildings used by hotel owners and managers to offer hospitality to their clients. The hospitality industry sells a bundle of services. Therefore, the key to success is client satisfaction. This satisfaction depends to a great extent on the comfort a client is offered in a given hotel, and comfort, in its turn, depends to a large extent on the performance of technology. Generally speaking, there are two kinds of comfort: physical and psychological. Both depend, at least partially, on technology. Examples include:

Physical comfort	*Psychological comfort*
Access to premises	Safety
Room surface-area and volume	Security
Heating, ventilating and air conditioning	Hygiene
Lighting, both natural and artificial	Privacy
Sanitary, electrical, kitchen equipment	Soundproofing
Leisure and sports installations	Safekeeping
Telecommunication equipment	
State of repair (maintenance)	

The impact of engineering on the physical comfort parameters given above is quite clear: if their performance is not satisfactory the clients will notice immediately and their own satisfaction is likely to fall or even disappear. The influence of engineering on the psychological comfort parameters is more subtle as can be seen in the following examples.

Safety	Minimizing physical plant risks and dangers through good design and sound construction techniques
Security	Exits, sprinklers, emergency lights, hidden-camera security systems; modern, high quality, computer linked key systems
Hygiene	Design and installation of easy to clean sanitary, dish washing, and laundry equipment; cleaning machines; cleaning products
Privacy	Door and window systems; design and installation of heavy duty curtain systems
Soundproofing	Sound insulation; double-glazed windows; vibration control at the source; expansion joints; acoustic wall and ceiling claddings
Safekeeping	Room safe deposit boxes

As the above discussion shows, almost every aspect of hotel operations is affected by engineering. It is therefore recommended that the hotel manager become familiar with:

- systems of measurement, both SI and Imperial;
- engineering terminology, especially as regards projects documents and drawings: plans, elevations, cross-sections, scale, symbols and graphs;
- elementary engineering calculations: surface-areas and volumes of common shapes, basic statistics, project accounting; and
- building codes and by-laws: construction industry standard procedures, especially as regards bidding, financing, payments, scheduling, penalty clauses and dispute settlement.

The remainder of this chapter will examine the most important aspects of hotel engineering and maintenance, starting from installations, and progressing through construction and planning. This chapter concludes with an examination of some new ideas on ecology and energy management.

TECHNICAL INSTALLATIONS IN HOTELS

There are many technical installations in hotels. Here we will consider only the five most common, and always with a special eye for their importance in the hospitality industry.

Sanitary installations

Drinking water, both cold and hot, is vital for any hotel operation. The natural cycle of water is a kind of closed circuit, alternating between evaporation and precipitation, in which the heat coming from the sun causes water from the sea to evaporate and accumulate in the sky. After following the caprices of meteorology water falls back to earth (i.e. precipitates) where it is used by the flora and fauna (including man) for their living needs. Finally, all water returns to the sea to restart the cycle. Man interferes with the natural cycle of water by using it for his needs. In the industrialized world, this interference has two major aspects:

- consumption: the daily average domestic consumption is in the order of some 250 l/person. To this, we have to add the industrial consumption (agriculture, chemical industry, medical and military activities, hospitality industry, and so on) of about 300 l/person per day, to give a total of about 550 l/person per day; and
- waste disposal: we use water directly as a vehicle to carry all sorts of waste, including heavy metals and toxic substances. Indirectly, water picks up residual waste, such as insecticides and fertilisers, from the percolation of agricultural and industrial fields.

Clearly, this enormous interference with the natural cycle of water is very dangerous, for the resources of the Earth are limited. In fact, only a tiny portion (0.5 per cent) of water is available in the form of fresh water. This is found in the rivers, lakes and water tables of the world. Water arrives at your tap after a long trip through nature and distribution networks. After use, it become wastewater and must be disposed of. Natural water is not readily usable as drinking water for, to be qualified as such, water has to meet World Health Organization (WHO) standards. These concern primarily: water mineralization, hardness, pH-value and microbial contents. If it is too hard, water must undergo a treatment called softening. Water also contains gases dissolved in it. The hydrogen potential (pH) is important because man can tolerate only very small variations in pH. Therefore, this parameter has to be very carefully monitored. Water may also contain micro-organisms of various kinds. Most water-borne microbes are harmless, but some are deadly and cannot be tolerated in drinking water (see Box 10.1). In hotels, there is a large demand for hot water from:

- guests;
- kitchen and restaurant;
- laundry requirements; and
- heating and air conditioning.

Hot water production, distribution and consumption are very difficult technical problems better left to specialists. However, the hotel manager must become familiar with

---

Box 10.1: The water pH parameter

Thanks to oxygen contained in water, fish can live totally immersed in it. They have the ability to absorb from the water-dissolved oxygen by virtue of their gills, which are nothing but modified lungs (actually, our lungs are modified gills!). By a no less wonderful phenomenon, hydrogen also manages to make its presence felt in water. This is called potential of hydrogen, pH for short, and is measured on the pH-value scale, beginning at 0 and ending at 14. Here is how water is classified according to its pH.

pH 0 to pH < 7	**pH 7**	**pH > 7 to pH 14**
Water is **acid** (corrosive)	Water is **neutral**	Water is **basic** (alkaline)

Humans can tolerate but small variations in pH. Usually this parameter is controlled by adding to water some comestible phosphates, especially if the water has to be heated.

Undesirable germs contained in water

Name	Disease caused
Salmonella	Typhoid and paratyphoid
Shigella	Bacillary dysentery
Amoeba	Amoebic dysentery
Vibrio comma	Cholera
Hepatitis virus (A and B)	Hepatitis

To ensure that drinking water is free from such bacteria chemical additives are used, chlorine being the most common. However, this may give a bad taste to water and may cause toxicity problems. Therefore, whenever this kind of treatment becomes necessary it is most sensible to entrust the task to water treatment specialists.

---

the rudiments of hot water technology (see Box 10.2). Sanitary equipment is of primary importance for hotels and this includes the plumbing network in the hotel itself. As for appliances, there are, on the market, literally thousands of different models for toilet bowls, sinks, bathtubs, shower stalls and taps. Their impeccable performance is necessary for client satisfaction. Therefore, the hotel manager, after acquiring a good basic knowledge of this topic, is advised to acquire the services of a specialist for this fundamental aspect of hotel installation.

Box 10.2: Water needs for hotel rooms according to hotel category

Type of establishment	Cold water l/registered guest	Hot water l/registered guest
Simple hotel *	70	100
Comfortable **	80	110
Middle class ***	100	140
First class ****	120	180
Deluxe *****	140	220

Heating, ventilating and air conditioning (HVAC)

The physical comfort of hotel guests depends to a great extent on heating, ventilating and air conditioning parameters. Heating provides the right temperature and humidity in hotel rooms (see Box 10.3) while ventilation provides new oxygen and evacuates bad odours. Air conditioning is, of course, the best system for controlling all aspects of air quality, but it is expensive to install and maintain effectively. There are three principal types of ventilation systems.

- Air extractions systems. An electro-mechanical ventilator removes spent air from the room and evacuates it outdoors. This creates a depression in the room thereby forcing new air to enter through fissures.
- Air propulsion systems. An electro-mechanical ventilator takes spent air from outdoors and pushes it in the room. This creates a pressure in the room thereby forcing new air to exit through fissures. This type of ventilation is not very efficient and is seldom used in hotels.
- Air extraction with propulsion systems. A combination of the first two types. This is the best ventilation type but requires more sophisticated installation than the previous types. Recommended and actually very often used for large rooms (conference halls, fitness rooms, indoor swimming pools and so on).

All these systems run best when installed as central, sectoral systems, as already recommended for water systems. Most HVAC installations depend heavily on water, especially hot water. Water is a precious commodity. Care must be taken for controlling its use and consumption and some useful ideas in this direction will be presented at the end of this chapter. All systems depend on some form of energy, the most common being: diesel light fuel (DLF), liquefied natural gas (LNG) and electricity. HVAC problems and solutions can get very complex. Here again it is recommended that specialists be acquired for design and installation of these systems.

Refrigeration

Whenever we want to create a cool, cold or frozen artificial climate in a contained volume we need refrigeration. In the hospitality industry, we need this quite often, for air conditioning and food storage needs. Theoretically this is easy, but practically, producing cold is not so simple. There are a number of technical ways of creating refrigeration but only one has emerged as the best. Hotel Managers must become familiar with the mechanical refrigeration cycle. The principle is simple. Compression increases energy levels, as expressed by corresponding increases in pressure and temperature. Conversely, decompression causes a drop in pressure and temperature. The performance of a refrigeration installation is influenced by many factors, the most important are as follows.

- Compressor power. A powerful compressor injects lots of energy in the refrigerant, therefore delivering very low temperatures.
- Condenser efficiency. A large condenser, with lots of internal ribs to increase its surface, condenses gas rapidly thus improving process speed.
- Evaporator power. Same remarks as for condenser.
- Refrigerant properties. As mentioned above some substances are better than others in delivering cold, but we have to be aware that the most popular, CFC, is no longer favoured because of its negative effects on the environment.

- Speed of circulation. The faster the refrigerant circulates the more quickly cold is accumulated in the refrigerator and thus the lower the temperature.

Box 10.3: Recommend temperature and relative humidity values

Sector	Ambient temperature, °C	Relative humidity %
Occupied guest rooms, day time	18 to 19	30 to 70
Occupied guest rooms, night time	16 to 17	40 to 60
Unoccupied guest rooms	10 to 12	30 to 70
Bathrooms	22 to 24	30 to 70 may be higher for short periods during use
Meeting rooms	18 to 19	50 to 70
Offices	16 to 18	30 to 70
Restaurants	18 to 19	50 to 70
Swimming pools	24 to 26	60 to 80
Fitness rooms	14 to 16	60 to 80

Control system modes for hotel room heating

Type of control	Notes
Manual	Flow regulating valves are placed at each heating body incoming pipe. This lets the guest choose the settings according to their whims. Since our customers are often impatient with the equipment response to their actions, this control system is not the best.
Individual automatic	Thermostats are placed on the walls of each room again allowing the client to select settings (on the thermostat instead of the heating body itself, that is why these systems are called automatic) and with similar drawbacks as the previous system. Again this control system is not the best. However, it is so widespread in existing hotels that the Hotel Manager must come to terms with it and try to make the best out of the situation.
Sectoral automatic	Thermostats are installed on the start branches of the sectoral circuits and the heating of the entire hotel is managed by a computer. This allows a much more rational approach to heating controls and optimizes energy and other resources. Therefore, for modern hotels, this control system is recommended.

There are certain substances that like playing this game indefinitely. They are called refrigerants and the best of them all is the famous Chloro Fluoro Carbon (CFC). Unfortunately, CFC has revealed itself as a major environmental hazard and its use curtailed. Today we use less dangerous substances and technology is struggling to equal or even surpass CFC performance using substitute substances, alternative processes or both.

Most domestic and commercial refrigerators come in the form of appliances, i.e. some kind of cabinet that can be plugged in and used right away. They contain all the components needed for their functioning and their capacities go from 150 to 3000 litres. By contrast, big commercial and industrial refrigerators, commonly called cold rooms and used extensively in hotels and restaurants, come as modular units and capacities are measured in m^3, going from 10 to 100,000 m^3 and even more. They can be purchased as individual, separate parts and then assembled and located virtually anywhere and, above all, they can be retrofitted in an existing hotel. They usually need the support of a centralized installation but are sold with their own evaporators.

Electrical installations and lighting

There are two kinds of electrical current, direct current (DC) and alternating current (AC). DC is the kind we get from batteries. Its tension is constant throughout time and may last as long as the battery is charged. Most practical applications however, require AC, the type of electricity we get from ordinary electric sockets. Electricity is characterized in terms of:

- amperage (A, amp): the current intensity;
- voltage (V, volt): the current tension;
- power (W, watt): the current capacity of doing work by combining amps and volts;
- resistance (Ω, Ohm): the resistance a conductor opposes to the passage of a current; and
- frequency (Hz, Hertz): the number of oscillations per second of an alternating current. In central European AC, the tension varies with time, producing oscillations of ± 220 volts at a frequency of 50 Hertz.

The dangers associated with electricity can result in severe impairment or even death. Consequently, safety measures in hotels are extremely important. All circuits must be properly grounded and provided with adequate circuit breakers. In all bathroom circuits, special ground-fault breakers must be used. All appliances must periodically be checked for electrical safety.

Electricity is used to produce light, heat, sound and mechanical work. Of these uses, the most visible, by its very nature, is of course lighting. In every hotel there are hundreds or even thousands of lighting bulbs. Good lighting design is part of customer comfort and also contributes to the hotel image (see Boxes 10.4 and 10.5). Therefore, we must accord to this topic a great deal of attention. The classical light bulb was invented in 1879 by the famous scientist and engineer Thomas Alva Edison and is still today the principal component of any lighting system. However, it has the major drawback of producing more heat than light. Of all possible ways of producing light by using electricity, we will mention here only two:

- incandescence (halogen lamps are special incandescent bulbs) this is the Edison way of producing light by heating a metal filament enclosed in a vacuum glass bulb; and
- fluorescence (neon tubes, economy lamps) this technique produces light by exciting a phosphor layer on the inside walls of a glass tube with ultraviolet light.

Box 10.4:   Recommended lighting levels for various hotel premises

Room	Parameter
Exterior accesses	100 lx
Underground parking, corridors, stair wells, elevators	250 lx
Bathrooms, public toilets, service rooms	300 lx
Bars, restaurants	350 lx
Entry halls, receptions, foyers	400 lx
Guest rooms, general lighting	400 lx
Guest rooms, desks	500 lx
Offices, business centres	500 lx
Kitchen, working areas	600 lx
Ironing and sewing rooms	800 lx

In general, hotels are big consumers of electricity and therefore care must be taken to control consumption and to negotiate a convenient tariff. Some useful ideas in this direction will be presented at the end of this chapter.

HOTEL CONSTRUCTION

In the course of their professional career, Hotel Managers will certainly be faced with hotel renovation, modernization, transformation and, possibly, new construction. In all these activities, it is necessary to be familiar with modern construction techniques and materials. Here we will illustrate some key points concerning new construction with the understanding that any of these topics are applicable, after adaptation, to all other forms of hotel construction mentioned above.

Construction begins with the inspection and eventual acquisition of a building lot. Apart from the obvious concern for 'location, location and location', as any good real estate agent will tell you, we must be careful about the soil capacity to bear construction loads. In all cases it is recommended that, prior to making an offer, the prudent Hotel Manager asks for a geological survey to make sure that the soil is sound.

Once the land is secured, architects and engineers are hired to conceive and design the buildings. The actual construction work is usually carried out by a general contractor. The most common construction procedure is to build first the shell and the exterior of the building (also called 'rough in' or 'rough work') and then the internal partitions and internal finishes. Water, electricity, telecommunication and sewer connections are part of the rough work whilst technical installations, discussed earlier, are part of the finishes.

There are a myriad of construction materials, from the very basic structural components to the last decoration detail. The Hotel Manager must be familiar at least with the most important. Stones (granite, marble), bricks, stucco, wood, structural metal (steel, aluminium, pipes, electrical wiring), carpeting, wall papers, ceramic tiles, paints are some to be aware of. In addition, exterior doors and windows, venetian blinds, interior partitions, interior doors, curtains systems and the likes must be carefully researched if rational decisions on these items are desired.

Box 10.5:   UK Hotel, Catering, International Management Association Guide to Electric Lighting

TECHNICAL BRIEF

No 7/97

Guide to Electric Lighting

1.   INTRODUCTION

1.1 Lighting accounts for between 15 and 25 per cent of total electricity consumption in hospitality premises. Use of electricity contributes to environmental phenomena such as global warming, acid rain and local area smog. Care in the choice of lighting and design of facilities to maximise the use of natural daylight can bring considerable cost savings and improve environmental performance.

1.2 The quantity of light incident on a surface, or illuminance, is measured in Lux (lumens per square metre). The illuminance will depend upon the amount of natural light available, the type of electric lamp used, what kind of fitting it is mounted in, how far it is from the particular spot being illuminated, and the reflective qualities of the surrounding surfaces.

Quality embraces the colour of light emitted and how faithfully it reveals and models people, objects and colour seen under it, as well as freedom from glare.

2.   COST-EFFECTIVENESS

2.1 The cheapest form of light to use is natural daylight and some companies have found that increasing use of daylight within facilities also enhances staff productivity. Locating desks next to windows, cleaning windows regularly, and decorating in light colours can all enhance the availability of natural daylight.

2.2 When electric lighting is necessary, companies can select between traditional filament lamps or "energy efficient" fluorescent lamps.

2.3 Filament lamps are relatively cheap to buy and exhibit good quality of light. They do, however, waste a relatively large amount of electricity in the form of heat rather than light and are relatively energy inefficient.

2.4 "Energy efficient" lamps are more expensive to buy, but they last much longer (up to ten times) and cost up to 60 per cent less to run because their efficiency is higher. They do, however, sometimes require specially adapted fixtures.

2.5 The cost-effectiveness of lamps that give approximately the same illuminance and quality of light can differ greatly. As an example when two lamps with equivalent output, a 100 watt filament lamp and a 25 watt compact flouresent (energy efficient) lamp were compared over a period of one year's operation (8760 hours), it was found that although the compact lamp cost five times more than the filament lamp to purchase, the electricity operating cost was only a quarter of the cost of operating the filament lamp, and therefore the overall costing incuding purchase and electricity used showed that the compact lamp cost half the cost of the filament lamp.

2.6 This cost comparison is in its simplest form. In other instances the calculation of lighting costs may include replacement of failed starter-switches, depreciation of capital costs of installations, and labour for lamp replacement and cleaning. Tariff selection and power-factor correction may also be relevant. The net annual cost of alternative schemes for satisfactory lighting in a given area may sometimes differ by a factor of as much as 3 or 4.

2.7 Greatest potential savings from the installation of energy efficient lights and the most rapid payback periods are achieved where lights are in constant use. Further cost savings can be made by enforcing a "switch-off" policy, cleaning light fixtures regularly, or by installing motion detectors, time switches, or other energy saving devices.

3.   USING COLOUR RENDERING TO ENHANCE LIGHT EFFICIENCY

3.1 Careful selection of colours and fabrics when refurbishing facilities can help to reduce lighting costs. Light colours are generally more reflective and reduce overall lighting requirements. Some surfaces also help to reduce glare and reflect light more efficiently than others.

3.2 When selecting fluorescent lamps, it is important to select those which complement the surrounding decor and provide a feeling of "warmth" in some areas. Colour rendering indices (CRI) are used to indicate the appearance of light and a CRI of more than 80 will give a "warm" appearance.

3.3 It is particularly important that fluorescent lamps used in a dining area should possess good colour rendering. Lamps in the kitchen and servery should have the same colour-rendering characteristics.

3.4 Different types of light provide a different colour appearance and it is important to ensure a good colour match when selecting new furniture or decor, or when changing lighting. A good colour match under one light source can become a disagreeable mis-match under another.

4. LIGHTING GUIDELINES-PUBLIC AREAS INSIDE BUILDINGS

4.1 Entrance Zone from Street - illuminance 300 to 600 Lux during daylight hours; 100-200 Lux at night.

4.2 Hall/Lobby - General illuminance 100 to 200 Lux. Appearance may be enhanced by using compact fluorescent down lights and spotlights on features such as floral displays.

4.3 Reception, Cashier's, Porter's Desks - Minimum illuminance 300 Lux.

4.4 Lounge Areas - General illuminance 50 to 200 Lux, the higher value in daylight hours. Various speciality lighting should be considered, including table lamps and ceiling illumination.

4.5 Bars - Lighting should be used to ensure that the bar is a focal point. Consider coloured lamps or filters. General illuminance as for lounges.

4.6 Restaurants, Dining Areas etc.-
General illuminance:

Fast food unit, ice cream parlour	300 to 500 Lux
Coffee bar, grill room	100 to 300 Lux
Traditional restaurant (night)	50 to 100 Lux
(day)	150 to 200 Lux

4.7 Food display Counters - On cold displays use good colour-rendering fluorescent tubes or dichroic (cool-beam) spotlights. On hot displays local light is usually provided by infrared (heat) lamps.

4.8 Cloakrooms - General illuminance 100 Lux. Up to 500 Lux near mirrors, with lamps positioned to avoid heavy shadows on the face.

4.9 Corridors and stairs - Average illuminance 100 Lux. Light fittings above steps should be mounted where they give good contrast in appearance between treads and risers.

4.10 Lifts, Escalators and Travelators - Average illuminance 150 Lux. 200 Lux at escalator entrance/exit. Avoid bright reflections from treads.

4.11 Bedrooms - Average illuminance 50 to 100 Lux. Bed-head and desk 300 Lux.

4.12 Bathrooms - Average illuminance 150 Lux. Additional lighting at mirror.

5. LIGHTING GUIDELINES-INTERIOR

5.1 Kitchens (500 Lux) and Serveries (300 Lux) - Light fittings must be totally enclosed, waterproof, and readily cleanable.

5.2 Storage Rooms (150 Lux) - Fittings as for kitchens. Wine cellars may be lit less brightly and must not be lit continuously.

5.3 Offices (500 Lux) - Use fittings that minimise reflections from VDU screens.

6. LIGHTING GUIDELINES-EXTERIOR

6.1 In exterior lighting prime considerations are resistance to weather, intruders and vandals; also switching arrangements (photo-electric switching will avoid wasting electricity in daytime) and high lamp efficiency. The quality of light is usually less important.

6.2 The range of illuminance required for safety of movement and general amenity is 10 to 30 Lux. Light levels should be increased in high risk areas.

ACKNOWLEDGEMENT

This brief has been prepared with assistance from Dr Rebecca Hawkins PhD.

FURTHER READING

Lighting Industry Federation (207 Balham High Road, London, SW17 7BQ) Various Leaflets.

Building Research Establishment Fact Sheet No. 189 "Energy Efficient Lighting" (BRE, Garston, Watford, WD2 JR).

British Standards Institution (389 Chiswick High Road, London, W4 4AL)
BS 8206 Part 1: Code of Practice for Artificial Lighting
BS 5266 Part 1: The emergency Lighting of Premises
CP 1007: Maintained Lighting for Cinemas

Chartered Institution of Building Services Engineers, (222 Balham High Road, London, SW12 9BS)
Code for Interior Lighting

The Electricity Association (30 Millbank, London, SW1P 4RD)
Shedding Light on Energy Efficiency (single copies free)

Department of the Environment, 1996
Good Practice Guide 189: Energy efficiency in hotels-a guide to cost effective lighting

The Hotel Manager must also know something of construction techniques, work scheduling, contract bidding, cost, quality and time control (see below), job site progress checks, acceptance tests and construction accounting. Certainly, the more competence a Hotel Manager has in these topics, the more likely will a project be achieved to the required standards.

HOTEL PLANNING AND DESIGN

Any hotel project begins with an idea, a more or less abstract desire of investing in the hospitality business. If the idea is good, it may progress through to a concept, a feasibility study, several draft design projects and finally a fully-fledged construction project, ready for construction. This is a lengthy and difficult process involving the Hotel Manager, a group of investors, marketing specialists, architects, engineers, bankers, public authorities, general contractors, hotel employees and ultimately hotel clients. Usually, a hotel project costs a lot of money. Therefore, a lengthy planning period, sometimes lasting several years, is essential.

For any given project, planning is the art and science of trying to forecast as many possibilities, problems and solutions as possible and then design a hotel building that satisfies all constraints and requirements, clearly a very difficult task. Still, a tangible effort has to be made to ensure that every facet of the project is examined and planned in such a way as to reduce the risk of trouble or, worse still, failure to a minimum. To help in planning a hotel, professionals have contrived several standard parameters, procedures and methods. The three major project parameters are as shown in Box 10.6.

Box 10.6:   Major project parameters in hotel planning and design

Cost control
The Hotel Manager must be familiar with construction costs and financing. The construction budget can, at best, be estimated to an accuracy of ±10 per cent. Assistance in this endeavour is available from architects and bankers and from previous information (e.g. statistics) relating to similar projects. As construction advances, the risk of cost overruns is high. Care must be taken to ensure that any departure from initial cost estimates is well documented and explicitly accepted by all parties.

Quality control
The Hotel Manager must make sure that the materials and the quality agreed upon in the bid documents are actually delivered on the job site. The architects, official agent, for the project owners, are the major liaison with the general contractors' work. But the Hotel Manager is responsible for the results.

Time control
This is the most difficult parameter to hold, especially in a large project. The biggest danger is the sequential nature of most construction jobs. For example, the concrete slab cannot be cast unless the framework is ready and the reinforcing steel is in place; the floating floor screed cannot be poured until the concrete slab is cast and dry; and carpeting cannot be spanned until the floor screed is dry in its turn. Thus, if any of these steps are delayed the schedule of the subsequent ones will be upset, with serious consequences. The Hotel Manager must be attentive to any such disruption and act energetically against all delay.

The Hotel Manager participates fully in the process of planning and design by requesting the architects to implement the results of the marketing research project. Moreover, the Hotel Manager is familiar with the typical hotel aspects and parameters that will determine the actual surface, volume, function and performance of the building. Box 10.7 shows standard recommended surface area parameters for hotel rooms and typical room and corridor width. Box 10.8 shows five activity centres of a hotel room together with some illustrative corridor layout. This information is passed on to the architects who sketch various proposals and discuss them with the Hotel Manager. After several trials the final project emerges. This is presented to investors and bankers for approval and financing and shortly thereafter construction can start. The process of hotel planning and design is long, difficult and sometimes painful, but is both necessary and rewarding; the result of good hotel planning and design is long-term operating success.

HOTEL SAFETY AND SECURITY

There are many hazards in a hotel. Electrical safety has already been discussed. Accidents, theft, aggressions, catastrophes and the like have also been implicitly treated above, when speaking of good planning, design and construction practices. Here we are especially concerned with fire hazards. Statistics tell us that every 11 minutes there is a fire in a hotel somewhere in the world. Of these, about 0.3 per cent are serious, meaning that at least one person dies, usually as a consequence of asphyxia. As regards fire origins, we have the following gloomy picture:

Origin	Frequency
Guest rooms	37.6 %
Halls, stairways	25.1%
Storage rooms	13.8%
Service, housekeeping	6.9%
Kitchen	6.1%
Technical rooms	5.2%
Outdoors	0.4%
Miscellaneous	4.9%

As regards fire causes, the most frequent are as follows:

Cause	Frequency
Cigarettes	40.7%
Mischievous activities	13.1%
Electrical installations	12.4%
Kitchen equipment	6.2%
Heating equipment	4.8%
Electrical equipment	4.2%
Waste fermentation	1.4%
Miscellaneous	17.2%

From the foregoing, it is possible to infer the most probable causes of fire hazards in a hotel. The basic physical measures to be taken to minimize the risk of fires are as shown

Box 10.7: Recommended surface area parameters for hotel rooms

Category	*	**	***	****	*****
Double room Surface (m²)	12	13	16	20	25 or more
Bathroom Surface (m²)	4	4	5	6	7 or more
Equipment	CW & HW; 1 BT or SH for 25 beds; 1 WC for 10 beds without WC	CW & HW; 30% of rooms with WC and BT or SH; 1 BT or SH for 20 beds without BT or SH; 1 WC for 10 beds without WC	CW & HW; 75% of rooms with WC and BT or SH; 1 BT or SH for 15 beds without BT or SH; 1 WC for 10 beds without WC	CW & HW; 100% of rooms with WC and BT or SH, of which 50% or more with BT	CW & HW; 2 S or 1 double S; plenty of storage; 100% of rooms with WC and BT or SH (or both), of which 90% or more with BT
Room width	3.15m to 3.30m	3.15m to 3.50m	3.30m to 3.80m	3.50m to 4.50m	4.50m or more
Corridor width	0.85m to 1.00m	0.90m to 1.00m	1.00m to 1.20m	1.20m to 1.50m	1.40m to 2.00m or more

Note: Total rough surface area
Add 10% of room's net surface to account for structural wall thickness, partition thickness, service shafts, and other net losses.

BT: Bathtub
CW: Cold water
HW: Hot water
S: Sink
SH: Shower
WC: Toilet bowl

Box 10.8: **Five activity centres in a hotel room and four illustrative corridor layouts**

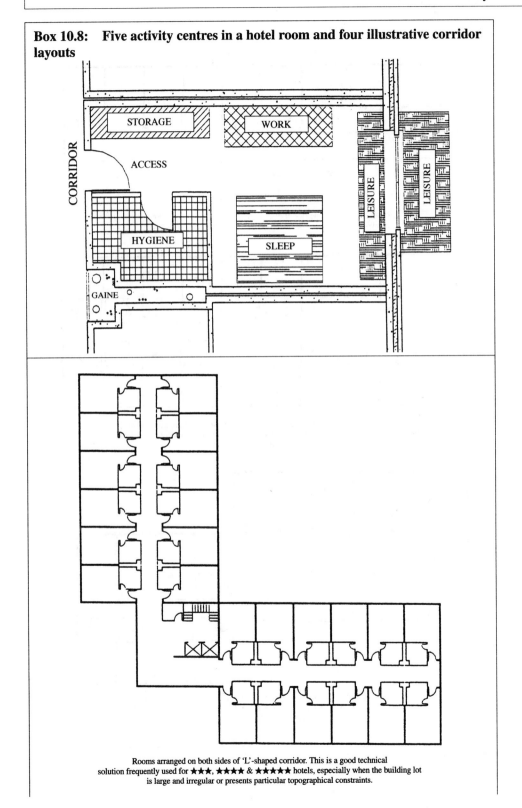

Rooms arranged on both sides of 'L'-shaped corridor. This is a good technical solution frequently used for ★★★, ★★★★ & ★★★★★ hotels, especially when the building lot is large and irregular or presents particular topographical constraints.

Box 10.8: *continued*

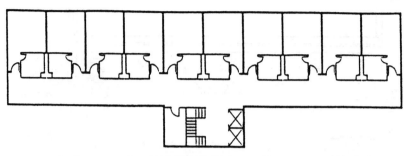

Rooms arranged on one side of corridor. While this solution is not optimal,
it is very simple and is often used for small hotels and, especially, motels.

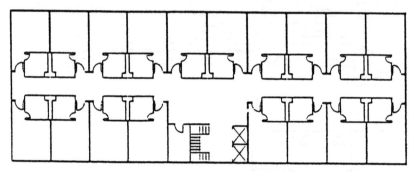

Rooms arranged on both sides of corridor. This is a classical solution, widely used in
the planning of ★★ & ★★★ hotels. Doors are often staggered in order to break long
corridors monotonous appearance

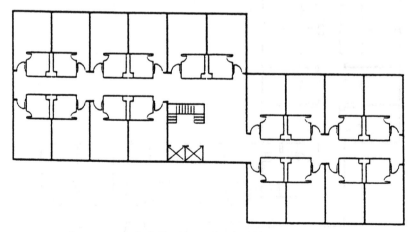

Rooms arranged on both sides of staggered corridor. This is a good technical solution
frequently used for ★★★, ★★★★ & ★★★★★ hotels, especially when the building lot
is large and irregular in shape.

in Box 10.9. This is but a small, incomplete list. The Hotel Manager can learn much more by consulting official fire protection manuals and by contacting the local fire department and fire marshal.

Box 10.9:   Measures to minimize the risk of fires

Fire detectors:
Compulsory in every hotel room, powered by independent energy sources (e.g., battery) and tested at least twice a year

Sound alarms:
Mandatory in public spaces, along with other safety measures

Fire alarms:
Must be placed at strategic points throughout the hotel premises

Fire extinguishers:
Are part and parcel of fire alarm posts, must be checked regularly (at least yearly)

Fire escapes:
Absolutely compulsory in every public building, especially hotels, hotel rooms and corridors

Sprinkler system:
Mandatory in public spaces. In hotel rooms, because of the huge damage it can cause in case of accidental or malicious tripping, this equipment is no longer recommended

---

PHYSICAL PLANT MAINTENANCE

When we look at hotels as buildings filled with all kinds of machinery, and when we consider that all this has to perform impeccably in order to satisfy the expectations of our clients, we realize how important it is to keep our hotels in good repair and in perfect working order for, without maintenance, the working life of a hotel is very short indeed and its residual value degrades very rapidly (see Box 10.10). Maintenance comes in many forms of which only the two most important are discussed here, i.e., regular maintenance and major maintenance. As for regular maintenance, its features are given in Box 10.11.

The advantages of Normal Response Maintenance (NRM), Emergency Response Maintenance (ERM), and Cyclical Planned Maintenance (CPM) are quite evident. The advantages of Preventive Planned Maintenance (PPM) are the following:

- establish current building conditions;
- estimate risks of failures and defects;
- establish causes of risks;
- draw up priority lists; and
- evaluate budgets and suggest new or updated maintenance work schedules.

As for major maintenance, it implies extensive work and it is usually carried out at critical times during the working life of a hotel. Hence, major maintenance involves major

Box 10.10: Typical degradation curves

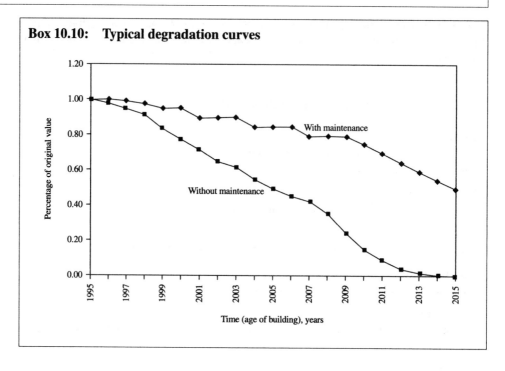

Box 10.11: Principal types of maintenance procedure

Normal Response Maintenance (NRM)
Done as required, usually during working hours. Examples: changing light bulbs, repairing leaking taps, adjusting thermostat settings, fixing furniture, minor painting jobs; and so on.

Emergency Response Maintenance (ERM)
Done as required, whenever an emergency occurs. Examples: fixing electricity blackouts, repairing broken water mains, repairing defective door locks, changing broken window panes, repairing defective motors, water pumps, heating elements; restarting computer networks, telecommunications, PA systems; and so on.

Cyclical Planned Maintenance (CPM)
Done periodically, regardless of the component's actual condition. Examples: daily, weekly, monthly, yearly check up or tuning of mechanical apparatus, changing oil, oil filters, spark plugs of motors and pumps, changing or cleaning air filters in air conditioning systems; cleaning, washing, sanitizing, repainting; and so on.

Preventive Planned Maintenance (PPM)
Done at predetermined intervals (usually yearly), to prevent failure or falling below standards. Examples: inspections, controls, diagnostics, audits; needs and priority assessments; planning remedial work and/or improvements, renovations, major changes; evaluating costs and benefits, establishing maintenance budgets; and so on.

building updating, renovation, extensions, additions, transformations, modernization, demolition and reconstruction or even the outright sale of the property, usually 'as is'.

It is obvious that maintenance requires much planning and even more diligence. It also costs a fair amount of money. Thus, the prudent Hotel Manager must establish a proper maintenance department and an adequate maintenance budget, usually between 3 per cent and 5 per cent of general operating expenses. In view of the tremendous advantages maintenance affords, establishing and executing it makes good business sense.

APPLIED HOTEL ECOLOGY

*how to be ecological

In the last few years, we have heard a lot on ecology. Terms such as: 'pollution', 'environmental protection', 'greenhouse effect', 'ozone layer depletion', 'sustainable development' and the like, have been heard repeatedly. Several specific measures have been taken to correct the most blatant environmental mistakes. But the general public remains as attached as ever to unabashed consumerism. In particular, the developing nations want to catch up fast with the living standards of developed nations and this is without too much concern for the environment. It is not our intention to engage here in a philosophical or ethical discussion. From an engineering point of view, the pursuit of industrial 'progress' without consideration for the environment is no longer defensible, the more so as, nowadays, there are ways and means to do a reasonably good job in this respect.

For the hospitality industry, environmental problems have always been acute and have now become extremely urgent. Hotels are traditionally big users of energy, water, consumer goods and luxury items. With the increase of operating costs and pending environmental legislation, we have to find innovative solutions to environmental problems without lowering the level of service to our clients. This apparent contradiction can be resolved and there are already several examples as follows.

- Alternative refrigeration. As mentioned earlier, CFC is now out of favour. Newer products and processes are being used and studied. Further progress in this field is imminent.
- Super insulation. Hotel Managers have discovered that insulation is as useful in cold climates as in warm climates. Double-glazed windows are now universally adopted.
- Biodegradable products. Plastics, long some of the worst environmental offenders, are getting much more environmentally friendly. Paints, glues, soaps and laundering products are now obtainable in environmentally friendly varieties.
- 'Bio' food products. Agriculture is improving not only its image but also its actual performance in this field.
- Economy bulbs. Hotel managers have long discovered that, where light quality is not important, they can substitute economy bulbs for ordinary incandescent lamps, thereby saving about 75 per cent of energy costs (see Box 10.12).
- Grey water technology. There is no reason to flush toilets with pure drinking water, recycled water is much better. In dish washing machines cycles scrubbing can be performed by recycled water. In both cases, energy savings are in the order of 30 per cent.
- Cogeneration. Heat and electricity can be produced simultaneously by a clever arrangement of modern machinery. In this case, the Hotel Manager cannot only

Box 10.12:   Electric bulbs comparison table

Economy bulbs   Incandescent bulbs

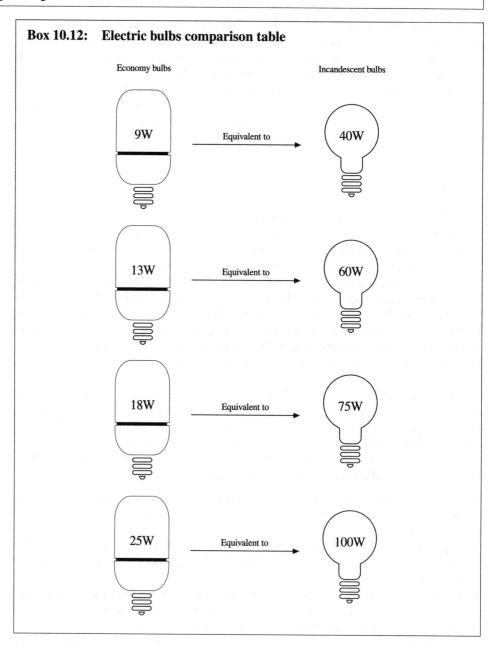

9W   Equivalent to   40W

13W   Equivalent to   60W

18W   Equivalent to   75W

25W   Equivalent to   100W

realize substantial savings but also profits, by selling surplus electrical energy back to the supply network! Whatever the case, attention to efficient energy use will be a key issue for businesses in the future (see Box 10.13).

Many other interesting ideas are in place and several hotels are already winning awards in environmental management. In the future we will certainly see new wonders such as extensive recycling, creative waste management (including bio-methanization), generalization of hydrogen technology and, inevitably, the development of safe nuclear technology (lets not forget that the sun is nothing but a huge nuclear furnace!). Whatever

Box 10.13: UK Hotel, Catering, International Management Association guide to efficient energy utilization

TECHNICAL BRIEF

No 36

Using energy efficiently

1 INTRODUCTION

1.1 Energy is an essential resource in the hospitality industry where it is used for heating and hot water, lighting, catering, ventilation, and many other functions. As a resource, energy needs to be carefully managed; unlike most purchases, it is largely invisible to those responsible for its consumption, and wastage may go unnoticed.

1.2 Using energy efficiently benefits premises owners and managers because efficiently run buildings cost less to operate. Government estimates suggest typical savings in energy costs of up to 5% (through good housekeeping and careful management), up to 10% (by installing low-cost items like improved controls or low-energy lighting) and up to 20% through capital investment in proven technology with short payback periods [see first source of information overleaf]. Occupants and guests benefit from well-controlled comfortable conditions. And the wider environment benefits because lower energy use conserves natural resources and reduces environmental pollution.

1.3 Your main aims in managing energy should be to ensure that you provide comfort conditions in your premises only when, where, and to the extent, they are actually required. Try to ensure your existing installations are maintained so that they operate with as little wastage as possible. And try to identify those low-cost improvements which will pay back their investment in as short a time as possible.

1.4 The hospitality industry is associated with service, and few occupants or hotel guests will tolerate reduced standards in the cause of energy efficiency. But many people are genuinely interested in green initiatives, and you may consider informing them of your commitment to reducing your environmental impact and asking them to use energy responsibly themselves. You may wish to cite your environmental commitment in your marketing and promotional literature.

2 APPOINT AN ENERGY CHAMPION

2.1 Initially it is important to ensure someone has the responsibility for managing energy - in a small organisation this may well be you. In larger premises, appoint an Energy Champion, someone with leadership and motivational skills who can work with staff to ensure energy is used responsibly.

2.2 In larger hotels or institutions an Energy Conservation Committee, reporting to the General Manager, may be appropriate. The committee's remit should include the establishment of an energy policy, and identifying and implementing actions to save energy, such as those given in this technical brief.

3 CONDUCT ENERGY HOUSE TOURS

3.1 A good place to start is by inspecting your premises systematically. When you make your regular house tours, include energy as one of the items you check. Better still, carry out house tours which focus specifically on energy issues. The checklist on the back of this guide will help to get you started. You may wish to take some of your staff around with you to obtain their ideas and suggestions.

3.2 Based on your inspections prepare an Energy Action Plan of the items needing attention. Divide them into three lists - good housekeeping (or no-cost) measures, items needing repairs and maintenance, and those which need capital investment. Identify your priorities within each of the three lists and decide on timescales for implementation.

4 INTRODUCE GOOD HOUSEKEEPING ROUTINES

4.1 Once you have identified clear and achievable good housekeeping actions, you should establish routines and responsibilities for undertaking them. For example, allocate lighting and equipment checks at various times of day and night to particular members of staff.

4.2 Staff are likely to be better motivated to save energy if they are given encouragement and feedback on how well they are doing. By monitoring energy consumption and reporting to staff on the savings achieved you will help to maintain the momentum of your energy efficiency campaign.

5 STAFF INDUCTION AND TRAINING

5.1 Energy issues should be incorporated into staff induction courses and in-service training. In larger premises, an energy efficiency campaign may be appropriate. Use posters, stickers, and articles in the staff newsletter, if you have one, to launch the campaign.

5.2 Patterns of wasteful behaviour can become entrenched and staff need to be motivated frequently if good practices are to continue. Vary your campaign and initiate a regular flow of fresh ideas. Move posters to new positions, and/or devise new ones. Consider poster competitions for staff. Incentive schemes may be appropriate in some organisations. Remember if all the savings are clawed back, there will be little incentive for staff to save energy.

6 METERING AND MONITORING

6.1 It has often been said that you cannot manage what you cannot measure. Knowing what you are paying, what you are using, and how it is used, are important aspects of energy management. Cost information is vital for assessing the business impact of energy costs and determining the potential contribution to profitability from energy savings.

6.2 Collect energy use data from utility invoices and/or by reading your meters. This will help you to judge whether changes in consumption are reasonable when compared with changes in occupancy and catering levels, weather conditions, and the facilities available.

6.3 Reading meters regularly (at the same time each day, week or month) will help you to identify sources of waste, such as excessive night-time or weekend consumptions. Ensure you investigate the causes and take appropriate action whenever excessive consumption levels are detected.

6.4 Use the consumption data you collect as the basis of negotiation with your utility suppliers to ensure you are on the most advantageous tariffs for your particular operation. In some cases it may be appropriate to use a tariff consultant to negotiate on your behalf, but check carefully the basis of their fee.

6.5 If you have independent operators on the premises, re-charge them for the fuel they use. This will place responsibility for energy with those who use it.

6.6 In the case of hotels, you can use your energy data to compare your energy performance against industry standards. The Department of the Environment's Energy Consumption Guide 36 shows good, fair and poor consumption and cost figures for three sizes of hotel - small, medium and large (see sources of information overleaf).

7 PURCHASES

7.1 Remember to include energy and environmental requirements in contracts for the purchase of goods and services from your suppliers.

8 RAISING EFFICIENCY THROUGH INVESTMENT

8.1 Once you have established routines to use the equipment and services you have as efficiently as possible, you should consider investing the savings you make through these no-cost measures in technical improvements.

8.2 When considering such improvements, assess their applicability, technical feasibility and reliability in use. How many examples are there of successful implementation in premises similar to your own? Check the history and reputation of the supplier. Seek independent advice if you need it from other hotel operators, trade associations or professional consultants.

8.3 Consider whether the hotel could benefit from an independent and comprehensive energy audit. This will assess current consumption levels against industry standards, review opportunities for savings, and set out a series of costed options for technical improvements.

8.4 If you plan to alter or refurbish you premises, make sure you include energy efficiency improvements. Such opportunities do not occur frequently - so don't miss the chance.

Box 10.13: *continued*

Checklist for an energy house-tour

Space heating system
Is the space comfortable - neither too hot nor too cold?
Are room thermostats and controls on minimum settings to provide comfort?
Are windows and doors kept closed when the heating is on?
Are radiators or heaters free of all obstructions?
Is heating turned off in areas that are not in use?

Hot water
Are leaking or dripping taps, baths, showers or wcs reported and repaired quickly?
Is the water temperature from appliances limited to being hand hot?
Are low-flow fittings and flow restrictors used where possible?

Lighting
Are light switches labelled or colour coded adequately to encourage switching off?
Are lights in the positions where they provide the most effective lighting?
Are windows and rooflights clean to ensure the maximum amount of daylight?
Do nets and curtains allow maximum use of daylight?
In restaurants and bars, is the lighting turned off outside opening hours?
Is the lighting switched off whenever it is not required (subject to safety)?
Can the required lighting levels be met by fewer lamps?
Are light fittings cleaned regularly to ensure maximum light output?
Are shades and diffusers translucent or clear to increase light output from fittings?
Do lamps have good reflectors to ensure maximum light output?
Are light colours used to improve reflected light from walls and ceilings?
Have 38mm fluorescent tubes been replaced by 26mm tubes?
Have tungsten lamps been replaced by more efficient compact fluorescent lamps?
Have automatic controls, such as timers and daylight sensors, been considered?

Mechanical ventilation
Do extract fans operate only during the periods of use?
Are extract fan grilles cleaned periodically?

Air conditioning systems
Are checks undertaken to prevent heating and cooling operating simultaneously in the same part of the building?
Does refrigeration plant operate only when outside temperatures justify it?

Miscellaneous equipment
Is equipment operated only when it is actually in use?

Building fabric
Are roof voids insulated to reduce heat loss?
Is draught stripping in a state of good repair?
Are self-closing mechanisms to external doors fully functional?

Swimming pool and leisure facilities
Is a cover used over heated swimming pools when they are not in use?
Are supplies to sauna, steam room, or showers shut off when they are not in use?

Externally
Is security lighting switched off during daylight hours?
Does external lighting use high efficiency light sources?

Fuel use, fuel costs, plant room, and controls
Is fuel use checked regularly and compared with targets?
Is accountability matched to responsibility through profit-centre operation?
Have tariffs been checked to ensure minimum cost of fuel purchase?
Are controls labelled to indicate their function and, if appropriate, their settings?
Have responsibilities for control setting, review and adjustment been established?
Is there a routine for checking control settings?
Are optimum start/stop controls and weather compensation controls set correctly?

Are boiler sequencing controls set correctly?
Are time switches set to minimum periods consistent with requirements?
Is the plant maintained in accordance with good industry practice?
Are checks conducted of combustion efficiency and flue gas temperatures?
Are hot water thermostat accuracy and temperature settings checked periodically?
Is the temperature of stored water kept to a minimum, subject to safety?
Are hot water storage tanks fully insulated and is the insulation in good condition?
Is hot water pipework fully insulated and is the insulation in good condition?
Have localised hot water generators been considered to avoid long pipe runs?
Are temperature controls for cooling set to avoid cooling "fighting" the heating?
Are fans and pumps running only when they are required?

Catering
Are kitchen staff informed of minimum heat up times for cooking equipment?
Are staff discouraged from using hobs or ovens for space heating?
Do kitchen staff switch off equipment when it is not needed?
Are taps turned off when not needed?
Are dishwashers run on full load only?
Are pans with the proper base size for hobs used?
Are lids kept on pans whenever possible?
When boiling, are hobs set to the minimum for simmering?
Is the storage of cooked food minimised?
To reheat relatively small quantities of food, are microwave ovens used?
Are hot cupboards well insulated and fitted with thermostats?
Are refrigerators and freezers placed away from sources of heat?
Are doors to refrigerators and freezers opened for the minimum periods?
Is food allowed to cool before being placed in refrigerators?
Are the doors to walk-in freezer store rooms kept closed?
Do refrigerator condensors have good air circulation?
And is dust cleaned off condensors periodically?
Are kitchen ventilation fans set to operate only when cooking is taking place?
Have induction hobs been considered?
Has low temperature dishwashing been considered?
Have current developments in efficient appliance design been reviewed?

Laundry
Are operating hours adapted to linen requirements and the availability of steam?
Is equipment being used only when fully loaded?
Is there a timely flow of used linen to laundry - so equipment is not left idle?
When the laundry is not operating, are steam and air supplies closed off?
Are supply and exhaust fans switched off when laundry is not operating?
Are there any leaks of water, steam and compressed air which require repair?
Are there gaskets or ill-fitting doors that need to be repaired?
Have low temperature detergents been considered?
Are manufacturers' instructions on detergents and temperatures followed?
Has tumbler operation been reviewed to prevent overdrying?
Are driers loaded quickly to retain heat?
Are production and cost figures kept and compared with industry norms?

Capital investment items for consideration

Automatic door closers on external doors, or revolving door or draught lobby
High efficiency lights generally throughout
Zoned heating system with co-ordination between room letting and space heating
New condensing boiler and modern programmer
Building energy management system
Combined heat and power system
Energy efficient catering appliances
Double glazing to windows
Roof and wall insulation

Free sources of information

Single copies of the guides to energy efficiency in hotels are available from BRECSU Enquiries Bureau - telephone 01923 664258.

This brief has been prepared with the assistance of BRECSU for the Department of the Environment

DISCLAIMER

This technical brief is intended as a guide only. While the information it contains is believed to be correct, it is not a substitute for appropriate professional advice. The HCIMA can take no responsibility for action taken solely on the basis of this information.

HCIMA 191 Trinity Road, London, SW17 7HN Tel 0181 672 4251 Fax 0181 682 1707

August 1997. This document has no copyright restrictions. Registered Charity No.326180.

Printed on environment-friendly paper

the future may bring, Hotel Managers live in the present and, as good corporate citizens, they must respond to the environmental challenge in a positive way.

REFERENCES AND FURTHER READING

Bangert, A. and Riewoldt, O. (1993) *New Hotel Design*, London: Laurence King.
International Hotels Environment Initiative (IHEI) (1996) *Environmental Management for Hotels: the Industry Guide to Best Practice*, London: Butterworth Heinemann, 2nd edn.
Kirk, D. (1996) *Environmental Management for Hotels: a Student Handbook*, Oxford: Butterworth Heinemann.
Rutes, W.A. and Penner, R.H. (1985) *Hotel Planning and Design*, New York: Whitney Library of Design.
Salvioni, L. (1993) *Ecologia in Albergo*, Milano: Publicazioni ZAO.

11 Conference and convention management

Udo A. Schlentrich

The meeting industry represents one of the least understood market segments of the hospitality industry. Yet, in terms of profitability and the ultimate success of a hotel or convention centre, it is imperative that management fully understands this market's structure, buying centres, venue and service requirements. The objective of this chapter is to introduce the reader to the meeting industry and to investigate its organizational structure, the buying process and successful marketing and service strategies used by the hospitality industry to attract this market segment.

INDUSTRY EVOLUTION

From the beginning of civilization people have gathered to exchange goods and to share experiences and knowledge. The early marketplace has evolved into today's sophisticated convention and exhibition centre. During medieval times, craft and trade guilds were formed to uphold standards and protect their members, much as international associations represent their members today. Early records of the Greek philosopher, Plato, give evidence that meetings were used to communicate information to groups of people gathered to acquire knowledge through the interaction of those present. Although today's conferences and exhibitions are larger and more international in nature, they are organized to fulfil the same basic objectives.

The need to communicate in order to exchange goods, information and know-how accelerated rapidly as a result of the Industrial Revolution which began in Great Britain in the 1760s. The resulting changes in social and economic organizations led to the rapid evolution and growth of trade associations, unions, educational institutions and, ultimately, international trade, each of which required the communication of information amongst its members.

National economies are becoming steadily more integrated as cross-border flows of trade, investment and capital increase. Consumers are buying more foreign goods and a growing number of firms now operate across national borders. Two forces have been driving this flow of goods and money. The first is technology. The costs of computing and communicating have been falling rapidly. The natural barriers of time and space that separate national markets have been decreasing steadily. The second driving force is trade liberalization. As a result of both the GATT negotiations and unilateral decisions, almost all countries have lowered barriers to foreign trade. Over the past decade, trade has increased twice as fast as output, foreign direct investment three times as fast, and cross border trade in shares, ten times as fast. Many companies and scientific research organizations have pursued strategic alliances and partnerships. Cross border mergers and acquisitions have been the growth area for business in the mid to late 1990s worth over $252 billion.

Most executives realize that one of the most important sources of competitive advantage is knowledge. In the global knowledge economy, the challenge for companies is how to continuously develop, share and leverage knowledge in order to create increased value for customers, employees and shareholders. Financial capital and other traditional factors of production have become commodities, and intellectual capital is now the real driver of future earnings. For business and public institutions to continuously exploit and renew their intellectual capital, some of the most effective tools of communication are conferences, conventions, exhibitions and trade fairs.

ECONOMIC IMPACT

According to the Convention Liaison Council, the impact of the meeting and convention industry on the US economy exceeds $82 billion per annum. The total economic impact of the meeting market worldwide is estimated to be $137 billion per year. The impact of the meeting industry on local economies is also significant. The 1997 Rotary International Convention attended by 30,000 delegates in Glasgow, for example, resulted in an economic benefit to Scotland of approximately £32 million. Twenty-five to thirty-five per cent of the occupancy of urban hotels is attributed to meetings and conventions, thus making this market segment extremely important to the hospitality industry.

Local economic impact

Conventions and exhibitions attract visitors from different parts of the country and the world who often would not normally visit a given destination. The destination thus receives supplementary income which results in the following primary benefits:

- delegate spending – it is estimated that between $525 and $970 is spent per delegate staying in a host community for an average of 2.6 days;
- employment - the International Association of Convention and Visitor Bureaus (IACVB) estimates that every $20,000 spent by delegates and attendees creates one new job; and
- positive image – new convention and exhibition centres often act as a catalyst in the process of inner-city renewal and thus play a vital role in uplifting a city's image. World trade centres, hotels, leisure facilities, restaurants and shopping arcades are often part of such a development process. Cities such as Birmingham, Chicago, Singapore and Frankfurt would not have experienced such positive growth had it not been for their ability to attract the international convention and exhibition market.

COMPONENTS OF THE MEETING INDUSTRY

The meeting industry encompasses many different types of service organizations and events. The principle components of the typical organizational and functional structure are presented in Figure 11.1.

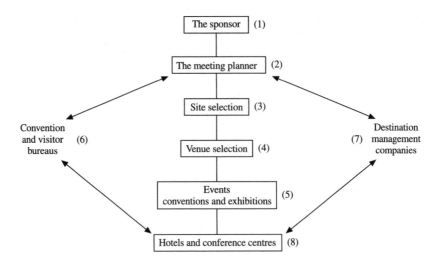

Figure 11.1 Components of the meeting industry

The sponsor (1)

Sponsors initiate the buying process for a particular meeting, convention or exhibition. They define the objectives of the meeting, target audience, location, type of facility and budget parameters for the event. Sponsors can be associations, corporations or exhibition organizers.

The meeting planner (2)

The meeting planner is either a part- or full-time member of the association or corporation, or an externally contracted professional charged with the planning and supervision of a particular event. Meeting planners will generally not make the final decision as to where a meeting will be held. However, they often greatly influence the decision when they make their recommendation to the sponsor.

Site selection (3)

Site refers to the location and environment where the event will take place. It may be a national or international site situated in an urban, resort or airport location. In selecting a site, the meeting planner has to take into consideration the following key criteria: meeting objectives; meeting format; number of delegates; size and type of various functions; overall budget; accommodation and facility requirements; interests and expectations of delegates; transportation; support structure and expertise of venue's staff; and available support services of convention bureaus and destination management companies. The meeting planner must also take into account important destination considerations such as stability (economic, social, political and employment); infrastructure (transportation and communication links); amenities (shopping, cultural attractions, leisure and entertainment); and environment (climate, health and safety) (see the following Case Study).

CASE STUDY: BIRMINGHAM: EUROPE'S PREMIER CONVENTION AND EXHIBITION DESTINATION

During the past ten years, the city of Birmingham has achieved what was thought to be impossible, namely, to stimulate its local and regional economy, to improve a derelict inner city and to change its once negative image into that of being one of the most dynamic cities in Europe. The city, fraught with economic and social problems, established a redevelopment master plan which at its very heart contained an exhibition and convention centre, a symphony hall and a national indoor arena. These facilities, managed by one management group on behalf of the Birmingham City Council, joined forces under an umbrella organization called the Birmingham Marketing Partnership whose objective is to promote and coordinate the city of Birmingham corporately as the gateway to the region in order to increase business and leisure tourism, exhibition and conference business and business investment. Two aspects of the nature of the Partnership helped ensure its success. First, it has been able to form a consensus committed to a sustained and consistent marketing message by inviting the most important decision makers and influencers from both the public and private sectors on to its Board of Directors. Second, the Partnership was constituted as a pro-active, entrepreneurial enterprise allowing it to react swiftly to changing conditions and exploit new marketing opportunities as they arose. Much of the Partnership's marketing and promotional success to date has been due to the many organizations in the city working closely together with a common aim. The committed long term support of Birmingham's City Council, the support organizations and commercial partners made it possible to create a powerful 'one voice' lobby. This lobby helped to obtain European Union funding and to attract new levels of business investments for hotels, restaurants and retail outlets.

Facilities
The facilities of the National Exhibition Centre (NEC) include the following elements.

- **The Exhibition Centre** – with a capacity of 158,000 m² and parking for 15,000 cars.
- **The International Convention Centre** – capable of handling conferences from 50 to over 2000.
- **The Symphony Hall** – which is home of the City of Birmingham Symphony Orchestra and available to meeting planners for special occasions such as opening sessions for up to 2200 people.
- The **National Indoor Arena** – with an international standard sporting arena having a seating capacity of up to 13,000. Larger conventions make use of this facility for their opening plenary sessions.

As a result of this superb infrastructure, Birmingham is able to attract international conventions, trade shows, exhibitions, product launches, sporting events, and classical and popular music concerts.

The Birmingham Summit
In 1998, the Birmingham Summit took place at the City's International Convention Centre attended by world leaders from Britain, the US, Canada, France, Germany, Italy, Japan and Russia. This meeting attracted approximately 1000 delegates and

up to 5000 journalists. In addition to the meetings held by the Heads of State, a programme of entertainment, exhibitions and special events were organized for visitors, many of which were also open to residents of Birmingham and the region. The economic benefit received by Birmingham as a result of this one week summit was estimated to be well over £10 million. More importantly, however, the Summit further enhanced Birmingham's claim to be one of Europe's leading convention and exhibition destinations. Prior to the event, Birmingham City Council Leader, Councillor Theresa Stewart, said:

> I am delighted that Birmingham has been chosen to host the Summit which will give us the opportunity to spotlight our achievements in regenerating the City. Birmingham will be seen on television screens all over the world. There is no doubt that the Birmingham Summit will give a tremendous boost to the City's economy. Thousands of hotel rooms have been earmarked for the Summit, and shops, restaurants and theatres will all benefit from the huge influx of visitors.

Economic impact

The Birmingham Convention, Exhibition, Symphony Hall and Sports Arena form an integral part of the city's overall economic development strategy to create additional employment and to act as a catalyst for the regeneration of Birmingham city centre. In addition, the venues specifically focus on attracting events and visitors to the region thereby raising its profile and image. A 1993 KPMG Peat Marwick study evaluated the economic impact of the NEC facilities on the city of Birmingham and the surrounding region. The report highlighted the following.

- Over two-thirds of the visitors to the venues originate from outside the West Midlands region, reinforcing the venue's objective of attracting additional expenditure to the region.
- Approximately 49,000 (37 per cent) of the estimated 134,000 international visitors to the venues used Birmingham International Airport as their port of entry into the UK.
- The hotels in Birmingham and the surrounding area generated approximately 1.3 million bednights (23 per cent of total bednights sold) from visitors attending NEC events.
- The different events held at the NEC attracted 4.5 million visitors.
- Total expenditure by these visitors in Birmingham and the West Midlands region amounted to £438 million.
- Total jobs created were 5,800 in Birmingham and 16,800 in the region.

Venue selection (4)

Venue refers to the specific facility where the event is to take place. For larger functions, the venue could be an international convention and exhibition centre, a convention hotel or a theme park resort. Other possible venues include cruise ships or country hotels. Once meeting planners have established the overall meeting programme, they embark on the site and venue selection process. Venues are commonly classified into one of two categories: venues with accommodation (Figure 11.2) and venues without accommodation (Figure 11.3).

The type of accommodation selected is dependent on the meeting objectives, the

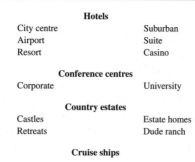

Hotels

City centre	Suburban
Airport	Suite
Resort	Casino

Conference centres

Corporate	University

Country estates

Castles	Estate homes
Retreats	Dude ranch

Cruise ships

Figure 11.2 Venues with accommodation

Meeting Venues

Convention and exhibition centres	University classrooms and theatres
Country and city clubs	Sports stadiums
Municipal buildings	Concert halls and theatres
Corporate offices and training centres	

Receptions

Museums and historic buildings	Castles and country estates
Ships and antique trains	Breweries
Tents	Race tracks

Figure 11.3 Venues without accommodation

desired amenities and facility mix and the service requirements. Venues are generally grouped into price categories such as deluxe, first class, mid-price, economy and budget. Hotels are the most popular venues for conferences, being used for more than 90 per cent of association and corporate meetings. Conference centres are gaining in popularity, especially for training sessions and seminars. Country estates and cruise ships are popular venues for incentive and smaller group meetings.

Nowadays, municipalities, civic organizations, universities and sporting clubs market their venues towards the meeting market as a means of generating additional revenue. For their reception and hospitality functions, sponsors increasingly like to utilize unusual venues to create a memorable setting and a welcome change of pace from the business sessions of the meeting programme (see the following Case Study).

CASE STUDY: OPRYLAND – A WORLD CLASS CONVENTION AND EXHIBITION VENUE

The Opryland Hotel Convention Center is recognized as one of the world's leading meeting and convention destinations. This unique facility offers the highest standard of accommodation, convention and entertainment services under one roof.

Location
The Opryland Hotel Convention Center is located in Nashville, Tennessee within seven miles of Nashville's international airport. It is situated immediately adjacent to the Opryland, US, Theme Park and the world renowned Grand Ole Opry.

Facilities

The original 600 room hotel first opened its doors in 1977 and has expanded over the years to 2870 rooms including over 200 suites. The hotel's dedicated meeting and exhibit space covers over 600,000 square feet and includes a 55,465 square foot ballroom, making it the world's largest convention centre located in a hotel. Since its opening, the hotel has maintained an 85 per cent year round average occupancy with a phenomenal rate of return business and personal referral. The hotel has earned global recognition for its consistently professional service, outstanding facilities and culinary skill. According to its President, Jack Vaughn:

> The industry has seen many changes since we hosted our first convention. Changes that have kept us striving for perfection, improvements and greater capabilities. We knew that to be a leader in the convention and trade show business, we had to grow with the needs of our guests. And to do that, we had to listen. Obviously, we did, because Opryland Hotel Convention Center has not only grown in actual size, it's grown to become the epitome of what a convention hotel should be, with everything you ever need, under one roof. We take pride in the distinctive environment we've created.

Design concept

The hotel and convention centre features breathtaking architecture at the heart of which are a 4.5 acre indoor garden, a river, a 110 foot wide waterfall, a unique 20,000 square foot antebellum-style mansion, more than 15 restaurants and bars, retail shops, and a complete mix of dedicated function space allowing for every type of gathering for groups from 10 to 10,000, including major conferences, conventions, and trade shows.

Amenities
- **Opryland Theme Park** – a musical theme park featuring rides and live shows
- **Grand Ole Opry** – a theatre staging live country music performances
- **General Jackson Showboat** – a 300-foot long, four deck paddle steamer which can be chartered to accommodate from 15 to 1000 people
- **Springhouse Golf Club** – an 18-hole championship golf course with function facilities to hold events for up to 500 people

Events (5)

The term 'event' describes the type of meeting being held. The following are the most common types of events.

- Assembly. This term is used to describe a large formal gathering during which the leadership of an association or corporation addresses its members.
- Award/Gala Dinner. Commonly, a gala dinner is an integral part of an association's closing ceremony for its annual convention. Its primary function is to socialize and celebrate. It is normally a black tie affair featuring entertainment, a recognized speaker and a festive setting.
- Clinic. A clinic is an educational session where participants learn by doing. It can either be attended by a small group interacting with each other or be led by teaching staff.
- Colloquium. This is a meeting involving academicians or scientists who deliver lectures followed by a question and answer session.

- Conference. In the UK, the word 'conference' is generally used to describe nearly every type of meeting. Conferences are usually general sessions with a high level of group participation. Conferences are mainly confined to members of the same company, association or profession. The typical level of attendance for a conference ranges from 30 to 150 delegates.
- Congress. The term congress is normally used in Europe to describe an event which in the US is called a convention.
- Convention. Webster's Dictionary defines a convention as the act of coming together, or an assembly, often periodical, of delegates or representatives, as of a political or religious group, commercial organization, professional association, fraternal society and so on. The term 'convention' is widely used in the US to describe larger meetings (250 to 30,000 delegates) with a formal structure usually extending over several days and often comprised of many different functions such as board of director meetings, general assemblies, symposiums, workshops, exhibits and so on.
- Exhibition (Exposition). An exhibition (called an 'exposition' in the US) is an event designed to bring together purveyors of products, equipment and services in an environment in which they can display or demonstrate their products or services to a group of attendees. Exhibitions are either free standing events, or are part of a convention.
- Forum. This term is used to describe a meeting where experts in a specific field give short presentations, usually expressing different views, followed by an opportunity for the audience to partake in the discussion. A forum may also be called a panel discussion.
- Incentive. Incentives are events which are specifically designed to reward the participants for high achievement. Incentive programmes are often staged at upscale international destinations and include high quality leisure and entertainment experiences. Spouses are usually invited. The main target group is the sales staff of insurance and automobile companies. The entire programme is paid for by the company.
- Lecture. A lecture is a formal presentation given by a specialist to an audience.
- Meeting. A meeting usually involves only a few participants (from 2 to 12) discussing business in a board room setting. However, the word 'meeting' is also used in a wider context to describe conferences, meetings and seminars in a collective manner.
- Poster session. A poster session is part of a major academic conference during which authors are given the opportunity to display abstracts of their papers on notice boards and are able to meet with delegates on a one-to-one basis to discuss their findings.
- Presentation. This term is used for a meeting in which a speaker describes a product, budget, or new business strategy in a formal setting. Attendees are usually given handouts of the topic being presented.
- Production/Show. These terms are used to describe events such as product launches which are often supported by live entertainment or elaborate multi-media shows.
- Programme. This is a term used to describe the entire schedule of events within a conference. However, it is also sometimes used to describe a specific training programme.
- Seminar. A seminar is a lecture and discussion period which allows participants to share experiences in a particular field. A seminar is guided by an expert facilitator. Seminars are usually one or two day events attended by 12 to 120 participants.

- Summit. This is a term used to describe a conference attended by heads of government or high level officials.
- Symposium. A symposium is similar in style to a seminar. It is normally concerned with a single subject and consists of an extensive two-way flow of information.
- Theme party. In order to create a change of pace and allow for informal networking, sponsors increasingly request theme parties to be part of a convention. It is here that hotels have an opportunity to differentiate themselves. Theme parties often reflect the characteristics of the local destination.
- Trade show/fair. A trade show or fair is an event during which suppliers present their products or services in an exhibit format (booths and displays). Visitors to the trade show are given the opportunity to inspect the product and receive demonstrations and brochures, as well as verbal information from vendors. Trade shows are either free standing events (such as motor, home, or boat shows) or are part of a convention. Trade shows can include as many as 10,000 exhibitors or as few as 20.
- Workshop. Workshops are usually events where large groups of people who have attended a lecture or presentation split into small workshop groups of 6 to 12 people to discuss a particular problem or assignment in detail. One member of the small group is usually designated as the leader, presenter or facilitator charged with reporting the findings or proposals of the workshop group back to the large group.

The meeting market is comprised of two primary categories of events namely conventions and exhibitions.

Conventions

Conventions are comprised of two major market segments, associations and corporate.

Associations

In order to attract the important association market, it is imperative to understand the different organizational and meeting requirements which apply to the various association sectors. The purpose of an association is to advance their members' interests which, according to the American Society of Association Executives (ASAE), can be broadly defined as to:

- advance the status and image of its members;
- provide for peer interaction and exchange of information;
- evaluate and advance the association members' interests (political, economic, social);
- evaluate and project future trends;
- train and update members' know-how;
- emphasize the value of membership; and
- provide entertainment and informal interaction.

Members of associations elect local, regional, national and international boards who, on a voluntary basis, direct the affairs of the association, representing their members' views. Larger associations employ a full-time staff at their national or international business office. The elected board members usually serve for a limited time period (one to three years) since they also hold full-time positions in their respective professions.

An association's main board is primarily concerned with the setting of policies and the direction which the association should be taking from a strategic point of view, whereas the full-time executive staff is responsible for the implementation of policy and the running of the association on a daily basis. The organizational structure of an association's main board is typically mirrored by the structure of the paid executive structure of the organization. An association's organizational structure might look as illustrated in Figure 11.4.

Types of associations

Associations can be classified into the following categories.

- Trade and professional associations. These associations are primarily interested in improving the economic and trading environment as well as promoting the image and status of their members. Educational and networking sessions are an integral aspect of the association meeting schedule. Members regard belonging to their association as a vital part of their profession. Conventions are held during non-vacation periods and budgets for hotel accommodation, entertainment and meetings are in the upper tier. National and international meeting dates and locations are often set three to five years in advance.
- Government organizations. Political parties, regional municipalities, and military and police organizations all belong to this segment. These meetings are usually held during fixed, predetermined dates. Meetings are often held in the same location annually. Expenses incurred are generally reimbursed, based on *per diem* guidelines. Entertainment is normally rather limited for these events.
- Labour unions. Union conventions and meetings are usually held in the summer or the beginning of autumn. All expenses are generally borne by the local or national union on behalf of their delegates. These conventions would only be held in venues which are unionized.

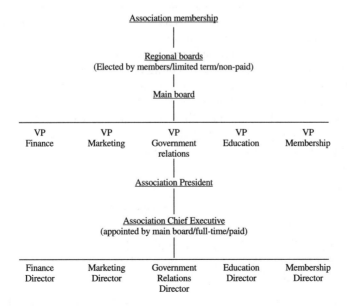

Figure 11.4 Example of the organizational structure of an association

- Scientific and medical associations. As a result of the continuous rapid changes in technology and the sciences, this sector organizes frequent conventions and meetings at the national and international level. Meetings usually include the presentation of papers, demonstrations, plenary sessions and exhibits. Main sessions involve all participants, require large theatres and are nearly always followed by smaller special interest symposiums which often involve sophisticated audio-visual equipment such as rear screen projection, closed circuit satellite television or multi-media presentations. These meetings are prestigious and the participants usually stay in up-market accommodation.

- Religious organizations. There are two major groupings of religious conventions: those held for clergy and support staff and those held for individuals practising a particular religion. Meetings for the first group are scheduled on a regular basis and are attended by approximately the same number of participants from year to year. Meetings for the second group are primarily family affairs and are therefore often scheduled during school vacation periods. As participants at these conventions finance their own attendance, hotels in the lower budget category are in higher demand. Participants often stay with local church members or use university student accommodation.

- Educational associations. These conferences are generally held on university campuses and require a large number of breakout meeting rooms for plenary sessions and the presentation of papers. Meetings are usually held when universities and schools are not in session. Budgets are relatively modest and associations attempt to obtain sponsorship for meal functions and social gatherings. Publishers often exhibit at these conventions.

- Avocational associations. These associations span a broad sector of interest groups. In contrast to members of previously mentioned associations who generally share vocationally related interests, members of avocational associations comprise members sharing sport, recreational, hobby, fraternal, cultural, civic or other social interests. Meetings are held at local, national and international levels and usually take place on weekends and during holiday periods. Members pay for their own expenses.

- Charitable associations. These organizations are divided into two primary groups. Their first group supports and raises funds for the advancement of a particular cause such as the arts, human rights or the fighting of poverty or disease. A major source of fund raising is the staging of charitable gala events and raffles. The second group is represented by research, lobbying or support organizations (for example, the Red Cross) who are actively involved in the operational aspects of addressing particular problem areas. These groups meet frequently both nationally and internationally to set the stage for future strategic development.

Association marketing strategies
Venue selection for the more prestigious national and international conventions is basically a three-step process:

- selection of 2 or 3 preferred sites, including field visits;
- preparation of final programme and budget; and
- presentation of final bid document and signing of contract.

A joint study by the ASAE (American Society of Association Executives) and the IACVB (International Association of Convention and Visitors Bureaus) confirms the important role which the paid association staff and executive team hold in the process of site selection. This study indicates that 58 per cent of the time the association executive conducts the site inspection, and 28 per cent of the time it is the meeting planner. When the final choices are presented to the association's main board, 57 per cent of the time the paid association chief executive is involved in the decision-making process to award the convention to a particular venue. Given the permanence of the paid staff versus the continuous change in composition of the main board, it becomes evident that the function of the full-time staff is extremely important and the convention centre or hotel needs to establish credibility with these professionals.

The bid to host a convention usually requires the co-operation and support of different partners, for example:

- local/national association board;
- local convention/visitors bureau;
- national tourist office;
- the venue itself (convention centre/hotel); and
- local community leaders (council/lord mayor).

International associations plan their site selection on a geographic rotation schedule, changing from year to year and from continent to continent. City selection within a region depends largely on the following criteria:

- site and standard of convention and exhibition facilities;
- accommodation mix and standard;
- transportation and access;
- security and health;
- quality of recreational facilities, shopping, restaurants and amenities;
- reputation of site management and staff (professionalism, stability, management/union relations); and
- value for money.

The bidding for a larger convention requires strong support, especially from the local association chapter. Critical support in the preparation of a bid document is provided by the national tourist authority. In the UK, the BTA (British Tourist Authority) offers financial and technical assistance to associations and venues in the preparation of bid documents. The BTA stages and/or participates in trade missions aimed at promoting the UK conference market. Individual cities and venues can participate in these missions to reach the association executive and meeting planner. Furthermore, BTA coordinates the following activities aimed at this important market.

- Familiarization trips are launched for potential overseas association clients to gain first-hand experience of locations and venues. Transportation companies, local hoteliers, conference organizers and officials from the conference and visitors bureau participate in hosting 'fam trips' to showcase their respective cities and facilities.
- Meeting and incentive travel workshops are staged in different parts of Britain, bringing together overseas conference and incentive buyers with hotel and conference operators.
- Publications, including directories such as *Britain – Where the Business Meets*, are distributed to potential buyers all over the world via BTA. The *British Business Bulletin* is another excellent vehicle to promote a conference venue. This newsletter

is distributed to all BTA and overseas trade offices. It is a regular digest reporting on business travel events and news updates.

Corporate

Corporate meetings represent the other major meeting sector. This market has also expanded rapidly during the last decade. The removal of trade barriers has resulted in the internationalization of business ventures. These trends are expected to continue well into the future. In their book, *Competing for the Future*, Hamel and Prahalad state: 'The future is to be found in the intersection of changes in technology, lifestyles, regulations, demographics and geopolitics' (Hamel and Prahalad, 1994: 95). Through mergers and joint ventures, corporations expanded both their manufacturing and service base, thereby increasing the need to communicate with their staff and clients. Although rapid communication methods such as satellite conferencing and email have gained in popularity, one of the most effective methods of communication is still the personal meeting. Many companies which rely heavily on training have developed their own dedicated conference centres (i.e. McDonald's, Holiday Inn, Exxon). However, the vast majority of corporate meetings take place in hotels or purpose-built conference centres.

Whereas attendance at association meetings is voluntary, attendance at corporate meetings is mandatory. The agenda for the corporate meeting is set by one person or an executive committee whereas the agenda for an association meeting is developed largely by its membership. The billing for corporate meetings includes all room, meal and entertainment expenses under one master account billed to the company whereas association billings for rooms and meals are paid for by the individual association member. The lead times for corporate meetings is relatively short, often governed by previously unknown events such as new product launches, changes in strategy, new legislation or acquisitions. Association meetings, on the other hand, are usually held annually as required by their constitution and are planned years in advance.

A survey by *Meetings and Conventions* magazine identified the types of meetings which corporations hold most frequently (Figure 11.5). It is worth briefly considering the top five of these in a little more detail.

Management meetings	25%
Training seminars	23%
Regional sales meetings	16%
New product introductions	10%
Professional/technical meetings	9%
National sales meetings	6%
Incentive trips	4%
Shareholder meetings	3%
Other meetings	4%

Figure 11.5 Types of corporate meetings
Source: Meetings and Conventions, 1996.

- Management meetings typically last one to three days and are attended by 10 to 25 participants. Their main purpose is to determine and communicate corporate budgets and products, and marketing and service strategies. Increasingly, however meetings are being used to form motivational links between management teams. One reason why management holds meetings away from corporate offices is to create a non-threatening, non-hierarchical environment. Although meetings are often held in an informal setting, they usually require state-of-the art facilities and high service standards. Recreational or informal 'get-togethers' are often integrated into the meeting agenda. Activities might include a round of golf, a cycling tour, a rafting trip or a round robin tennis tournament. After the evening meal, participants often gather into smaller groups for case studies or team projects with activity breaks such as darts, table tennis or snooker.

- Training seminars typically last from three to five days and are usually attended by 30 to 50 participants. These meetings are very focused, involving classroom style presentations, small teamwork groups and individual projects to be completed by the participants. Organizers of these sessions are looking for a high standard of food quality, up-to-date conference rooms and state of the art audio-visual equipment.
- Marketing and sales meetings are held primarily to motivate, familiarize and educate participants about a company's products and services. Meetings often include award ceremonies for high producers, promotional presentations by advertising or public relations agencies and peer interactions along the lines of a theme or particular marketing slogan. National marketing meetings often require elaborate audio-visual support and are usually attended by 150 to 600 participants.
- Professional and technical meetings are similar to training sessions, often involving experimentation and demonstrations.

A 1997 survey of meeting planners indicated which factors were most influential in the hotel selection process (Figure 11.6).

Incentives

Incentives have long been recognized by companies as a motivational tool to reward their employees for outstanding accomplishment. The largest share of the incentive market is derived from insurance companies and car dealerships. Companies reward achievements such as customer satisfaction, reaching financial targets or reducing staff turnover with incentive travel rewards. It is expected that the use of incentives

Hotel reputation	92%
Quality of food and service	87%
Meeting rooms (size, mix, decor, A/V)	86%
Dedicated conference manager (CSM)	78%
Previous experience with staff and facility	75%
Guest rooms (size, decor, desk)	72%
Convenient access/transportation links	65%
Competitive pricing (value for money)	62%
Physical appeal of hotel and surrounding area	62%
Efficient check-in/check-out	57%
Exhibit space	32%
On site recreation	28%
Convenience for shopping, museums, etc.	12%

Figure 11.6 Factors influencing hotel selection

Source: Schlentrich, 1997(unpublished data).

will continue to increase as companies find it an effective and personal way to reward staff and management.

In the UK, the incentive market is estimated to be worth more than £150 million, whereas in the US it generates over $2 billion annually. Incentive trips are usually organized by travel agents or destination management companies. The average incentive group includes 40 to 60 participants. Spouses are usually invited to take part in the trip which is fully paid for by the company. The average length of an incentive trip is one week and is usually scheduled when a company's business will allow participants to be absent from work.

Incentive organizers seek venues (hotels, cruise ships or country estates) which offer quality facilities and are able to create a memorable experience. Almost all incentive programmes involve special entertainment, themed food and beverage functions, and either spectator or participative events (such as visits to a show, rafting trips, shooting). It is not uncommon for larger companies to charter jets or an entire cruise ship for their incentive programme. Companies also frequently stage hospitality functions and short incentive weekend programmes planned around prestigious sporting events such as the British Open, Ascot, Henley or Wimbledon. Resort hotels such as Gleneagles in Scotland, the Princess in Acapulco and the Greenbriar in the US have developed special incentive programmes in order to attract this profitable market segment.

Corporate marketing strategies

Whereas it is relatively easy to target the executives responsible for arranging association meetings, small and mid-size corporations generally do not employ a full-time executive responsible for planning corporate meetings. Corporate executives from the human resource, marketing, finance or research department could be involved in planning meetings. It is often the department head's secretary or executive assistant who is responsible for negotiating meeting details. The level of their understanding of event planning can vary greatly from being highly professional to requiring personal assistance during each step of the planning process. Larger companies increasingly outsource their business travel service requirements (including the planning and supervision of conferences), in order to achieve financial savings and the delivery of a higher standard of service.

Exhibitions

Exhibitions are increasingly being held in conjunction with the annual meeting of an association. Exhibitions allow manufacturers and suppliers to directly reach a target audience which otherwise would be difficult and expensive to reach. According to a study by the American Society of Association Executives (ASAE), more than 50 per cent of association meetings hold exhibitions to supplement their income. Fifty per cent of the time, exhibitions were held in hotels and 40 per cent of the time, in convention or exhibition centres (see Figure 11.7 which shows the largest European exhibition centres).

Trade show

A trade show or fair is a form of exhibition where commercial suppliers promote their products or services to a specific profession or market segment. Trade shows are the most dynamic of all direct media marketing, the only situation in which a concentration of

	Square Metres
Hanover	475,600
Frankfurt	273,000
Cologne	260,000
Milan	249,000
Paris (Porte de Versailles)	222,000
Seldorf	198,000
Basel	172,000
Paris (Nord Villepointe)	164,000
Birmingham	158,000
Munich*	140,000

*Opened in 1998

Figure 11.7 Largest European exhibition centres
Source: Schlentrich, 1997(unpublished data).

prospective customers come together from many different regions during a limited time period to gather information and place orders. Initially, marketing executives dismissed the idea of trade shows as an educational experience, but they soon realized that trade shows are a cost effective means of reaching a broad spectrum of customers. Trade shows are usually held during the same period and in the same location each year (i.e. the Geneva Car Saloon, the Frankfurt Book Fair, the Las Vegas Computer Show). There are 'closed' trade shows which are only open to the professional trade, and 'open' shows which are targeted to a sector of the general public. Popular open trade shows (such as annual car, travel or home shows) attract millions of visitors each year around the world and are a profitable and important element of the exhibition industry. Trade shows may be organized by trade or professional associations, exhibition centres or professional exhibition companies.

The marketing of trade shows is becoming more and more sophisticated. The organizer's objective is to identify potential buyers through market research and to interest them in attending a particular show. Visitor statistics are recorded for each event by market segment and customer origin. Exhibitors of each show fill out confidential order and purchasing reports, allowing venues to quantify the total value of orders placed. Trade shows are a $21 billion a year industry with over 9000 shows held annually, attracting over 45 million visitors worldwide. In 1992, the average amount spent in the UK per out of town visitor attending a trade fair was £707.

Marketing and servicing the meeting industry: convention and visitor bureaus (6)

City governments and civic leaders have long recognized the importance of tourism as a vital link to employment, prosperity and overall positive city image and have therefore established convention and visitor bureaus to promote their cities. Convention and visitor bureaus coordinate and promote the diverse interests of city governments, travel suppliers (such as convention centres, hotels, restaurants, transportation companies and attractions) and trade and civic organizations. Bureaus act as information centres and promotional agencies.

Choosing a site and venue for a convention is one of the most complex and important tasks for a meeting planner. Meeting planners use extensively the services provided by CVBs in order to obtain detailed information about a specific location such as available meeting venues, hotel accommodations and other public facilities and services. The professionalism and image of a destination's CVB can greatly influence the site selection decision. For larger events, the CVB usually also provides other valuable services to the convention organizer such as:

- the preparation of a formal bid document in conjunction with the local convention venue, hotels, transportation and other service providers;
- the handling of room allocations for large city-wide conventions;
- the organization of government or city sponsored receptions; and
- the planning of pre- and post-convention programmes for convention delegates.

Destination management companies (7)

For larger conferences, the meeting planner frequently contracts with the local destination management company (DMC) whose responsibility it is to coordinate the following activities:

- delegate airport pickup and ground transportation;
- storage of convention or exhibition materials which are received in advance;
- selection of convention suppliers such as speakers, florists, photographers, decorators, security, caterers, entertainers and other personnel;
- development of spouse programmes; and
- organization of pre- and post-convention trips.

Hotels and conference centres (8)

Hotel and conference centre marketing executives employ a variety of strategies to attract the conference client to their property, the most important of which are the development of a marketing plan and the development of a service strategy.

Marketing plan

The marketing plan of a hotel or conference centre defines the responsibilities and actions to be taken over a given period of time (usually one year) to achieve the desired business and marketing objectives. The marketing plan is not just a working tool for the marketing department, but also influences the product and service delivery process of the operational departments, which impact the hotel and its overall image. Since customer demands and the competitive environment are constantly undergoing change, the marketing strategies should be continuously reviewed. The key elements of the marketing plan should take into consideration the following:

- occupancies and average rates to be achieved for each market segment;
- marketing budget required to achieve revenue projections;
- how venue is to be positioned in the marketplace;
- how to achieve a competitive advantage;
- how to attract conference buyers; and
- how to achieve consistent customer satisfaction and loyalty.

Marketing tools

Hotel and conference venues use some, and often all, of the following marketing tools to promote and solicit conference bookings.

- **Research.** The most productive sales strategy to achieve conference bookings is target marketing. Target marketing involves research into the meeting patterns of corporations and associations, such as when and where meetings take place, who makes the buying decision, what the budget is, and what services and facilities are required. In 1972, Omni International Hotels pioneered the concept of market research targeted to the meeting market. A database was established with input from the local, regional and national sales offices. Marketing research coordinators communicated detailed lead data to sales executives on a monthly basis who contacted the decision makers of particular companies or associations. This approach resulted in effective conversion rates (sales efforts versus bookings). Hotel post-conference information was fed back to the market research coordinators, thus keeping the database up to date.

- **Advertising.** Advertising for conferences is most cost effective and efficient when announcing a new product or facility, thus providing the reader with interesting new information. Trade publications, such as *Meetings and Conventions*, are an appropriate media.

- **Brochures.** A conference brochure is often the first impression that a meeting planner gains about a venue. Too often, brochures are cluttered and information is not clearly organized. A brochure should contain a descriptive section with information about the destination and the region in which it is located. It should include quality colour photographs of the facility, its setting, the conference facilities and suites and guest rooms. A brochure should also include an informative section (which is usually printed in black and white) providing floor plans, room layouts, technical data, menu proposals and pricing. As this information changes frequently, it is suggested that it be printed in a loose leaf flyer format.

- **Newsletters and direct mail.** Hotel and conference centres often develop a mailing list which facilitates periodic contact via a direct mail campaign or in-house newsletter to reach existing clients and target groups. Mailing lists can also be purchased from outside agencies or obtained from industry associations.

- **Telemarketing.** Telemarketing has increasingly become an integral part of a direct sales marketing strategy. It is primarily targeted towards the smaller, short lead time group meeting market.

- **Personal sales calls.** Due to the travel time and costs involved, personal sales calls have to be effectively planned and pre-scheduled.

- **Exhibitions and consortia promotions.** National and regional tourist boards frequently invite hotels and conference venues to partake in industry exhibitions staged nationally or internationally. Venues can reduce the cost of such an exhibition by joining other conference suppliers within their region in such promotions. The local Convention and Visitor Bureau usually coordinates such joint promotions.

- **Public relations.** Image and public relations campaigns are an effective means of keeping the name of a property in the forefront. News releases and stories sent to publications about a venue's achievements, special awards, new service features or products can be used to obtain positive publicity.

- **Branding.** Frequently, hotel chains brand their conference facilities and services in order to gain a competitive edge. Hilton International, for example, has branded their convention facility and service concept ('Meeting 2000'). All aspects, from meeting room design, lighting, audio-visual equipment, comfort of meeting chairs, coffee breaks and meal preferences were researched. Operational training and service standards were established to ensure consistency.

- **Pricing.** In order to provide meeting planners with an all-inclusive meeting package, venues develop standard pricing packages which include use of meeting facilities, meals, coffee breaks, supplies and audio-visual equipment, thus eliminating the often negative element of surprise inherent in the 'a la carte' method of pricing.

- **Facility visits.** Inviting prospective buyers to visit a hotel or convention centre in person is an ideal way to convince them to book business. Since they are expensive to plan and cumbersome to execute, familiarization visits (fam trips) should be targeted to decision makers and important clients.

- **Video.** High quality video presentations are an effective way to promote a venue either during personal sales presentations or during exhibits. (Videos sent overseas must conform to the destination country's video format.)

- **Websites.** This medium can be an effective marketing tool as meeting planners are increasingly using websites to gather information. Hotel chains such as Sheraton, Hilton, Marriott and Holiday Inn have dedicated meeting and conference websites.

Service strategies

As quality demands and sophistication of meeting planners increases, venues will need to rise to the challenge of improving their product and service delivery system. Service quality can only be achieved through well motivated, highly trained and empowered staff and management. Many hotel companies still have the attitude that staff training is expensive and, in view of high staff turnover rates, ineffective. There is strong evidence, however, that companies which invest in training and the creation of a positive work environment combined with fair pay will retain their staff and achieve superior service performance, all ultimately leading to a superior industry image and customer loyalty (Figure 11.8).

HILTON HOTELS CORPORATION CONVENTION SERVICE COMMITMENT

As the recognised industry leader in Convention Service operations, Hilton Hotels Corporation has a commitment to each client we serve. Through a property-wide unification, of service standards, Hilton is dedicated to the success of every meeting we host. Fundamental to the success of our endeavour are:

STAFF

Long term professionals, who are knowledgeable, experienced, and dedicated to each group they serve.

FACILITIES

Efficient convention properties which continuously demonstrate flexibility, always striving to meet the needs of our clients.

PRODUCT

A successful convention every time, as service is Hilton's number one product.

PROFIT

Dedicated effort to maximise revenue potential within the convention market segment – rooms, catering and beyond to all additional opportunities.

COMMUNICATION

The vital link necessary during a convention's pre-planning stages on site, and beyond, to a group's next meeting at Hilton.

TEAM WORK

A unified hotel team, anticipating needs, completing requests and fulfilling arrangements to the satisfaction of our guests.

CONTINUOUS IMPROVEMENT

Looking back, identifying how Hilton could improve on our product – looking ahead, through innovation, industry change, and Hilton's belief that meeting the challenge of the future enables us to stay ahead of the competition.

SELL HILTON

The rebooking of a convention – the ultimate measure of our success.

Figure 11.8 Hilton Hotels Corporation convention service commitment

Convention Service Manager

Once the meeting planner has finalized negotiations regarding a specific convention with the sales director of a given venue, the meeting planner will submit the event proposal and budget to the sponsor for final approval and the signing of the venue contract. At this point, the sales director will transfer the account to the Convention Service Manager (CSM) who will work closely with the meeting planner in coordinating all operational and administrative aspects pertaining to the meeting (Figure 11.9). The meeting planner will thus have one contact person at the venue (hotel or convention centre). The position of the CSM is relatively new and has gained in importance as the convention industry has grown and become more complex. Under the old organizational structure, the meeting planner often had to deal with up to ten different department heads, resulting in considerable inefficiency and communication problems.

A typical convention can include more than 30 functions. For each function, a detailed function sheet needs to be completed, listing the requirements for each function (such as timing of the event, number of attendees, seating layout, audio-visual requirements, food and beverage to be served, entertainment, decorative features, billing instructions, etc.). The information on the function sheet is then communicated to the various hotel departments. It is the responsibility of the CSM to ensure that what has been contracted for with the meeting planner is delivered to his satisfaction.

The Meeting Planner
(representing sponsor)

The Convention Service Manager
(representing venue)

Administration	*Rooms Division*	*Food & Beverage*	*Engineering*
Sales & Marketing	Reservation	Kitchen	Technical
Accounting	Telephone	Banquet	Decoration
Purchasing	Front desk	Restaurants	Audio-visual
	Concierge	Bars	
	Housekeeping	Room service	
	Security	Stewarding	

Figure 11.9 The Convention Service Manager (CSM)

FUTURE INDUSTRY TRENDS

Acquisitions

The meeting industry has been transformed during the past few years by a rush of mergers and acquisitions in the hospitality industry, notably the acquisition of Westin ($1.2 billion) and ITT Sheraton ($13.3 billion) by Starwood. In 1998, the UK brewing and leisure group, Bass, which already owned Holiday Inns (2400 hotels), acquired the upscale international hotel chain, Intercontinental Hotels (117 hotels) for $3 billion. These acquisitions allow the mega-hotel corporations to aggressively market their meeting and conference facilities, providing sponsors with attractive rates and a global network of facilities in different price segments. Affiliation with referral organizations is one means by which independent hotels and conference venues can counteract the threat which the large corporations pose.

Technology and design

Conference sponsors and organizers increasingly require a higher level of service sophistication and state of the art facilities for their meetings. The use of interactive media, computerized projection equipment, and media walls with rear screen projection capabilities have become standard requirements. The Doubletree Hotel Group recently launched a new hotel concept targeting the business and small conference market. A highlight of this new concept is a multi-purpose Business Club Room, which alternately serves as a well-equipped office, a self-service business centre, a meeting space for small groups, and a cafe, combined in one convenient location. According to Doubletree, 'We have set out to reinvent the three-star business hotel. Our research indicates that today's road warrior doesn't want to eat, sleep and work in the same room'. In developing this new concept, Doubletree has entered into an innovative partnership with three leading companies experienced in delivering quality products in their respective fields: Kinko's (providing the latest technology in business equipment), Au Bon Pain (offering freshly baked food long after most hotel restaurants are closed), and Steelcase Inc. (a premier manufacturer of business furnishings and workspaces configured with productivity in mind).

Although the marketplace has widely adopted the use of the internet and satellite conferencing as a means of communication, research confirms that face-to-face meetings are still one of the most effective means of communicating, promoting and selling one's products and services.

REFERENCES AND FURTHER READING

American Express (1994) *European Business Travel and Expense Management Report*, Brighton: AMEX.

Birmingham Marketing Partnership (1996/97) *Annual Report and Accounts*, Birmingham: Birmingham Marketing Partnership.

Blackwell, S. *et al.* (1985) *Fundamentals of Association Management*, Washington, DC: American Society of Association Executives.

British Tourist Board (1994) *Britain – The Great Incentive Venue*, London: BTA.

Dotson, P.C. (1988) *Introduction to Meeting Management*, Birmingham, AL: Convention Management Association.

Hamel, G. and Prahalad, C.K. (1994) *Competing for the Future*, Boston, MA: Harvard Business School Press.

Hanson, B. (1998) 'C-Corps, REITs continue to outperform Dow', *Hotel and Motel Management*, **213**(3), 12.

Hildreth, R.A. (1990) *The Essentials of Meeting Management*, Englewood Cliffs, NJ: Prentice Hall.

Hoyle, L.H., Dorf, D.C. and Jones, T. (1989) *Managing Conventions and Group Business*, East Lansing, MI: Educational Institute of the American Hotel and Motel Association.

Kotler, P., Bowen, J. and Makens, J. (1996) *Marketing for Hospitality and Tourism*, Englewood Cliffs, NJ: Prentice Hall.

KPMG Peat Marwick (1993) *The Economic Impact of the ICC, the NIA and the NEC on Birmingham and the West Midlands*, Birmingham: KPMG Peat Marwick.

McGee, R. (ed.) (1985) *The Convention Liaison Council Manual*, Washington, DC: The Convention Liaison Council.

Meetings and Conventions (1996) *Corporate Meeting Survey*, Secaucus, NJ: Ziff-Davis Publishing.

Penner, R.H. (1991) *Conference Center Planning and Design*, Whitney, NY: Watson-Guptill Publications Inc.

Rutherford, D.G. (1990) *Introduction to the Conventions, Expositions, and Meetings Industry*, New York: Van Nostrand Reinhold.

Schlentrich, U.A. (1993) 'Trends in World Hospitality', *Hospitality*, 135, 1146.

Schlentrich, U.A. (1996) 'Business Travel Marketing', in Seaton, A.V. and Bennett, M.M. (eds), *Marketing Tourism Products: Concepts, Issues, Cases*, London: International Thomson Business Press, 318–49.

Scottish Exhibition Centre, Ltd. (1995/96) *Corporate Review*, Glasgow: SECC.

Weirich, M.L. (1992) *Meetings and Conventions Management*, Albany, NY: Delmar Publishers Inc.

WEBSITES (ALL ADDRESSES BEGIN WITH HTTP: //WWW.)

Doubletree Hotels Corporation:	doubletreehotels.com/
Hilton Hotels Corporation:	hilton.com/
Marriott International:	marriott.com/
Sheraton Hotels:	sheraton.com

12 Facilities management and design

David A.C. Gee

This chapter provides an account of the management and maintenance of hospitality premises. As the scale and complexity of new building increases, so the need for new approaches to both their procurement and management during occupation has become necessary. These approaches, now rapidly developing into a professional 'facilities management' activity, are outlined in this chapter. As facilities management impinges on a wide range of related areas, there is scope here to provide only an introduction to the subject, further reading being suggested at the end of the chapter.

FACILITIES MANAGEMENT IN A HOSPITALITY CONTEXT

Many businesses in the hospitality industry own the premises (or facilities) from which they operate. Others lease premises which they fund out of operating income, enabling capital thus saved to be employed in other areas of the business. Still yet others who own their premises and provide hospitality services on these premises may out-source day to day operational management and similar activities to external providers. These and similar developing business arrangements feature significantly in the hospitality industry today (see Chapter 2). However, it is important to recognize that facilities (land, buildings, plant, equipment and furnishings) represent a considerable investment for organizations and that facilities are critical to business success by providing an important vehicle for attracting custom and for the production and provision of goods and services. At the same time, newly-built facilities today are infinitely more complex and sophisticated than in the past and facility users (be they customers, employees or business owners) make increasingly greater, and sometimes conflicting, demands upon them. Operators constantly seek ways of using space more effectively and reducing their operating costs. At a time when business activity is changing and fast-moving, a more pro-active approach is now being taken towards the management of facilities. Perhaps more so than in many other industries, hospitality managers recognize that instead of being an inhibitor or constraint on business activity, facilities are a vital asset to the organization's continued viability – indeed they are almost a tool for creativity.

What is it, therefore, that we should expect facilities to provide in the hospitality business context? The following criteria are suggested as a starting point.

- Sensual elements, such as those aspects concerned with appearance, space, privacy, social activity, image. Buildings impact upon our senses in a wide variety of ways – they tell us something about our culture, about our organizations; they can provide claustrophobic and oppressive environments or welcoming spaces where people can gather, interact or simply watch one another. Facilities can create a continuum of

opinion amongst users ranging from attraction, security and a feeling of well-being, to hostility, fear or even revulsion.
- Functional elements, such as those aspects associated with operational and cost effectiveness and with productivity. Buildings are expected to deliver an economic return on the resources expended on them. We seek to provide an appropriate amount of space and amenity relative to the people and activities the building is designed to house. Working conditions, workflow and organization are as important for staff as levels of comfort, convenience and reliability are for guests. Equally, the ability of facilities to meet the demands of wear and tear is as important as the ease with which these same facilities can be maintained and improved.
- Health and safety elements, which include compliance with statutory requirements.

PROFESSIONAL FACILITIES MANAGEMENT

The increasing importance to organizations of using and managing their property resources has given rise to the development of facilities management as a professional activity. The International Facility Management Association (IFMA) in its first decade of activity has become an important professional body; it functions in a fully international context and within the UK and many countries there are facilities management organizations which foster the professional development of members. Facilities management is now offered as part of many degree programmes by universities and specialist courses now lead to higher degree qualifications.

To many organizations, facilities management is generally viewed as providing a wide range of support services peripheral to the organization's main core activity. In the hospitality industry, however, as facilities themselves are regarded very much an integral part of that core activity, facility management functions need to be tailored to meet the specific needs of the individual organization. These functions would normally (but not exclusively) include:

- project planning and management;
- planning and managing space;
- aspects relating to facility ownership and occupation, leases and business tenancies, environmental health, safety, security issues;
- maintenance management related to internal and external areas of buildings, including energy management, budgeting and cost control;
- the procurement and management of outsourcing agreements; and
- insurance.

PROJECT PLANNING AND MANAGEMENT

The acquisition of a new building or the adaptation of an existing property is a major challenge for any organization. For those commissioning a new development, it brings them into contact with a wide range of specialists whose professional work is often perceived as quite different from that of the management of a hospitality business. With increasingly exacting requirements for a new hospitality building, the client (i.e. the prospective building owner and/or operator) will ultimately take delivery of a new property, whose design has involved considerable dialogue with architects and other design specialists and whose construction has involved large labour forces and vast amounts of materials. Some of the construction work is large scale, dirty and unglamorous, whilst other work is exacting and highly technical in nature. The whole process is generally undertaken over a long, but pre-planned, time scale and within clearly prescribed cost parameters.

Should anyone feel daunted at the prospect of undertaking some large scale and costly project which is alien to their experience, solutions may be at hand. For very small projects (and here one is thinking in terms of developments under £250,000 or so), a direct approach to an architect may well be likely to provide the best solution. Professional institutes publish lists of their members and in making their own inquiries the prospective client would doubtless sound out opinion from those who have used the services of specific designers. With large sums of money at stake, it is important that both parties feel comfortable with each other; the client needs to be assured that the completed development will meet their expectations. Clients should also expect some guidance on the role and expected contribution they might make throughout the process. The client for larger scale projects would normally appoint a project manager to represent their interests in the procurement process. Today, businesses use project leaders to implement new programmes as diverse as new computerized control systems and staff sales training programmes. Change is so much the hallmark of business operation that the one-off introduction of, say, a new operating procedure cannot be left to chance and whims of individual line managers – the consequences of a poorly managed project can have ramifications on sales, on employee relations, on service quality and also on profitability. Project managers in building design and construction work have a vital role to play in the delivery to their employer of a development which meets all the employer's requirements and where there has been no overshoot in development cost and contract period.

Clearly the prime impetus for development stems from an organization's need to expand its business within existing or in new locations. An organization's assessment of existing and potential markets, of its existing products, of new products it might develop, of its general attitude towards development – these and other considerations help the organization to crystallize its thoughts on expansion. An organization's existing property inventory will suggest where these premises might be remodelled or expanded; market studies might suggest other locations for the development of new units or the acquisition of existing hospitality properties.

For the client, defining needs and expectations of a new property requires the identification of the hospitality product (in all its complexities) relative to markets/customers to be attracted. Market intelligence seeks to provide answers to the size, nature and expectations of the market the organization identifies as its target, and to evaluate the reaction of markets to new products the organization might develop. Such considerations are not without risk, indeed it might be said that the interplay of location (affected by climate, access, attractions, and many other factors), markets, timing, services and facilities provided by a new development are more problematic than for up-dating an existing product in an existing location.

Interpreting the findings of market intelligence, translating these into project requirements and expressing these aims in the form of a design brief, provides a critical benchmark against which subsequent design work, and ultimately the completed project, can be judged. For most organizations new to this type of work, the development of a design brief can be a lengthy and exhaustive process – future success of the business in a new building will be dependant as much on identifying and expressing problems as determining the number of guestrooms, bars or storage spaces. The owner of a new property sees the building as a saleable/rentable asset, the operator views it as a vehicle for generating revenues, controlling costs and facilitating profitability whilst the consumer (hotel guest) has expectations of seeing their requirements satisfied in meeting psychological and sensual needs. A brief, therefore, should begin to express information in terms of physical requirements (lists of accommodation for people and 'things'); functional information (relative to activities and functions which have to be housed, coordinated and controlled – such as flows of people, materials, and so on); psychological information (which attempts to qualify physical requirements in terms of the feelings and expectations of all users); life expectancy; versatility; development; and subsequent running costs (including maintenance, energy and other costs). Bedrooms are often regarded as an important benchmark by hotel users when judging the operation as a whole. Guests generally spend more time in their room than in other parts of the hotel, and thus tend to form opinions about convenience, comfort, privacy, safety and other aspects affecting their stay. Thus time spent at the briefing stage in assessing guest expectations is likely to be well spent if those involved 'think customer', and place themselves in the guests' shoes as these customers attempt to adjust heating, ventilation, lighting, seating and other amenities provided. Errors and omissions in the design brief cannot often be corrected in the completed building except at high cost in terms of time, money and disruption or loss of business.

By focusing on the individual 'customer' (and that 'customer' is just as likely to be a hotel employee as a hotel guest) in formulating the design requirements for a guest room or workplace environment, briefing considerations must not ignore wider issues. Departmental factors (such as the layout and relationship of areas, space allocation for departments, the accommodation of special plant, machinery and equipment) and factors affecting the organization at a corporate level (such as the need to fulfil corporate policies and standards which can range from image to cost parameters, from operational imperatives to service standards) need to be fully recognized in the design brief. Often the dilemma for clients and designers forming a brief is that having designed the pieces of the jigsaw (i.e. individual spaces), these pieces can rarely be arranged so that they fit together exactly and conveniently. Alternatively, where a broad-brush approach is taken towards an overall scheme layout, it is not uncommon to find that the subsequent design of individual work spaces and guest areas is seriously compromised – compromise which can provide day-in and day-out frustration during the operational life of the facility.

In a short chapter of this kind, a detailed account of alternative design and development procedures cannot be given. Clients already experienced in new building and development will have learnt much from that experience to guide them in subsequent development work. The client who is new to development however should seek advice from professionals at an early stage – for apart from the difficulties of translating marketing intelligence into project requirements and subsequently into a design brief, other factors need to be balanced out – factors such as the complexity of the design solution; the ability to control variations in the design which may have to be initiated even during construction work; quality control both in terms of materials used but also in standards of workmanship employed; price, time and programme certainty; areas of responsibility; and how risk can be avoided (or at least minimized). Traditional routes which can be employed by the client to obtain their building where often much of the work is undertaken sequentially are still appropriate in many circumstances, however increasingly 'design and build', 'management contracting', 'construction management' and 'design and manage' routes might be viewed as more appropriate for some developments.

MANAGING SPACE

Hospitality managers view space from two perspectives. First, space designed to accommodate the needs of the organization's customers – in other words, spaces where income can be generated from the sale of services, products and amenities. For example, whilst guest (bed)rooms may be designed primarily to fulfil the function the description suggests (sleeping, working, relaxing, entertainment and so on), the operations manager tends to view a guest room as 'space' – space which is versatile in the uses to which it might be put. So with minimal scene shifting a guest room could be transformed into a private dining room, conference room, meeting room or a range of other uses. It is not unknown for undercover car parking to be transformed (with suitable 'props') into exhibition space or even a concert venue. Second, hospitality managers are concerned with space designed to house the administrative and other areas needed to receive, store, produce and deliver goods and services to customers. Whilst at one time, workplace areas tended to be haphazard in their design and layout, managers increasingly recognize that the design and layout of the workplace is critical to efficient business operation and productivity. Ergonomic aspects such as anthropometry, kinetics and physiology now play a vital role in all design work (and not just in workplace areas) and the importance of psychology not only relates to employee motivation but also to customer decision-making, affecting purchases made.

Frequently many spaces in hospitality buildings are poorly utilized, inconveniently located or surplus to the core activity requirements of the organization. Re-modelling space in an existing building can frequently be done cost-effectively although the disruptive effect on existing business must be carefully evaluated. Such face-lifts can do much to revitalize business by enabling the introduction of new sales outlets and new themes. In other situations, space which fronts the pavement of a prime shopping street in a town centre might provide greater income to the property owner if let to retailers. Basement areas could be leased to others for purposes as diverse as hair and beauty salons, leisure and fitness studios, and car parking. With overall development costs for hospitality properties ranging from £1750 to £2500 per square metre (and more) the importance of utilizing spatial resources to their full potential is all too evident.

LEGAL ASPECTS RELATING TO FACILITY OWNERSHIP AND OCCUPATION

The legislation governing property ownership and occupation is considerable and well outwith the scope of this chapter. However, one issue likely to face the facilities manager on a regular or periodic basis concerns leases and business tenancies. Whether leasing premises or offering premises for lease, hospitality managers should always seek professional legal advice. The law affecting land and property is complex and the potential for misunderstandings and disagreements between parties in such situations might not be fully appreciated at the outset by landlord or tenant. Without formal written agreement there exists the possibility of disputes ranging from simple issues like the dates for the payment of rent to more complex problems affecting the definition of 'fixtures and fittings' or the scope for sub-letting. Thus, agreements must be professionally drawn up to ensure that the rights and interests of all parties are properly safeguarded.

SECURITY

Hospitality businesses seek to attract custom unhindered. Indeed, too many security checks, whilst tolerated by travellers at airports might be seen as overkill if applied to a hospitality situation. Nevertheless, the hospitality business has a responsibility to protect the people using its premises; to protect its assets; to protect information held by the business; and to encourage the normal functioning of the business. Crime rates on hospitality premises are not inconsiderable and the nature of crime committed is changing from simple theft and pilferage to crimes involving more serious offences such as fraud, drugs, personal attack and even hostage taking. Whilst some forms of crime are born of opportunist action, deliberate, calculated and organized crime is also developing apace. Initial decisions affecting a building taken at the design stage can accommodate crime issues, but additional measures are inevitably required at all stages during the life of a business. Even the most sophisticated room security key-card system can be thwarted by careless oversight on the part of front office staff. Undesirables are often difficult to identify and an environment which encourages an open-house type of atmosphere invariably attracts petty thieving, prostitutes and fraudulent activities.

Managing security threats can be tackled by the introduction of preventative, thwartive or deterrent measures. Care must be taken to ensure that in the hospitality context, the image of a uniformed factory-type security officer is not allowed to prevail to alienate genuine law-abiding guests. Security measures which are 'designed-in' to new buildings are inevitably less costly than incorporating systems into an existing property, and they are certainly much less obtrusive and perceived by undesirables as much more likely to be effective. The positioning of a new building within a site can have a deterring effect on break-ins, as can access points to buildings which do not provide privacy for criminals seeking access. The use of 'sleeping policemen' type humps on vehicle carriageways, of gradients and bends, of high quality lighting along with security cameras and infrared detection systems all conspire to discourage access to premises by undesirables.

Whilst all businesses to a greater or lesser extent implement procedures affecting safety and security, they should also consider the extent to which planning can be made for disaster situations. Of course, such situations normally comprise unexpected events which are by definition not normally part of the routine safety and security activities of the organization. However, in the hospitality industry a modest outbreak of food poisoning which links the business into the food chain can cause serious disruption to normal functioning. More dramatically, the impact of terrorist action can leave unprepared management and staff vulnerable. It is unrealistic to plan in anticipation of every conceivable threat but it is important to recognize that unexpected disasters do happen. In formulating plans designed to cope with different situations, many areas of commonality will feature. These might include building evacuation procedures, and the responsibilities and authority accorded to an individual member of staff for dealing with the press or liaising with emergency services. By recognizing and preparing for disasters, management provides some reassurance to customers, staff and others that the impacts of a disaster are at least anticipated.

ACCIDENTS, FIRE AND SAFETY

Many aspects of building management are constrained by legislative requirements. Whilst many assume that 'accidents will always happen', the managers of hospitality premises should distance themselves from such an opinion. Most, if not all, accidents are avoidable, even if the measures might be extreme. For example, one cannot be injured whilst crossing a road, if you decide never to cross a road in future. Due care and attention to the amount of traffic, its speed and other factors help to keep us safe most of the time. Carelessness on our part or on the part of a driver might cause a rare accident.

Guests and employees on hotel premises do not frequently have accidents, but a significant proportion of fires which occur in hotels, originate during sleeping hours (double the occurrence of that in one's own home). Many arise as a result of cigarettes, with others starting in kitchen areas which are often linked to fat fires and fume extract systems. The siting of appropriate fire fighting equipment and the provision and implementation of staff safety training are likely to have the most impact on fire safety. Regular maintenance and servicing of plant, machinery, escape routes and fire fighting equipment adds to the preventative measures. Operators of hospitality premises are recommended to seek advice from the local fire authorities and from commercial suppliers of equipment.

ENVIRONMENTAL HEALTH

The provision and maintenance of a safe environment not only make sound business sense, but is also required by law. In this area the law is extensive, complex and frequently changing. Much of the legislative force is made under the provisions of the Occupiers' Liability Acts 1957 and 1984, the Public Health Acts, the Health and Safety at Work etc. Act, 1974 and the Offices, Shops and Railway Premises Act 1963. Matters with which the facilities manager should be concerned are as diverse as ventilation and temperature in workplaces; liability towards trespassers; staff safety training; personal protective equipment for employees; and sick building syndrome. The operations manager must be familiar with these and many other aspects relating to environmental health and safety.

INVENTORY MANAGEMENT AND ASSET MAINTENANCE

The adage that 'if it is not screwed down, it will disappear' is especially apposite for those with responsibility for hospitality facilities. The experienced hospitality manager is unlikely to be fazed by vanishing teaspoons, television sets and table-cloths – experience of such losses is a common one amongst those in the industry. Asset registers held on computer, asset tagging and physical inventory checks, not only help retain assets in one's ownership, but also assists assessment of asset condition and the frequency and extent of repair and maintenance needs. Maintenance checks are, in addition, frequently a requirement for insurance purposes and also in the fulfilment of statutory requirements.

Maintenance activity is often perceived by managers as unglamorous and an activity best left to the hotel maintenance staff. This is a dangerous view to hold as the assets of even a modest business as represented by its buildings, land, plant, equipment and furnishings is likely to run to at least £1 million and a city-centre high quality operation may well have a book value of £50–£100 million, or more. Plant, machinery, furnishings and equipment in many hospitality businesses can often account for one-quarter to one-third of the fixed assets of an organization, somewhat of a misnomer when such assets are not always as 'fixed' as their designation implies. Apart from sustaining utility and value in assets, the maintenance of facilities substantially helps attract and retain custom and contributes positively towards the public's image of the organization. Customers are much more likely to be drawn to a clean and attractively maintained property than to one which is in need of a fresh coat of paint and a drop of oil on the seized-up sign outside.

The choice of materials made at the design stage and the standards of workmanship employed during construction frequently affect the durability of assets. Both features influence the frequency and extent to which maintenance may be necessary at a later stage during the life of the building. User behaviour can be influenced by decisions made at the design stage, but the operational manager can also exert influence on the way facilities are used on a day to day basis. Laid out pathways through a forest walk are much more likely to discourage walkers from straying than signage which exhorts them 'not to walk on the grass'. Strategically placed litter bins tend to be more effective than 'do not drop litter' signs.

As few consumer durables are purchased today without an operating manual, so a new building should be supplied with a Premises Owners' Manual which can inform the occupier how they might get the best of a new building. In addition, it can inform on recommended maintenance and servicing schedules which facilitates the apportionment of adequate funds to support maintenance activity whether it is planned preventative or corrective work or that which is required in an emergency situation. An Owner's Manual can inform on recommended procedures, for example, for the removal of felt pen markings from polished surfaces (the application of methylene chloride with a soft cloth is infinitely preferable than the use of abrasive powders or steel wool which would leave permanent scratch marks!).

The need for maintenance is generated principally through use – a woollen sweater will ultimately develop holes at the elbow irrespective of how careful the wearer might be. Experience suggests that the users of hospitality facilities are generally not as careful as they might be at home, and the throughput of guests in city centre hotels is such as to severely test the wearing capabilities of, for example, even the most durable of carpets. Climate also affects the speed with which buildings and building materials deteriorate – wind, rain, snow and temperature variations may affect water penetration in buildings in exposed locations. The effects of solar radiation in a hotter climate can accelerate the deterioration of roof claddings.

Changing standards whilst not strictly a maintenance issue are generally handled as part of a maintenance schedule – as facility users develop more exacting standards, so improvements may be made additional to routine maintenance activity. Thus as assets age, maintenance and enhancement costs increase as the useful life span of an asset is extended beyond that which might be normally expected.

ENERGY MANAGEMENT

Environmental issues have assumed considerable importance as global warming and general pollution increases. Whilst for hospitality businesses the expenditure on energy at around 4.3 per cent of turnover might seem unimportant relative to labour and raw material costs, official reports have suggested that savings of around 20–35 per cent could be achieved by modest capital expenditure and careful 'housekeeping'. In financial terms a saving of between £21,000 and £35,000 on an annual energy bill of say £100,000 is likely to find itself enhancing pre-tax profits by much the same amounts. To achieve a similar increase in profit by more conventional means of increased sales would require income to rise by around 12–15 per cent (or say, £340,000) to compensate. Energy is used in a wide range of ways from space heating (which generally takes the lion's share of up to 50 per cent), to hot water, catering and lighting.

Whilst good housekeeping measures achieved by staff training and the development of work systems produce large savings, conventional equipment fitted with better forms of control or new equipment designed specifically to provide energy savings are also desirable. Heat exchangers, better insulation, radiator thermostat controls, photocells to control lighting – these and other measures will ensure that energy consumption and cost is modified.

OUTSOURCING

Few businesses are sufficiently self-sufficient that they do not rely on some outside organization to provide an input, whether it is buying office supplies, sourcing materials for manufacture or using a firm to clean the office windows. Increasingly today, where an organization contracts others to provide services previously handled in-house, it often makes sound economic and organizational sense to consider this option. Some hotel property owners, rather than manage the property themselves, may choose to outsource the total management activity whilst retaining ownership of the property and sharing in the success of the business it houses. Whilst the outsourcing of a core activity is still relatively uncommon, the majority of organizations outsource some part of their business operation to a greater or lesser degree.

Most business operators prefer to retain the core activity, for which they have an obvious interest, whilst seeking the outsourcing option for peripheral activity. Activities which call for special skills, knowledge or equipment or which are undertaken infrequently or haphazardly are typical of those areas where an organization might consider the use of an outside provider in preference to employing, training and equipping its own labour force. Whether it is linen and laundry services; security; specialist cleaning; pest control or even the total facility management function, criteria that are uppermost are cost and the extent to which the use of an external provider will not disrupt the organization's core activity. For example, the level and type of security required for a factory unit located in an industrial estate is very different from that required in a luxury hotel property – the potential for theft may be much the same in financial terms, but hotel custom might be jeopardized unless more discreet security systems are used as opposed to more obvious indications on factory premises. Determining the nature of services which might be outsourced, finding a suitable provider and drawing up the specification for services to be provided – all are important features to be addressed by the operations manager and embodied in contractual arrangements.

The acquisition of plant and equipment may fall within the remit of the facilities manager. As an alternative to the outright purchase of such plant and equipment, hiring and leasing arrangements may provide a more attractive proposition. Hiring is normally associated with short periods (i.e. where an electricity generator may be required at short notice or for a specific event). Leasing tends to relate to longer time-scale arrangements (from one to five years) and may be attractive to businesses wishing to use equipment prone to obsolescence. Such arrangements allow the organization to lease 'next generation' office copiers, dishwashers, furnishings, motor vehicles with each new lease period. Furthermore, it is increasingly common practice, especially in the case of technically sophisticated equipment, for agreements to take the form of a service lease; this ensures that the interests of the owner of the equipment are safeguarded by his right to provide any maintenance and servicing which may be required.

INSURANCE OF ASSETS

Security issues, along with other perils, can be handled by insurance. Insurance will not, by itself, reduce the security issues facing an organization, but it can provide some form of compensation for the problems that have been created, it is unlikely to fully recompense the operator for the longer term damage such breaches in security might occasion. Whilst this section does not wish to side-step the issue of insurance for business premises, the issue is so complex that clients are advised to seek specialist advice either through a broker or by directly consulting an insurance company. Some form of protection in relation to general insurance is given by the Insurance Brokers (Registration) Act of 1977 and clients should, for their own peace of mind, consult brokers covered by the Insurance Brokers Registration Council (IBRC) or members of the British Insurance and Investment Brokers Association (BIIBA). Brokers can offer a wide range of advice covering buildings, contents, money, liability insurance and consequential loss and loss of profits as a result of business interruption. Whilst in theory insurance can provide a measure of assurance to clients for all forms of calamity, the cost of premiums may be such that many businesses may be more content to take on some risks out of their own resources.

COMPUTER TECHNOLOGY AND FACILITIES MANAGEMENT

Few hospitality organizations operate today without the aid of information technology. Computers are now regarded a part of everyday life and a wide range of hospitality software is available which enables businesses to control and record information from guest-room reservations to food purchases, from wage and salary records to complex sales analyses, from guest-room key control to automated check-in/check-out. The critical factor for managers to address is that in choosing a computer system they determine the precise range of tasks a system should be expected to perform and the range of information required in order that effective management control can be exercised.

In the context of facilities management, it is only within the last few years that information technology has been developed to provide managers with tools to assist day to day operation. Building management systems (BMS) can be used to provide a database of services and installations within buildings, and a number of computer-aided facilities management systems (CAFM) are now available. Their introduction has been somewhat slow generally in the UK as experienced facilities managers have tended to feel more comfortable with manual systems. There is little doubt however, that with new and increasingly complex buildings being developed more Premises Owners Manuals (see under 'Inventory management' above) will be provided in a computer literate format enabling CAFM systems to be introduced at the start of a building's life. Computer based facility management systems can be applied to a wide range of building management situations including space management and planning, the management of assets (including asset registers, asset tagging and maintenance scheduling), security issues, fire security, energy management (space heating, water heating and lighting control).

REFERENCES AND FURTHER READING

Association of Insurance and Risk Managers in Industry and Commerce (annual publication), *Company Insurance Handbook*, Aldershot: Gower.

Boisot-Waters Cohen (1987) *Business Property Handbook*, Aldershot: Gower.

Braham, B. (1990) *Computer Systems in the Hotel and Catering Industry*, London: Cassell.

Briner, W., Geddes, M. and Hastings, C. (1990) *Project Leadership*, Aldershot: Gower.

Costello, J. (ed.) (1991) *Intelligent Buildings International*, London: IBC Business Publications.

Doswell, R. and Gamble, P. (1987) *Marketing and Planning Hotels and Tourism Projects*, London: Hutchinson.

Energy Efficiency Office, *Energy Efficiency in Buildings*, London: HMSO.

Gordon, J.E. (1991) *Structures: or Why Things Don't Fall Down*, London: Penguin.

Grigg, J. and Jordan, A. (1993) *Are You Managing Facilities? Getting the Best Out of Buildings*, London: N. Brealey Publications/Industrial Society.

Hughes, D. (1984) *Guide to Hotel Security*, Aldershot: Gower.

James, R.W. and Alcorn, P.A. (1991) *A Guide to Facilities Planning*, Englewood Cliffs, NJ: Prentice Hall.

Jones, C. and Jowett, V. (1998) *Managing Facilities*, Oxford: Butterworth Heinemann.

Lawson, F. (1995) *Hotels & Resorts – Planning Design & Refurbishment*, London: Butterworth Architectural.

Loss Prevention Council (undated) *Protection of Premises Against Terrorist Attack*, London: LPC.

Masterman, J. (1993) *Building Procurement*, London: Spon.

NEDO (1988) *Faster Building for Commerce*, London: NEDO/HMSO.

Pannett, A. (1992) *Principles of Hotel and Catering Law*, London: Cassell.

Reid, E. (1984) *Understanding Buildings*, London: Construction Press.

Sabbagh, K. (1990) *Skyscraper: the Making of a Building*, London: Macmillan.

Saxon, R. (1993) *The Atrium comes of Age*, London: Architectural Press.

Scarrett, D. (1991) *Property Management*, London: Spon.

Scarrett, D. (1995) *Property Asset Management*, London: Spon.

Seeley, I. (1990) *Building Maintenance*, London: Macmillan.

Spedding, A. (ed.) (1987) *Building Maintenance: Economics and Management*, London: Spon.

Spedding, A. (ed.) (1994) *CIOB Handbook of Facilities Management*, Harlow: Longman.

Turner, A.E. (1990) *Building Procurement*, London: Macmillan.

Underwood, G. (1984) *The Security of Buildings*, London: Architectural Press.

Part III
Issues in hotel accommodation

Current trends in hotel accommodation design
13

Cailein H. Gillespie

This chapter addresses trends in international hotel design, interior design and redesign. *Collins Concise Dictionary* shows that 'trends' are characteristically viewed in terms of 'general tendency or direction' and 'fashion or mode'. The entire field of design in the hotel and hospitality industry is an important area for research because around the world there has grown a small but prominent collection of extraordinary and individualistic hotels, and to a lesser degree hotels owned by corporations, providing a cameo of changing cultural and social trends in design. Hart and Service (1988) writing about the effects of managerial attitudes to design see the term 'design' suffering from the same umbrella usage as 'fashion' and 'marketing' and thus having the potential in its corrupted use to undermine its contribution to overall quality and value. However, many hotel properties have become authoritative symbols of the strength of the worldwide tourist industry. There has, in tandem, grown an equally select and international band of hotel designers, interior designers and signature designers, whose prominence has spawned major investment by hotels, and interest from a small but prominent and élite clientele. The latter have bought into the harmonization of look, image, location and social value, overall packaging identity and individuality that distinctive properties provide. Exemplary marketing has also made these distinctive properties match the rhythm of good living to such an extent that in some social circles, design has become a kind of addiction and hotels are revisited almost devotionally. Many elements of new design are also important for hotels in the middle and lower tiers who often copy as many design elements as are fiscally prudent.

Elliott and Johns (1993: 6) looking at the influence of international tourism trends on the design of leisure resorts saw 'the finest as able to transcend fashions in architecture and tourism and generate lasting innovation'. With so many hotels and rooms available, competition in selling hotels and their amenities has become paramount, to the point where it is impossible to determine how many hotel rooms are being built or refurbished annually around the world. Many hotels like the Schlosshotel Vier Jahreszeiten in Berlin (total interior design by Karl Lagerfeld); The Lanesborough Hotel on Hyde Park Corner, London (renovation and interior-design by Ezra Attia Associates who were also responsible for work at the Schlosshotel Vier Jahreszeiten); or Morgans, in the Murray Hill area of New York (interior-design by Andrée Putman), have all invested in what could be termed 'high design'. However, hotels are for people, and are ultimately required to provide a service. These properties have not invested in short lived fashion or design indulgence, but in interior design which promotes the ethos of superlative hotel service.

Neal A. Prince (1986: 26) one-time Staff Vice President, Interior and Graphic Design, for Inter-Continental Hotels Corporation, states that 'hotels being primarily people oriented are usually also fashion oriented'. Design has often therefore been treated with a degree of scepticism, and has been tarnished by its association with fashion, style, trends and popular life-style which have undermined its contribution, design being represented as lightweight and ever-changing. However, some of the most commercially successful hotel and hospitality properties and companies are intensely design conscious, and invest major resources in the effective management of design. Table 13.1 shows recent spending on design, interior design and redesign for a sample of hotel properties and companies.

Table 13.1 Some examples of expenditure on hotel design

	Property or company	Spend
1	Savoy Group	£72 million
2	Sofitel (in Europe per annum since 1993; expected completion 1998)	Ff. 200 million c., US$40 million
3	The Dorchester London	over £100 million
4	The George V Paris	£50 million
5	Mandarin Oriental	invest anything from 3–10% of Gross Revenues on renovation and of equipment. In 1997 this equated to close to US$40 million
6	The Royal Lancaster Hotel, London	£10 million refurbishment
7	Thistle Hotels	£55 million investment in 1997
8	Inter-Continental Hotel, Paris	Ff. 280 million c., US$58 million
9	The Breakers Hotel and Resort Palm Beach, Florida, USA	US$100 million, refurbishment, interior-design, redesign over 5 years without borrowing
10	Hotel Princesa Sophia, Barcelona	£8 million refurbishment
11	Grosvenor House Hotel, London	£3.5 million upgrade of the Crown Club executive floor
12	The Athenaeum Hotel, London	£10 million refit and refurbishment
13	Forte Posthouse	An investment of £60 million on upgrading in 1997–8. By the year 2000, c. 56 of the UK's 83 Posthouses will have redesigned bedrooms and refurbished meeting rooms, leisure and dining facilities
14	The Mount Royal Hotel Marble Arch, London	£15 million refurbishment of rooms, public areas and meeting rooms
15	Cliveden Hotel in Bath, England	£3.5 million refurbishment of rooms, meeting facilities and public areas

These individual properties and companies tend also to possess other strengths, for example, in strategic, financial and quality management, marketing (in future, design will become an even more integral part of marketing and positioning), and mass communication/public relation skills. Walsh *et al.* (1988) in the context of manufacturing, state that design is a crucial factor in international competitiveness. The description is equally relevant to today's hotel industry. Design concerns choices and decisions that determine the quality and value of products. As Walsh *et al.* note, there is often an overlap in the definitions of design, quality and value, one distinction being that design is what the supplier 'puts in' whilst quality and value is what the customer perceives in, and obtains from products. The critical point here is that the end user cannot be disassociated from any design project.

Walsh *et al.* (1988: 202–3) examined the role of design in the competitiveness of manufacturing companies and found that quality or 'non price' factors were more significant than price in establishing the internal competitiveness of firms. They found that good design communicated quality and enhanced value for money and customer demand. They saw commercial success as contingent upon 'a whole chain of causation, design-quality-value for money', but noted that links in the chain themselves depended on other elements like management skills; coordinating design activities with other tasks in the company, particularly marketing, manufacturing and finance; and ensuring the provision of comprehensive design briefs. The importance of corporate strategy to design excellence, satisfaction of customers, meeting financial goals, and a systems approach to planning were all stressed. Walsh *et al.* (1988: 215) conclude that 'investment of resources in design could be a key factor in commercial success, but did not guarantee it. The qualifications were, that it also depended on what a company meant by good design and importantly, what it did to help the product sell'.

This chapter, which concerns current trends in hotel accommodation design, looks at design which can transcend fashions in architecture and tourism to generate lasting innovation. It briefly examines these issues in the lower and mid-share of the international hotel market, but also focuses on 'boutique' and 'specialist hotels' (defined within the chapter) part of the 'luxury market' where design has had a special and major impact; and on the corporate (chain) hotel operating in the luxury market. The principle concern of the chapter is to evaluate how pervasive design has become in international hotels, and how, attendant on this, hotels in the UK have exploited three sets of features in the luxury hotel sector in particular, in order to enhance design. These are:

- symbolism – particularly the use of symbolism as an emotional marketing tool offering a subtle language of persuasion (employed by companies like Mandarin Oriental; Rosewood; Four Seasons; Ritz Carlton and others, even in sales videos);
- the (perceived) convergence of business and leisure requirements of consumers; and
- the deployment of advanced technology.

A short case study of The Savoy Group's £72 million investment in design and refurbishment gives a potted account of a typically large refurbishment programme. The chapter concludes with a view of likely future trends.

The chapter draws on primary research in the form of interviews and a questionnaire survey conducted as part of a wider project into design parameters. Both interviews and the survey were directed towards a variety of personnel involved in hotel design including managing directors of groups; general managers; senior executive managers; architects; design managers and interior designers. In addition, over a period of nine months the author spent the equivalent of six weeks in international hotels which were, during this period, in the process of, completing the design or redesign process or had just completed it, and talked with management, staff and guests. Quotations employed for this research are signalled by the use of the term 'personal communication' (abbreviated to 'pc') when introduced for the first time in what follows. We begin with a brief examination of the spread of design in the hotel market.

THE LOWER AND MID-SHARE OF THE INTERNATIONAL HOTEL MARKET

There is worldwide demand for budget hotels, where cost reductions are crucial to charging reduced room rates. Many hoteliers at this level feel that they cannot therefore afford costly designers, and design in any case tends unusually to be standardized and planned to accommodate families. In budget hotels the guest rooms represent c.85 per cent of the total build area of the hotel. In the middle tier, more hotel and resort owners work with professional architects and designers to maximize their marketing thrust, and in many, hotel room charges can fluctuate with the days of the week or season of the year.

In the short term, many hotel owners and investors are currently seeking for ways to update the look of their hotels without major investment and they thus often keep a weather eye on the luxury market, making the most of what is achievable on their budgets. However, if they invest in interior decoration as opposed to quality interior design, it can only accelerate renovation schedules. Gimmickry and cheap or ill-conceived and ill-planned features tend to date and/or wear rapidly. After all, interior design is the only integral aspect of hotel planning which is visual, tactile and possesses the ability to be experienced by the guest. It is therefore important for investors and hoteliers to have architects, interior designers and signature designers who understand the nature of hotels and who can specialize in this area.

This is not to say that the four and five star market has it all their own way, for the middle tier has responded to the challenge in ways that have virtually reinvented this market segment. For example, Four Points by ITT Sheraton, Jury's Hotels and others are marketing design and technology to raise their market share, and with a strong mid-tier demand around the world this should ensure rapid return on capital expenditure for these new design-led concepts. Some mid-tier hoteliers may be willing however to spend more on guest rooms, meeting facilities, public and other areas to make them as well-equipped as possible in order to save on labour costs. New concepts in the mid-tier, all suite and economy sectors, and concepts such as combined hotel/timeshare properties, will make up a high proportion of the design, redesign and interior decoration work available well into the 21st century.

BOUTIQUE HOTELS

The term 'boutique hotel' was coined by the US hotelier Steve Rubell, but the cult of exclusivity in boutique hotels was quickly built around properties like Anouska Hempel's Blakes Hotel in London's Chelsea, the Hempel in Bayswater, London, owned by a Japanese investment company, the Royalton in New York owned by Ian Schrager, the Montalembert in Paris and many others. This relatively new and non-formulaic concept set out to provide opportunities for differing types of customer experience and introduced laser-like targeting of particular groups. The vocabulary of the 'fashionable' or 'boutique hotel' has in many ways become a social badge with a composite of dimensions, including a range of tactical promotional techniques, which include the 'hotel-as lifestyle' product, allowing the guest to buy into and add layers of microfeeling to their stay in a hotel. Well designed boutique hotels offering 'chain similar' facilities can often provide individual style and there are now sophisticated networks of boutique and specialist hotels giving their larger rivals a run for their money. Some of these boutique hotels employ marketing consortiums like Design Hotels International and Art o'tels, each hotel exhibiting the complete work of an important artist (i.e. the hotel as gallery). Even Hyatt, in an attempt to de-brand has opened a small boutique style hotel, 'The Hyatt Regency Paris Madeleine', offering 81 rooms and nine suites with business facilities. Stephen Rushmore (1997: 16) President and

Founder of HVS International reckons that 'the top hotels offer unparalleled attributes and that brand affiliation isn't necessary for hotels whose provision is superior in terms of product and service'. Chic small hotels in crowded markets can exploit demand if they focus on customer profile, for example Ken McCulloch's One Devonshire Gardens in Glasgow, Scotland. Niche-market hotels which promote their uniqueness can be cost effective by disposing of costly non-essentials, to concentrate on budget and operational expertise, and their presentation is often the secret of their competitive advantage.

SPECIALIST HOTELS

The principal difference between boutique and specialist hotels is that the latter properties are the key concept of their owner. Boutique hotels are unequivocally focused on distinctive interior design and contemporary works of art. They tend to be small (although a number sometimes have up to 80 rooms) and can be privately owned or part of modest chain groups. The specialist hotel genre provides unique, more one-off high design properties which are invariably non-corporate. Both are aimed at connoisseurs of contemporary design and style, and generally involve themselves in target group segmentation, where design has acquired a vital role in defining and distinguishing hotels in contexts of global competition, commercial value and individualization and diversification.

A lucrative market has emerged centred around escapist environments where the building only plays one part, albeit an important part. Specialist hotels currently avoid the ennui of soulless functionality and bed-in-a-box hotels. Culture informs us that a hotel must look like a hotel and most of us buy into this value system when in fact there could be much more cross-fertilization and room for individuality. This trend for individuality promises to bring higher style and nonconformist design elements into hotel rooms of the future, principally because hoteliers look for any advantage to help their properties get noticed in crowded markets. Desire to advance and stimulate new design are two aspects of trends which are making hotel construction the paradigmatic task it was in the *belle époque* (1885–1914).

Specialist provision provides one-off-hotels which are non-corporate. They are usually niche-market properties providing non-standard solutions to lodging for business and leisure travellers. The properties tend to be aspirational and constructed by entrepreneurial types, trend setters who can seize the imagery of the icon and utilize symbolism and metaphor. They create room for a whole range of feeling and guests should arrive with a lack of preconception and constraint for they may encounter individuality, simple elegance, adventure, visual stimulation, theatricality, explosive dramatic experience, and leave with a strong and positive memory of that experience. On the negative side, guests can also experience design indulgence or pretension, monastic sterility cloaked as minimalism, poorly integrated features, contemporary design that denies familiarity, alienating guests' seeking functionality with echoes of home comforts, and gimmickry and over-fashionable features.

Signature designers tend to be used for these properties. They provide a creative function by distilling the client's brief, but there also needs to be a distinctive partnership between the management and service of the hotel. First visits tend to be out of curiosity, and many specialist hotels fail to please because strategies in designing the experience have not been sufficiently developed. However another obstacle to incompletely realized design often stems from the pressure to save money by revising standards. Compounding the problem can be clients who do not value quality or professional design and who appear unable to buy into the use, by specialist hotels, of semantics and symbolism.

LUXURY CHAIN HOTELS

Some guests may never have the opportunity to experience the full range of luxury and design in a given hotel, for in many cases it is hidden away on executive floors, in penthouse suites or in separate wings of the building. Luc Vaichäre and Didier Lefort (cited in MacInnes 1996: 103), both international hoteliers, contend that 'luxury is basically communicated by an idea and not simply through the addition of numerous aesthetic elements'. Luxury however, is subjective and some individuals view hotels in terms of quality and quantity of services rather than an architectural success story, others however actively pursue ostentation. Table 13.2 shows a range of services that could well be expected from properties in the 'chain' luxury market.

Upscale hotels are likely to make heavier investment in infrastructural items and better quality goods. Higher standards at competitive rates at all levels are now demanded, and a variety of experience to satisfy what should be considered to be a captive audience provided. Atesh Chandra, Vice President Administration, The Breakers Hotel and Resort Palm Beach, Florida (a five star five diamond beach front property), thinks that large five star and deluxe hotels need places to explore and a future trend could well be in the hotel retail sector with dual or multi-function public spaces (pc).

Table 13.2 Designing hotel services in the luxury market

24 hour room service	Non-smoking rooms
24 hour concierge	Dual line telephones
Remote control TV, cable & in-room movies	Satellite
Bill viewing systems on TV	ISDN Line
Voice mail	US/UK modem points
Bedside panel operating full lighting control	Electronic DND signs
CD Player/complimentary loan of CDs	Printers on request
VCR or complimentary loan service	Quality room amenities
Jogging/walking map	Personal in-room safe
Phone jacks in room are computer compatible	Valet parking
In room fax/designated number	Secretarial services
Limousine, car rental	Airline reservations on request
Minibar	Executive/business/club floors
Express check-out	Bathrobes
Current US and European publications	Personalized shopping itineraries
Laundry dry cleaning and pressing service	Fitness room/gym
Foreign exchange	Shoe cleaning service
Essentials shop, other shopping opportunities	Theatre tickets etc. via concierge
Twice daily maid service	Evening turndown service
Massage, health and beauty treatments	Hairdryer

Many also have private rooms and intimate spaces for tycoons and business people, as in for example The Peninsula Hotel, Hong Kong or The Willard Hotel in Washington. In essence, hoteliers and designers need to completely understand each other's problems and approaches, so that the end product is able to satisfy their needs, and those of their clients, for both require to understand the operational function of each and every area requiring design input. George Fong, Vice President, Design and Construction, for Rosewood Hotels and Resorts when asked if hotel design and interior design like fashion, directed culture, or reflected it, stated 'Our hotels are designed to be timeless, rather than trendy because we cater to the affluent and sophisticated world traveller rather than a specific section of the market'. When asked what he looked for from a designer Mr Fong stated that 'a designer should always understand the needs of the guest first, nothing is more important to the success of a hotel than the satisfaction of the guests. Some of the key elements in the designers' profile are flexibility, creativity, team work, budget awareness, and the capability to translate vision to reality' (pc).

In the five star and deluxe category, the trend is toward room bays in a standard range of 31 square metres or more. Robert Riley Managing Director of Mandarin Oriental Hotels is finding that guests who patronize five star and deluxe hotels are demanding more spacious rooms. Mandarin's standard is typically 45 square metres. Rather than using modular furniture, a popular choice in the 1970s, Mandarin attempts to create a more residential feel to their rooms by using an eclectic selection of furniture of a kind and quality found in the discerning client's home (pc). Kenzo Watanabe, Senior Executive Director of Kanko Kikaku Sekkeisha, Architects and Designers, states that 40 square metres is becoming the norm in guest room sizes of upper middle-class hotels and has even worked on rooms for deluxe hotels of 50 and 60 square metres (pc). George Fong states that at Rosewood they are designing their hotels to provide large guest rooms from 500 square feet and up, and future bathrooms of 120 square feet and beyond.

Despite the emphasis placed on design in this sector, such emphases vary. For example, Robert Riley, Managing Director of Mandarin Oriental Hotels reported considerable reliance on the expertise of the group's interior design team. In the past they used Hirsch Bedner Associates for major hotel renovations, and Tony Chi (New York) for several food and beverage concepts. Employing and remunerating these consultants, not to mention implementing their changes reflects the Mandarin view that their guest profile demands a sophisticated, quality design. George Fong of Rosewood was more cautious, noting that: 'The design element is only part of the success of our hotels. No matter how beautiful and unique a hotel is, if the element of service is not extended to guests, there will always be dissatisfaction'. John Elliott, Managing Director, Wimberly Allison Tong and Goo Inc, Architects and Planners, London, states that:

> provided one is fully familiar with the needs of the owner and operator, that are profit driven, it is possible for the creative designers to subtly alter the design, practicality and service equation to make something new, different *and* enduring by being one creative step ahead.

CONTINUITIES WITHIN THE LUXURY MARKET

Boutique and specialist hotels are examples of usually fairly small 'luxury' hotels. Most hotels in the luxury sector have developed or are developing their own language of design offering exclusivity teamed with a non-formulaic approach, many also precisely target particular market groups and segments, namely high-end business and banking personnel, individuals from the worlds of theatre, fashion, music, the arts, publishing, design, television and film, as well as the monied (old and new) and aspirational users.

As noted earlier, design trends in the luxury sector are characterized by three principal sets of factors. First is the role that symbolism plays in all luxury hotels, where guests buy into new worlds of experience, bound up with status and in some cases escapism and fantasy. Second, is a perceived convergence in market trends, in particular between business and leisure use in the sector. Currently many hoteliers in the luxury market believe there to be no essential differences between the requirements of these two segments. The third area is the deployment of technology, boutique and specialist hotels invest across the property, whereas larger luxury hotels may do this but invest mainly and quite heavily in executive or club floors or wings, offering the further exclusivity of separate check-in, usually on the floors that guests will be occupying. There is also a trend towards offering separate lounges and in some cases dining or meeting facilities; separate concierge; and separate business centres, virtually offering a hotel within a hotel.

Boutique and specialist hotels do not appear to need to market themselves in exactly the same way as large 'chain' luxury hotels, the best of which create a genuine warmth which allows the guest to access the semiotics of exclusivity. The smaller properties tend to be marketed by the guests themselves through word of mouth. They also often have the added caché of being likely to generate a lot of publicity in design and lifestyle magazines. Guests would appear to subliminally accept the designer and hoteliers proficiency in manipulating the semiotics of exclusivity, fashion, design and improved technology reflecting the élitist nature of the boutique/specialist sub-sectors. Whereas boutique and specialist hotels target niche markets, larger luxury 'chain' hotels need a broader spread of careful marketing primarily because of their larger size and a commercial need to operate in a range of different markets at the one time, and not simply as business hotels during the week and leisure operators at the weekend. The whole idea of luxury is also very subjective in that one hotel company's deluxe or luxury rooms would be another's standard or superior. Luxury hotels also tend to invest in larger room bays, and have more places to explore, for example shopping malls, and multi-function public spaces.

Hotels as subjective symbolism: offering a language of persuasion

Philippe Stark one time fashion designer for 'Pierre Cardin' furniture, now an international product and interior designer (quoted in MacInnes, 1996a: 108–9) admires Asia because as he states, 'people know how to work with symbol. They have more semantics than us'. Stark has stated 'I work with semantics and symbol and around enjoyment'. What hotel guests purchase by their careful selection of property and product act as signifiers, demonstrating to others and themselves what kind of people they are, and by choice they enter a world where they adopt and are imbued with the perceived values of the hotel, which can also be discerned as a sign of an individual's sensitivity, a kind of self portrait, but also of the hotel's proficiency in effortlessly manipulating the semiotics of exclusivity, fashion, design and improved technology.

Human communication depends on the symbolism of language and the language of fashion and design provides a rich weave of symbolic carriers. Most hotels of the upmarket variety, which place great emphasis on design, can provide their guests with new worlds of experience bound up with personal status symbols and many have become theatres of life characterized by escapism and fantasy. Design becomes an identification signal that informs members of the international élite that they have come to the right place, but it is also an 'emotional marketing' tool.

Many specialist hotels offer a definite sense of place. Designing hotels with a sense of place is integral. Many individuals when travelling actively seek an authentic experience of the place being visited, and those working with value design which incorporates and celebrates elements that make the location unique, tend to be revisited. For instance, while Hyatt hotels and resorts around the world have designed over a dozen properties, no two look alike. Future hotels and resorts, as three of Wimberley Allison Tong and Goo's Directors in interview with Nicola Turner (1996: 110) stated, 'will hopefully support travellers aspirations for such transformative encounters as cultural enrichment, relaxation, education, rejuvenation and creative expression'.

Sarah Tomerlin Lee (cited in Bone 1997: 71) the prolific and internationally acclaimed designer who has worked on over 40 prominent hotels which have included the Doral Saturnia Spa in Miami, the New York Helmsley and the Willard Inter-Continental Hotel in Washington, has always attempted to ensure her work reflects a conceptual connection to the space she designs for. She feels that nowadays hotels are attempting to 'lasso the fantasies of tourists'. Gerald Allison of Wimberley Allison Tong and Goo (pc) states that 'travellers are looking for more than a place to stay, they are seeking something that will add to their knowledge and enjoyment'.

A convergence between business and leisure

Many of the world's top hoteliers believe there to be no fundamental distinction between the requirements of the business person and the tourist, although most believe that they should be able to choose distinct facilities. Convergence between these two is therefore a matter of sophisticated flexible dual provision. A major indicator of the belief in business and tourism convergence is in the effort of hoteliers in this sector to both blend and customize rooms. Leading hotel strategists are currently designing incentives to motivate both prospective business and leisure buyers. These will be experiences, not products, to the extent that some major hotel companies have started shedding corporate image in favour of offering a service customized approach to hotelkeeping rather than a product. Marriott, Stakis, Hilton, Hyatt and others are currently dabbling in de-chaining in an endeavour to erase the characterless, standardized international look for which they were famed (Manser, 1997: 9–12). George Fong thinks that 'hotels have become more and more important in the business world where travellers spend a lot of their time. Most, if not all business travellers stay at hotels which provide them with three key elements: good service, convenient location and value for money. On average the business traveller spends more time in the bathroom than in the bedroom except for sleeping and expect separate showers, bright lighting, generous vanity space, and a spacious open area' (see Box 13.1).

Leisure travellers in the luxury market are more inclined to seek a powerful sense of place. They tend to pursue local culture and anticipate that the encounter will carry through into the hotel design and interior design. Business travellers, however, are more concerned with how a hotel caters to their business needs. Of importance are: office style furniture with a spacious desk and storage space for stationery supplies; neat orderly well lit rooms with the latest in technology including print, copy and fax

---

Box 13.1:   Trends in guest bathrooms

Upgrading guest bathrooms will be a major issue in conversions especially in five star and deluxe hotels. Robert Riley Managing Director of Mandarin Oriental states that 'the bathroom is expected to have four fixtures, bath, separate shower, vanity and toilet, and if possible a separate dressing area' (pc). The next generation hotel bathroom will be expected to have more counter space; better quality flooring with counter surfaces such as marble, granite or Corian; more mirrors, including makeup mirrors; more residential taps and fixtures. New technology will be expected to upgrade hackneyed guest bathrooms into cosseting mini-spas. Whirlpool tubs are expected to be fairly standard. Larger tiling is also likely to have a more contemporary appeal. Bathrooms are getting larger, and some, as Robert Riley reported, are allowing for a dressing area, complete with a walk in closet and vanity unit. Good lighting and mirrors will be *de rigueur*. The separate tub and shower will become standard, even in the four star market. The next generation of bathtubs may even be capable of surrounding guests with softly coloured light that can be changed to fit their mood. Instead of pulse or spray options, shower heads will offer guests choices ranging from gentle mists to a vigorous thalasso-massage. Computerized shower heads could well be programmed in future to accommodate guests of varying heights. Individuals not wishing to get their hair wet will be able to programme the unit to shower them just from the shoulders down, and 'smart' units will be able to remember each guest's preference. Sound systems will also be capable of enhancing the relaxing atmosphere, and there is even the possibility of aromatherapy systems to set the right mood, and fibre optics already installed in some deluxe hotels will be used in the taps and shower heads to illuminate water cascades.

---

capability for producing presentation quality documents from the room, surge protection for PCs, and modem and printer cables. Robert Riley, Managing Director of Mandarin Oriental feels that in terms of the design of the room, the business traveller demands a spacious work area in the room. If possible, the room should be designed with a work area suitable for receiving clients, but this will usually only be possible in a suite arrangement. Of course plug points, telephone jacks and good lighting need to be easily accessible from the desk, especially for users of lap-top computers.

George Riley of Mandarin Oriental recognizes that to some degree the days of big dinners and entertaining clients in the bar until late into the night have just about ceased to exist although there are global variations. Both leisure and business travellers will frequently dine in hotel restaurants in Asia. In the US and Europe, the profit margins are so small in hotel restaurants that they are normally limited to two outlets. He recognizes that people are living healthier lives and that opportunities have arisen to generate additional revenues by creating health clubs and spa facilities where pampering treatments such as massage, facials, reflexology and aromatherapy are offered.

Business and leisure travel are increasing, and more individuals are now combining both. Wimberley Allison Tong and Goo expect, however, that the leisure market will grow rapidly, at least through the remainder of the century. They see this reflected in the design and operations of hotels, with business and convention hotels adding recreational and family-oriented amenities, and resorts adding conference and meeting facilities. John Elliott, Managing Director, Wimberly Allison Tong and Goo Inc. Architects and Planners, London, reckons that the growth market in leisure and business tourism varies from place to place, but sees the leisure industry growing broadly at 15 per cent per annum. He also believes that new resorts are needed to respond to new economies; that new city hotels have responded to growth in business travel; and that there is a growing blurring of the distinctions between resort and business hotels (for example Claridge's in London's Mayfair district is an example of a new (sic), 100 year-old hotel whose clientele use it for business and as a city centre resort with shopping and culture as the resort facilities) (pc).

Technological investment in hotels

Doren and Blackman (1993: 26) report a staggering increase in utilization of hotel technology over the decade, although they argue that hoteliers do not utilize technology to its fullest advantage. This has markedly changed in the luxury market to the extent that hoteliers who cannot as yet afford fully integrated systems are at least planning or wiring for it in their redesign of premises. George Fong Corporate VP Engineering for Rosewood Hotels and Resorts, highlighted the role played by new technologies in the redesign/refurbishment programmes for their hotels:

> New technologies play a significant part in the design of our new projects. The Lanesborough in London became the first hotel in Europe to have a fully integrated information technology system with six different computer systems interfacing with each other. We use new technologies to enhance the guest experience and to allow the hotel staff to provide better and friendlier service.

John Elliott, Director of Wimberley Allison Tong and Goo, the architects and lead consultants for recent renovations of Claridge's hotel in London, was of a similar view. He noted that:

> in order to be successful, hotels must function as efficient 'factories'. Claridge's has become one of the most efficient 'factories' in the world as a result of our recent refurbishment. Savings on energy, BMS, waste management, man hours and space creates more from less. The control of the design and construction process is now utterly dependent upon computer software and IT communication. Technology creates the time and money to ensure that customer service is the basis of every first class hotel.

In larger properties energy management systems will be important and centralized energy management systems will be designed to further dramatically cut costs (Hensdill, 1997: 81).

An architectural study of the hotel industry conducted by Katherine MacInnes (1996: 102–3) demonstrated a trend in luxury and fantasy, which was linked with the desire by guests to experience the latest technology. MacInnes in her study also touched upon the dwindling differences between the demands of international executives and holiday makers outlined earlier in this chapter. In the UK, Fran Johnson reporting for the *Caterer and Hotelkeeper* (1997: 78–9) believes technology is playing a significant role in hotel bedrooms but, noted that the same technology was not available below the mid-market.

Future common place technologies could quite possibly involve card locks evolved to the extent that they are able to read the guest's hand or thumbprint. It may even be possible that in recognizing the guest's need for safety and security, cameras could scan guest room corridors and that some guests might be able to access this video system to view who is at the door. Soundproof rooms or rooms with white-noise generators, combating corridor and elevator noise are also no longer science fiction but science fact. A number of revolutionary features are in the pipeline, for example, smart paint is already being tested which will adjust the colour of guests' room walls. Smart glass, reacting like sunglasses will be able to adjust automatically to light levels in the room. It will be introduced to serve the dual purpose of reducing glare and to lessen sun damage and fading of interior design fabrics.

The more technology on display in the rooms, the more the design of the room is impacted. The craze for thematic and atmospheric design will most likely drift in and out of fashion, but the job of procuring materials, textures, lighting and effective hidden technologies will be much more important.

CASE STUDY: THE SAVOY GROUP

The Savoy Group includes five UK properties: The Berkeley, The Connaught, Claridge's, The Savoy and The Lygon Arms. In 1997 it completed a major redesign and refurbishment of its hotels. In undertaking this task the maxim of the Group's Managing Director, Ramón Pajares, was simple: 'respecting the past and understanding the future'. He assembled a formidable team of British designers and after a spend of £72 million the results are impressive. The commissioning of designers who could provide both technical and design excellence and with whom the Group could build a relationship was paramount to achieving a cohesive and financially viable end product. The redesign had to be sensitive to different cultures and different markets. Failure to meet guest expectations could easily present opportunities for competitors, as hotels in the luxury market have little margin for aesthetic design error (Schmid, 1990: 8–11).

At the close of the restoration programme the hotels had used:

- 20 miles or 32km of carpet;
- 200,000 litres of paint;
- 150,000 square metres of plaster work;
- 44,000 metres of restored cornicing;
- 10,000 square metres of curtain fabric;
- 4 metric tons of nails and screws;
- 200,000 metres of pipes/plumbing;
- 10,000 metres of new air conditioning ducts;
- 2,000 new telephones; and
- 120,000 metres of wire.

Success of the project lay in a fusion of preservation, regeneration and rebirth, and the best of the past has been fused with an innovative dynamic approach to both the present and the future. Individual unit managers understood the challenge to provide service that would respond to new demands yet cater sensitively to existing and long-term clients as thoughtfully as ever (a challenge for all hotels facing such major renewal). The renovation was an intermix of cosmetic renovation, minor and major property renovation and customer-driven renovation.

The Savoy Group Design Manager, Lesley Knight, described her role as involving the management of all interior design projects including the brief, monitoring, design development, the reviewing of all interior design drawings and specifications, factory inspections and ensuring that minimum standards were upheld. She was also involved with the design of smaller projects within the Group which could be undertaken without the involvement of a project team (pc). The Savoy Group used nine individual designers to give each room in each hotel a soul and individuality. The Savoy Group relies heavily on the design element and foregrounds fashion, design and exclusivity in deliberate and distinctive ways to create and reinforce the conception of desired ambience. The Group used prominent interior designers like Tessa Kennedy, who worked on the Berkeley and Claridge's hotels; David Linley and Nina Campbell; Veere Grenney who worked on Claridge's and The Savoy; Lynne Hunt of Hunt, Hamilton, Zuch, who worked on Claridge's executive deluxe bedrooms and standard singles, a guest lift, the Olympus suite health club and the Pavilion and Wellington suite at The Berkeley (Lynne also worked on numerous bedrooms at The Savoy); John Stefanidis who worked on 40 bedrooms at Claridge's and bedrooms on the third and fourth floors at The Berkeley; and Richmond International, specialists in hotel design who worked on The Berkeley, Claridge's and The Savoy Hotel.

Knight considers the five most important elements in hotel design and redesign to be:

(1) a reflection of the luxury and quality demanded by their guests;
(2) fitness for purpose;
(3) longevity of design;
(4) longevity of fabrics and materials; and
(5) individuality of design.

Refurbishment for the Savoy Group takes place as required, but generally major refurbishment is every 5–7 years. The time-span for the repayment of refurbishment cost is considered confidential information, but in hotels with high occupancy this can be paid back fairly speedily. When asked what she looked for in a designer, Knight responded by saying 'I look for loyalty, discretion and confidentiality. An understanding of our requirements, ability to follow up projects, creativity and a perception of value'.

The difference designers made to The Savoy Group were in terms of their individuality and creativity. Knight feels that design is not just a commercial activity but a cultural one, i.e. concerned not simply with consumerist issues of luxury life-style and fashion, but with designing for social need and public good. She views the current trend as one for style with simplicity without loss of comfort, but feels that Savoy Group hotels encompass more than the furnishing of accommodation and provision of services: 'They have an aesthetic, sensory dimension which can be evaluated by management, staff and guests in terms of a holistic experience, beautiful surroundings, service and cache'. Knight believes that what separates the Savoy Group from its competitors is: a leading brand name; 100 years of experience in providing high level service; individuality of design; provision of up-to-the minute technological facilities; and an excellent reputation worldwide.

CONCLUSIONS: FUTURE TRENDS

In design terms, the luxury hotel market is likely to continue to become more heterogeneous. Investment in hotel projects is huge, as was seen in Table 13.1, and financial realism will be a likely companion of all future developments, as for example, hotel bedrooms alone are a highly perishable product and today's innovation is tomorrow's standard. Architects and designers have also improved their understanding of how space is utilized, by whom, and in what contexts. Most of the leading hotel chains are looking at ways to refurbish traditional guest facilities to meet today's fluid market demands. This is resulting in new rooms being less formulaic in design. Hotels are likely to become more individualistic and, as previously stated, individual properties within companies will no longer function alike. Product differentiation will be forefronted and design will be influential in cultivating identity for emerging brands. One constraint in refurbishment is the question of whether refurbishing should take place as required (this tends to be more 'soft' (furnishing) refurbishment) or on a rolling plan.

Many leading hotel companies including Le Meridien, Peninsula, Mandarin Oriental, Hilton, Hyatt, Sheraton, and The Savoy Group refurbish on a rolling plan. Rosewood Hotels and Resorts and Mandarin Oriental constantly refurbish their hotels, each property has a yearly capital budget for ongoing renovations. They also undergo major renovations which include redesign so as to seek to keep ahead of competition as well as attempting to provide guests with a unique experience and the improvements they demand.

Design will continue to support how a guest room will be used. In the immediate future many redesigned rooms will by necessity have to be constructed around existing hotel spaces, and highly interchangeable new design components will be inevitable to accommodate essential amenities without constricting available space. Renovations will be calculated to extend a hotel's market base, by incorporating for example, business components to a resort hotel or additional diversionary aspects to a city centre guest room. The Chicago-based Hyatt Hotels Corporation, which is highly individualistic and a pioneer of distinctive and dramatic design, has already carefully analysed alternatives for customizing the function of its guest rooms and bathrooms.

As hinted at earlier, resort hotels may well be at the forefront of architecture and design in the 21st century. Leisure rooms of the future will be required to meet the needs of non-traditional families requiring more privacy. As individuals live longer it is quite feasible that more grandparents will travel with families and children, that there will be different types of family unit, and more single parents. Leisure hotel rooms will also have to have the basics of business needs. Instead of a desk there could be a table and more comfortable chairs, large enough for in-room dining but flexible so as to act as office facilities. Like city centre hotels, resort rooms will be pressured to become more energy efficient. Wimberley, Allison, Tong and Goo's Gerald Allison, cited in *Interior Design* (Anon., 1996: 162), foresees 'an environmental air conditioning system that will use heat sensors to sense and maintain pre-selected body temperature and certain humidity levels'. Allison reckons that 'Resort development may move away from ocean front and golfing venues and into less well trammelled areas, to, feasibly, the rain forests, mountain ranges and even the Arctic'. Adventure tourism sites like these will also have to be very much more environmentally sensitive.

It can be argued that trends in international hotel accommodation design affect construction and interior costs, and so more financially careful businesses are conceivably less likely to commission designs offering a full range of amenities. In addition, international hotel companies experiencing occupancy levels in excess of 90 per cent in boom periods find it hard to free rooms for essential refurbishment. This can cause a dilemma, for with deteriorating stock requiring redesign the hotelier may have to pay for refurbishment in less profitable times in the future. The rising cost of design, redesign and interior design is forcing many hotels to find ways to stabilize or reduce this impact. It can also be seen that technological innovation, changes in lifestyle, inclination toward experiences as opposed to products, towards designing hotels that satisfy a variety of markets and cost controls are major factors driving hotel design trends. A better philosophy for hotels to adopt is one of cost containment as opposed to cost cutting, for if costs are cut at the expense of quality and service, hoteliers can anticipate repercussions. Design at corporate level is often perceived as a strategic tool, through which technical ability is transferred into competitive advantage by emphasizing customer needs (Olins, 1986: 52–5). Pannell Kerr Forster Associates (1993) recognized that other emotive factors include fashion, image and style. Luc Vaichäre and Didier Lafort saw luxury communicated through the idea and not simply through addition of design elements. Design, redesign and interior design will be an even more integral part of marketing and positioning, for today, in terms of their design and range of services, hotels are trying to lasso the fantasies of business people and tourists. Josef Ransley a UK designer (cited in *Interior*, Anon., 1996a: 72), believes that current design trends stem from hoteliers' quest for greater individuality. He states: 'the industry has become so competitive, hoteliers realise they have to offer customers something different so they are going for contemporary classics that offer theatre and entertainment'.

Discriminating hotel guests tend to desire something that will give pleasure. They want a better or equal quality of life to that which they get in their own home, and for others the hotel experience may be the only time they will enjoy the same treatment as the wealthy. The quality and value that the customer perceives is all important. As Walsh *et al.* found in their study, good design communicates quality, value for money and demand, but all importantly it is what hotels do to help the product sell that makes the difference and how that is communicated to them is crucial. The specialist and boutique hotel markets have seized (as shown earlier) on the imagery of the icon and utilize symbol and metaphor, and their marketing offers a rich language of persuasion. Shrewd niche marketing has brought dividends and could easily be applied to the deluxe and four to five star market.

REFERENCES AND FURTHER READING

Anon. (1996) 'The Full-Service Business Room of the Future', *Interior Design*, June, 162.
Anon. (1996a) 'Leading Hotel Designers Register a Change of Direction', *Interior*, **4**, 72.
Bone, E. (1997) 'Without Reservations', *Metropolis: Architecture, Design and Travel*, July/August, 71.
Collins Concise Dictionary (1989) London and Glasgow.
Doren, K. and Blackman, D. (1993) 'Communication Systems and Connectivity for the Intelligent Bedroom of the Future', *International Journal of Contemporary Hospitality Management*, **5**(2), 25–6.
Elliott, J. and Johns, N. (1993) 'The Influence of International Tourism Trends on the Design of Leisure Resorts', *International Journal of Contemporary Hospitality Management*, **5**(2), 6–9.
Hart, S.J. and Service, L.M. (1988) 'The Effects of Managerial Attitudes to Design on Company Performance', *Journal of Marketing Management*, **4**(2), 217–29.
Hensdill, C. (1997) 'Automated Energy Management' *Hotels*, **8**, 81.
Johnson, F. (1997) 'Bedroom desires', *Caterer and Hotelkeeper*, 20 November, 78–9.
MacInnes, K. (1996) 'The Entertainment Business: Hotels into the 21st Century', *World Architecture*, **51**, 102–3.
MacInnes, K. (1996a) 'Mutual Dependence', *World Architecture*, **51**, 108–9.

Manser, J. (1997) 'Chuck out the Chintz', *Design Week*, July, 9–12.

Olins, W. (1986) 'The Strategy of Design', *Management Today*, May, 52–5.

Pannell Kerr Forster Associates (UK) (1993) 'Factors Influencing the Design of Hotels', *International Journal of Contemporary Hospitality Management*, **5**(2), 10–12.

Prince, N.A. (1986) 'The challenges of contemporary hotel design', in Skyme, R. (ed.) *Hotel Specification International, A Guide to Hotel Design and Interiors*, New York and Tunbridge Wells: Pennington Press.

Rushmore, S. (1997) 'First Person', *Hospitality Industry International*, **18**, 16.

Schmid, A.M. (1990) *International Hotel Redesign*, New York: PBC International, 8–11.

Turner, N. (1996) 'Fast Forward', *World Architecture*, **51**, 110–11.

Walsh, V., Roy, R. and Bruce, M. (1988) 'Competitive by Design', *Journal of Marketing Management*, **4**(2), 201–6.

Human resource management in hotel accommodation services

14

Dennis P. Nickson

The Hotel and Catering International Management Association's (HCIMA) inaugural presidential conference, held in April 1997, took as its title 'The Human Asset – Use it or Lose it' and this notion appositely captures the key issue facing many hotels in relation to how they manage people. The warnings of the then HCIMA president, Diane Miller, that the industry was 'haemorrhaging' talented staff – whilst paradoxically at the same time suffering chronic skills shortages in areas such as housekeeping and reception – reflected the fact that the hospitality industry continues to be seen and, indeed, experienced by many staff as offering an unsatisfactory employment experience. Support for this view is also supplied by the Institute of Personnel and Development's (IPD) 1997 survey of labour turnover which found that the hotel and leisure industry had the highest turnover rate (34.56 per cent) of over 20 industrial sectors. Indeed, this may be something of an understatement, with Dr Anne Walker, the then director of the Hospitality Training Foundation (HTF), suggesting a truer figure may be nearer 60 per cent, a figure that costs the industry £4 billion a year, or 10 per cent of annual turnover, as well as 339,000 people leaving the industry (HCIMA, 1998).

Thus, despite the rhetoric of hotel employers that people are the industry's most important asset, many remain unconvinced that such a view is borne out by evidence and that whilst these conditions prevail the industry will in fact continue to lose their human assets (Lucas, 1996; Price, 1994; Wood, 1997). Clearly then, organizations and managers in the hotel industry face real challenges in recruiting, selecting, developing and maintaining a committed, competent, well-managed, and well-motivated workforce which is focused on offering a high quality service to the increasingly demanding and discerning customer. This chapter will seek to address some of the key human resource issues that have to be tackled in order that organizations can maintain such an environment. To do so it will critically review some of the problems that lead many to characterize hospitality employment as generally unrewarding and unappealing, whilst also looking at some examples of human resource management (HRM) policies and practices which may offer cause for greater optimism in the way people are managed within the hotel industry. One final point is to add a caveat to the reader about the amount of detail a chapter of this nature can go into. This chapter necessarily offers a snapshot of some key HRM issues but the reader is directed elsewhere if they wish to consider a more extensive and detailed exposition of these issues (see for example Goldsmith et al., 1997; Riley, 1996).

THE ACCOMMODATION SECTOR – THE IMPORTANCE OF CONTEXT

To fully understand the nature of the HRM issues facing organizations offering accommodation services it is worth briefly describing some key features of the UK hotel industry and, relatedly, the main components of accommodation services.

The scope of the UK hotel industry

Knowles (1998) suggests that within the UK there are approximately 27,000 hotels which range from first class and luxury hotels providing extravagant full service on a 24 hour basis, to the more homely comforts of bed and breakfast establishments. Despite the growth in major chains who are increasingly visible within the market (e.g. Granada/Forte, Hilton, Holiday Inn, Queens Moat House, Whitbread/Marriott) the vast majority of businesses are small and medium sized enterprises (SMEs). For example, in the UK 81 per cent of hotels have fewer than 25 employees (Department of National Heritage, 1996) and the largest number of hotels are in the four to ten room category. As a consequence of the fragmented nature of the industry and the preponderance of small firms there are a number of difficulties in addressing HRM problems, such as relatively low pay and low levels of training activity. Indeed, this is exacerbated by the fact that many smaller hotels will not have a HRM/personnel department or manager. Thus much of the work that is reported on good practice is often in relation to larger organizations and less so to SMEs (Anastassova and Purcell, 1995; Price, 1994). There is, therefore, the potential for a dichotomous approach to the development of human resource capital between large and small organizations particularly in the sense that many smaller firms may not have the wherewithal to develop their employees or to sustain a progressive approach to HRM – although importantly, good practice does still exist within small hotels (Department of National Heritage, 1996). Moreover, a number of recent industry and government initiatives aimed at improving HRM practices are addressed explicitly at the small business sector and these will be discussed later in the chapter.

Rooms division – issues of organizational structure

A corollary of the above discussion on the nature of the UK hotel industry is the recognition that there is likely to be wide divergence between the organizational structures of large and small hotels. Generally, the larger hotel will have a departmentalized structure with rooms division consisting of a separate front office/reception area and a housekeeping section which will be responsible for the servicing of rooms. Such a division of labour is unlikely to exist within the small hotel and it is common for a small number of individuals to be responsible for all areas of the hotel and to spend their time between several tasks encompassing both back and front-of-house. Regardless, though, of whether the hotel is large or small, employees will require a range of technical and social skills and behavioural and attitudinal attributes to allow them to function effectively. To appreciate some of these skills and attributes we should note the range of rooms division functions typically found in a large hotel (Knowles, 1998: 147–8):

- front office/reception – the focal point of the hotel with the greatest amount of guest contact and usually consisting of a front desk, cashier, mail and information sections;

- reservations;
- telephone/switchboard;
- housekeeping – often the section with the largest number of personnel and responsible for ensuring the cleanliness and aesthetic appeal of any hotel property;
- uniformed services – an adjunct to the services provided by reception and a term used to describe collectively hotel employees providing front-of-house personal services for guests and likely to include concierge, parking attendants, door attendants, porters, limousine drivers and bell persons; and
- night audit.

A key feature of areas such as reception and uniformed services is the high level of guest contact and the concomitant need for high calibre employees to offer excellent service to the guest. However, even those areas that do not have direct contact with the guests on a regular basis are equally crucial to the success of a hotel in providing an important service that will influence the guests' perceptions of the quality of their stay. To appreciate, then, how all employees within the rooms division may be managed effectively, attention now turns to the key tenets of HRM, and the way these may be operationalized through policies and practices.

HRM – RHETORICS AND REALITIES

Of all the neologisms which have entered the managerial lexicon in recent years, human resource management has arguably had the most impact, at least at the level of rhetoric. The apparent (and appealing) simplicity of the oft-repeated statement 'our people are our most important asset' offers a seductive blueprint for people management which clearly signals to employees their central role within the organization and its quest to be successful. Increasingly, research adds credence to this claim with Hiltrop (1996) noting the growing evidence of 'best' practice HRM policies being associated with high (financial) performance in organizations. Similarly, West and Patterson (1998) report the results of a seven year research programme, albeit in medium-sized manufacturing firms, in the UK to conclusively argue that effective people management equals strong business performance and a healthier bottom-line profit. Indeed, within the intensively competitive market of the UK hotel industry these considerations would seem to have a particular resonance, such that the effective utilization of human resources is now suggested as being crucial in giving hotels a competitive advantage (Eccles and Durand, 1997). Moreover, due to its labour intensive nature the largest cost for a hotel – at around 30 per cent – is payroll and related expenses so, pragmatically, hotels should be seeking greater productivity and value for the large amount of money they invest in labour (Knowles, 1998).

However, despite this growing consensus of the importance of people management to organizational success, too often there is only a nominal commitment to the high ideals of HRM. As we have already noted many academics and practitioners remain deeply sceptical of the extent to which hospitality organizations have adopted such approaches, as exemplified by high labour turnover figures. Moreover, this scepticism has recently been given full voice by government. The Department of National Heritage (1996) report *Tourism: Competing with the Best, No. 3, People Working in Tourism and Hospitality* offered a bleak and damning picture of a self-perpetuating vicious circle of recruitment difficulties, shortages of skilled and qualified staff, relatively low pay, high staff turnover and a relatively unattractive image as an employing sector. On balance, then, the prognosis for HRM in the hotel sector seems poor. Equally, though, that should not mask examples of good practice and to appreciate these, and how organizations may take a more proactive and strategic approach to managing people, we can now move on and look at several key HRM processes.

HRM in the hotel sector

This section draws particularly on the work of Anastassova and Purcell (1995), Cheng and Brown (1998) and Nankevis and Debrah (1995). Respectively they report research on HRM in the Bulgarian hotel industry; the role of effective and strategic HRM practices in reducing labour turnover in Australian and Singaporean hotels (notwithstanding the long-standing debate between hospitality academics and practitioners on whether high labour turnover is necessarily deleterious to an organizations performance, see Wood (1997) for a review of this debate); and finally on HRM practices in a number of large chain-owned and independent Australian and Singaporean hotels. Based on this work we can identify several key areas of HRM, namely:

- recruitment and selection;
- orientation/induction and socialization;
- flexibility and job design;
- training and development;
- remuneration; and
- performance management/appraisal.

Each will now be discussed in turn.

Recruitment and selection

As Law and Wong (1997: 27) note 'Acquiring the best human resources is a significant challenge for the hospitality industry as the performance of a hotel depends very much on its employees'. Similarly Cheng and Brown (1998) propose that if an organization makes the correct selection decision it is likely to minimize labour turnover rates and this recognizes the increased need to select the 'right kind' of people who are likely to 'fit' into the organization and its culture. In order to do this the hotel will have to ensure it can attract the interest of quality staff and then employ a variety of selection techniques to fully assess the ability and suitability of individuals and whether they have the requisite skills or aptitudes to fill any particular position. This process is likely to be more successful if the hotel utilizes key HRM tools such as job analysis, a job description and a person specification. Taken together these allow the hotel, and any potential employees, to be sure of the functional aspects of the job and the tasks it will entail along with the attributes and characteristics of the 'ideal' person for the job. Indeed, it is the latter aspect that is increasingly suggested as being important in a variety of service-oriented jobs. Henkoff (1994), in recognizing that a number of unskilled or semi-skilled jobs within the rooms division department may not necessarily require high levels of education, experience or technical expertise advocates that decisions on a person's suitability should, in part, be on the basis of their personality, attitudes and character. Clearly, there will still be certain jobs were a level of technical expertise, skills or knowledge is a *sine qua non* for employment, but equally hotels may seek to assess whether potential employees have the resilience, resourcefulness, empathy and creativity to be considered as front-line workers in particular. Thus, Cheng and Brown (1998) note the increased use of what they term 'behavioural interviewing', which is a variant on the traditional selection interview and places increased emphasis on the behavioural aspects of potential employees and whether they have the 'right' sort of personality for the person-oriented hotel industry. The use of behavioural interviewing is suggested by Cheng and Brown as denoting a more strategic approach to selection, and is bracketed with other methods such as targeted selection, networking and encouraging a strong internal labour market – the process of filling supervisory positions and above from within existing hotel employees with the intent of providing career paths and clear development opportunities. These methods may then be complementary to more traditional methods identified by Cheng and Brown, such as advertising, walk-ins, selection interviews and reference checking.

Orientation/induction and socialization

Cheng and Brown (1998: 145) opine that 'Generally, induction is still regarded as exerting a significant and direct impact on the successful retention of employees'. In part this reflects the notion of the so-called 'induction crisis', that is the greater propensity of people to leave organizations in the first six weeks or so of employment. To ensure a smooth transition to organizational life hotels should see induction as a natural extension of the recruitment and selection function (Mullins, 1995). Thus induction is likely to have a twofold rationale. First, to acculturate and assimilate employees into the organization and its prevailing culture; and second, a more specific orientation within departments to familiarize new employees with daily operational procedures. Together these should allow new employees to be fully apprised of what the hotel is about and their role in the successful running of their section or department and the hotel generally. In terms of the detail of how this could be achieved, Mullins (1995: 196) suggests that an induction programme to the hotel could include the following aspects:

- the nature of the unit, its facilities and services and type of customers;
- requirements of the job and to whom responsible, and any subordinate staff;
- main terms and conditions of employment, including circumstances which could lead to dismissal, and disciplinary and grievance procedures;
- introduction to working colleagues, and the work and functions of other relevant departments;
- the management structure including responsibilities for the personnel function;
- the physical layout of the unit and the use of equipment;
- any special policies or procedures, and any house rules such as no eating or drinking, or no-smoking areas;
- fire, health and safety regulations;
- trade union membership, staff representation, consultation and communications, suggestion schemes;
- social and welfare facilities; and
- opportunities for training and personal development.

In relation to the more specific task of familiarizing new employees within new departments many hotels now seek to encourage a mentoring system, whereby an experienced employee helps the new employee to settle in and also takes responsibility for their initial training.

To exemplify some of these issues Henkoff (1994) reports on a model induction process used by Marriott hotels. All of Marriott's new employees (or associates as they are known in order to engender a greater sense of belonging to the company) attend an initial eight hour training session that would encompass many of the above issues and also includes a lunch served by long-standing employees of the hotel. Alongside this general introduction to the company the new employees are also assigned a mentor or 'buddy' within their departments, who is responsible for helping them through the next 90 days. New employees also undergo refresher courses after the first and second month in the hotel. Finally, after 90 days the hotel treats all employees to a banquet to celebrate their successful induction into the hotel.

Flexibility and job design

Guerrier and Lockwood (1989) suggest that a key concern in the labour intensive hotel industry is how flexibility may be used to improve productivity via the more efficient use of human resources. They outline a number of issues which hotels need to consider in their use of flexibility, and these are: job design; motivation; skills and abilities to do a job and the possible need for greater training; and the issue of scheduling and the need to match labour supply to fluctuations in customer demand, with such fluctuation being apparent on a daily, weekly, seasonal and annual basis. Thus it is the latter issue of scheduling which really provides the context in which the other issues may be played out. As Jones and Lockwood (1989: 59) suggest 'The scheduling problem, then, is to match as closely as possible the available supply of labour to the demands of the customer'. In response to this, hotels may adopt one or more of the following methods of flexibility:

- numerical flexibility – the adjustment of the number of workers or number of hours worked in response to demand, by utilizing temporary, part-time or casual workers;
- functional flexibility – seeks greater flexibility in the utilization of skills and movement between a variety of jobs and tasks at a similar level (horizontal flexibility) or different levels (vertical flexibility);
- pay flexibility – may be linked to functional flexibility to encourage the acquisition of more skills or rewarding scarce skills for multi-skilled or high performing staff; and
- distancing strategies – involving the contracting out of certain operations, for example the management of leisure facilities, laundry, in order to redistribute risk or uncertainty elsewhere.

The issue of flexibility within the hotel industry has generated an extensive literature (see Wood, 1997, for a review) and several key points can be extrapolated from this work. First, many authors note the widespread and long-standing use of, in particular, numerical flexibility. Many commentators regard this as 'inevitable' given the unpredictable and volatile nature of demand in the industry. Second, and relatedly, there is concern about the impact on quality of the use of numerically flexible labour. Walsh (1991) notes that part-time, temporary and casual workers will often be central to a hotel's operation and erroneously may be characterized and treated as 'peripheral' employees. Consequently hotels also need to induct, socialize, train and fairly reward such workers, thus recognizing their important role. Third, despite the fact that functional flexibility appears to offer increased job satisfaction and the attainment of greater skills, Riley (1992) notes that functional flexibility remains something of a

'Cinderella' idea and the creation of genuinely multi-skilled hotel operatives remains largely unrealized.

Whilst Riley remains rightly sceptical about the creation of a genuinely multi-skilled hotel operative who has no strong overall departmental orientation, there is nonetheless growing evidence to suggest a number of hotels are seeking to redesign jobs to offer greater autonomy and scope to employees. For example, Henkoff (1994) reports on Marriott's attempts to create a Guest Service Associate (GSA) who can check the guest into the hotel, pick up their key and paperwork from the rack in the lobby and then escort them straight to their room. As one of the employees interviewed by Henkoff (1994: 52) describes it: 'I am a bellman, a doorman, a front desk clerk and a concierge all rolled into one. I have more responsibilities. I feel better about my job, and the guest gets better service'. Similarly Marriott has been at the forefront of attempts to empower front-line staff to respond more promptly to guest problems without constant recourse to managerial approval (see Clutterbuck and Kernaghan, 1994: 237–42; Lashley, 1997). In a similar vein Jones and Lockwood (1989: 55–6) describe the redesign of the chambermaids' jobs within a large hotel, which involved allowing them to check their own rooms and return them to reception. This 'self-checking' offered greater control and responsibility to the chambermaids and an enhanced sense of job satisfaction (see Chapter 9). These initiatives exemplify hotels' attempts to design jobs that promote employee autonomy, flexibility and a problem-solving, positive attitude and would seem to offer the potential for a more proactive approach to managing people.

Training and development

As we already noted, high levels of labour turnover in the hotel industry exist paradoxically alongside severe skill shortages. To address this twin-track problem a number of training and development initiatives have been developed at the governmental, industry and organizational level which have sought to encourage the dissemination of good practice and the promotion of hospitality as a rewarding industry to work in.

Governmental initiatives

Over recent years various governments have introduced a range of training initiatives to encourage greater commitment to training and staff development and improved skill levels throughout the UK economy. Such initiatives have been particularly useful within the hotel industry due to the existing low skills base.

National Vocational Qualification (NVQ – S(cottish)VQ north of the border) is a workplace-based accredited qualification that ranges from the level one foundation course to senior management level, which is level five. Hales (1996) suggests that the case for developing and implementing NVQs is largely based on two factors: first, their contribution in enhancing the competitiveness and performance of the UK economy by widening access to training and qualifications; and second, the benefits to participants, i.e. employees, in terms of increased recognition for workplace ability and competence, with the effect of increasing job satisfaction, motivation, a sense of achievement and standards of work. He also goes on to report on five case study organizations in the hotel sector. All of the case study organizations were small businesses employing between 22–44 employees and four of them had adopted and continued to use NVQs, with one adopting and then subsequently dropping them. Hales' research suggested that those hotels which had adopted and persevered with NVQs noted a pay-off in terms of better employee attitudes and behaviour, increased service quality and an overall improvement in business performance. However, he does remain sceptical about the extent to which NVQs may penetrate the small hospitality business sector generally, unless they are given active encouragement. On this point, a way forward for smaller hotels may be through networking approaches to allow businesses to 'pool' resources and expertise to sustain the uptake and delivery of N/SVQs.

A further initiative is Investors in People (IiP) which attempts to link staff development with development of the business and which has enjoyed a reasonably high take up rate within the hospitality industry. *Hospitality* ('Investors in People', September/October 1997: 14) recently reported that over a quarter of a million hospitality employees or 22 per cent of all industry employees are now within IiP accredited organizations, although this is slightly lower than the national average of 30 per cent. Importantly, IiP is equally applicable to large and small businesses. For example, the HCIMA, in conjunction with Training and Enterprise Councils (TECs) in England and Wales, Local Enterprise Companies (LECs) in Scotland, and IiP UK Ltd, has developed a self-help pack *Shaping Your Team for Success* which is designed to particularly help small business to achieve IiP accreditation at minimum cost. In relation to its impact on business performance *Tourism Training Scotland* (1996: 4) reports a survey of 35 Scottish tourism companies – including a number of small and medium sized hotels – which suggested that several benefits were attributable to the achievement of IiP, these being (and see also Goldsmith *et al.*, 1997: 86–90):

- improved business performance;
- improved customer satisfaction;
- better employee performance; and
- reduced labour turnover.

The last of the national training initiatives worthy of mention is Modern Apprenticeships that are primarily aimed at young people aged from 16 to 19. Modern Apprenticeships offer a framework for work-based training and assessment and are also linked with N/SVQs. The scheme ordinarily runs over three years and has a number of sequential steps. Initially the trainee is inducted into the industry and organization and the Modern Apprenticeship programme, before gaining recognized qualifications in areas such as health and safety and customer care. The intermediate stage, leading to the achievement of S/NVQ Level 2, develops jobs skills within the chosen specialism, which includes accommodation services. Lastly, the trainee develops supervisory or advanced technical skills, which culminates in the award of an S/NVQ at Level 3. Mason (1997) suggests that there are currently 7000 Modern Apprenticeships in the hospitality industry, including schemes at Marriott, Holiday Inn, Hilton, Jarvis Hotels and De Vere Hotels, although again Modern Apprenticeships can be taken in all sizes of establishment. Moreover SMEs can access funding from local L/TECs or alternatively form consortiums with other SMEs to share training, assessment and coordination resources. Mason believes the usefulness of the scheme lies in the embedding and maintenance of a training culture as the current generation of Modern Apprenticeships move into managerial positions and in turn seek to encourage their own staff.

Industry level

As we have already noted a number of the governmental initiatives described above are likely to bring organizations into contact with professional bodies within the hospitality industry, such as the HCIMA. The other organization which plays a key role in attempting to systematize and formalize training structures within the industry is the Hospitality Training Foundation (HTF), which was previously known as the Hotel and Catering Training Company (HCTC) and the Hotel and Catering Training Board (HCTB). The HTF has recently launched Hospitality 2000 which is a campaign premised on challenging the hospitality industry to meet a number of training and skills targets by the end of 2000. Thus, having firstly identified that there are over a quarter of a million businesses in the hospitality industry, the HTF suggests that *inter alia*: 75 per cent of employers should be aware of the purpose and benefits of N/SVQs, IiP and the Modern Apprenticeship Scheme; at least half of employers should be offering N/SVQs; 10,000 young people should be working towards a Modern Apprenticeship; 1000 organizations should have IiP; and 60 per cent of employees will have qualifications relevant to their job (Anon., 1997). Therefore, the HTF is concerned with advising and assisting employers with the training of staff, ranging from management development to training for unemployed people, and again is a particularly useful source of help and advice for small and medium sized hotels seeking information on aspects of staff training and development.

As well as professional associations, employers' organizations are increasingly recognizing, first, the need to encourage talented people into the hospitality industry and then, second, actually to retain these new workers. For example, at the industry level, concern over skills shortages in the UK hospitality industry has led to a new campaign to attract the brightest school leavers into the industry. Called 'Let's Make it First Choice', the campaign seeks to address what it considers 'myths' about low pay and long hours and instead present a more upbeat view of the hospitality industry as offering 'exciting' career prospects. This will involve senior managers in the industry visiting the top 400 schools in the UK three or four times a year to talk about careers in hospitality in the hope of encouraging talented young people into the industry as a first choice and not as a last resort (Shrimpton, 1996).

Furthermore the British Hospitality Association (BHA) has recently instigated a 'good employers' scheme which is targeting 8000 small hotels. The 'Excellence Through People' (ETP) programme is seeking to identify best employment practice within the industry. The BHA acknowledge that the ETP scheme is, in effect, their response to the damning indictment of the industry portrayed in *Tourism: Competing with the Best: No. 3, People Working in Tourism and Hospitality* (BHA, 1998). Under the Government-funded scheme hotels pay £75 to join ETP and eventually gain accreditation by demonstrating good staff training, effective communications and a competitive employment package, as well as signing up to a 10-point code of practice. A key aim of the virtuous circle the BHA is aiming to create is a reduction in, what the chairman of the BHA described as, 'the maddeningly high (and expensive) rate of labour turnover' (BHA, 1998: ii). Eventually, all of those organizations accredited will be included in an annual directory of good employers for job centres and careers officers, and once in the directory employers will have to seek annual verification to ensure standards do not slip. It remains to be seen what the actual impact of this laudable scheme will be, but again it evidences an attempt to be more proactive in addressing HRM problems within the hotel sector.

Organizational level

Cheng and Brown (1998: 145) assert that 'There is a clear recognition ... of the strategic contribution made by training to the retention of staff'. Consequently a number of hotels are now attempting to develop structured training and development programmes which seek to signal to their employees their concern with fully developing them. This may entail involvement in one or more of the schemes outlined above and this may also be supplemented by training programmes run within the hotel, to for example, encourage functional flexibility. Such in-house training is likely to encompass both on the job and off the job training and within the rooms division particular skills that would be useful to staff are likely to include: customer care, information technology skills, quality management, telephone etiquette and language skills. Again, despite the active encouragement to small businesses within many of the schemes outlined above, there may be a disjuncture between large and small organizations in relation to the level and scope of training. At a practical level to address this problem Welch (1996) reports on agitation in the UK by the Joint Hospitality Industry Congress (JHIC) – an umbrella body for the industry's leading trade and professional associations – to encourage greater local co-operation between smaller and larger organizations, for example, allocating places to people from small family-run enterprises on larger companies' training courses at a reduced or affordable cost.

Remuneration

The International Labour Office (1989) (cited in Baum, 1995) and Riley (1993) outline a number of structural features of the tourism and hospitality industry which are likely to have downward pressure on wage levels, the most important of these being as follows.

- Small unit structure of the industry – the industry in most countries is highly fragmented and heterogeneous, being an amalgam of small to large businesses. However as already noted the majority of hotels are small businesses.
- Fluctuations in levels of business activity – there is constant fluctuation in consumer demand across large and small time periods.
- Cost pressures induced by competition.
- A reliance on vulnerable and 'marginal' workers (Wood, 1997) – for example, drawing on sections of the labour market that have little bargaining power, such as young people, students, married women returning to work and ethnic minorities.

Consequently, within hotels and catering, levels of remuneration and reward are generally low and this is supported by a range of empirical evidence (see Goldsmith *et al.*, 1997: 179–202; and Wood, 1997: 46–62 for a more comprehensive review). For example, the Department of National Heritage (1996) suggests that average gross earnings in the hospitality industry in the UK are 40 per cent lower than for the service sector as a whole, and that gross earnings within retail, which shares the common characteristics of having many low or unskilled workers, were 20 per cent higher than hospitality. Interestingly, and perhaps reflecting these considerations, in the aforementioned IPD labour turnover survey, retail was well down the list with a turnover figure of 14.57 per cent. As low pay is often cited as the primary reason for people leaving an employer in the hospitality industry, low levels of remuneration can be seen to play a key role in high levels of labour turnover which has a range of attendant costs to the organization, such as lost productivity, loss of customer service skills, time taken to train and inculcate new members of staff to the organizational culture and the possible loss of repeat business, as regular customers like to see familiar faces.

In response to some of these issues the newly elected Labour Government is seeking to enact minimum wage legislation that they argue will have a major beneficial effect on pay levels and morale within the UK hospitality industry (The Labour Party, 1996). Although there is much concern within the industry about the possible effects on the competitiveness of the industry and the potential for job losses with the introduction of the national minimum wage (NMW), Chris Smith, the Secretary for Culture, Media and Sport (previously known as the Heritage Secretary), has argued that the opposite is likely to be true, with the NMW enhancing Britain's competitive position and encouraging more people to work within the industry. Wood (1997a: 343) in a recent review of the NMW debate argues persuasively that the arguments of those both for and against are rather more reliant on belief than any genuinely conclusive factual evidence, and thus 'nobody really knows what effect a minimum wage would have on jobs and economic performance'. Consequently the argument about the NMW 'is primarily a moral one' and whether individuals, organizations or industries are in favour or against is likely to reflect a prevailing ideological and political world view.

Notwithstanding the view of Wood (1997a), in seeking to allay the concerns of the industry, the Labour Party, in its policy document on the strategy for tourism and hospitality, made a commitment to include industry representatives on its Low Pay Commission (LPC) that sets the rate at which the minimum wage will exist. Indeed, there was much speculation that Peter Jarvis, the outgoing Chief Executive of Whitbread, would head the LPC but the government eventually appointed Professor George Bain, the then head of the London Business School. He heads the tripartite body, consisting of employers representatives, employee representatives and independent experts, which will set the minimum wage. At the time of writing (September 1998) the minimum wage has been set at £3.60 per hour for workers over the age of 21. In effect, this may have little real impact on larger hotels as a number of them are likely to be paying a similar national minimum hourly rate for operative staff. For example, *Income Data Services* (Report 752/January 1998) report that Forte Hotels and Jarvis Hotels now both operate a minimum rate of £3.50. More generally, throughout the hotel sector, it remains to be seen what impact the NMW has in relation to job creation, competitiveness and perceptions of the industry as an employer.

Performance management/appraisal

Mabey and Salaman (1995: 189) propose that performance management is concerned with establishing 'a framework in which performance by individuals can be directed, monitored, motivated and refined'. On that theme the Department of National Heritage (1996) suggest that, in order to pursue a 'virtuous circle', organizations need to have a long-term commitment to excellence and customer satisfaction with their employees being the key to success within this process. Thus, having recognized that excellent employers will pay above the industry average wage, and provide other benefits such as pension schemes, save as you earn schemes, employee discounts, and so on, the report goes on to suggest a number of other employment practices (which are currently seen in a range of hotel chains such as Granada/Forte Hotels, Novotel, Whitbread/Marriott) that recognize the importance of intrinsic rewards that encompass issues of performance management and appraisal and include the following:

- Recognition and the need for positive feedback. For example, passing on positive feedback from customers to employees and also having a well-designed appraisal system which can be useful in building trust between the employee and the organization. Mullins (1995) suggests that appraisal is key in improving organizational performance. However such appraisal systems have to be well-planned, clearly understood by both the appraiser and appraisee and conducted in as objective a manner as possible. On that basis the appraisal system would ordinarily seek to review performance, including job performance, personal standards, quality of work, communication skills, teamwork, problem-solving and decision-making; set future objectives wherein the appraiser and appraisee would agree on future achievements and what organizational and management support may be needed to facilitate this; and training and development needs which offers greater detail on what training needs have to be met to ensure long-term self development. One final point is the pragmatic one of whether small and medium-sized hotels should have an appraisal system. Goldsmith *et al.* (1997) suggest that there are certain minimum requisites or parameters for organizations to be able to successfully develop appraisal systems, for example, there should be at least 20 full-time non-managerial employees. Thus, on the criteria outlined by Goldsmith *et al.*, it may well be that hotels have to be at least medium sized to develop an appraisal system.

- Motivating and involving the staff in the business and communicating with them. For example, 'away days' to discuss key issues – one employer entrusted his staff with developing an organizational mission statement, paying staff to sample products offered by other companies, and empowering staff to have the confidence to contribute to the running of the organization and the willingness to take decisions.
- Understanding the importance of team-work. For example, formally assigning workers to a team can encourage a sense of belonging for employees and increase feelings of loyalty within the team.
- Turning jobs into careers and although this is easier for larger organizations who can encourage a strong internal labour market by promoting from within, it is also something which smaller firms can address. For example, the report relates how one small hotelier has set up an apprenticeship scheme with two other hotels and the local TEC so apprentices can move between the hotels to experience different jobs.

A CRITICAL REVIEW OF ACCOMMODATION WORK: A WORD OF CAUTION ON HRM

In reflecting the upbeat view held by a number of practitioners and academics of HRM, and its efficacy in managing employees in a humane and efficient way, this chapter has, at times, taken something of an idealized view of the benefits of adopting this new managerial philosophy. Therefore, it is important to add a word of caution amongst some of the more prescriptive elements to the chapter. In part, this has been an aim throughout the chapter and there have already been several allusions to poor personnel practice. A further and more specific caveat is also provided by Wood (1997) in his review of accommodation workers. In discussing this diverse group of employees Wood notes that the main focus of the limited research conducted about accommodation workers has been on chambermaids and reception staff.

A key finding from this research was the extent to which both groups of workers undertake difficult and demanding jobs, often without commensurate rewards. For example, Wood draws on this research to suggest that room-cleaning is physically demanding and dirty work, repetitive, boring and limited in variety and scope, and undertaken at times when employees are unlikely to encounter customers. Moreover the employers expectation that room cleaners should clean between 11–16 rooms a day was felt by many employees to be unreasonable. Indeed, some research findings suggested this expectation was exacerbated by a lack of management interest in chambermaids, which was exemplified by things such as consistent staff shortages, failure of other hotel staff to help and a lack of appropriate materials to adequately perform their task. As a counter-argument to some of these issues it should be noted that Wood is drawing on research evidence from the 1970s and the mid-1980s, which largely predates the rise of the HRM phenomenon. Nonetheless, it would be naive in the extreme to imagine that the 1990s has ushered in a complete sea-change in the nature of the room cleaner's job. A measured view would recognize Wood's (1997: 94) contention that 'many women who undertake room cleaning do so because of a shortage of alternative employment' and as a consequence 'find their employment a source of considerable misery'. HRM cannot, in this instance (or indeed in any other) offer a panacean solution to these issues, but by incremental and sensible steps – for example, the redesign of chambermaids jobs discussed earlier – at least begin to address some of these concerns.

Similarly, Wood also notes the pressures apparent within the work of the reception desk. Most obviously as the most overt public face of the hotel the receptionists usually bear the responsibility for guests' first impressions – which are likely to be crucial in shaping how they perceive the rest of their stay – and the first port of call for discontented and dissatisfied guests. Added to this Wood notes a variety of other responsibilities likely to be undertaken by the receptionist including: bookkeeping, letter writing, inventory taking, typing, record keeping, answering queries, filing, taking reservations, dealing with mail and lost property, dealing with room changes, taking payment of customers' bills, banking monies, holding responsibility for room keys and producing reports and statistics. Receptionists, then, face a potentially stressful time in acting as a conduit and centrepoint for the hotel in seeking to placate irate guests and also communicate complaints which may have arisen in other parts of the hotel. Wood, notes that this mediating role is further clouded by the ambiguous status enjoyed by receptionists in the hotel. For example, research suggests that senior kitchen and restaurant staff may see them as low in status, whilst lower kitchen staff see them as arrogant and self-important.

In summary, then, there is a need to place these considerations alongside some of the more evangelical claims for HRM. Thus, Wood's work is particularly useful in injecting a healthy dose of reality into discussions about the nature of accommodation work and the difficult challenges faced by managers in managing these employees.

THE EUROPEAN DIMENSION

One final area which the chapter will briefly discuss is the European dimension and particularly the continuing role played by the European Union (EU) in their attempts to regulate employment conditions across Europe.

A level playing field?

Initiatives emanating from the EU exemplify an attempt to create a convergent level playing field of employment rights, both legally and voluntarily based, which will underpin an economically integrated and successful EU. Lucas (1996a) in reviewing the impact of European social policy on the tourism and hospitality industry is sceptical of its overall effect in the UK, whilst at the same time acknowledging that several measures have influenced the way that organizations approach areas such as equality, pensions and health and safety. For example, the 48 Hour Working Time Directive, introduced as a health and safety measure, looks set to have major implications for hotels with the effects of its main provisions including the ending of coercing employees to work more than 48 hours, and an entitlement to three weeks' paid holiday, rising to four weeks in 1999 (and see Goldsmith *et al.*, 1997: 128–9). Moreover the recent agreement of the Labour government to opt-in to the Social Chapter of the Maastricht Treaty will mean hospitality organizations within the UK will have to consider the implementation of Directives on European Works Councils, parental leave and a wide-ranging Directive on part-time work. The hospitality industry, to date, has remained resolutely opposed to many of the EU Directives, and again it remains to be seen to what extent they may improve the employment conditions and HRM techniques in the hotel sector (Huddart, 1997).

CONCLUSIONS

At one level HRM is the simple task of, in the epigrammatic words of Jones and Lockwood (1989: 49), placing the right person, in the right job, at the right place at the right time and within the right environment. To do this the hotel needs to address issues such as recruitment and selection, induction, flexibility and job design, remuneration and performance management to encourage greater effort and efficiency from staff. To date, it seems the weight of evidence would suggest that by no stretch of the imagination do hotels universally address these issues by practising a form of HRM premised on the view that people are *the* key to organizational success. Increasingly though there may be a recognition that the long-term costs of a self-perpetuating vicious circle of recruitment difficulties, shortage of skilled and qualified staff, relatively low pay, high staff turnover and a relatively unattractive image as an employing sector are unsustainable. Consequently there is much talk about the need to move towards a virtuous circle approach of high quality products and services, high training standards, good terms and conditions of employment, high skills and low labour turnover. Arguably then the procurement and management of quality personnel is the most important challenge facing hotels today. Thus HRM can be seen to play a key strategic dimension within a hotel's attempt to be successful and these issues will continue to have a particular resonance in the high guest-contact areas in accommodation services.

REFERENCES AND FURTHER READING

Anastassova, L. and Purcell, K. (1995) 'Human resource management in the Bulgarian hotel industry: From command to empowerment', *International Journal of Hospitality Management*, **14**(2), 171–85.

Anon. (1997) 'Customer service in the next century', *Hospitality*, March, 9.

Baum, T. (1995) *Managing Human Resources in the European Tourism and Hospitality Industry*, London: Chapman and Hall.

British Hospitality Association (1998) *Creating Hospitality's Virtuous Circle of Employment*, special supplement to *Hospitality Matters*, January.

Cheng, A. and Brown, A. (1998) 'HRM strategies and labour turnover in the hotel industry: A comparative study of Australia and Singapore', *International Journal of Human Resource Management*, **9**(1), 136–54.

Clutterbuck, D. and Kernhagan, S. (1994) *The Power of Empowerment – Release the Hidden Talents of Your Employees*, London: Kogan Page.

Department of National Heritage (1996) *Tourism Competing with the Best, No. 3 People Working in Tourism and Hospitality*, London: Department of National Heritage.

Eccles, G. and Durand, P. (1997) 'Improving service quality: Lessons and practice from the hotel sector', *Managing Service Quality*, **7**(5), 224–6.

Goldsmith, A., Nickson, D., Sloan, D. and Wood, R.C. (1997) *Human Resource Management for Hospitality Services*, London: International Thomson Business Press.

Guerrier, Y. and Lockwood, A. (1989) 'Managing flexible working', *The Service Industries Journal*, **6**(3), 406–19.

Hales, C. (1996) 'Factors influencing the adoption of NVQs in small hospitality businesses', *International Journal of Contemporary Hospitality Management*, **8**(5), 5–9.

Henkoff, R. (1994) 'Finding, training and keeping the best service workers', *Fortune*, 3 October, 52–8.

Hiltrop, J. (1996) 'The impact of human resource management on organizational performance', *European Management Journal*, **14**(6), 628–37.

HCIMA (Hotel and Catering International Management Association) (1998) *The Hospitality Yearbook*, Crawley: William Reed Directories.

Huddart, G. (1997) 'Brussels doubts', *Caterer and Hotelkeeper*, 18 December, 70–1.

International Labour Office (1989) *Conditions of work in the hotel and catering and tourism sector, such as hours of work, methods of remuneration, security of employment*, Geneva: Hotel, Catering and Tourism Committee of the ILO.

Jones, P. and Lockwood, A. (1989) *The Management of Hotel Operations – An Innovative Approach to the Study of Hotel Management*, London: Cassell.

Knowles, T. (1998) *Hospitality Management – An Introduction*, Harlow: Longman, 2nd edn.

Labour Party (1996) *Breaking New Ground: Labour's Strategy for Tourism and Hospitality*, London: Labour Party.

Lashley, C. (1997) *Empowering Service Excellence – Beyond the Quick Fix*, London: Cassell.

Law, R. and Wong, M. (1997) 'Evaluating the effectiveness of interviews as a selection method', *Australian Journal of Hospitality Management*, **4**(1), 27–32.

Lucas, R. (1996) 'Industrial relations in hotels and catering: neglect and paradox?', *British Journal of Industrial Relations*, **34**(2), 267–86.

Lucas, R. (1996a) 'Social policy', in Thomas, R (ed.) *The Hospitality Industry, Tourism and Europe: Perspectives on Policy*, London: Cassell, 135–65.

Mabey, C. and Salaman, G. (1995) *Strategic Human Resource Management*, Oxford: Blackwell.

Mason, A. (1997) 'Apprenticeships – do they work?', *Hospitality*, September/October, 26–7.

Mullins, L. (1995) *Hospitality Management – A Human Resources Approach*, London: Pitman, 2nd edn.

Nankevis, A. and Debrah, Y. (1995) 'Human resource management in hotels: A comparative study', *Tourism Management*, **16**(7), 507–13.

Price, L. (1994) 'Poor personnel practice in the hotel and catering industry: Does it matter?' *Human Resource Management Journal*, **4**(4), 44–62.

Riley, M. (1992) 'Functional flexibility in hotels – is it feasible?', *Tourism Management*, **13**(4), 363–7.

Riley, M (1993) 'Labour markets and vocational education', in Baum, T. (ed.) *Human Resources in International Tourism*, Oxford: Butterworth-Heinemann, 47–59.

Riley, M. (1996) *Human Resource Management in the Hospitality and Tourism Industry*, Oxford: Butterworth Heinemann, 2nd edn.

Shrimpton, D, (1996) 'Industry drive to lure young stars', *Caterer and Hotelkeeper*, 8 August, 7.

Tourism Training Scotland (1996) *Annual Report 1996*, Glasgow: Tourism Training Scotland.

Walsh, T. (1991) 'Flexible employment in the retail and hotel trades', in Pollert, A. (ed.) *Farewell to Flexibility*, Oxford: Blackwell, 140–50.

Welch, J. (1996) 'Hotels told to improve image', *People Management*, 25 July, 10–11.

West, M. and Patterson, M. (1998) 'Profitable personnel', *People Management,* 8 January, 28–31.

Wood, R.C. (1997) *Working in Hotels and Catering*, London: International Thomson Business Press, 2nd edn.

Wood, R.C. (1997a) 'Rhetoric, reason and rationality: The national minimum wage debate and the UK hospitality industry', *International Journal of Hospitality Management*, **16**(4), 329–44.

15

Yield management in hotels

Una McMahon-Beattie, Kevin Donaghy and Ian Yeoman

On a cold winter's night, 24th December to be precise, Joseph and Mary were in town looking for accommodation. All of the hotels were extremely busy that night, as it was the holiday season. Joseph was extremely worried about Mary, as she was nine months pregnant. Anyway, Joseph and Mary called at the local hotel to find out if there was 'any room at the inn'. The story begins.

Receptionist	*How can I help you?*
Joseph	*Do you have any room tonight?*
Receptionist	*It is extremely busy tonight, as it is the holidays.*
Joseph	*We have been travelling all night, surely you must have some accommodation somewhere.*
Receptionist	*Let me check with the Front Office Manager.*

In the back office

Receptionist	*There is a couple on the front desk, that need accommodation tonight.*
Front Office Manager	*Well, lets see what's available. All the rooms have been booked. In fact we are overbooked tonight by three rooms. Just a minute, there are still ten arrivals to check-in. These arrivals are not guaranteed. Release those rooms for resale immediately.*

Back at the front desk

Receptionist	*You are very lucky, I have seven rooms available.*
Joseph	*How much will that be?*
Receptionist	*£100*
Joseph	*That's expensive. The last time I stayed here, it was only £60.*
Receptionist	*Joseph and Mary (checking his customer records data) … that's right. You stayed here last Easter. But that was a special promotion. You had booked the accommodation over four weeks in advance. Easter is generally a very quiet period.*
Mary	*That's right, we'll take the room.*

Accommodation is a unique product, as Joseph and Mary have found out. That product can only be sold once. Accommodation cannot be stored for future sales like manufactured products. Demand is variable, never constant. Therefore, the management of accommodation requires a special range of skills, knowledge and procedures, namely yield management.

Yield management (YM) is a management tool or technique which is currently being utilized by an increasing number of group and independently owned hotels in order to maximize the effective use of their available accommodation capacity and improve financial success. Yield management is not an entirely new innovation and most hoteliers practice it in some form, such as in the adjusting of room rates to temper fluctuations between peak and off-peak seasons, mid-week and weekend rates. This chapter, therefore, examines the use and application of yield management in hotels in effectively maximizing revenue and profit generation in this highly competitive and capital intensive industry.

HISTORICAL DEVELOPMENT OF YIELD MANAGEMENT FROM AIRLINES TO HOTELS

The airline industry has been credited with the development and refinement of yield management following deregulation of the US airline industry in the late 1970s. The resulting heavy competition led to a price cutting war with some airlines going out of business (Ingold and Huyton, 1997). Kimes (1997) cites the example of People's Express which emerged briefly as a low price, no frills airline. In response, large carriers such as American and United began to offer a small number of seats at even lower fares whilst maintaining the higher priced fares on the remainder of their seats. This strategy allowed American and United to attract the price sensitive customers and still retain their high paying passengers. As a result People's Express went into bankruptcy. Consequently, yield management was introduced as a method of utilizing capacity and maximizing revenue or 'yield' where airline companies sought to fill their planes with the optimum mix of passengers.

In similar highly competitive circumstances, yield management began to be adopted in the hotel industry around the middle of the 1980s. At this time the industry was being confronted with excess capacity, severe short-term liquidity problems and increasing business failure rates. Major hotel chains such as Hyatt, Marriott, Quality Inn and Radisson endeavoured to redress these difficulties by adopting yield management (Donaghy and McMahon, 1995). Opportunities for applying yield management in small to medium sized hotels are also actively being developed following a report for the European Union (Arthur Andersen, 1996).

DEFINITION

In general terms, Kimes (1989, 1997) has described yield management as the process of allocating the right type of capacity or inventory unit to the right type of customer at the right price so as to maximize revenue or 'yield'. Applying this to airlines, yield management can be considered to be the revenue or yield per passenger mile, with yield being a function of both the price the airline charges for differentiated service options (pricing) and the number of seats sold at each price (seat inventory control) (Belobaba, 1987). Larsen (1988) further crystallizes the meaning of yield management in the airline context by dividing it into two distinct functions: overbooking and managing discounts.

In hotels, yield management is concerned with the market sensitive pricing of fixed room capacity relative to a hotel's specific market segments. Kimes (1989) states that yield management in hotels consists of two functions: rooms inventory management and pricing. The goal of yield management is the formulation and profitable alignment of price, product and buyer. As such, Donaghy *et al.* (1995: 140) define yield management in hotels as a 'revenue maximisation technique which aims to increase net yield through the predicted allocation of available bedroom capacity to predetermined market segments at optimum price'. It is the predicted nature of yield management which is the key to its ongoing successful financial management of hotels in today's increasingly competitive market. On a strategic level, Jones and Kewin (1997) have extended the definition of yield management to incorporate historical performance, demand forecasting, and decision making to enable revenue optimization. This definition further highlights the differentiation between the strategic and tactical role that yield management plays in managing capacity. In a more holistic fashion, Lieberman (1993) interprets yield management as a tool with the capacity to yield a net result of enhanced revenue and customer service through a melding of information systems, technology, profitability, statistics, organization theory, business experience, and knowledge.

Yield management should not be viewed as a panacea for hoteliers operating in the difficult circumstances of today's market. It does not replace the basic managerial tasks or functions such as forecasting, setting strategies for the future, feedback on performance and the establishment of corrective action (Lee-Ross and Johns, 1997). It should not replace managerial decision making, but provide more information so that decision making can be more effective in its implementation.

PRECONDITIONS, INGREDIENTS AND BOUNDARIES OF YIELD MANAGEMENT

Yield management suits the hotel industry where capacity is fixed, where the demand is unstable and where the market can be segmented (Kimes, 1989). As with many service organizations, a feature of hotels is that they have low marginal costs and usually sell their perishable product to their customers well in advance of consumption. Developing these ideas further, Kimes (1997) has outlined a number of preconditions for the success of yield management and suggested a number of factors or ingredients which are prerequisites for the implementation of yield management as a functioning, workable system.

Preconditions

- Fixed capacity. Hotels tend to be capacity constrained with no opportunity to inventory their products or goods. Simply put, many hotel services and products are perishable. Capacity can be changed by, for example, adding a number of new bedrooms or a new function suite but this usually involves a large financial investment in terms of equipment and plant.
- High fixed costs. The industry is characterized by high fixed costs and, as explained above, the cost of adding incremental capacity can be very high and is not quickly adjusted. Adding new bedrooms to a hotel not only entails a large capital outlay but may involve a long planning and construction period.
- Low variable costs. The costs incurred by, for example, selling a bedroom to a customer in otherwise unused capacity is relatively inexpensive and incurs only minor servicing costs.
- Time-varied demand. Since hotel capacity is fixed, organizations cannot easily adjust their capacity to meet peaks and troughs in demand. Kimes (1997) explains that when demand varies, hotels can benefit from controlling capacity when demand

is high and relaxing that control when demand is low. As with airlines, utilization of reservation systems can assist in managing demand since they log requests for rooms in advance.

- Similarity of inventory units. As a general rule, yield management systems operate in a situation where inventory units are similar. However, it should be noted that service firms like hotels can differentiate their units by, for example, offering add-on luxury features or the possibility of upgrades.

Ingredients

- Market segmentation. Hotels normally have the ability to divide their customer base into distinct market segments such as leisure, business, long and short stay (see Chapter 3). Business or corporate clients who are usually time sensitive are willing to pay higher rates whilst leisure travellers who tend to book longer in advance are price sensitive.
- Historical demand and booking patterns. Detailed knowledge of a hotel's sales and booking data per market segment should help managers predict peaks and troughs in demand and assist the hotelier in more effectively aligning demand with supply.
- Pricing knowledge. Kimes (1997) describes yield management as a form of price discrimination. In practice, hotels operate yield management systems which depend on opening and closing rate bands. In order to stimulate demand in periods of low demand, hotels can offer discounted prices whilst during periods of high demand low rates can be closed off. Additionally, by offering a number of rates in the hotel the manager will, ideally, profitably align price, product and buyer and increase net yield (Sieburgh, 1988).
- Overbooking policy. Overbooking is an essential yield management technique. Overbooking levels are not set by chance but are determined by a detailed analysis of what has happened in the past and a prediction of what is likely to happen in the future. Predicted no-shows, cancellations, and denials all form part of a complex calculation carried out in advance. In this way the risk of disappointing a customer who has booked in advance is minimized.
- Information systems. Effective management information is essential for successful yield management whether the hotelier is operating a manual or computerized system. However, information technology can assist greatly in the sorting and manipulation of required data. The use of artificial intelligence (AI) has enormous potential for handling the complexities of yield management because of its abilities in complex problem solving, reasoning, perception, planning and analysis of extensive data (McCool, 1987; Berkus, 1988; Russell and Johns, 1997). Expert systems (ES) are 'knowledge based' software packages that reflect the expertise in the area of the application and these type of systems have extensive capacity in dealing with non-numeric, qualitative data (Sieburgh, 1988). However, Kimes (1997) and Donaghy et al. (1997a) warn that yield management systems need to be integrated to property management systems, reservation systems and group systems. If this is not the case incomplete or inaccurate information may be entered into a yield management system.

Boundaries

There exists some concern over the applicability of yield management to the hotel industry. Hansen and Eringa (1997) cite evidence to show that yield management within the hotel sector is distinct from yield management within the airline industry. Both Orkin (1988; 1988a) and Kimes (1989) have stated that it would be dangerous for hotels to follow directly the yield management practices in the airline industry. They have identified a number of boundaries.

- Multiple night stays. An airline seat can be used on one flight and one day only. With hotels, guests can arrive on a low rate and stay through a number of high rate days. This obviously leads to a problem with determining the right rate to charge the customer.
- Multiplier effect. If a hotelier focuses on the revenue that can be generated from the accommodation function, they may be ignoring the revenue that could be generated in other departments of the hotel such as restaurants, conference and banqueting, and leisure facilities.
- Lack of a distinct rate structure. Airline passengers are familiar with the restrictions and barriers which, for example, prevent a business traveller benefiting from those rates structured for the leisure traveller. Hotels, whether independent or group, rarely have such restrictions.
- Decentralization of information. It is often the case that hotel bedrooms in group hotels are sold at too low a rate because the central reservation system is not linked into the unit hotel's property management system.

MEASURING YIELD

Traditional methods of performance measurement in hotels such as occupancy rate and average room rate have tended to focus on the volume or value aspects of accommodation sales. However, high occupancy rates are no indication of financial success since the rate per room charged to the customer may be highly discounted and well below the rack rate. Whilst the average room rate gives an indication of the level of revenue generated per sold room, it gives no indication of the actual number of rooms sold. Indeed, as the hotelier increases one, they tend to decrease the other. Furthermore, where room night productivity becomes a valuation technique for sales and reservation staff, lower paying group business will increase whilst higher paying transient business is turned away (Orkin, 1988; 1988a; Jones and Hamilton, 1992). Yield management, on the other hand, aims to optimize both occupancy and average room rate simultaneously and this can easily be seen in Orkins' (1988) yield efficiency statistic:

Yield Efficiency = Revenue Realized / Revenue Potential
= (Rooms Sold × Average Room Rate) /
(Room Rate × Available Rooms)

Orkin (1988) defines revenue realized as 'actual sales receipts' and potential revenue as 'the income secured if 100 per cent of available rooms are sold at full rack rates'. Therefore, a 250 bedroom hotel with a £145 rack rate which sells 190 rooms at an average of £98 yields:

$$\frac{190 \times £98}{£145 \times 250} = 51.37 \text{ per cent}$$

The nearer the percentage is to 100, the better the yield.

YIELD MANAGEMENT DECISION VARIABLES

Huyton and Peters (1997) identify the variables that hotel managers use to make yield management decisions. These variables are based upon the principles of forecasting; systems and procedures engaged; and the strategies and tactics utilized.

- Forecasting. Forecasting is the foundation of yield management. This forecasting must be done on a daily basis, with 30 day, 60 day, 180 day and 365 day projections. A continuous examination of demand and supply variables is required in order to take effective yield management decisions. The factors that may effect demand and supply include; past business forecasts, sales mix, special events, weather and competitors' behaviour.
- Systems and procedures. A computerized system manages all the variable decisions in order to recommend appropriate pricing decisions. Appropriate systems and procedures enable the hotel manager to store, track and make appropriate decisions. These systems and procedures are concerned with everything from telephone inquiries through to how a reservations clerk works a VDU screen and makes an appropriate decision, thus providing a reference framework for suitable decisions to be taken.
- Strategies and tactics. Decisions are made in relation to pricing policy and market demand. Therefore on high demand days, management concentrates on decisions regarding average room rate. This will involve restricting access to accommodation from groups and low spend customers, whereas on low demand days management is concerned with market mix in order to maximize occupancy. In both scenarios, hotel management will have to design a policy that relates to overbooking. Overbooking occurs when customers cancel accommodation, check-out early or don't show up on the day of arrival. As accommodation can only be sold once in the hotel industry, the hotel manager needs to set a level, i.e. a number of rooms, at which they are prepared to overbook. This level will depend on the forecast for the given period, the number of anticipated 'no shows', cancellations and early check-outs.

BUILDING A YIELD MANAGEMENT MODEL

Building a model of yield management that takes into account yield management decision variables is a key skill of a successful hotel manager. But many managers have attempted to do just this and failed. Yeoman and Ingold (1997) identify reasons why yield management decision models have failed as follows.

- Organizational culture. Many hotels are not geared to a team approach in management decision making. Many organizations have a clear hierarchy of decision-making authority, and a team approach is inconsistent with this.
- Quality of decisions. Many operations managers follow the satisficing heuristic in decision-making, i.e. they follow a course of action that yields an outcome that is 'good enough' rather than the best possible option. Most yield decisions are influenced by social and political factors which are underpinned by the weight given to qualitative rather than quantitative information. The biggest influence is seen to be time pressure with insufficient time available to make quality decisions.
- Overconfidence. Hotel managers do not have the foresight to see how events might unfold. Decisions are taken based on one particular anchoring when operations managers search for the information to support a favoured course of action.

- Flexibility of decision makers. Many hotel managers involved in revenue management decisions adopt systems and procedures that are appropriate in one circumstance but not in another.

MODELS OF YIELD MANAGEMENT

Taking the above factors into consideration, many authors have designed operational frameworks to guide the use of decision making process for managing yield within hotels. The work of Donaghy *et al.* (1997; 1997a) identifies the key stages in yield management and provides a workable method for assessing the application of yield within both the hotel and the external environment and provides an excellent starting point for developing an effective yield focused model (see Figure 15.1). To implement

Stage 1 – Personnel
- Develop employee understanding
- Highlight customer/hotel interface problems
- Appoint forecasting committee
- Sort available customer and market data

Stage 2 – Analyse demand
- Identify competitors and sources of demand
- Define hotel's strengths and weaknesses
- Predict demand levels and booking patterns
- Constantly monitor external factors

Stage 3 – Market segmentation
- Identify market (existing or total market)
- Segment market (demographic and geographic)

Stage 4 – Guest mix
- Determine most desirable guest mix based on (i) propensity to spend and (ii) volume usage

Stage 5 – Analyse trade-offs
- Extensive calculations of monetary leakage
- Avoid displacing higher spending guests

Stage 6 – Establish capacity levels
- Set capacity to meet demand of market segments

Stage 7 – Introduce YM system
- Groups and consortia need tailor-made systems
- Small or independent hotels adopt revised version of above to achieve maximum benefits

Stage 8 – Customer re-orientation
Training courses come into practice by realizing
- Hotel's YM objectives
- Meeting customer needs

Stage 9 – Operational evaluation
- Revise room allocation
- Evaluate how demand changes
- Identify additional factors which determine demand

Stage 10 – Action
- Implement any changes required immediately

Figure 15.1 Key stages in a formal YM system
Source: Donaghy *et al.*, 1997.

the key stages outlined in Figure 15.1 effectively and subsequently to achieve the aims of an increased and sustainable net yield, yield management activities must be based on a comprehensive awareness of continually changing market configurations.

Jones and Kewin (1997) acknowledge the fragmentation and duplication noted by Donaghy *et al.* (1997) relating to effective working practices of yield management. In attempting to further clarify this without adding further duplication, Jones and Kewin (1997) have drawn upon the work of the following authors in developing their Hotel Yield Management System Model (Yeoman and Watson, 1997; Donaghy *et al.*, 1995; Jauncey *et al.*, 1995; Jones and Hamilton, 1992; and Russell and Johns, 1997). This model by Jones and Kewin (1997) (Figure 15.2) highlights five inter-related systems:

- strategic decision making systems;
- tactical decision making systems;
- information systems;
- technological systems; and
- human resource systems.

To understand this model by Jones and Kewin (1997) Figure 15.3 outlines the model again, though this illustration notes those operational components within each element/system.

Thus, the model proposed by Jones and Kewin (1997) has effectively drawn together the various strands identified by authors to date. It incorporates the operational key stages outlined by Donaghy *et al.* (1997; 1997a) and the earlier work by Jones and Hamilton (1992) which identified seven key elements of yield management (developing a yield culture, analysis of demand, price value determination, market segmentation, demand pattern analysis, tracking of declines and denials, and system evaluation).

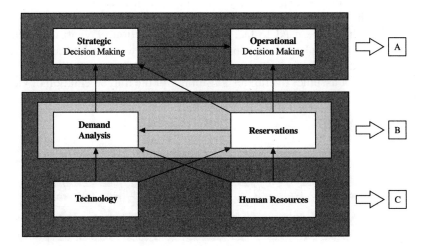

Figure 15.2 Hotel Yield Management System Model
Source: Jones and Kewin, 1997.

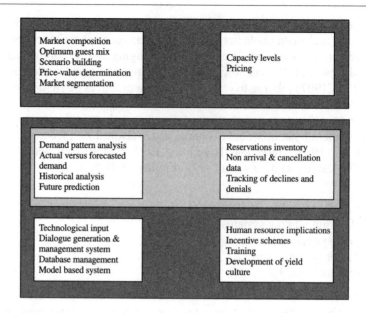

Figure 15.3 Hotel Yield Management System Model outlining operational component within each element/system

A COORDINATED APPROACH: THE YIELD MANAGER

It is increasingly more apparent in the recent literature that yield management can most effectively be implemented through a yield manager. The advantage of such a position is that the disparate activities which contribute to overall yield (sales, marketing, reservations and general management) may be more easily focused toward one common unified goal rather than remaining components of a number of fragmented departmental objectives. Research undertaken by the authors (Donaghy *et al.*, 1997a) established that the effective implementation of yield management is contingent upon a coordinated approach. Evidence clearly suggests that a three stage 'implementation process' (Figure 15.4) should be used to facilitate the introduction of yield techniques. The effectiveness of the implementation process was found to be influenced by the extent to which one individual assumes responsibility for yield management.

The coordinator assumes overall responsibility for the implementation of yield management and must ensure that functional specialists and yield specialists work and

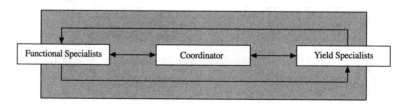

Figure 15.4 Implementation process
Source: Donaghy *et al.*, 1997a.

learn from each other. The fundamental role of the coordinator is to enable the implementation of yield management by appointing functional specialists and yield specialists. Hotel managers believe that the coordination role should be undertaken by the hotel general manager. Functional specialists are those individuals within the hotel who are involved in the packaging and sale of the accommodation product, i.e., the hotel room and accompanying facilities and services. Ideally, functional specialists should include the entire middle management team including all departmental managers and supervisors. These individuals form the core of this team due to their specialist knowledge of their respective areas. However in the study by Donaghy et al. (1997a), hotel managers believe that this will only be an effective method of implementation if this team of specialists is headed by a yield manager who assumes responsibility for managing the functional specialists. Five key requirements for an effective yield manager were identified:

- knowledge of the area geographically;
- experience of strategic planning essential;
- leadership and negotiation skills;
- experience in service sector marketing; and
- computer literacy.

The distinct advantage of having a yield manager is the coordinated and systematic approach to introducing yield techniques. Whilst the general manager facilitates the process in itself, the yield manager acts as a project manager, liasing between hotel general manager, functional specialists and the yield specialists – those external organizations contracted to deliver training or provide technological support. Research has also established that this integrated team strategy led by the yield manager avoids a prescriptive approach to yield implementation and ensures that yield applications are tailored to meet specific requirements of hotels and respective markets.

CONCLUSIONS

Yield management offers hotels an opportunity for a focused methodology for improving revenue that integrates the characteristics of the hotel industry. The hotel sector is both distinct and diverse in the characteristics of the unit of inventory compared to the manufacturing sector. The benefits of yield management have been drawn from the airline industry, but tailored to suit hotels. Many hotels are facing financial pressures which encourage hotel managers to devise imaginative and new ways of managing accommodation. Yield management provides that edge, as a means of supporting the hotel manager in taking decisions on how much accommodation to sell to which customer and at what price.

REFERENCES AND FURTHER READING

Arthur Anderson (1996) *Yield Management in Small to Medium Sized Enterprises in the Tourism Industry*, Brussels: European Commission DGXXIII, Tourism Unit.

Berkus, D. (1988) 'The Yield Management Revolution – An ideal use of Artificial Intelligence', *The Bottomline*, June/July, 13–15.

Belobaba, P.P. (1987) *Air Travel Demand and Airline Seat Inventory Management*, unpublished Ph.D. thesis, Massachusetts Institute of Technology, USA.

Donaghy, K. and McMahon, U. (1995) 'Yield Management – A Marketing Perspective', *International Journal of Vacation Marketing*, **2**(1), 55–62.

Donaghy, K., McMahon, U. and McDowell, D. (1995) 'Yield Management – an overview', *International Journal of Hospitality Management*, **14**(2), 139–50.

Donaghy, K., McMahon-Beattie, U. and McDowell, D. (1997) in Yeoman, I. and Ingold, A. (eds), *Yield Management: Strategies for the Service Industries*, London: Cassell, 183–201.

Donaghy, K., McMahon-Beattie, U. and McDowell, D. (1997a) 'Implementing Yield Management: Lessons from the Hotel Sector', *International Journal of Contemporary Hospitality Management*, **9**(2/3), 50–4.

Hansen, C.N. and Eringa, K. (1997) 'Criteria success factors in Yield Management', paper presented at the 2nd International Management Conference, University of Bath, 9–11 September.

Huyton, J. and Peters, S. (1997) 'Application of Yield Management to the Hotel Industry' in Yeoman, I. and Ingold, A. (eds) *Yield Management: Strategies for the Service Industries*, London: Cassell, 202–17.

Ingold, A. and Huyton, J. (1997) 'Yield Management and the Airline Industry' in Yeoman, I. and Ingold, A. (eds), *Yield Management: Strategies for the Service Industries*, London: Cassell, 143–59.

Jauncy, S., Mitchell, I. and Slamet, P. (1995) 'The Meaning and Management of Yield Management in Hotels', *International Journal of Contemporary Hospitality Management*, **7**(4), 23–6.

Jones, P. and Hamilton, D. (1992) 'Yield Management: Putting People in the Big Picture', *Cornell Hotel and Restaurant Administration Quarterly*, **33**(1), 88–95.

Jones, P and Kewin, E (1997) 'Yield Management in UK Hotels: Principles and Practice', paper presented at 2nd International Yield Management Conference, University of Bath, England, 9–11 September.

Kimes, S.E. (1989) 'The Basics of Yield Management', *Cornell Hotel and Restaurant Administration Quarterly*, **30**(3), 14–19.

Kimes, S.E. (1997) 'Yield Management: An Overview', in Yeoman, I. and Ingold, A. (eds), *Yield Management: Strategies for the Service Industries*, London Cassell, 3–11.

Larsen, T.D. (1988) 'Yield Management and Your Passengers', *Asta Agency Management*, June, 46–8.

Lee-Ross, D. and Johns, N. (1997) 'Yield Management in Hospitality SMEs', *International Journal of Contemporary Hospitality Management*, **9**(2/3), 66–9.

Lieberman, W.H. (1993) 'Debunking the myths of Yield Management', *Cornell Hotel and Restaurant Administration Quarterly*, **34**(1), 34–41.

McCool, A. (1987) 'Some considerations in developing expert systems for the hospitality industry', *International Journal of Hospitality Management*, **6**, 191–8.

Orkin, E.B. (1988) 'Boosting our bottomline with Yield Management', *Cornell Hotel and Restaurant Administration Quarterly*, **28**(4), 52–6.

Orkin, E.B. (1988a) 'Yield Management makes forecasting fact not fiction', *Hotel and Motel Management*, 15 August, 112–18.

Russell, K.A. and Johns, M. (1997) 'Computerised Yield Management Systems; Lessons Learned from the Airline Industry' in Yeoman, I. and Ingold, A. (eds), *Yield Management: Strategies for the Service Industries*, London: Cassell, 120–7.

Sieburgh, J.A. (1988) 'Yield Management at Work at Royal Sonesta', *Lodging Hospitality*, October, 235–7.

Yeoman, I. and Ingold, A. (1997) 'Decision-making', in Yeoman, I. and Ingold, A. (eds), *Yield Management: Strategies for the Service Industries*, London: Cassell, 101–19.

Yeoman, I. and Watson, S. (1997) 'Yield Management: A Human Activity System', *International Journal of Contemporary Hospitality Management*, **9**(2), 80–3.

Hotel valuation techniques 16

Joseph E. Fattorini

INTRODUCTION

The role, method and validity of hotel valuations in the UK has been the subject of debate for some years as part of a wider discussion surrounding the valuation of commercial property more generally. However, a number of concerns and incidents have thrust hotel valuations in particular into the limelight. Towards the end of the 1980s a number of hotel buyers paid what later appeared to be excessive prices for hotel property leading them to experience dire financial problems in the recession of the early 1990s. More specifically, controversy over the valuation of the Queens Moat House Group led to a DTI investigation that has yet to be concluded, and in the wider field of leisure property, there have been several cases of negligence being bought against surveyors (for example, *Corisand Investments Ltd* v *Druce &· Co* 1978; *Craneheath Securities* v *York Montague*, 1993) (Sayce, 1995). In hotels, as in all commercial property valuation, the debate has also been influenced by the publication of The Mallinson Report (Royal Institute of Chartered Surveyors [RICS], 1994) which presented a number of proposals dealing with the way in which appraisals and valuations are carried out, presented and justified by valuers.

The response of the hotel industry as well as valuation professionals to these events and experiences has been to devise guidelines and recommended practice for the valuation of hotel property. In the hotel industry's case the outcome was the *Recommended Practice for the Valuation of Hotels* published by the British Association of Hotel Accountants (BAHA) (1993). This recommended practice was the outcome of a committee established by BAHA in 1991 with the intention of establishing a common basis for hotel valuation. It was hoped that this would restore the confidence of banks and other investors in the hotel sector. Of the various methods available to valuers, the BAHA committee recommended the ten-year discounted cash flow approach (DCF), which is the main valuation methodology discussed in this chapter. A response (RICS, 1994a) and further guidelines were subsequently issued by RICS which related more widely to the valuation of leisure property, including hotels (RICS, 1994b).

The guidelines issued by BAHA and RICS are intended to be advisory and not prescriptive, although they both give strong indications of their preferred practice. Neither is particularly detailed on the subject of the valuation process or the theoretical basis for the methodologies they recommend. Greater discussion of the detail of valuation methodology has taken place in journals and the limited number of texts on the topic. In the context of the UK hotel market, Sayce (1995) and Menorca (1993) are particularly useful in this respect. However the majority of texts in the hospitality valuation field are from the US and in particular from Stephen Rushmore, President of Hospitality Valuation Services, a hotel appraisal and consulting firm. His work *Hotels and Motels: A Guide to Market Analysis, Investment Analysis and Valuations*

(Rushmore, 1992) covering all stages of valuation analysis and calculation has become the standard and seminal work in the area (see also his earlier paper, Rushmore, 1990, which is useful as a description of various financial calculations used in hotel valuation). Similarly, Mellen (1983) is an earlier description of a simultaneous valuation technique now widely used and adapted in the case of hotels. That such a wide body of work on hotel valuation has come out of the US should neither surprise us, nor invalidate it for use in the UK. The US has long been a more sophisticated market for hotel property than anywhere else in the world and hotel property has been seen as a form of financial investment for some time. Needless to say, this has bought greater scrutiny to bear on the values put on hotel property and the returns provided by operators, all leading to more complex, and hopefully more trustworthy, valuation methods.

WHY HAVE A VALUATION REPORT?

Before embarking on the research and analysis involved in valuing hotel property, a valuer must first establish why the valuation is being carried out. Clearly a common reason may be that the current owner wishes to sell. In this case they will wish to find out what price a typical buyer would pay for the property, known as its 'open market value'. Open market value (OMV) 'is defined as the best price at which the sale of the hotel or interest in the hotel might reasonably be expected to have been completed unconditionally for cash on the date of the valuation' (BAHA, 1993: 20). This presumes a willing seller, that the hotel is well marketed to a wide range of buyers and offered for sale in current market conditions.

Alternative forms of valuation may be employed to establish the cost to rebuild the hotel, for insurance requirements or to establish a value for the balance sheet as required for audited accounts, known as asset valuation in the UK. Similarly, some valuations are performed to establish a value when renegotiating financing, when preparing for a flotation on the stock market or raising money for expansion or improvement of the property itself. Given the wide range of uses to which valuation reports might be put, valuers must always be clear about what their purpose in performing the valuation is, and those who commission valuation reports must always be clear in their instructions (for a discussion on the duty of care to be exercised by a valuer in the context of hotels see the discussion of the comments of Gibson J. in *Corisand Investments Ltd* v *Druce & Co.*, 1978, in Hattersley, 1990).

DIFFERENT VALUATION METHODS

We have already noted that the recommended valuation method for hotels in the UK is the ten-year discounted cash flow (DCF). A number of other valuation methodologies exist and some are used widely in the valuation of different forms of commercial and domestic property. Equally some can be very useful in performing check valuations on hotels or for specific forms of valuation. Before discussing the ten-year DCF method it is worth reviewing some of these alternative valuation methodologies.

Influences on the valuation methodology

As has been noted elsewhere in this book, hotels are increasingly held as financial investments and as such are valued by their owners on the basis of the income that they generate (for a wider discussion on the changing emphasis of real estate from 'capital asset' to 'financial asset' see Torres and Volk, 1995). In many forms of commercial property the income generated is relatively stable and so valuations are derived from a 'stabilized' or average income figure which is multiplied or, to use the jargon, 'capitalized' into a total value for the property. However, in hotels the income can vary widely. Income in hotels is particularly related to both revenue from rooms and levels of occupancy, which are themselves closely related to the state of the wider economy (this topic is discussed in Chapter 5). This combination of an inconsistent income stream, which is strongly affected by the wider economy, makes valuations based on a single 'stabilized year' figure from which a valuer could establish the total property value frequently inaccurate. Despite this, the simplicity of valuations based on the multiplication or capitalization of a single, stabilized year remains popular, even if they only act as a check valuation on other, more complex methods.

Furthermore the opacity of the market for hotels can make valuations based on comparative value (as in the way houses are valued) very unsafe. As these are commercial transactions, vendors and buyers are usually keen to keep prices paid a secret, and truly comparative properties can be very hard to find. Not only do hotel characteristics (and thus relative values) change between brands, but the outlook for different properties changes depending on the markets they serve. Thus two similarly branded hotels cannot provide a true comparison because they serve different markets (say London and Frankfurt) whilst hotels in the same market cannot be compared as they are differently oriented or sized (such as the comparison between a small, independent, luxury hotel and a large, branded four star property both situated in a single market like Glasgow).

In the following discussions of methodologies we can see how these and other factors influence the choice of valuation methodology used.

Depreciated replacement cost

The depreciated replacement cost approach (or more simply the 'cost approach') assumes that purchasers will pay no more for a property than the cost of building a similar property with similar utility (Rushmore, 1992: 208). It is arrived at by estimating the construction cost of the hotel at today's prices and then subtracting a depreciation charge to reflect the age of the hotel. Rushmore (1992) suggests that depreciation can come from any of three factors:

- physical deterioration – the physical wearing out of the property;
- functional obsolescence – a lack of desirability in the layout, style, and design of the property as compared to a new property serving the same function; and
- external obsolescence – a loss in value from causes outside the property itself.

The approach can be useful as a check valuation when assessing the viability of a proposed development or in very new units. Even so, a number of factors weigh against it as a valuation methodology in older more established units. Hotels are particularly susceptible to deterioration and obsolescence in the manner described above and this can often be very hard to quantify and justify. More fundamentally, this approach does not reflect investor rationale. Investors are buying the property on the basis of a future stream of profits, not its replacement cost, and to be valid the valuation methodology must reflect this.

Sales comparison

Based on the assumption that a hotel buyer will only pay as much as they would for a similar hotel, the sales comparison approach: (a) involves comparing the hotel with other similar properties that have recently been on the market; and (b) arriving at a likely sale price. Clearly this approach relies on having timely, verifiable, comparable data on which to base valuations. For homogeneous properties like housing this is widely available and properties are directly comparable. However, this is not the case in the hotel market where properties and buyers/sellers are considerably fewer (meaning fewer transactions to base valuations on) and where properties and buyer/seller motivations are considerably more heterogeneous.

That is not to say that the approach has no value. If a number of recent transactions are known they can provide a useful check valuation. Alternatively, this information can be used in the form of a database such as the Hotel Valuation Index, collated by Hotel Valuation Services International, a hotel consultancy company based in the US. This can then provide a benchmark of property values or an indication of trends in the market. A similar benchmark index, based on operating performance rather than comparative sales (and confusingly also called the 'Hotel Valuation Index') is published in the journal *Hotel Report*.

Income capitalization

As hotel ownership is a form of investment, the ideal method of valuing a hotel should be one that reflects the rationale of the investor who is not simply buying a hotel, but is also buying a stream of future earnings. Income capitalization therefore works by valuing the hotel on the basis of what income it generates. This is the basis of our principal valuation methodology, the ten-year discounted cash flow. It is also the basis of the simpler earnings multiple method which we shall deal with first. To understand how both the methods work it is worth establishing the basis of investment methodology, using the following example adapted and corrected from Isaac (1998: 12–13).

Where an investor has a ready sum of money and has established a required rate of return, it is possible to calculate the income from a proposed investment in the following way:

$$Income = Capital \times \frac{i}{100} \text{ where } i = \text{rate of return required}$$

For example, if the investor has £10,000 and requires a rate of return of 8 per cent the income is:

$$Income = £10,000 \times \frac{8}{100} = £800 \, p.a.$$

Yet in the case of hotel and other property investments we know, or at least have a prediction of the income we will receive but do not know what the capital value of that income is. To do that we must change the formula so that the capital becomes the subject:

$$Capital = Income \times \frac{100}{i}$$

So if we want to know how much to pay for an investment that produces £800 per year, and our required rate of return is again 8 per cent:

$$Capital = £800 \times \frac{100}{8} = £10,000$$

What we have done is turned the income into a capital sum, or 'capitalized' it. We can further refine this calculation and express it in a slightly different way. As the income we are interested in here is the cash we will receive, we must ensure that the income capitalized is 'net' of any expenses to give us a net income figure (NI) further modifying the calculation to:

$$Capital = NI \times \frac{100}{i}$$

Also, in real estate practice, rates of return are commonly expressed in the form of a multiplier, referred to as 'Years Purchase'. Thus in the case of our calculation above:

$$\frac{100}{8} \text{ becomes } 12.5$$

This produces the final equation:

$$C = NI \times YP$$

Those interested in this topic will find Isaac (1998) and Baum *et al.* (1997) useful general introductions to property investment and the income approach to property valuation.

Earnings multiple method

The earnings multiple method (also known as the single capitalization rate, multiplier or band of investment – one stabilized year approach) is often favoured by valuers. It is not hard to see why; not only does it reflect the rationale of real hotel buyers, it is also quick and easy to use, easily understood and widely used in the valuation of commercial property other than hotels. The calculation is essentially the same as that outlined above. The issue for the hotel valuer using this method is how they derive their net income (NI) figure and multiplier rate.

The net income figure in this approach is the level of income that the property could reasonably sustain over its lifetime. As in the discounted cash flow approach described later, valuers should complete a full market analysis before arriving at a net income figure. This should include factors such as the development of competing property, but should exclude exceptional factors (for instance, the Olympic Games) which would exert a significant, but unsustained influence over the pattern of profitability in the hotel. Equally, in the case of new hotels, valuers should ignore the time taken to build up to a stabilized level of earnings.

To illustrate the method let us assume we are valuing a modern, four star, 100 bedroom hotel in a reasonably attractive, London, location. The hotel has enjoyed strong revenues over the past few years and is expected to perform reasonably well over the millennium and therefore suggests a sustainable net income figure of £1,458,000. We must now calculate the multiplier which will allow us to 'capitalize' this income. In this case we will assume that the purchaser is buying the property entirely out of equity (out of their own pocket) and will assume that they are looking for a return of 9.8 per cent. We can convert this percentage rate into a multiplier by inverting the terms:

$$\frac{9.8}{100} \text{ becomes } \frac{100}{9.8} \text{ or } 10.2$$

Leaving us to simply complete the calculation:

$$C = NI \times YP$$

or

$$C = 1,458,000 \times 10.2 = 14,871,600$$

$$\text{rounded to} = £14,800,000$$

Discounted Cash Flow

As we have noted above, whilst the earnings multiple method reflects investor rationale, is easy to understand and implement and widely used in commercial property valuation, it has a drawback. Hotels do not enjoy steady income flows as they are very susceptible to changes in the wider economy and this is reflected in their performance. This means that a single figure is insufficient in quantifying future earnings. What we need is a valuation methodology that can reflect varying income flows over a number of years and then capitalize those earnings in terms of their worth to the hotel owner today. The discounted cash flow method does this.

Before a valuer can begin the valuation method itself, they must provide net income figures to be discounted. The process begins with a market survey, followed by analyses of the property and its financial performance. At this stage the skill and experience of the valuer is paramount, as judgements which will have a material impact on the final value placed on the hotel are made at this time.

The market survey

Physical inspection

An initial physical inspection of the property is vital, and at this stage the valuer asks several key questions:

- is the hotel and its services appropriate for its market positioning?
- what is its general condition? and
- what level of investment will be required to bring it up to/maintain the required standard and when will the cash for these investments need to paid?

As large and complex physical properties, this stage will often require the help of a qualified surveyor and others who can make informed judgements on the physical condition of the property.

Location

'Location, location, location' may be an oft-used aphorism in discussions of the hotel industry, but for the hotel valuer a number of quite specific issues arise. Prominence, accessibility and 'findability' are vital in most urban, airport and roadside hotels as well as proximity to transport links, business locations or shopping and leisure facilities. Alternatively in countryside, rural and leisure oriented locations, being remote, secluded and quiet can be the hotel's primary asset. The importance of location as a factor in consumers' choice of hotels is reflected in a range of research devoted to the topic. One paper worthy of particular note is Bull (1994: 14) whose research suggests that 'it should be possible to put 'implicit price-location contours' on an area map for any particular quality of hotel or motel'. This would allow a valuer to estimate the price premium hotel guests appear prepared to pay for the benefit of staying within a certain radius of a location. This clearly has benefits in the assessment of proposed hotel developments.

Market overview

Having established the basic details about the hotel the valuer now needs to consider what the future holds for the property. This begins with an analysis of the market and economy generally. Hotels are susceptible to a very wide range of influences from the economy, and many of these are discussed in detail in Chapter 5. Amongst them are questions like:

- is the economy in a cyclical upturn or downturn?
- is the structure of the customer base changing?
- what is happening in the wider real estate market? and
- what are the key demand generators and what is influencing them?

This information is all collated and assessed as part of environmental scanning and environmental information collection in valuers and many hotel firms as a matter of course. It is vital in drawing up sustainable cash flow statements for the property.

Hotel market

Like the market overview above, this information is collected regularly by valuers and many hotel companies. It deals with the specific market in which the hotel to be valued operates. It will consider:

- what is the hotel's market position? Is it upscale, budget, luxury?
- what is the hotel's competitive profile? Who are its primary and secondary competitors?
- what is the hotel's demand profile? Who uses the hotel and why?
- can current (accommodated) demand be analysed in terms of market segment?
- is there unaccommodated demand from consumers who would like to come but cannot afford it or find rooms? Can this be induced (demand)? and
- what is likely to happen in the future? Are new competitors expected to arrive in the market? Are customers expected to change to competitor brands?

From this data it is possible to project likely demand in the future for:

- the whole market; and
- specific market segments.

This can be used to build scenarios, perform sensitivity analyses and penetration analyses which indicate how far a hotel penetrates each market segment. Again, a great deal of research has gone into how best to analyse these factors. Useful work in this area, particularly for the development of new hotels has been done by Morey and Dittman (1997).

Property details

Having picked up a general picture of the physical state of the hotel in the physical analysis, the valuer must now find out the detail of the property. Issues addressed include:

- the tenure – is the hotel a freehold, leasehold or building lease property? What effect does this have on value?
- what is the condition of the site and the property's building dimensions? and
- what are the statutory requirements for this type of property and are they being addressed in this case?

Again, hotel valuers may well need to call on the assistance of surveyors, lawyers or others at this stage.

Financial analysis

Financial analysis is carried out on historical accounts, allowing the valuer to form a basis for their income projections which will take into account the information gathered in the preceding stages. This can be a complex process and is covered extensively in Rushmore (1992). Several basic stages of the analysis are suggested by Hattersley (1990):

1 categorize income and expenditure and compare with published data and in-house historical performance;
2 estimate/calculate tenant's capital for the contents of the hotels, cash required to run the business and the cost of stock;
3 estimate/calculate occupancy rates;
4 analyse cash flow and cash flow sources;
5 consider the basis for depreciation and estimate the timing of actual cash outflows to buy new fixtures, fittings and equipment; and
6 estimate the level of stock (food, beverage, sundries and so on) required.

From this analysis it is possible to estimate future income using all the information garnered in the analysis so far. In the case of the discounted cash flow approach the earnings are estimated for each of the next (usually) ten years. From this earnings figure the valuer must deduct certain fixed charges, for example:

- management fees (if payable);
- insurance;
- property taxes;
- ground rent (if payable);
- expenditure/provision for renewals and replacements of furniture, fixtures, plant and machinery; and
- capital expenditure.

In the 'earnings multiple' method of valuation discussed earlier, the estimate of 'maintainable earnings' (in the case of our example £1,458,000) is also net of these deductions.

Residual value

The final piece of information needed before the valuer can construct a cash flow for discounting is a residual value. The discounted cash flow method works on the basis of a purchaser receiving an income stream for a number of years as noted (usually ten) followed by a hypothetical sale. The value attributed to the sale is usually a multiple of the final year's earnings. This is estimated on the basis of the market and the experience of the valuer. Whilst this can appear somewhat imprecise, as we shall see, the process of discounting future cash flows reduces the significance of any error in residual value calculation.

The valuation calculation; ten year discounted cash flow

The end result of this analysis and forecasting is a cash flow statement ready for discounting similar to Table 16.1. The figures are based on the same property described in the earlier application of the earnings multiple method, in other words a modern, four star, 100 bedroom hotel in a reasonably attractive, London, location. The hotel has

Table 16.1 Discounted cash flow valuation statement

All figures in future values £000s	1999	2000	2001	2002	2003	2004	2005	2006	2007	2008
Revenue	3,633	4,033	4,114	4,279	4,450	4,628	4,813	5,006	5,206	5,414
Less departmental expenses (includes cost of sales)	1,162	1,220	1,269	1,320	1,373	1,428	1,485	1,544	1,606	1,670
Departmental income	2,471	2,813	2,845	2,959	3,077	3,200	3,328	3,462	3,600	3,744
Less operating expenses (includes administration, marketing, management fees, maintenance and energy costs)	761	807	839	872	907	943	981	1,020	1,061	1,103
House profit	1,710	2,006	2,006	2,087	2,170	2,257	2,347	2,442	2,539	2,641
Less fixed expenses (includes property taxes and insurance)	327	353	367	382	397	413	430	447	465	484
(Plus residual value)										23,900
Net free cash flows	1,383	1,653	1,639	1,705	1,773	1,844	1,917	1,995	2,074	26,057

Residual value is capitalized at a rate of 9%, alternatively expressed as a multiplier or years purchase (YP) of 11.1. Therefore with the final year's net free cash flow of £2,157,000 the residual value is calculated using the calculation C = NI x YP (where C is the residual value):

C = £2,157,000 × 11.1 = £23,942,700
rounded to = *£23,900,000*

enjoyed strong revenues over the past few years and is expected to perform reasonably well over the millennium. However we have accounted for the 'millennium hangover', suggesting that revenues will not be so strong in 2001, and then stabilizing thereafter. For the years 2002 to 2008 earnings are assumed to grow at a stabilized rate of 4 per cent. Finally, residual value is calculated on the basis of a 9 per cent capitalization rate, or alternatively a multiplier/years purchase (YP) of 11.1. This means that we expect the property to be worth 11.1 times its final year's earnings.

Ten-year discounted cash flow using a single discount rate

The basis for any discounted cash flow calculation, is a calculation of how much future cash flows (in our case the net income figures) are worth to an investor *today*. In this, the more basic form of discounted cash flow calculation, we will assume that the property is being bought outright and in cash. Calculating the discount rate in this case is done in two stages.

First the investor must consider the three elements that make up the discount rate. The first of these is compensation for the effects of inflation and the second, the risk free rate of return. These two factors are incorporated in the current market rate for long-term government bonds (gilts). In this example we shall use a rate of 5.8 per cent. The third element is the risk premium. This is the return required by the investor to reflect the greater risk involved in investing in this project as opposed to risk free investments (government bonds). It is arrived at after considering factors such as the age, condition and location of the hotel, the condition of the economy and the 'quality' or trustworthiness of the predicted future earnings. For this property the investor feels that a rate of 4 per cent would be appropriate, which, added to the 5.8 per cent rate above gives a figure of 9.8 per cent. In our example this is the required rate of return.

The next stage is to convert this rate into a discount factor. This is done using the calculation:

$$\frac{1}{(1 + i)^n} = \text{the discount factor}$$

where

- i is the rate of return; and
- n is the projection period in years.

Thus in this case in year 1:

$$\frac{1}{(1 + 9.8\%)^1} \text{ or } \frac{1}{(1.098)^1} = 0.91$$

and in year 2:

$$\frac{1}{(1.098)^2} = 0.830$$

This is sometimes referred to as the 'present value of £1 at x per cent'. In other words, and in this case, £1 received a year in the future, at a rate of return of 9.8 per cent is worth 91.1p today. £1 received two years in the future at a rate of return of 9.8 per cent is worth 83p today. The net income figures are then multiplied by their corresponding discount factors to give the present value of the net income. This is shown in Table 16.2.

Table 16.2 Discounting factors and present values

Year	Net income in £000s	Discount factor at 9.8%	Present value
1999	1,383	0.911	1,260
2000	1,653	0.830	1,371
2001	1,639	0.755	1,237
2002	1,705	0.688	1,173
2003	1,773	0.627	1,112
2004	1,844	0.571	1,053
2005	1,917	0.520	997
2006	1,995	0.473	944
2007	2,074	0.431	894
2008	26,057	0.393	10,240
		Total property value	20,280,000
		rounded to:	£20,200,000

It will be noticed that this valuation is considerably higher than that achieved by the earnings multiple method (£20,200,000 against £14,800,000 – a difference of over 25 per cent). This is despite both methods having the same required rate of return, 9.8 per cent. Clearly the disparity lies in a much rosier outlook of earnings growth in the discounted cash flow method than in the earnings multiple approach. Were the valuation real, the valuer would wish to check their assumptions under both methods in order to attempt to resolve this disparity.

SUMMARY

This chapter has briefly discussed several key methods of valuing hotel property and considered the two most reliable (earnings multiple and discounted cash flow) in rather more detail. The discussion is intended to be introductory and interested readers are directed to the reading indicated in the text. Those seeking to study the area further are directed in particular to the Hotel Valuation Formula developed by Mellen (1983) and discussed extensively by Rushmore (1990, 1992). This algebraic formula allows for discounted cash flow valuations where the hotel is partly debt financed and is a development of the basic discounted cash flow approach discussed above.

REFERENCES AND FURTHER READING

BAHA (1993) *Recommended Practice for the Valuation of Hotels*, London: British Association of Hotel Accountants.
Baum, A; Mackmin, D and Nunnington, N (1997) *The Income Approach to Property Valuation*, London: International Thomson Business Press, 4th edn.
Bull, A.N.O. (1994) 'Pricing a Motel's Location', *International Journal of Contemporary Hospitality Management*, **6**(6), 10–15.
Hattersley, M. (1990) 'Valuation of Hotels', *Journal of Valuation*, **8**(2), 143–65.
Isaac, D. (1998) *Property Investment*, Basingstoke: Macmillan.
Mellen, S.R. (1983) 'Simultaneous Valuation: A New Capitalization Technique for Hotel and Other Income Properties', *The Appraisal Journal*, April, 165–89.

Menorca, E.S. (1993) 'Hotel Valuations: the Income Capitalisation Approach', *Journal of Property Valuation and Investment*, **11**(3), 211–16.

Morey, R.C. and Dittman, D.A. (1997) 'An Aid in Selecting the Brand, Size and Other Strategic Choices for a Hotel', *Journal of Hospitality and Tourism Research*, **21**(1), 71–99.

RICS (1994) *The Mallinson Report: Report of the President's Working Party on Commercial Property Valuations*, London: Royal Institution of Chartered Surveyors.

RICS (1994a) *The Valuation of Hotels: the Royal Institution of Chartered Surveyors Response to the Recommended Practice for the Valuation of Hotels*, London, Royal Institution of Chartered Surveyors.

RICS (1994b) *Manual of Valuation Guidance Notes*, London: Royal Institution of Chartered Surveyors.

Rushmore, S. (1990) 'Hotel Valuation Techniques', *The Real Estate Finance Journal*, Summer, http: //www.hvs-int.com/frcareer.htm.

Rushmore, S. (1992) *Hotels and Motels: A Guide to Market Analysis, Investment Analysis and Valuations*, Chicago, IL: Appraisal Institute.

Sayce, S. (1995) 'Leisure Property: A Question of Profit?', *Journal of Property Finance*, **6**(1), 7–27.

Torres, M. and Volk, C. (1995) 'Awareness Growing of Valuing Real Estate', *Pensions and Investments*, 3 April, 45.

Hotels and entertainment   17

Howard L. Hughes

The focus of this chapter is the provision of live entertainment in hotels. It is common-place for hotels to provide entertainment in the form of television and radio in guest rooms and background recorded music in public areas such as bars, restaurants and reception but performances in hotels by musicians, actors, comedians, dancers and the like are relatively rare. A hotel is 'an operation that provides accommodation and ancillary services to people away from home' (Jones and Lockwood, 1989: 19). Those ancillary services are usually interpreted as food and drink in restaurants and bars. In addition hotels may provide facilities for banqueting and conferences and possibly for sport and fitness activities. Live entertainment, however, is considered to be the function of theatres and nightclubs.

ENTERTAINMENT, HOLIDAYS AND HOTELS

Holidays

For many leisure tourists it is likely that entertainment is a significant part of the holiday experience. Entertainment is a feature of most holiday destinations whether in hotels or elsewhere (see Figure 17.1). A survey of British holiday-makers showed that in over a third (38 per cent) of their holidays in England they had been to see some form of live entertainment, including discos (Research Surveys of Great Britain, 1985). A similar proportion (32 per cent) of overseas visitors to Britain visit the theatre during their stay (British Tourist Authority and English Tourist Board, 1996). In one particular UK seaside tourist town, Blackpool, 70.8 per cent of holiday-makers had seen live entertainment during their stay (Hughes and Benn, 1997). It is unlikely that much business tourism has an entertainment component in quite the same way though it may feature as part of the process of establishing and maintaining good business relationships. Many conferences will have a supporting programme of social activities that may extend to entertainment. Individual business-people may well also have a demand for entertainment which is incidental to their business visit.

Although people do go to see live entertainment whilst on holiday, the influence of entertainment on choice of holiday destination is less easily established. In some instances entertainment will be a significant attraction of a destination and in others it will be an amenity which is incidental to other more significant attractions (see Figure 17.1). There have been a number of studies which have attempted to assess the influence of entertainment (see Hughes and Benn, 1995). In some obvious instances such as Edinburgh's International Arts Festival visitors are drawn by that specific attraction (Gratton and Taylor, 1992). In other situations where a more general holiday is sought the role of entertainment is less powerful or direct. In the case of Blackpool, the

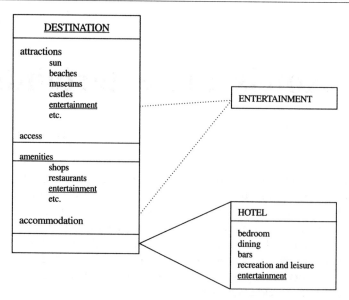

Figure 17.1 Simplified model of the components of the vacation destination and of the hotel and the relationship with entertainment

largest seaside tourist town in the UK, holiday-makers rated entertainment as one of the most important reasons for their visit to the town though it, like Las Vegas, does has a particular image associated with spectacular entertainment (Hughes and Benn, 1997). Some holiday trips are motivated largely by the desire to visit a show; leisure trips to London by British people often include seeing a musical as well as shopping and visiting other tourist attractions. For destinations such as London, it is common for entertainment and hotels to be linked in a package of accommodation and tickets to a show in a theatre. This may be put together by a tour operator specializing in this field; there are a number of such operators focusing particularly (but not solely) on London.

Overseas visitors to Britain consistently rate 'theatre' as an important reason for the visit. In 1995, over a third considered that it was 'very' or 'quite important' in the decision to visit though higher proportions gave that evaluation to historic attractions such as museums, castles, churches and cathedrals (British Tourist Authority and English Tourist Board, 1996). London, which has about a quarter of all professional theatres in the UK, also relies heavily on entertainment as one of its tourist resources (Hughes, 1998 in press). Some caution must be exercised, however, about the power of entertainment, in isolation, to attract holiday-makers to a destination. It may be significant only in conjunction with other attractions. There are many inter-related factors affecting the decision and it is likely that no one factor by itself will be decisive.

Entertainment is undoubtedly a part of the tourist product in that it characterizes most tourist towns, and holiday-makers visit shows of one sort or another whilst on holiday. Whether or not it is a fundamental attraction of a destination will depend on the individual destination and holiday-maker. There is nonetheless an obvious link between entertainment and hotels in the same way as there is between any tourist attraction or activity and the accommodation that is necessary for the tourism to occur. There are instances however where the link is more direct and the hotel itself provides entertainment.

Hotels

Nature of entertainment

The whole hospitality experience may be conceived of as a 'theatrical' experience. 'The theatre analogy may be applied to describe the role play between the frontline employee … and the guest' (Larsen and Aske, 1992: 22). The restaurant situation which is where guest–employee interaction is probably greatest is particularly identified as not just being 'like show business. It is show business … . The result is audience-participation theatre of the most demanding kind' (Romm, 1989: 37). These sorts of models of hospitality serve to draw attention to the interactive nature of the relationship and the importance of involvement and they result in an emphasis on the development of the social skills of staff (Gardner and Wood, 1991).

Apart from the theatre analogy there are situations where the theatre experience is more explicit. There are restaurants (usually non-hotel) where staff themselves perform in the sense of dancing, singing, juggling, as part of the serving experience. The provision of entertainment separate from the meal-service may take many forms ranging from recorded background music through accompanying live music groups to 'dinner theatre' where the entertainment becomes the focus after the meal is complete. Music in restaurants (and places such as supermarkets) can influence behaviour; it may establish identity and work to attract appropriate clientele. The type, volume and tempo of the music are all believed to affect eating-patterns (Lewis, 1991). The tone and identity of a restaurant and the length of customer stay at the table may be influenced by the music that is played there.

The provision of entertainment in hotels is similarly varied and it is convenient to categorize it as in Figure 17.2. Entertainment may be either live or recorded and may be either a background to activity such as eating or drinking or may be the main focus of activity as in a theatre. Karaoke is an amalgam of live and recorded entertainment and is usually a focus-activity rather than background. Any entertainment may also take place in a variety of places including dining rooms and bars or more specialist nightclubs and the like. Some of these, especially discos and nightclub entertainment may be open to non-residents. With respect to recorded music it is common for it to be relayed as background into public areas including restaurants (quadrant A of Figure 17.2). Recorded music can also be very significant in its own right in the form of discos (quadrant C) or as a contribution to karaoke (C or D). Music is evidently an important component of this recorded entertainment but it is also frequently associated with live entertainment in hotels.

Music performed by soloists, bands, quartets, groups, and so on may be background in hotel dining rooms (quadrant B). Live entertainment is also provided separately from the dining experience in a wide variety of forms though music is probably still the most common. An examination of brochures, advertisements and other media illustrates the range; it includes lounge pianists, 'tea dances', children's entertainers (including magic and puppetry), and musicians of all types (classical, jazz, folk, country and western) as a focal point rather than background as well as comedians, dancers and illusionists (quadrant D). Some hotels offer 'entertainment weekend-breaks' based on concerts or shows in the hotel itself or in conjunction with some other venue such as a theatre, concert hall or stately home.

The distinguishing feature of the British 'holiday camp' (popular from the 1930s through to the 1950s) was its all-inclusive provision; the holiday-maker did not need to leave the site during the holiday as all facilities were provided. The camps were

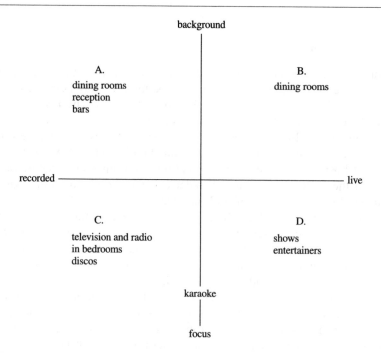

Figure 17.2 Hotels: the provision of entertainment

renowned for their on-site entertainment and employing their own teams of entertainers who would often be employed to undertake other jobs as well. Perhaps the most famous were the Butlin's 'Redcoats'; many entertainers who later found fame on television, radio and film began their careers as Redcoats (Ward and Hardy, 1986).

Some issues

Parker and Kent (1986: 13) consider the issue of entertainment in hospitality from a particular US perspective and conclude that 'the selection, hiring and monitoring of live entertainment can be a perplexing task for the hospitality manager'. They offer an approach to determining the financial returns from putting on entertainment and advise seeking the advice of a booking agent when choosing acts to hire. They consider that the complexities of the entertainment task arise in part from obligations with respect to copyright and the hire of union labour.

The provider of entertainment in the UK needs to be aware of a number of similar practical issues. Any place where 'public entertainment' occurs is required to be licensed by the local council (Cotterell, 1993; Manchester, 1994). This requirement is covered in England and Wales by the Local Government (Miscellaneous Provisions) Act 1982; London and Scotland are covered by different legislation but with similar provisions. A licence is required for any public dancing, music or other forms of entertainment whether it is performed for or by the public and whether or not the music is live or recorded. A licence is not always required, however; for example, if the music is incidental to some other activity or if the entertainment is in a members' club. Premises licensed for the sale of intoxicating liquor are not required to obtain a separate entertainment licence if, for instance, music played is not live. In some parts of the country local councils also have the power to license private places of entertainment. The concern of the licensing authority, before a licence is issued, is to determine matters of public safety and public order.

Royalties have to paid on all music played, whether recorded or live. The Performing Rights Society (PRS) collects such royalties on behalf of composers and lyricists from all places where there are public performances of music that is still in copyright. A licence is issued to the owner of premises on payment of an annual fee based on a number of factors. During 1993 the PRS collected £48 million royalties, of which the largest single amount (22.3 per cent) was from public houses. Hotels, restaurants and cafes were the third largest contributor at 12.3 per cent of the total (Performing Rights Society, 1994).

Hotel choice

Given the usual division of activity between hotels and theatres it is unlikely that entertainment will feature as a significant factor in the choice of hotel. Hotels that do provide it presumably assume that it will have some influence on choice. Studies make a distinction between those attributes of a hotel that are 'determinant' (which determine choice) and others, which though of some significance, do not influence choice (Lewis, 1984). Location is an important attribute of a hotel but it may not be 'determinant' when there are several proximate hotels. Similarly, en-suite facilities may be important to guests but when most hotels have them choice is based on some other attribute. (See Callan, 1996, for a related analysis of business travellers' hotel choice decisions). Choice of hotel will be influenced by the image that is created in the consumer's mind. This 'positioning' seeks to differentiate a hotel from its competitors by, for instance, offering different services or by modifying the potential customer's perceptions of the services offered (Lewis and Chambers, 1989). Hotels are 'largely equipment-based' (Jones and Lockwood, 1989: 21) in that guests' contact with the hotel building, its decor and furniture is usually greater than it is with staff; there is scope for positioning through these physical aspects of hotels but it is limited by the fixity of past investment in the fabric, fixtures and fittings and the expense of new investment.

Studies of determinants of hotel choice have not identified entertainment as being important though undoubtedly there may be instances where it is. A similar situation arises with respect to leisure facilities. There has been an assumption that such facilities in hotels do have an important role in establishing competitive advantage: 'to provide an effective differential advantage, leisure provision will need to be a part of the hotel's overall branding strategy' (Vierich and Calver, 1991: 15). These leisure facilities are associated with sport and fitness. There has undoubtedly been an increase in the number of hotels in all locations that offer leisure facilities in the form of swimming pools, gyms, saunas and also golf courses, squash courts and the like. The rationale has been to create a competitive advantage. The attraction has usually been greatest, in city centre and country hotels, for weekend leisure guests whose usage of the facilities is usually higher than that of business guests (Gratton and Taylor, 1987). Any advantage to an individual hotel has usually been short-lived in that most medium-sized and larger hotels now offer such services. The usage of facilities of guests may not always be high but it is possible that their existence may have some influence on hotel choice and guests have the option of use. Apart from their role in attracting guests, hotel managers have also expected leisure services to generate extra revenue; their introduction may be part of a move towards different markets willing to pay premium room rates

(Hales and Collins, 1988). Additional income may also result from local, non-resident, membership schemes and it is this which has been expected to make facilities profitable in most cases. There is little real evidence to suggest that these leisure facilities (or entertainment) feature amongst the attributes of hotels that are determinant in choice (see Callan, 1996).

CASE STUDIES

Las Vegas

The resort hotel is comparable to the British 'holiday camp' in that it too seeks to be all-inclusive (Lundberg, 1994). The services offered and the standard are considerably different, however, from those of the holiday camp and focus on recreational facilities such as swimming pools, golf courses and similar sporting amenities. The resort hotel in the UK tends to be positioned as a country club with up-market clientele (Roper, 1996). Entertainment does not feature highly in these but a particular type of resort hotel, the casino hotel, does put emphasis on entertainment. Such hotels are especially associated with Las Vegas (Nevada, USA) where 'entertainment shares billing with gaming and hotel rooms' (Lundberg, 1994: 187). The main attraction of Las Vegas is gaming; until recently Nevada was the only state to legalize casino gaming in the US. Las Vegas receives about 29 million visitors a year (Las Vegas Convention and Visitors Authority, 1996) and claims to have 12 of the 13 largest hotels in the world; the MGM Grand, for instance, has just over 5000 rooms.

Casinos are usually based in hotels which also provide a variety of live entertainment in order to attract and retain gaming customers (Christiansen and Brinkerhoff-Jacobs, 1995). Most Las Vegas entertainment is associated with hotels; the musical 'Starlight Express' was, for instance, staged at the Las Vegas Hilton. The entertainment ranges from musicians in bar and lounge settings (usually without entry charge) through circuses and illusionists to national and international artists in large purpose-built theatres and concert arenas. Some of these operations are so huge that effectively they operate as separate enterprises. Caesar's Palace (1500 rooms) has a 4500 seat indoor theatre and a 15,300 seat outdoor events stadium; MGM Grand has a similar size events centre as well as its own 33 acre theme park. At Circus Circus there is free circus in addition to a 5 acre indoor theme park.

There is even a genre of show, glitzy spectacular floor-shows with dancers and singers, that is referred to universally as a 'Las Vegas-type show'. The 'Official Visitors Guide' to Las Vegas refers to 'other parts of the casinos (where) entertainers adorned in glittering costumes join forces in lavish stage spectaculars … . Extravaganzas costing millions to produce surround visitors in a fantasy of shapely dancers, intricate choreography and special effects' (Las Vegas Convention and Visitors Authority, 1996: 40). Las Vegas is also a centre for many associated spectacular events including boxing.

Just under half of Las Vegas visitors attend a show during their visit (GLS Research, 1995) though it appears that this proportion has been falling (Dandurand and Ralenkotter, 1985). Roehl (1996) attempted to determine the effect that casino amenities such as entertainment might have on gambling expenditure; this was for a sample of Las Vegas residents rather than for visitors. Over half of these 'non-visitors' attended some form of entertainment though it was difficult to demonstrate that there was any significant relationship between amount of spending in the casino and spending on entertainment (or in restaurants). Roehl could surmise only that such amenities encouraged residents to visit a particular casino and to stay on the premises.

Entertainment was initially regarded in Las Vegas as a loss-leader in order to attract high-spending gamblers (Dandurand and Ralenkotter, 1985; Thompson *et al.*, 1996). There is now, however, more emphasis on entertainment as a profit centre; this, in conjunction with rising costs, has resulted in a shift from the star-centred shows towards smaller scale variety (or revue) shows and musicals.

The city has also in recent years sought to re-position itself as a family holiday destination. In order to do this, more family-oriented entertainment has been offered in the form of virtual reality experiences, theme parks and free open-air events such as an erupting volcano outside the Mirage hotel and a pirate battle performed outside the Treasure Island hotel. The emphasis on Las Vegas as a gaming centre has been reduced but it is still the hotels that maintain a connection with entertainment, albeit in a different form.

These developments have had mixed fortunes (Loverseed, 1995) and, whilst the appeal of Las Vegas has broadened, some forms of entertainment may have had an adverse effect on gaming (Christiansen and Brinkerhoff-Jacobs, 1995). There are several other concerns associated with this re-positioning, such as the increased number of 'non-gamblers' and 'low-roller' gamblers in the city and the loss of its distinctive character (Thompson, Pinney and Scibrowsky, 1996). In addition, 'the problem with this scenario is that casino executives are not skilled in providing these types of experience' (Thompson *et al.*, 1996: 72) and there have been some noticeable failures.

Las Vegas is a unique case and it would not be justifiable to draw conclusions about the hotel–entertainment relationship from it alone. The relationship is unclear because of the particular nature of the link between the two in this destination; entertainment along with gaming has been an integral part of the hotel product. The case study does suggest, however, that there may be two separate issues: the influence of entertainment on the choice of tourist destination and the influence on the choice of hotel.

Blackpool

The town

The remainder of this chapter discusses the results of a study of hotels and entertainment that was based in Blackpool. This is the largest seaside tourist town in the UK: just over 4 million staying visits in 1989 (the date of the last comprehensive estimate). There is also a very large day visitor market: nearly 13 million day visits in 1989. Blackpool's Pleasure Beach (an amusement park complex) is currently the most popular of all English visitor attractions (Hanna, 1994).

Blackpool is a tourist town which has an image of liveliness and vitality and it has been described as a town offering scope for 'working class conspicuous consumption – economically modest but indiscreetly vulgar' (Thompson, 1983). Its reputation has always been slightly down-market with entertainment that often verged on the 'bizarre'. A contemporary observer refers to Blackpool as: 'a mistress with whom one might spend a week of frisky … fun' (Martin, 1996: 25).

Blackpool has a long tradition, along with many other seaside towns, of live shows and of entertainment in theatres including pier theatres. 'The two main piers, North and South, have played host to the greats of British comedy as generation after generation of entertainers have won their spurs and crowned their glory in Blackpool' (Fanshawe, 1996). There is currently a large entertainment industry in the resort much of which is in the hands of commercial providers (Hughes and Benn, 1998). Unlike Las Vegas, most of this entertainment is not connected with the hotels. There are two large conventional theatres (2980 seats and 1200 seats respectively), three pier theatres (300 to 1500 seats) and a number of venues at two entertainment complexes, the Tower (1800 seats) and the Pleasure Beach amusement park (ranging from 450 to 2300 seats). There are also numerous bars and clubs where some form of entertainment is offered.

The survey

As noted earlier in this chapter most visitors to Blackpool go to see entertainment during their stay. Just over 20 per cent, however, of the shows they saw were in 'small' venues such as hotels, social clubs and bars (Hughes and Benn, 1997). The provision in hotels was the subject of a specific study carried out during April–July 1997. The aim was to determine the implications for management of providing such entertainment and to determine the rationale for this provision. In this study guests were not asked to rate the significance of entertainment in their hotel choice; the concern was to obtain management and ownership perspectives on the service offered. There are relatively few 'chain' or large hotels in Blackpool; this is similar to the situation in most seaside tourist towns where 'small' independently-owned hotels dominate. There are no hotels comparable in size to the mega-resorts of Las Vegas and the largest hotels are no more than 400 rooms.

In order to carry out the investigation it was necessary to identify those hotels in Blackpool that offered some form of live entertainment. The most accessible, suitable listing of hotels was the Blackpool holiday guide, published annually. In this guide a number of hotels state that they offer entertainment to guests. The extent of entertainment provision is, though, under-stated in the guide; some hotels known to offer entertainment do not include this fact in the guide information and not all of Blackpool's hotels, especially smaller ones, appear in the holiday guide. A total of 87 hotels were identified from the guide, and from other diverse sources, as offering entertainment to guests (this is equivalent to approximately 22 per cent of the 400 hotels in the guide). These 87 were sent a short self-completion questionnaire addressed to the manager or proprietor.

The questionnaire required the respondents to give details of the hotel (room size, classification) and to confirm that they did provide live entertainment. Other questions dealt with the type of entertainment provided, the timing in the week and year and the reasons for provision. The respondents were also asked for their views on the importance of the entertainment in attracting visitors to their hotel and on the usage and effects of the services provided.

There was a 33.3 per cent response to this mail-out: 29 completed questionnaires were returned (see Table 17.1). There is no comprehensive data relating to the accommodation stock in Blackpool and it cannot therefore be claimed that these results are representative but the size range of the 29 respondent hotels does approximate that of all hotels identified as offering entertainment. In addition, 8 of the 29 respondents agreed to follow-up interviews (see Table 17.1 for size range of hotels of the interviewees). The purpose of the interviews, which took place with proprietors or hotel managers, was to gain more information about topics raised in the questionnaire and to discuss practical issues in providing live entertainment.

Table 17.1 Hotel entertainment in Blackpool: characteristics of hotels represented in survey and interviews

	Questionnaires (n=29)	Interviews (n=8)
<25 rooms	3	1
25–49 rooms	14	3
50–75 rooms	7	3
>75 rooms	3	1
Not known	2	–
Range:	15–361 rooms	22–107 rooms

Survey and interview results

The information from the guide and other sources suggests that it is the larger hotels that are more likely to provide entertainment and more likely to do so in a professional manner. Relatively few hotels with less than 25 rooms offered any entertainment. The larger hotels in the sample of 29 were the ones most likely to provide entertainment year round and every night of the week. These hotels were also likely to have an established programme of entertainment. Typically the smaller ones did not have regular provision and the programme was more *ad hoc* and flexible.

Every hotel's programme was dominated by singers, live music and cabaret variety acts and comedians, usually described as 'easy listening' and 'middle-of-the-road' (see Table 17.2). Acts were usually professional (23 out of the 29 hotels used local professionals) and it was considered there was little difficulty finding performers in Blackpool. More often than not the acts were booked through personal contact though agents were also used; because of the size and concentration of the entertainment industry in the town there is a significant number of agents in the area. Performers typically appear in a 'circuit' by appearing in several different hotels over the course of a week or season or even the same night.

The entertainment is usually staged late evening – from about 10.30pm – and lasts between 45 minutes and 2 hours. The acts and the timing were geared to the guests – invariably a more mature audience; in a few hotels where guests were predominantly aged 60 or over the shows were earlier in the evening. Where guests were typically

Table 17.2 Types of entertainment offered (number of Blackpool hoteliers offering each type)

Singer/group	23
Variety/cabaret	16
Comedian	13
Live music	11
Children's	5
Magician	4
Dancers	1
Other	1

younger one hotel manager provided entertainment before 9.00pm – pre-clubbing – and did not provide it at all later in the evening.

The organization of the entertainment was usually carried out by the owner/manager; only one hotel (the largest) had a specific entertainment manager. The programme was often flexible and hoteliers booked acts at relatively short notice (often a week or less) according to the number and type of guests in during any one week; hoteliers also responded directly to guests' demands. No entertainment would be offered if guest numbers fell too low. The larger hotels tended to have programmes that were planned for the whole season. The entertainment was aimed at resident guests rather than non-residents and a high take-up was usually reported in the questionnaire responses with most hoteliers claiming that over half of their guests saw the entertainment (see Table 17.3).

Table 17.3 Guests in each hotel that 'use' the entertainment (number of Blackpool hoteliers indicating each proportion)

More than three-quarters	9
Half to three-quarters	15
Less than half	5

Most hoteliers considered that the cost of entertainment was minimal compared with other outgoings. There was little specialist provision of facilities or equipment (and thus little extra cost) and most performers brought their own backing and sound system. In some cases hotels have their own nightclub comparable with any non-hotel club and a small number (the larger ones) have purpose-built stage areas. More usually, however, hotels utilize bar or lounge areas. It is rare for the provision to be in a dedicated or 'purpose-built' area.

The timing of the shows (late evening) suggests that hoteliers regarded the entertainment as a supplement to the town's theatre provision. In Table 17.4 it can be seen also that most questionnaire respondents considered that their guests would still go to shows elsewhere in Blackpool during their stay and the hotel provision would not affect this. The larger hotels were more likely to see their entertainment as an alternative to programmes elsewhere in the town though this hotel provision tended to be in their own public (fun-pub) bars rather than resident-only provision. Additionally the shows helped encourage guests to return to the hotel after an evening out (or to stay in the hotel) and spend in the bar.

Table 17.4 Views of Blackpool hoteliers on hotel entertainment (number of hoteliers indicating each response)

	Agree/ strongly agree	Unsure	Disagree/ strongly disagree
Guests see only hotel entertainment in Blackpool	3	7	18
Attracts guests to the hotel	15	10	4
Guests are less likely to go to theatre shows	6	7	16
Raises bar revenue	17	9	3
Attracts non-residents	5	3	21

The impact on bar takings was rated highly by a majority of questionnaire respondents (16 out of 29) as a reason for providing the entertainment (see Table 17.5). This however, was rarely referred to in the interviews; if anything the interviewees were sceptical about the ability to significantly increase bar revenue. The other main reason given for providing entertainment was the ability to keep ahead of other hotels, to give a competitive edge. This was rated highly as a reason by 13 out of 29 (see Table 17.5). This explains why hoteliers offer the service; they also believed that entertainment is an important influence on guests. It was believed by 20 out of the 29 hoteliers to be 'very important' or 'important' in the visitors' decision to choose the hotel (see Table 17.6). In response to a related question entertainment was believed by 15 of the 29 respondents to attract guests to the hotel but, significantly, 10 were unsure. During the interviews some hoteliers commented on the fact that entertainment was so common in the town that any one hotel probably would not suffer by not providing entertainment. Others, however, firmly believed that their own guests did expect in-hotel entertainment and that older guests, in particular, found it much more convenient than going out at night. Interviewees felt it was a selling point though perhaps not a unique one. Many visitors to Blackpool expect the provision.

Table 17.5 Reasons for providing entertainment (numbers of Blackpool hoteliers ranking the reason 'very important' or 'important')

To boost bar revenue	16
To keep ahead of other hotels	13
Poor entertainment in theatres	7
Own personal interest	6
Because other hotels do it	6

Table 17.6 Importance of hotel entertainment in visitors' decision to stay in hotel (as evaluated by hoteliers) (number of hoteliers indicating each response)

Very important	7
Important	13
Not very important	8
No influence at all	1

DISCUSSION AND CONCLUSIONS

Hotels are not generally associated with offering performances by entertainers. Live entertainment is, however, part of the holiday experience and the opportunity to experience it (on whatever scale) usually contributes to the identification of a place as a holiday destination. The absence of such an opportunity may have a detrimental effect on the number of tourists (Hughes and Benn, 1997a). There are clearly many destinations which depend heavily on the entertainment they offer. It may be less important to those destinations whose product is based on sun and sea but even there entertainment can be a significant part of the holiday experience.

Given the division of function between the accommodation and entertainment industries it is not immediately obvious why hotels should wish to provide entertainment. The most obvious reason would appear to be to keep guests on the premises to achieve some other aim and this is most evident in the case of the gaming resort hotel. There is also a certain attraction to a hotelier in attempting to ensure that as much of a holiday-maker's expenditure as possible is captured by his/her organization. If a holiday-maker typically spends on meals, drink, souvenirs, recreation, leisure and entertainment, a hotelier may seek to provide opportunities for all or any of these in the hotel. The overall effect may be an addition to turnover and to profits. Some entertainment activities, such as discos and nightclubs (not necessarily live entertainment), may be important profit-generators in their own right, especially if open to non-residents. This is similar to leisure facilities provision where viability arises from usage by those other than hotel guests. It may be, however, that guests may have little desire to confine their holiday experience to within a hotel though the entertainment may succeed in raising bar revenue.

Hotels will put on entertainment as a means of boosting business perhaps at weekends in the same way as they might put on any 'specialist' weekend. This is not to claim that entertainment is widely considered to be a determining attribute of hotel choice. There is little evidence to confirm that, in general terms, hotel entertainment will be influential on choice of hotel. This obviously depends on the situation and, in destinations such as Las Vegas and Blackpool, the hotel provision does seem to be of significance. Hoteliers in Blackpool believe that it serves the purpose of maintaining a competitive edge; to keep up with or ahead of the competition. Further research would need to consider this view from the perspective of hotel guests.

Certain categories of holiday-maker, such as the older guest or those with young children, may be looking for in-hotel entertainment. Certain destinations which are entertainment-focused may also give rise to expectations of in-hotel entertainment though this is not always the case, as evidenced by London. It may be that hotels also provide entertainment when there is a deficiency of entertainment elsewhere. In many tourist (especially seaside) towns local government owns and funds theatres and is often responsible for the production of shows (Hughes and Benn, 1997a). Increased pressure on local government finances is partly responsible for a contraction of entertainment in seaside tourist destinations and there are few such towns where the private sector is willing to provide large-scale entertainment. The significance of hotel entertainment may thus increase.

The nature of the entertainment in hotels varies considerably. It can be a relatively 'easy' and cheap service to provide in that it need be no more than the hire of a single entertainer with a requirement for few specialist facilities other than a sound system. A group of hoteliers may jointly finance the hire of entertainers for performance in one of those hotels if they were convinced that, in their circumstances, entertainment was an attraction. Many hotels provide conference facilities requiring facilities similar to those required for live entertainment and, as such, little extra investment may be required. Exhibitions and presentations often involve some 'theatrical' input which may be provided by an outside agency; many hoteliers are thus involved in the provision of facilities, if not services, which are close to the provision of entertainment for guests. The basics may already be there to provide 'shows' if desired.

Such diversification into other activities is limited in its extent, it is in an associated activity and the skills required for operating a theatre have something in common with running a hotel. They are not, however, sufficiently transferable to ensure anything other than successful entertainment on a small scale. The analogy of hospitality service as a theatrical experience does not translate into the ability to be a professional impresario. The limited expertise of hotel management or limited effort that can be devoted to entertainment may lead to a relatively costly activity. If entertainment is not a net profit generator it will only be acceptable if it serves some other purpose. There is a danger too that it distracts hotel management from its main activity and leads to more complex management. In such circumstances hotel management may consider engaging a specialist manager, contracting out the services to an agency or, as in the case of shops, to concessionaires.

Live entertainment is usually associated with theatres and concert halls. A hotelier may find it difficult to meet the expectations of a public that is accustomed to the standards and high-tech nature of television programmes and the professional theatre; a hotel's provision may not be regarded highly in comparison. It is likely that the hotel operation will be able to compete with professional theatrical productions only through considerable investment and specialist management.

The continuing demand for live entertainment is unclear. It may be that, in the future, spectacle and the extraordinary will be increasingly sought in other forms such as fairs, theme parks, amusement parks and interactive, virtual-reality arcades and their associated technological products. The demand for the variety-type show and the musical (in both the seaside and city tourist towns) appears to be enduring but the emphasis on technological input increases and makes it more difficult for hoteliers to compete in the entertainment sphere.

In the right circumstances and with careful management the provision of live entertainment can be an asset to a hotel. It is clearly not something that every hotel should add to its portfolio of services and it is not appropriate to re-define the hotel product to include entertainment any more than it is to include leisure facilities. Live entertainment remains an ancillary activity which it may be appropriate to provide in certain circumstances. Knowledge about entertainment in hotels is, however, limited and there is a need for more research on the extent and nature of the provision across the country, perhaps by more individual case studies. Similarly it is necessary to find out more about the importance of entertainment in the holiday experience and in the choice of both destination and hotel.

REFERENCES AND FURTHER READING

British Tourist Authority and English Tourist Board (1996) Overseas visitor survey 1995, London: British Tourist Authority and English Tourist Board.

Callan, R. (1996) 'An appraisement of UK business travellers' perceptions of important hotel attributes', *Hospitality Research Journal,* **19**(4), 113–27.

Christiansen, E. and Brinkerhoff-Jacobs, J. (1995) 'Gaming and entertainment: an imperfect union?' *Cornell Hotel and Restaurant Administration Quarterly,* **36**(2), 79–94.

Cotterell, L. (1993) *Performance: the Business and Law of Entertainment*, London: Sweet and Maxwell, 3rd edn.

Dandurand, L. and Ralenkotter, R. (1985) 'An investigation of entertainment proneness and its relationship to gambling behaviour: the Las Vegas experience', *Journal of Travel Research,* **XXIII**(3), 12–16.

Fanshawe, S. (1996) 'What's a nice girl like him doing in a place like this?', *Mail on Sunday Night and Day*, 18 August, 40–2.

Gardner, K. and Wood, R. (1991) 'Theatricality in food service work', *International Journal of Hospitality Management,* **10**(3), 267–78.

GLS Research (1995) *Las Vegas visitor profile study 1995*, Las Vegas: GLS Research.

Gratton, C. and Taylor, P. (1987) 'Hotel leisure centres: the Trusthouse Forte example', *Leisure Management,* June, 25–6, 30.

Gratton, C. and Taylor, P. (1992) Cultural tourism in European cities: a case study of Edinburgh, *Vrijetijd en Samenleving*, **10**(2/3), 29–43.

Hales, C. and Collins, P. (1988) 'A leap in the dark?', *Hospitality*, November, 18, 20.

Hanna, M. (1994) *Visits to Tourist Attractions 1993*, London: British Tourist Authority and the National Tourist Boards.

Hughes, H. (1998 in press) 'Theatre in London and the inter-relationship with tourism', *Tourism Management*, **19**, 5.

Hughes, H. and Benn, D. (1995) 'Entertainment: its role in the tourist experience' in Leslie, D. (ed.) *Tourism and leisure: perspectives on provision*, Eastbourne: Leisure Studies Association, 11–21.

Hughes, H. and Benn, D. (1997) 'Entertainment in tourism: a study of visitors to Blackpool' *Managing Leisure: an International Journal*, **2**(2), 110–26.

Hughes, H. and Benn, D. (1997a) 'Tourism and cultural policy: the case of seaside entertainment in Britain', *European Journal of Cultural Policy*, **3**(2), 235–55.

Hughes, H. and Benn, D. (1998) ' Holiday entertainment in a British seaside resort town', *Journal of Arts Management, Law and Society*, **27**(4), 295–307.

Jones, P. and Lockwood, A. (1989) *The Management of Hotel Operations*, London: Cassell.

Larsen, S. and Aske, L. (1992) 'On-stage in the service theatre', *International Journal of Contemporary Hospitality Management*, **4**(4), 12–15.

Las Vegas Convention and Visitors Authority (1996) *Las Vegas Official Visitors Guide*, Las Vegas, NV: Las Vegas Convention and Visitors Authority.

Lewis, S. (1991) 'Sound advice', *Restaurants and Institutions*, 3 April, 109–10, 112, 114.

Lewis, R. (1984) 'Theoretical and practical considerations in research design', *Cornell Hotel and Restaurant Administration Quarterly*, **24**(4), 25–35.

Lewis, R. and Chambers, R. (1989) *Marketing Leadership in Hospitality: Foundations and Practices*, New York: Van Nostrand Reinhold.

Loverseed, H. (1995) 'Gambling Tourism in North America', *Travel and Tourism Analyst*, **3**: 40–53.

Lundberg, D. (1994) *The Hotel and Restaurant Business*, New York: Van Nostrand Reinhold, 6th edn.

Manchester, C. (1994) *Entertainment Licensing: Law and Practice*, London: Sweet and Maxwell.

Martin, A. (1996) 'Piers of the realm', *Sunday Times Magazine*, 25 August, 20–5.

Parker, G. and Kent, W. (1986) 'Utilising live entertainment in hotels, restaurants and clubs', *International Journal of Hospitality Management*, **5**(1), 13–22.

Performing Rights Society (1994) *PRS Yearbook 1994–95 and Report and Accounts*, London: Performing Rights Society.

Research Surveys of Great Britain (1985) *Holiday Entertainment Survey: a Report on Live Entertainment in Summer 1985*, London: RSGB for the English Tourist Board (unpublished).

Roehl, W. (1996) 'Competition, casino spending and use of casino amenities', *Journal of Travel Research*, **XXXIV**(3), 57–62.

Romm, D. (1989) 'Restauration theatre: giving direction to service', *Cornell Hotel and Restaurant Administration Quarterly*, **29**(4), 31–9.

Roper, A. (1996) 'Resort hotels' in Jones, P. (ed.) *Introduction to Hospitality Operations*, London: Cassell, 50–60.

Thompson, G. (1983) 'Carnival and the calculable: consumption and play in Blackpool', in Thompson, G. *et al.* (eds), *Formations of Pleasure*, London: Routledge and Kegan Paul, 124–37.

Thompson, W., Pinney, J. and Scibrowsky, J. (1996) 'The family that gambles together: business and social concerns', *Journal of Travel Research*, **XXXIV**(3), 70–4.

Vierich, W. and Calver, S. (1991) 'Hotels and the leisure sector: a product differentiation Strategy for the 1990s', *International Journal of Contemporary Hospitality Management*, **3**(3), 10–15.

Ward, C. and Hardy, D. (1986) *Goodnight Campers! The History of the British Holiday Camp*, London: Mansell.

Index